Sustainable Operations of Logistics and Supply Chain Management

Scrivener Publishing
100 Cummings Center, Suite 541J
Beverly, MA 01915-6106

Sustainable Computing and Optimization

Series Editor: Dr. Prasenjit Chatterjee (dr.prasenjitchatterjee6@gmail.com)

The objective of the series is to bring together global research scholars, experts, and scientists in the research areas of sustainable computing and optimization to share their knowledge and experiences on current research achievements in these fields. Since the series was launched in 2021, it has provided a golden opportunity for the research community to share their novel research results, findings, and innovations to a wide range of topics and applications. The series promotes sustainable computing and optimization methodologies to solve real-life problems mainly from engineering and management systems domains.

Publishers at Scrivener
Martin Scrivener (martin@scrivenerpublishing.com)
Phillip Carmical (pcarmical@scrivenerpublishing.com)

Sustainable Operations of Logistics and Supply Chain Management

Edited by

K. Mathiyazhagan

Thigarajar School of Management, Madurai, India

Krishna Kumar Dadsena

Indian Institute of Management Ranchi, India

Rajesh Kumar Singh

Management Development Institute (MDI), Gurgaon, India

Aakanksha Kishore

Operations Management at FORE School of Management, New Delhi, India

and

Andrea Appolloni

Department of Management and Law, University of Rome Tor Vergata, Rome, Italy

Scrivener Publishing

WILEY

This edition first published 2025 by John Wiley & Sons, Inc., 111 River Street, Hoboken, NJ 07030, USA and Scrivener Publishing LLC, 100 Cummings Center, Suite 541J, Beverly, MA 01915, USA

For more information about Scrivener publications please visit www.scrivenerpublishing.com.

Wiley Global Headquarters
111 River Street, Hoboken, NJ 07030, USA

For details of our global editorial offices, customer services, and more information about Wiley products visit us at www.wiley.com.

The manufacturer's authorized representative according to the EU General Product Safety Regulation is Wiley-VCH GmbH, Boschstr. 12, 69469 Weinheim, Germany, e-mail: Product_Safety@wiley.com.

Library of Congress Cataloging-in-Publication Data

ISBN 978-1-394-23851-4

Cover background image: Generated with AI using Adobe Firefly
Cover design by Russell Richardson
Cover boat image courtesy of Wikimedia Commons

Set in size of 11pt and Minion Pro by Manila Typesetting Company, Makati, Philippines

Printed in the USA

10 9 8 7 6 5 4 3 2 1

Contents

Preface

In an era of unprecedented technological advancements and growing environmental consciousness, the traditional paradigms of logistics, supply chain management, and sustainability are undergoing transformative shifts. This book, a compilation of ground-breaking research, aims to illuminate the multifaceted dimensions of modern logistics and supply chain management, particularly in the context of sustainability, artificial intelligence, and the circular economy.

The intricate tapestry of modern logistics and supply chain management is woven with threads of innovation, sustainability, and resilience. As we stand on the cusp of transformative advancements, the urgency to address the environmental, economic, and social implications of these systems has never been greater. This book seeks to explore the evolving dynamics of logistics, offering a comprehensive analysis of emerging technologies, operational challenges, and forward-thinking strategies shaping this domain.

Sustainability forms the bedrock of contemporary logistics. As industries increasingly embrace green practices, they must navigate a labyrinth of obstacles, from high implementation costs to resistance to change. This book delves deep into these challenges, presenting actionable strategies that encourage the adoption of sustainable solutions. It highlights how organizations can transcend operational constraints by fostering collaboration, leveraging technology, and developing innovative frameworks that integrate environmental consciousness into core business practices.

At the heart of this transformation lies the synergy between technology and sustainability. The integration of artificial intelligence, big data analytics, and machine learning into logistics operations has redefined efficiency and precision. By utilizing advanced algorithms and predictive models, companies are better equipped to optimize routes, reduce emissions, and enhance resource utilization. This book sheds light on how these tools enable businesses to transition toward smarter, greener logistics systems while addressing the intricacies of their application and potential barriers.

The disruptions brought about by global events, such as pandemics, have underscored the fragility of supply chains. This work provides an in-depth exploration of the causes and impacts of these disruptions, offering resilience strategies to fortify logistics networks against future crises. Through detailed audits and scenario analyses, it examines how agility, risk diversification, and digital integration are critical to mitigating the vulnerabilities exposed in recent years.

Central to sustainable logistics is the concept of circularity, where the lifecycle of resources is extended through reuse, recycling, and efficient waste management. This book explores how circular economy principles can be embedded into supply chains, addressing challenges such as the procurement of used products and the optimization of reverse logistics. By presenting practical solutions and case studies, it demonstrates how businesses can align operational goals with environmental stewardship.

The human dimension of logistics is another critical focus. From understanding how individual traits influence decision-making to improving the working conditions of those driving supply chain operations, this book emphasizes the importance of a people-centric approach. By addressing social impacts alongside environmental and economic considerations, it provides a holistic perspective on achieving sustainability in logistics.

Economic viability remains a cornerstone of any sustainable initiative. This work explores how organizations can balance the costs associated with green logistics while achieving long-term financial gains. By integrating sustainability into working capital management and evaluating the lifecycle costs of various logistics strategies, it provides actionable insights into creating economically resilient systems that do not compromise environmental goals.

As industries continue to evolve, so too must the frameworks guide their operations. This book examines innovative approaches to inventory management, procurement, and last-mile logistics, offering models and methodologies that account for real-world complexities. Whether it is optimizing defective inventory, integrating digital procurement functions, or aligning last-mile and reverse logistics, these solutions aim to enhance efficiency and sustainability across the supply chain.

Ultimately, this work is a testament to the interconnectedness of logistics systems with broader societal goals. It recognizes that achieving sustainability in logistics is not merely an operational challenge but a critical step toward addressing global issues such as climate change, resource scarcity, and economic inequities. By fostering collaboration between policymakers, industry leaders, and researchers, this book seeks to inspire transformative changes that extend beyond individual organizations to benefit communities and the planet.

As this book demonstrates, the intersection of sustainability, technology, and logistics is ripe with opportunities and challenges. From eco-innovation frameworks to resilience strategies for supply chain disruptions, the insights provided here chart a path toward a future where logistics is not only efficient but also environmentally and socially responsible.

This preface sets the stage for an intellectual journey into the transformative realms of logistics and supply chain management. Each chapter offers a unique perspective, pushing the boundaries of knowledge and practice in the quest for a sustainable tomorrow. Whether you are a researcher, policymaker, or industry practitioner, this book invites you to explore, learn, and contribute to the evolution of sustainable logistics.

We hope that this book will inspire further research and innovation in this exciting field and contribute to the development of practical solutions that can be implemented on a global scale. Finally, our gratitude goes to Martin Scrivener and the team at Scrivener Publishing for their support in bringing this volume to light.

The Editors
August 2025

Part 1

GREEN LOGISTICS AND SUSTAINABILITY PRACTICES

1

Navigating the Complexities of Green Logistics Management: Challenges, Strategies, and Future Directions

Hafiz Wasim Akram

Department of Marketing, Entrepreneurship, and Logistics, College of Commerce and Business Administration, Dhofar University, Salalah, Dhofar Governorate, Oman

Abstract
Green logistics management is essential in minimizing the environmental impact of supply chain activities. This chapter explores the challenges faced in adopting green logistics practices, focusing on diverse regulatory compliance, high initial investments, technological integration, and organizational resistance. It highlights how global regulatory variations and dynamic changes increase compliance complexity and costs, posing significant hurdles for companies, especially SMEs. The chapter also discusses the substantial financial burden and uncertain return on investment associated with green logistics initiatives. Technological advancements offer solutions, yet integrating them with existing systems requires considerable investment and adaptation. Organizational resistance due to entrenched cost-efficiency priorities and the rapidly evolving consumer expectations further complicate the implementation of sustainable practices. Strategies to address these challenges include adopting advanced technologies, fostering collaboration, leveraging government incentives, and prioritizing consumer engagement and education. By overcoming these obstacles, companies can achieve sustainable logistics operations, enhancing their environmental performance and contributing to a more sustainable future.

***Keywords*:** Green logistics, environmental sustainability, regulatory compliance, technological integration, organizational resistance, consumer expectations, supply chain complexity, sustainable practices

Email: hakram@du.edu.om

K. Mathiyazhagan, Krishna Kumar Dadsena, Rajesh Kumar Singh, Aakanksha Kishore and Andrea Appolloni (eds.) Sustainable Operations of Logistics and Supply Chain Management, (3–24) © 2025 Scrivener Publishing LLC

Introduction

Environmental sustainability has come into focus for most of the industries across the world in recent decades [1]. The serious damage which industry has done to the environment in recent decades has led to an increased demand for less environmentally damaging forms of production. The contemporary movement of eco-friendly transport has embraced green logistics, a new concept which incorporates the strategic and logistical management of logistics processes that reduce the environmental impact [2]. Green logistics is a way to balance out the cost-effective logistics with environmental protection calls [3]. It is the handling of waste, carbon emissions [4], and energy, which is a continuous, tedious, and lengthy task. It is very important and urgent in dealing with supply chain waste, carbon emissions, and power consumption. Green logistics as a concept is nested in the larger framework of sustainable development which means economic growth that satisfies the needs of the present generation without jeopardizing the capacity of future generations to satisfy their own [5]. This rule has been growing popular with organizations aiming at enhancing environmental functioning and also for complying with strict regulatory rules. Consequently, green logistics has ceased to be a fringe aspect of business strategy and become one of the key components instead.

The increased demand for green logistics practices is being driven by several key factors in all sectors [6]. Key to this transformation of greener logistics is regulatory pressures. All around the world, governments are enacting tougher environmental legislations. Meeting these regulations will mean significant shifts in logistics operations and will require companies to practice more sustainable behavior. Secondly, they have seen a significant awareness and demand for greener produce. Consumers nowadays are becoming more conscious about how their purchases are more environmentally sustainable, and are increasingly supporting companies that are going out of their way to act in a more sustainable manner [7]. Such a transition in consumer behavior has encouraged businesses to implement green logistics practices for promoting their own brand and also meeting customer standards. Other technological advances directly support green logistics. New transportation, energy, and information technologies have introduced new means to mitigate the environmental impacts of logistics [8]. Indeed, the innovations in electric vehicles, renewable energy, and big data analytics have made it possible for businesses to not only improve the efficiency of their logistics operations, but also their impact on the community.

Green logistics practices can provide so much more than environmental sustainability. The biggest benefit is cost savings. Through routing solutions, fuel savings and waste elimination, processes can be streamlined and operational costs can be dramatically reduced [9]. For instance, replacing gas guzzlers with more efficient alternatives and diversifying into bio energy can provide significant cost savings in fuel costs. Moreover, decreased waste *via* improved inventory management and recycling efforts can bring down disposal costs and improve overall resource allocation. Improved corporate identity and increased brand value is another big gain. Businesses with a strong sustainability record are able to distinguish themselves while appealing to an increasing number of shoppers who care about the environment. This good-good products image can help to gain the loyalty of the customers and, hence, generate more sales. In addition, green logistics practices ultimately lead to higher employee satisfaction which in turn boosts employee retention, since many workers nowadays prefer to work for companies that act in a socially responsible way with regard to the environment [10]. Green logistics also helps in risk management by reducing the risks related to environmental legislations and climate changes.

Several trends and future directions are emerging in the field of green logistics [11, 12]. A key trend is the growing use of digital technologies and data analytics to improve the efficiency and sustainability of logistics operations. Using IoT Devices, Big Data analytics and AI, companies are now able to track and optimize their logistics in real time. IoT sensors can monitor vehicle performance and environmental conditions, and AI algorithms can optimize routes and reduce fuel use. The circular economy in logistics is another burgeoning trend. Advocates of the circular economy work to prevent waste, and to get used matter as resource-saving as possible back into the cycle. This means designing supply chains to enable products and materials being returned and reused, so as to minimize the environmental impact of production and consumption [13]. More and more companies are experimenting with nontraditional circular economy principles such as the product-as-a-service and reverse logistics business models.

Green logistics is also picking up the pace with sustainable transportation solutions. Electric and hybrid vehicles are starting to make a presence, and new fuels are being considered, including hydrogen and biofuels [14]. These modes of transport are sustainable ones, helping to bring down greenhouse gas emission rates and to make the nation less reliant on gas and diesel. Technological developments in automated driving systems also offer the potential to improve the productivity and environmental performance of logistics operations. Green logistics are being driven forward by the spirit of cooperation and partnerships [15]. For the first time companies are required to realize that in order to achieve their sustainability goals, the need to engage in active conversation with the ecosystem of other stakeholders including suppliers, customer, government agencies and non-governmental organizations. Collaborative initiatives, including green logistics networks and industry alliances, share best practices, resources, and knowledge, allowing organizations to collectively address environmental challenges driving systemic change [16].

Thus, green logistics management is an essential part of the sustainability movement. Regulatory pressures, consumer demand, and advancements in technology are all driving the rise of green logistics, with associated benefits including but not limited to cost savings, a stronger brand, and improved risk management. But there are many hurdles to overcome in implementing green logistics practices, such as needing an expensive up-front investment, complexity in the operations, and technological challenges. The future of green logistics as green logistics progresses, we can see how changes in the logistics industry influence the environmental sphere which leads to green logistics evolving to include digital technologies, circular economy principles, sustainable transportation projects and of course — partnerships. At its core, and despite the challenges these trends present, pursuing a more sustainable logistics operation can contribute to a more sustainable and long-term future for everyone.

Thus, the chapter addresses several problems that drive the need for green logistics:

1. **Environmental Degradation**: The damage industries have caused to the environment has led to a demand for less harmful production. Green logistics emerges as a response, balancing economic and environmental priorities.
2. **Regulatory Pressures**: Governments worldwide are implementing stricter environmental regulations, pushing companies to adopt sustainable logistics practices to comply and avoid penalties.
3. **Consumer Demand for Sustainability**: Rising consumer awareness and preference for environmentally responsible brands encourage companies to adopt green logistics to enhance brand image and customer loyalty.
4. **Technological and Operational Challenges**: Green logistics involves significant operational complexities, including managing waste, reducing carbon emissions, and optimizing energy use—tasks that require costly investments and advanced technology.

5. **Need for Collaboration**: Effective green logistics requires stakeholder cooperation, including suppliers, government agencies, and NGOs, to share best practices and drive systemic change.

Challenges in Green Logistics Management

This section will summarize many different problems in the field of green logistics, which is caused mainly by mixed regulations and compliance costs that hinder the uniform implementation of activities globally. Technological improvements and use of green technologies will be another focus, examining the various challenges and costs faced. This section also covers the economic hardships faced by them, with the heavy costs of setting up and the doubtful profitability. The section will further delve into the operational challenges stemming from the complexity of supply chain and the ongoing need to balance efficiency and sustainability. We will then explore resistance to change & the struggle to make the strategic leap towards sustainability in the area of cultural & organizational challenges.

a) ***Diverse Regulations and Compliance Costs***

There is thick spread of regulatory activities and companies have to deal with the compliance which is a biggest challenge for the companies for the green logistics management [17]. As regulations related to environmental protection and sustainability are not standardized worldwide [18, 19], organizations operating in international logistics must establish complex compliance frameworks stretching across various regions and countries. For instance, the European Union (EU) will likely require large cuts in carbon output at some point, with programs such as the Green Deal pushing the development and utilization of renewable energy sources [20]. By comparison, regulations in other regions may be not so strict or have different structure all together, and then companies find themselves with local exceptions. Sostakeholders have a level of regulatory diversity which makes it challenging for them to have green logistics policies worldwide. Companies need to adapt their logistics strategies to conform to the different local environmental regulations — a time-consuming and resource-intensive process. The challenge is further compounded by the fact that environmental regulations change continually in response to actual or expected shifts in emissions and pollution loading [21]. With new environmental issues, new scientific approaches and new political paradigms, regulatory frameworks are in constant evolution. All of this is enormously resource intensive and demands a very high level of proficiency.

Whether because of this or separate concerns, compliance can consume resources at an unsustainable pace, especially for smaller and medium-sized enterprises (SMEs) with no dedicated resources for compliance measures. More importantly, a series of periodic changes can cause hiccups in the normal operation of a business as it accommodates logistics to conform to fresh protocols, almost always with little or no warning. The cost associated with compliance with the regulations pose as a significant challenge in the management of green logistics.

Meeting environmental regulations typically comes with significant costs, including investments in new technologies and infrastructure, and funding expenses for monitoring, reporting and auditing [22]. For example, the conversion to an electric or hybrid fleet in order to comply with emissions regulations is very costly. Likewise, investing in energy efficient technologies in warehouses and distribution centers — for instance, by adding solar panels or upgrading HVAC systems — can be capital-intensive. SMEs are particularly susceptible to high compliance costs and often lack the funding required to invest in green logistics initiatives. Also, continual compliance costs can be substantial as well. This, in turn, requires companies to continuously monitor their practices under a set of environmental standards, meaning more professional staff has to be employed or hired from the outside [23]. Also, the requirement for relatively intricate environmental paperwork and reporting necessary to demonstrate compliance may result in increased administrative burdens and costs as well. Costs of non-compliance place an institution at risk of being subject to fines, penalties, and/or becoming blacklisted. Hence, financial responsibility is an important point of concern for firms aiming to adopt green logistics practices.

Managing the balance between various regulations and their associated costs in a strategic manner needs careful planning and allocation of resources. The new trend will likely be a proactive strategy to regulatory compliance where sustainability objectives are a core part of overall business strategy for companies [24]. This consists in comprehensive risk assessments being carried out for the anticipation of regulation-related issues and the set-up of plans aimed to resolve them when they happen. Furthermore, technology may be a key solution to compliance costs. By utilizing this type of data analytics and logistics management software, companies can track their environmental performance, reduce their reporting burden, and develop cost saving opportunities. Furthermore, it may seek to collaborate with industry peers, governments, donors and NGOs to better understand what the regulatory landscape looks like and how we can best work together to reduce compliance costs.

Thus, there are many challenges to overcome in managing green logistics. Their operations span a dynamic and organic environment of regulation, transitioning in contrast to an ample landscape of fiscal consequence. It is both critically strategic and proactive to tradeoff between technology and collaboration to best of one's ability streamline compliance and cut costs. By overcoming these challenges, organizations will not only achieve regulatory compliance but will also improve the overall sustainability performance that will promote achieving a more sustainable future for the logistics industry and society.

b) ***Technological Advancements and Integration of Green Technologies***
The incredible increase in the speed of emerging technology which is used in the current environment is one of the key issues in implementing green logistics management. New technologies promise impressive results to mitigate the environmental impact of logistics activities, but keeping up with these innovations and implementing them in ongoing practices can be overwhelming [25]. In the logistics industry, we have witnessed spectacular changes due to the evolution and development of technologies like Electric vehicles (EVs), Autonomous transportation, and Renewable energy systems [26]. Nonetheless, such technologies necessitate a huge investment and regular up-gradation. One of the most significant hurdles that companies face in order to be competitive is large investments companies have to make in research and development (R&D), something that can be incredibly difficult to do for those classified as Small and Medium Enterprises (SMEs). The limited lifespan of technology also means that investments made today may need replacing sooner than expected, increasing the cost involved [27].

There are significant modifications to infrastructure and processes to implement green technologies into logistics operations. For instance, the conversion to an electric vehicle fleet requires the installation of charging stations and the creation of a new local electricity network to ensure an increased electricity load. Likewise, deploying renewable energy sources is a series of changes to established facilities [28]. Stepping through these infrastructure changes are potentially cumbersome and can cause operational downtime if not done right. Also, implementing more advanced logistics management software and data analytics platforms to streamline supply chain operations will require retraining the staff and perhaps breaking down the existing workflows. The complexity of these changes means that the implementation of environmentally-friendly logistics practices can be distressed with increased costs and delays, providing a major obstacle to companies wishing to become greener. Incorporating green technologies however faces another challenge of compatibility with that of existing systems and processes. A good number of logistics operations run on legacy systems that are likely to be incompatible with new technologies [29]. This is because older vehicles and equipment may not be compatible with modern emissions control technologies or telematics systems, and other such advancements [30]. Meanwhile, advanced energy management software may not mingle easily with existing warehouse management systems. Greater customization and potential costs are involved in achieving interoperability with new and old technologies that need to be modernized or deprecated. This is combined with the need to continue operations while introducing new technologies results in a heavily phased implementation that reduces the disruptions however prolongs the transition.

The role of the human factor in the successful integration of green technologies is also not to be underestimated. New technology may be more difficult to train employees how to operate and maintain, adding to the time and manpower it takes on. Resistance to change — employees are often used to the old methods, and do not want to try something new [31]. Change management is necessary to manage this resistance and make a successful move the change process. This includes communicating clearly about the benefits of green technologies, setting up comprehensive training programs, and encouraging a culture of sustainability within the organization. Furthermore, reduction in green technology adoption challenges such as sustainability and the associated barriers requires the support and commitment of leadership. Thus, technological development and adding green technologies to the system cause major complications for green logistics management. Innovation happens too quickly, requires heavy investment in R&D and continuous upgrade of systems and processes. Adapting infrastructure and retaining compatibility with current systems makes the integration of green technologies more complex and expensive. Sustainable logistics operations will not be possible without the adoption of green technologies, despite the challenges. Through strategic solutions to these challenges, organizations can use technological progress to improve their environmental performance and help build a more sustainable future.

c) ***Economic Challenges in the form of High Initial Investment Uncertain Return on Investment (ROI)***

One of the hardest hurdles to jump in the process of the green implementation of green logistics practices is the huge initial investment. Several green logistics measures are capital intensive, including investments in eco-friendly vehicles, upgrading existing sites and the use of renewable energy sources. For example, switching to an electric — or even hybrid — vehicle fleet incurs large, upfront expenses to purchase the vehicles and install electric charging facilities [32]. In the same way, harnessing solar or wind power to run your distribution center/manufacturing center requires considerable investment in installation and reworking existing energy systems [33]. Such large investments are very expensive, especially for small and medium-sized businesses (SMEs) which do not always have large reserves of capital. In fact, the initial costs of green logistics are high, not just in terms of hard assets. Besides that, companies have to spend money on research and development (R&D) to identify and implement new technologies and practices. This covers investments in pilot projects for the deployment of new solutions and their evaluation of viability and impact. While this transition might come at a price, there will be costs to hiring and training new employees to handle these technologies and to ensuring current workforce has the skill sets needed to support a move to greener initiative [34]. In addition, the cost of R & D, costs of training cause the financial cost and companies do not have enough resources to focus on green logistics, and manage other business issues.

This can make the decision-making process even more complex, with the uncertainty of the ROI associated with green logistics initiatives [35]. As green backlogs can demonstrate considerable environmental savings, return on investment is not always guaranteed, nor may it be for some time. These include the benefits resulting from less fuel use, reduced energy bills, and the payback period of investments in renewable energy systems that can often be several years. The long-term nature of ROI can be especially difficult for organizations that rely on short-term financial cycles and need to prove immediate financial performance to stakeholders. The ROI on green logistics projects is also subject to influence from a wide of external factors including legislative frameworks, technological innovations, market developments and so on [36]. Energy costs can also affect the return on renewable energy investments and new technologies may quickly make recent solutions obsolete, requiring new investments. Because companies invariably have little to no idea what their green logistics initiatives will earn, it is difficult to project the ROI, and it prevents companies from investing in green logistics. In addition, the absence of common indicators of the effectiveness of green logistics initiatives and the problems of quantifying the economic effect of sustainability efforts aggravate the situation, forcing organizations to often evaluate the financial return of implementing their measures simply by guesswork.

Faced with high initial investment due to the long-term ROI of some green logistics measures, companies need to be smart about it. To cope with these challenges in green logistics management, an organizational-strategic approach must be developed. This includes developing and implementing extensive cost-benefit analyses to ensure proposed initiatives are financially sustainable and provide a means to identify cost saving and efficiency opportunities. By taking advantage of government incentives and subsidies for green technologies, some of the upfront capital costs can also be clawed back, thus reducing the cost impact on organizations thinking of embarking on green logistics initiatives [37]. Business must take charge of creating the business case for green logistics that goes beyond the immediate financial returns. It focuses on things like better corporate reputation, more customer loyalty, and better compliance with regulations. Green logistics initiatives should be positioned as an essential part of the broader sustainability strategy and the future success of the business by the company in order to have stakeholder backing and the financing required with which to actuate the agendas. Furthermore, the same way investment in comprehensive monitoring and reporting programs is fundamental in tracking performance will prove the value of green logistics initiatives and assist decision-makers in making sustainable choices in future investments.

d) ***Operational Challenges in the form of Supply Chain Complexity and balancing Efficiency and Sustainability***

Today, global supply chains have grown into complex networks crisscrossing several continents, engaging diverse actors, and relying on a range of transportation modes [38, 39]. The complexity that exists in the system implies that ensuring that green logistics practices are carried out in an effective manner is something of a challenge. Supply chains are interconnected, so alterations in one part of the system can lead to reverberations that resonate across the network. As an example, the implementation of green transportation alternatives such as electric vehicles could help lower a firm's carbon footprint but may lead to additional costs and shipping times—or both—thereby impacting the profitability of the end-to-end supply chain [40]. In addition, multiple suppliers, manufacturers, and logistics providers may require coordination, each with their sustainability practices and standards, further complicating matters. Getting all stakeholders to agree on the greens in the green logistics can be cumbersome, and it usually means suffering through interminable rounds of negotiation and the eventual agreement to demonstrate unity based on sustainability metrics that have been so diluted as to be almost meaningless.

In addition, the global nature of supply chains makes the skills and behaviors needed to run them even harder — and we all know that global supply chains come with the added bonus of variation and the need to predict the future. On the other hand, supply chain disruption (caused by geopolitical instability and natural disasters, or changes in market demand) may interferes with green logistics practices as it can be challenging to stick with consistent supply chains [41]. As an example, a rapid surge in demand may simply require the utilization of faster, less environmental means of transportation in order to optimize expectations, meaning sustainability goals might be compromised. It is important that metrics are put in place to track and respond to these ever-changing influencers, making real-time data more demand and a prerequisite for any form of correct management but not always as cost-effective or tech-friendly. This means that businesses can find it hard to balance the considerable costs of some green logistics projects, next to the immediate need to make the supply chain work at its most resilient and efficient.

Other challenge for green logistics is to balance efficiency and sustainability. Classical supply chain businesses have high costs, minimize lead times, and optimize throughput [42]. The obstacles being capital and fixed costs, but as one can imagine, these goals often come into conflict with sustainability, meaning they are all about reducing carbon footprints and waste and replacing of non-renewable resources. For example, whilst optimal service time routing minimizes the fuel usage and emissions produced by vehicles, it may increase the delivery time of a product, and in contrast, using environmentally-friendly services will reduce the amount of fuel used but may introduce additional costs. Balancing efficiency with sustainability is a trade-off that needs to be taken into a strategic consideration which can address the short-term operational goals and its long-term environmental impacts simultaneously [43].

A good solution to this problem can be the assimilation of advanced technologies like Artificial Intelligence (AI), Machine Learning, and the Internet of Things (IoT). These innovations can also be used to improve supply chain visibility, and thus, more-prescient, and efficient resource utilization [44]. For instance, AI can optimize transportation routes so that less fuel is wasted but delivery times are kept at an overall acceptable level. This can lead to better, more adequately scheduled maintenance, as data collected through IoT helps prevent parts or entire systems from breaking down, and it may even help in better resource management. Nonetheless, implementation of these technologies entails substantial initial costs and a structural culture change to become more innovative and sustainable. Collaboration is another key component in trying to manage efficiency and sustainability in a supply chain [45]. When it comes to saving money and time, there are also physical solutions to the ecological problem—collaborative logistics practices (such as shared transportation networks and joint warehousing), which allow for more economical seizure of resources and, as a consequence, greater emission savings. In collaboration, companies are able to benefit from economies of scale as well as the ability to reduce empty miles and enhance the overall supply chain. But cooperation asks that the partner organizations trust each other and share the core objectives and measurements for sustainability. But the move to this kind of collaboration would be quite difficult, especially in highly competitive industries where most companies have no intention of sharing information and resources.

There is no journey in green logistics that is straightforward. Hence, the solution is in innovation, collaboration and in the strategic intersection of efficiency and sustainability. As a solution, it is critical for companies to advocate a broad spectrum of visionary sustainability as the integral part of their overall business and supply chain strategy. It requires investment in cutting-edge technologies and a reconsideration of traditional supply chain processes, as well as fostering sustainability throughout the organization. Leadership engagement (usually at the top level) is need because it defines the culture inside the organization and required to champion the green logistics initiatives. The legal environment and relevant government support measures can also greatly promote the development of green logistics [46]. Policies by governments to encourage sustainable practices such as subsidies for using public transportation, and for investing in green technologies, along with strict emissions standards, can help. These standards maintain equitable conditions that will prompt companies to incorporate sustainable habits in their corporate environment, whilst still enabling them to remain competitive. On top of that, with more and more companies realizing their operations need to align with consumer values the push from a consumer perspective toward environmentally conscious products can force companies to make green logistics a top priority. Green logistics is to transition into two essential elements of education and training. Organizations should invest in training and development in order to provide employees the knowledge and capability to facilitate green logistics projects [47]. This includes education on how to operate sophisticated equipment, informing individuals about existing environmental regulations and the promotion of a vision of continuous improvement. Creating an agile workforce of skilled, sustainability-conscious employees enables companies to successfully navigate the complexities of green logistics and strike the desired balance between efficiency and sustainability.

e) ***Cultural and Organizational Challenges***

Despite the virtues of green logistics, organizational resistance is one of the toughest obstacles. There is a culture within many companies that is influenced by cost-efficiency and the more traditional ways to operate. For this reason, one may face resistance from employees and management, who have the impression that green logistics may not offer benefits or may negatively affect the bottom line. Resistance can be seen in many forms including refusal to embrace new technologies, doubts about the affordability of sustainable solutions, and efforts to perpetuate the existing situation. Organizational resistance usually is driven by financial motivations [48]. Taking the steps to implement green logistics frequently entails large upfront costs associated with new technology, infrastructure, and training. It includes switching to electric vehicles for transport, transferring supply chain routes to optimize sustainability or setting up efficient systems of energy in warehouses, which all require a lot of money. If businesses are only making small profits, they might not want to expend resources on these initiatives, particularly if ROI only becomes obvious in the longer term. Furthermore, without a consistent regulatory mechanism that should accompany it, any commitment that companies might make to green logistics is itself on shaky ground. Leadership must communicate in clear terms that green logistics will yield long-term sustainability and financial benefits, and since this can face resistance within the organization, this can be a significant obstacle to overcome [49]. Illustrating the cost savings achieved by increased efficiency, waste reduction, reduced waste and a reputation of sustainability associated with the best practices will align organizational goals with sustainability goals. Also, a culture of innovation & learning should be created. It will encourage employees to adapt to new practices, technologies etc. Whatever the approach toward implementing green logistics may be, training and educating employees in the organization on the importance of the green logistics and its positive environmental impact could reduce the resistance and gain their support.

The change in consumer behavior has led to pressure on businesses to incorporate green logistics practices to continue to meet these demands [50]. Yet meeting sustainability expectations together with the need to consider costs, convenience and rapid delivery is not easy to navigate. Today, consumers expect companies to be open about how their operations are affecting the environment and make a real effort to reduce their impact. This expectation applies from the sourcing of raw materials to the completion of final delivery across supply chain. As such, business must guarantee that their logistics are not only efficient but also sustainable [51]. Living up to this will demand drastic changes to current modes of operations — from cutting down packaging waste to weaning off fossil fuels, and scaling back carbon emissions across the supply chain. But these changes are often difficult to make without sacrificing other aspects of the business like cost-effectiveness and operational efficiency. In addition, the willingness to pay a premium for sustainable products from consumer perspectives may differ significantly. So even as some consumers are prepared to chip in for a healthy planet, others may again prioritize cost and convenience over sustainability. This variation could make it difficult for companies to develop a standardized approach to green logistics. Companies, thus, have to strike a balance ensuring that they can meet the expectations regarding bettering the environment and perhaps assets by greenly and that they can stay accessibly or conveniencing consumers in a broader view of the market. Communication and marketing should get into this gap and there should be an education to let people know how important it is to use sustainable technologies and after this there will be a big demand for green logistics.

In order to address the issue of organizational resistance and consumer changing requirements, companies would have to adopt a strategic and multi-dimensional green logistics strategy [52]. One approach is to link sustainability more closely with business and supply chain strategy. This includes having clear sustainability targets, measuring progress with key performance indicators and ensuring that goals are met., which is created as a byproduct to the operations of the business. Integrating sustainability in the organization makes the green logistics strategy more consistent and deep-rooted. Another important strategy is collaboration. By working together with suppliers, logistics providers, and other stakeholders, firms can develop and apply sustainable business practices. Collaboration could bring about shared resources, cost reductions, and even innovation in green logistics [53]. This can range from co-creating industry standards for sustainability, sharing best-practice approaches, and making joint investment in initiatives like shared transportation networks or renewable energy projects. By partnering, they could increase the effectiveness of their work and develop a more strong ecosystem for supply chain. Lastly, technology and innovation are critical in solving the green logistics challenge [54]. For tracking and managing supply chain operations, smart technologies like Artificial Intelligence, Big data analytics and Internet of things help companies to get the visibility to their total logistics and provide enough data to alter the routes to and fro, reduce energy consumption, reduce wastes, chain processing orders and customer experiences [55, 56]. In turn, research and development of new low-impact solutions will support improvements and even help organizations pre-empt shifts in consumer expectations. Adopting technology helps companies to not only take green logistics practices to the next level but also maintain an edge in the market.

Conclusion

Given the extended nature of global supply chains, one of the primary hurdles facing green logistics management is complexity. These networks are spread over multiple countries, appeal to many actors, and comprise all types of systems, and so contribute to the global environmental burden. The networked nature of supply chains implies that changes in one tier of the system can cause ripple effects across the network, making it challenging to implement green logistics practices in a uniform and systematic way. In order to counter this complexity, the companies must look at the comprehensive model, giving the bigger picture of the entire supply chain ecosystem. The technology available to provide visibility and increased efficiency in operations today, with the likes of AI, ML, IoT etc., allows enterprises to obtain broader, faster, and deeper support from the ecosystem components for increased security. These technologies enable real-time visibility across the supply chain and identify areas of inefficiency and wastage that produce upstream and downstream solutions to mitigate their environmental impact. Moreover, suppliers need to be encouraged to work together with their supply chain partners. Companies should specify common sustainability objectives and indicators, and support these with collaborative activities that can consolidate efforts and make progress towards more sustainable logistics.

One of the main barriers that the adoption of green logistics faces until now is related to the organizational resistance. Old business models and modes of operation have historically favored cost efficiency and short-term profitability over sustainability. Combined with financial barriers and minimal enforcement of the long-term advantages of green logistics, this resistance is strengthened [57–61]. This will also mean a shift in organizational culture and leadership commitment in order to overcome this resistance. It is clear that, the adoption of sustainable practices is led by governance. Leaders should make an unambiguous case for change by communicating clearly as to how green logistics delivers long-term benefits, and how sustainability goals are aligned with business objectives. Additionally, investments in training and education are critical. Providing employees with the information and tools they need to put green logistics into practice can help eliminate pushback and cultivate a more common understanding along the organization. Furthermore, businesses may want to consider alternative business models that centralize sustainability in their core operations. This could generate new revenue streams and reduce their environmental footprint — for example, by adopting circular economy principles, which involve designing products to be reused, recycled, and repurposed.

There is a tough new consumer landscape for green logistics management, but it is definitely also an opportunity. With the trend of increasingly environmental-minded consumers, more informed and expectant of companies to be environmentally responsible and ethical. This, however, is a complex challenge in striking the balancing act between continuing to meet these expectations whilst still ensuring cost-effectiveness and operational efficiency. In order to satisfy evolving consumer wants, both of these need to be top of mind within a company. Transparency in communicating the logistics impact of their environmental strategy builds trust with consumers and preserves their loyalty. At the same time, one should make consumers part of sustainability journey, by providing them with environmentally friendly product and service offers and using messages to promote sustainable consumption. This can mean sustainability in packaging, container recycling, carbon-neutral delivery options, and generally showcasing how sustainable their products can be. Companies, large and small, especially those selling direct to consumers, should take note, and also find ways to align their logistics strategies with their consumers to set them apart in the market and drive demand for more sustains solutions.

Strategic Path Forward

The drive toward green logistics is neither easy nor does it hold back any temptation, but, it is an avenue to find new ways of being opportunistic, collaborative and competitive. To address these challenges, organizations need a strategic and comprehensive approach that incorporates sustainability throughout all logistics aspects. Investment in advanced technologies is a must. It is the insights which can be provided by other technologies like Artificial Intelligence (AI), Internet of Things (IoT), and big data analytics, that can be used to streamline supply chain operations and minimize waste, and energy and resource use [62, 63]. So if companies embrace these technologies, they can have efficiency and sustainability at the same time. Also, there is a need to build a cooperative culture. Collaborating with suppliers, logistics providers and other actors is incumbent for shared resources, savings, and innovation. Solutions driven by collaboration could further strengthen the effectiveness of individual initiatives and a more resilient ecosystem of the supply chain. Policy regulations and governmental motivation also play a crucial role in the road to green logistics. Government intervention can promote sustainable behaviors through measures that make the environmentally friendly options more attractive, such as subsidies investments in green technologies and enforce higher limits on emissions. With said measures, one can foster a fair competition and make companies embrace the transition to sustainability. Also, enterprises need to invest in the marketing and communications of such initiatives and increase awareness amongst consumers to bring the importance of green logistics on the forefront. Companies that generate a strong demand for sustainable products and services enables market transformation and vice versa.

References

1. Rajeev, A., Pati, R.K., Padhi, S.S., Govindan, K., Evolution of sustainability in supply chain management: A literature review. *J. Clean. Prod.*, 162, 299–314, 2017.
2. An, H., Razzaq, A., Nawaz, A., Noman, S.M., Khan, S.A.R., Nexus between green logistic operations and triple bottom line: Evidence from infrastructure-led Chinese outward foreign direct investment in Belt and Road host countries. *Environ. Sci. Pollut. Res.*, 28, 37, 51022–51045, 2021.
3. Akram, H.W., Abbas, H., Ciddikie, D., Green Manufacturing: A Comprehensive Exploration of Sustainable Practices and Industry 4.0 Integration, in: *Green Manufacturing for Industry 4.0*, pp. 159–178, Productivity Press, New York, 2024.
4. Gautam, P., Kishore, A., Khanna, A., Jaggi, C.K., Strategic defect management for a sustainable green supply chain. *J. Clean. Prod.*, 233, 226–241, 2019.
5. Schaubroeck, T. and Rugani, B., A revision of what life cycle sustainability assessment should entail: Towards modeling the net impact on human well-being. *J. Ind. Ecol.*, 21, 6, 1464–1477, 2017.
6. Rodrigue, J.P., Slack, B., Comtois, C., Green logistics, in: *Handbook of Logistics and Supply-Chain Management*, vol. 2, pp. 339–350, Emerald Group Publishing Limited, Howard House, Wagon Lane, Bingley BD16 lWA, UK, 2017.
7. Gierszewska, G. and Seretny, M., Sustainable behavior–the need of change in consumer and business attitudes and behavior. *Found. Manage.*, 11, 1, 197–208, 2019.
8. Chatti, W., Moving towards environmental sustainability: Information and communication technology (ICT), freight transport, and CO2 emissions. *Heliyon*, 7, 10, e08190, 2021.
9. Hoang, A.T., Varbanov, P.S., Nižetić, S., Sirohi, R., Pandey, A., Luque, R., Ng, K.H., Perspective review on municipal solid waste-to-energy route:

Characteristics, management strategy, and role in circular economy. *J. Clean. Prod.*, 359, 131897, 2022.
10. Malik, S.Y., Hayat Mughal, Y., Azam, T., Cao, Y., Wan, Z., Zhu, H., Thurasamy, R., Corporate social responsibility, green human resources management, and sustainable performance: Is organizational citizenship behavior towards environment the missing link? *Sustainability*, 13, 3, 1044, 2021.
11. Islam, M.S., Moeinzadeh, S., Tseng, M.L., Tan, K., A literature review on environmental concerns in logistics: Trends and future challenges. *Int. J. Logist. Res. Appl.*, 24, 2, 126–151, 2021.
12. Kumar, D., Singh, R.K., Mishra, R., Wamba, S.F., Applications of the Internet of Things for optimizing warehousing and logistics operations: A systematic literature review and future research directions. *Comput. Ind. Eng.*, 171, 108455, 2022.
13. Rini, K.A., Optimal policy for a green production system with quality inspection and warranty cost under environmental regulations. *Process Integr. Optim. Sustain.*, 5, 4, 859–873, 2021.
14. Sandaka, B.P. and Kumar, J., Alternative vehicular fuels for environmental decarbonization: A critical review of challenges in using electricity, hydrogen, and biofuels as a sustainable vehicular fuel. *Chem. Eng. J. Adv.*, 14, 100442, 2023.
15. Fritz, M.M. and Ruel, S., What does "sustainable supply chain management" really mean? A contribution to bridging the gap between research, education and practice. *Int. J. Logist. Manag.*, 35, 2, 332–363, 2024.
16. Harala, L., Aarikka-Stenroos, L., Ritala, P., Coopetition for a circular economy: Horizontal initiatives in resolving collective environmental challenges, in: *Stakeholder Engagement in a Sustainable Circular Economy: Theoretical and Practical Perspectives*, pp. 311–362, Springer International Publishing, Cham, 2023.
17. Yang, Y., Chen, J., Lee, P.K., Cheng, T.C.E., How to enhance the effects of the green supply chain management strategy in the organization: A diffusion process perspective. *Transp. Res. Part E Logist. Transp. Rev.*, 175, 103148, 2023.
18. Akram, H.W., Abbas, H., Sulaiman, M.B., Logistics & Supply Chain Resilience in Context of Oman, in: *Reference Module in Social Sciences*, Elsevier, Amsterdam, 2024b, https://www.sciencedirect.com/science/article/pii/B9780443137013000554.
19. Umar, M. and Safi, A., Do green finance and innovation matter for environmental protection? A Case OECD Economies. *Energy Econ.*, 119, 106560, 2023.
20. Cassetti, G., Boitier, B., Elia, A., Le Mouël, P., Gargiulo, M., Zagamé, P., Nikas, A., Koasidis, K., Doukas, H., Chiodi, A., The interplay among COVID-19 economic recovery, behavioural changes, and the European Green Deal: An energy-economic modelling perspective. *Energy*, 263, 125798, 2023.

21. Neira, M., Erguler, K., Ahmady-Birgani, H., Al-Hmoud, N.D., Fears, R., Gogos, C., Hobbhahn, N., Koliou, M., Kostrikis, L.G., Lelieveld, J., Majeed, A., Climate change and human health in the Eastern Mediterranean and Middle East: Literature review, research priorities and policy suggestions. *Environ. Res.*, 216, 114537, 2023.
22. Charoenwong, B., Kowaleski, Z.T., Kwan, A., Sutherland, A.G., RegTech: Technology-driven compliance and its effects on profitability, operations, and market structure. *J. Financ. Econ.*, 154, 103792, 2024.
23. Zhang, W., Zhang, W., Daim, T.U., The voluntary green behavior in green technology innovation: The dual effects of green human resource management system and leader green traits. *J. Bus. Res.*, 165, 114049, 2023.
24. Emeka-Okoli, S., Nwankwo, T.C., Otonnah, C.A., Nwankwo, E.E., Corporate governance and CSR for sustainability in Oil and Gas: Trends, challenges, and best practices: A review. *World J. Adv. Res. Rev.*, 21, 3, 078–090, 2024.
25. Richey Jr., R.G., Chowdhury, S., Davis-Sramek, B., Giannakis, M., Dwivedi, Y.K., Artificial intelligence in logistics and supply chain management: A primer and roadmap for research. *J. Bus. Logist.*, 44, 4, 532–549, 2023.
26. Mittal, G., Garg, A., Pareek, K., A review of the technologies, challenges and policies implications of electric vehicles and their future development in India. *Energy Storage*, 6, 1, e562, 2024.
27. Khan, U., Zevenhoven, R., Stougie, L., Tveit, T.M., Life cycle cost analysis (LCCA) of Stirling-cycle-based heat pumps vs. conventional Boilers. *Clean. Environ. Syst.*, 8, 100105, 2023.
28. Sinsel, S.R., Riemke, R.L., Hoffmann, V.H., Challenges and solution technologies for the integration of variable renewable energy sources—a review. *Renew. Energy*, 145, 2271–2285, 2020.
29. Farooqui, A., Bengtsson, K., Falkman, P., Fabian, M., Towards data-driven approaches in manufacturing: an architecture to collect sequences of operations. *Int. J. Prod. Res.*, 58, 16, 4947–4963, 2020.
30. Chavan, L. and Jindal, P., Revolutionizing the Automobile Industry: A Blue Ocean Strategy Approach, in: *Balancing Automation and Human Interaction in Modern Marketing*, pp. 248–262, IGI Global, USA, 2024.
31. Rehman, N., Mahmood, A., Ibtasam, M., Murtaza, S.A., Iqbal, N., Molnár, E., The psychology of resistance to change: the antidotal effect of organizational justice, support and leader-member exchange. *Front. Psychol.*, 12, 678952, 2021.
32. LaMonaca, S. and Ryan, L., The state of play in electric vehicle charging services – A review of infrastructure provision, players, and policies. *Renew. Sustain. Energy Rev.*, 154, 111733, 2022.
33. Gulagi, A., Alcanzare, M., Bogdanov, D., Esparcia Jr., E., Ocon, J., Breyer, C., Transition pathway towards 100% renewable energy across the sectors of power, heat, transport, and desalination for the Philippines. *Renew. Sustain. Energy Rev.*, 144, 110934, 2021.

34. Javaid, M., Haleem, A., Singh, R.P., Suman, R., Substantial capabilities of robotics in enhancing industry 4.0 implementation. *Cogn. Rob.*, 1, 58–75, 2021.
35. Sonar, H., Mukherjee, A., Gunasekaran, A., Singh, R.K., Sustainable supply chain management of automotive sector in context to the circular economy: A strategic framework. *Bus. Strat. Environ.*, 31, 7, 3635–3648, 2022.
36. Trivellas, P., Malindretos, G., Reklitis, P., Implications of green logistics management on sustainable business and supply chain performance: evidence from a survey in the Greek agri-food sector. *Sustainability*, 12, 24, 10515, 2020.
37. Joyce, C. and Stanford, J., *Manufacturing the Energy Revolution: Australia's Position in the Global race for Sustainable Manufacturing*, The Centre for Future Work at the Australia Institute, 2023.
38. Akram, H.W., Abbas, H., Saeed, A., Make-in Oman for Boosting Economic Development and Supply Chain, in: *Reference Module in Social Sciences*, Elsevier, Amsterdam, 2024c, https://doi.org/10.1016/B978-0-443-13701-3.00056-6.
39. Royle, K., Cycling in the time of the biodigital: Small acts towards a conscious uncoupling from non-regenerative digitised economies, in: *Bioinformational Philosophy and Postdigital Knowledge Ecologies*, pp. 161–181, Springer International Publishing, Cham, 2022.
40. Patil, A., Shardeo, V., Dwivedi, A., Moktadir, M.A., Bag, S., Examining the interactions among smart supply chains and carbon reduction strategies: To attain carbon neutrality. *Bus. Strateg. Environ.*, 33, 2, 1227–1246, 2024.
41. Roscoe, S., Aktas, E., Petersen, K.J., Skipworth, H.D., Handfield, R.B., Habib, F., Redesigning global supply chains during compounding geopolitical disruptions: the role of supply chain logics. *Int. J. Oper. Prod. Manag.*, 42, 9, 1407–1434, 2022.
42. Dey, B.K., Bhuniya, S., Sarkar, B., Involvement of controllable lead time and variable demand for a smart manufacturing system under a supply chain management. *Expert Syst. Appl.*, 184, 115464, 2021.
43. Sharma, A., Pathak, S., Borah, S.B., Adhikary, A., Collaboration strategies in buyer-supplier relational (BSR) networks and sustainable firm performance: A trade-off story. *Int. J. Prod. Econ.*, 253, 108558, 2022.
44. Al-Debei, M.M. and Bus. Anal., J., The era of business analytics: identifying and ranking the differences between business intelligence and data science from practitioners' perspective using the Delphi method. *J. Bus. Anal.*, 7, 2, 94–119, 2024.
45. Alzoubi, H., Ahmed, G., Al-Gasaymeh, A., Kurdi, B., Empirical study on sustainable supply chain strategies and its impact on competitive priorities: The mediating role of supply chain collaboration. *Manag. Sci. Lett.*, 10, 3, 703–708, 2020.

46. Zhang, W., Zhang, M., Zhang, W., Zhou, Q., Zhang, X., What influences the effectiveness of green logistics policies? A grounded theory analysis. *Sci. Total Environ.*, 714, 136731, 2020.
47. Cheng, Y., Masukujjaman, M., Sobhani, F.A., Hamayun, M., Alam, S.S., Green logistics, green human capital, and circular economy: the mediating role of sustainable production. *Sustainability*, 15, 2, 1045, 2023.
48. Thompson, B.S. and Rust, S., Blocking blockchain: Examining the social, cultural, and institutional factors causing innovation resistance to digital technology in seafood supply chains. *Technol. Soc.*, 73, 102235, 2023.
49. Paddeu, D., Parkhurst, G., Rosenberg, G., Carhart, N., Taylor, C., Promoting sustainable urban freight through stakeholder engagement to co-create decarbonisation pathways in the UK. *Res. Transp. Econ.*, 104, 101424, 2024.
50. Sharma, M., Luthra, S., Joshi, S., Kumar, A., Jain, A., Green logistics driven circular practices adoption in industry 4.0 Era: A moderating effect of institution pressure and supply chain flexibility. *J. Clean. Prod.*, 383, 135284, 2023.
51. Akram, H.W., Akhtar, S., Ahmad, A., Anwar, I., Sulaiman, M.A.B.A., Developing a conceptual framework model for effective perishable food cold-supply-chain management based on structured literature review. *Sustainability*, 15, 6, 4907, 2023d.
52. Singh, R.K., Strengthening resilience in supply chains: the role of multi-layer flexibility, supply chain risks and environmental dynamism. *Int. J. Logist. Manag.*, 35, 6, 1807–1826, 2024.
53. Prataviera, L.B., Creazza, A., Perotti, S., A call to action: a stakeholder analysis of green logistics practices. *Int. J. Logist. Manag.*, 35, 3, 979–1008, 2024.
54. Gupta, A. and Singh, R.K., Applications of emerging technologies in logistics sector for achieving circular economy goals during COVID 19 pandemic: analysis of critical success factors. *Int. J. Logist. Res. Appl.*, 27, 4, 451–472, 2024.
55. Lee, K.L., Wong, S.Y., Alzoubi, H.M., Al Kurdi, B., Alshurideh, M.T., El Khatib, M., Adopting smart supply chain and smart technologies to improve operational performance in manufacturing industry. *Int. J. Eng. Bus. Manag.*, 15, 18479790231200614, 2023.
56. Kumar, D., Agrawal, S., Singh, R.K., Singh, R.K., IoT-enabled coordination for recommerce circular supply chain in the Industry 4.0 era. *Internet Things*, 26, 101140, 2024.
57. Dadsena, K.K. and Pant, P., Analyzing the barriers in supply chain digitization: sustainable development goals perspective. *Oper. Manag. Res.*, 16, 4, 1684–1697, 2023.
58. Dadsena, K.K., Pant, P., Paul, S.K., Pratap, S., Overcoming strategies for supply chain digitization barriers: Implications for sustainable development goals. *Bus. Strateg. Environ.*, 33, 3887–3910, 2024.
59. Mathiyazhagan, K., Govindan, K., NoorulHaq, A., Pressure analysis for green supply chain management implementation in Indian industries using analytic hierarchy process. *Int. J. Prod. Res.*, 52, 188–202, 2014.

60. Mathivathanan, D., Mathiyazhagan, K., Rana, N.P., Khorana, S., Dwivedi, Y.K., Barriers to the adoption of blockchain technology in business supply chains: a total interpretive structural modelling (TISM) approach. *Int. J. Prod. Res.*, 59, 3338–3359, 2021.
61. Sonar, H., Sharma, I., Ghag, N., Singh, R.K., Barriers for achieving sustainable agri supply chain: study in context to Indian MSMEs. *Int. J. Logist. Res. Appl.*, 1–20, 2024, https://doi.org/10.1080/13675567.2024.2345359.
62. Goodarzian, F., Ghasemi, P., Appolloni, A., Ali, I., Cárdenas-Barrón, L.E., Supply chain network design based on Big Data Analytics: heuristic-simulation method in a pharmaceutical case study. *Prod. Plann. Control*, 1–21, 2024, https://doi.org/10.1080/09537287.2024.2344729.
63. Mukherjee, S., Nagariya, R., Mathiyazhagan, K., Baral, M.M., Pavithra, M.R., Appolloni, A., Artificial intelligence-based reverse logistics for improving circular economy performance: a developing country perspective. *Int. J. Logist. Manag.*, 35, 1779–1806, 2024.

2

Navigating Green Logistics: Identifying Challenges and Potential Solutions

Rohith Ram R., Ram Prasad K.* and M. Nishal

Department of Mechanical Engineering, Sri Venkateswara College of Engineering, Tamil Nadu, India

Abstract
Adoption of green logistics is gaining traction at an unprecedented rate. Despite this there exists a myriad of unidentified challenges in addition to a dearth of enablers to aid in the overcoming of said challenges. Employing appropriate methods to overcome specific challenges is of monumental importance now more than ever, mapping these factors provides great potential upside to companies of all monetary denominations in achieving long term sustainability. This work focuses primarily on providing industries with a concise view on hurdles they may encounter throughout the implementation process in addition to tools and measures to counter these, ensuring organizational sustainability goals are met.

Keywords: Reverse logistics, green logistics, sustainable supply chain management, decarbonization in supply chain management

2.1 Introduction

In the all-encompassing sphere of logistics, types of services provided are primarily associated with certain hallmark examples these set in place the groundwork for effective logistics decision making. The concept of logistics in production can be presented in terms of the flow of raw materials procurement, component supply throughout the production cycle and of the finished products. For instance, an automobile manufacturer may

**Corresponding author*: ramprasadk2008@gmail.com

K. Mathiyazhagan, Krishna Kumar Dadsena, Rajesh Kumar Singh, Aakanksha Kishore and Andrea Appolloni (eds.) Sustainable Operations of Logistics and Supply Chain Management, (25–38) © 2025 Scrivener Publishing LLC

purchase parts from different suppliers, integrate them into automobiles *via* efficient value addition chain, and then supply the finished automobiles to the dealers or directly to consumers.

Retail logistics on the other hand deals with the flow of goods from manufacturers to retailers and includes distribution to the end consumers as well as providing provisions for after-sales service(s). For instance, electronic manufacturers organize logistics to ship products to dealers, who have their own logistics systems to transport goods to end users.

Cold chain logistics services involve the distribution and storage of products that are sensitive to change in temperature for instance, perishable goods. These include but are not limited to food products and drugs. A cold chain logistics firm may be expected to deliver fresh fruits from production sites to grocery chains all over the world and should ensure that the products are shipped in an optimal temperature range and humidity level in order to meet quality standards, viability in the market and ensure safety of the consumer. In addition to this, there are third-party logistics (3PL) service providers who deal with the selling of various services to other businesses for example, the Amazon logistics service department takes responsibility for sorting, packing, and delivering orders. This enables sellers to concentrate on creation of new products and promotion of the same.

The determining factor in the selection of the three logistics formats is what body determines the logistics service level. In the self-operated format, the customer of the product determines the service level of the equipment selling the product. On the other hand, in the contract outsourcing format of 3PL enterprise or platform outsourcing is determined by 3PL enterprise or the platform. According to the transport and location service provider the objective of the firm is to provide services that are cost effective to the customer while simultaneously providing the best service possible, meaning that the maximum level of servicing should be sustained so as to accommodate a large number of customers. This service levels affect the product seller's repurchase rate of the product that in turn determines the profit made [1]. While taking into consideration the aforementioned factors and adhering to green logistics (GL) principles creates a new challenge in terms of accommodating reverse logistics needs in the supply chain. It is essential to ensure potential challenges and possible solutions are mapped in industry specific settings to ease the adoption of green logistics principles.

2.2 Green Logistics

Green logistics refers to the concept of implementing sustainable practices within logistics and supply chain operations to reduce environmental impact. The goal of green logistics is to conduct transportation, material handling, warehousing, and other supply chain activities in a way that minimizes carbon emissions, waste generation, and overall environmental footprint. Key aspects of a GL approach involve improving transportation efficiency through route optimization, load consolidation and backhauling, adopting cleaner vehicle technologies like electric trucks and automation, utilizing renewable energy sources at facilities, promoting recycling and reducing packaging, engaging suppliers in sustainability efforts and giving preference, when possible, to environmentally friendly products and materials. Implementing measures like these from sourcing all the way to the end-of-life for the product, aids organizations to develop resource-efficient, low-carbon logistics networks that are better aligned with environment protection objectives [2].

Green logistics is a subfield of green supply chain management where the main aim is to lower the detrimental effect of logistics operations conducted within the supply chain on the environment. They include practices that support sustainability in the flow of goods, services, and information through the improvement of the systems. Interorganizational cooperation is key in ensuring GL and supply chain management. Companies working with their trading partners to support pool point, cluster delivery and thereby cutting down on empty miles is the need of the hour. Such partnerships encourage pathways to the organization of supply chains that minimize CO2 emissions and expenses associated with logistics activities. Moreover, green supply chains rely primarily on data and technology. Through data analysis and technological reinforcement, it is possible to control and manage the logistics activities in real time. This includes but is not limited to, precise location tracking, route planning, and predictive analysis to assist in decision making to ensure a net neutral impact on the environment [3].

The concepts of GL are essential due to increasingly pertinent environment challenges posed at a global scale [4]. The primary problem with conventional logistics processes is the negative influence it has on the environment. Green logistics systems can potentially be put in place to reduce the negative impact organizations have on the environment. Achieving substantial reductions in greenhouse gases emitted during logistics activities is of the utmost priority to ensure sustainability in the long run.

In addition to this GL is also concerned with the generation and management of waste throughout the transportation cycle. A myriad of industries would benefit greatly from the implementation of GL frameworks. In the online retail and e-commerce sectors GL may prove highly beneficial in terms of identification of optimal transportation networks, optimal inventory management, and minimization of packaging. Ensuring sustainable packaging and designing environmentally friendly systems for last mile delivery could potentially improve customer satisfaction and improved brand image. Construction and building materials is another industry/product that requires extensive revision through the lens of GL principles. Construction processes deal with product supply chain networks that consume resources while generating a disproportionately high amount waste.

Through the integration of green supply chain management principles ensuring environmental sustainability in the long run becomes significantly straightforward but this requires identifying and addressing challenges in the process.

2.2.1 Overview

In today's consumer centric world, the flow of goods across the globe allows for a true free market. This necessitates environmentally conscious logistics that supports decentralized manufacturing and is sustainable in the long run.

The conventionally modus operandi of designing and operating a logistics chain that facilitates the movement of goods from sourcing materials, to production, to retailers and finally to consumers in a linear fashion is null and void when taking into account the principles of green logistics. In lieu of utilizing an obsolete framework that focuses solely on cost effectiveness, lead time minimization and transparency in terms of: material, information and cash flow; systems must be designed taking into account additional factors such as: energy efficiency, accommodation for reverse logistics and overall sustainability [5].

Reverse logistics entails creating provisions for the end consumer to move goods either to a manufacturer or a party that further processes the goods as detailed in Figure 2.1. This serves two primary functions:

- allowing for rectification, recalls and maintenance of the goods
- recycling of the goods

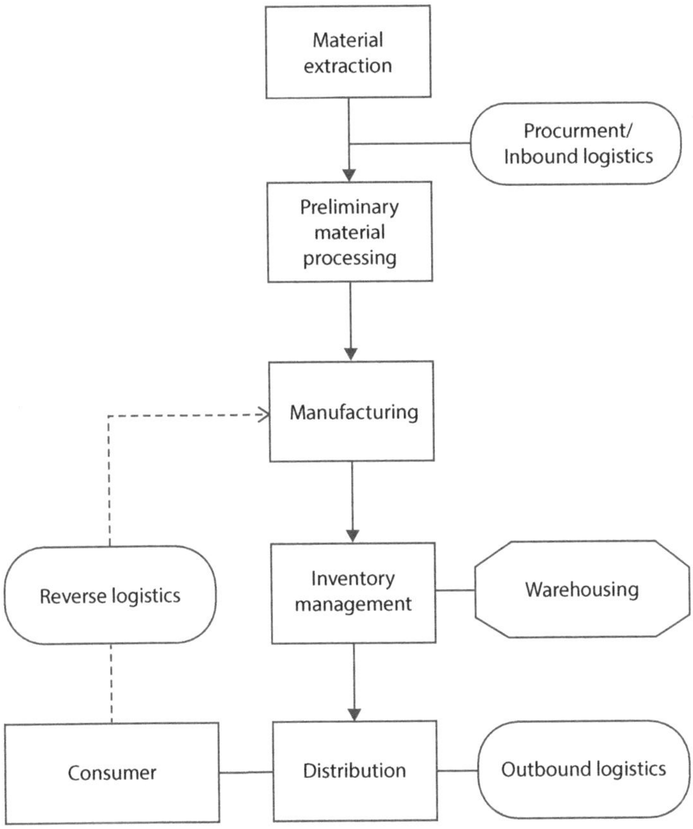

Figure 2.1 Process outline of green logistics.

2.3 Hindrances

It is essential to taken into account the challenges involved in planning, implementing, and controlling a green logistics chain to ensure its smooth operation [6], this encompasses gaining an understanding of what entails GL. It is the set of practices that makes all parties involved cognizant of the environmental impact caused by the system and its subsequent betterment towards environmental sustainability.

The net goal of GL is to ensure decarbonization of the process by accounting for challenges posed through its initiation and operation; these include but are not limited to:

Empty miles: In freight networks empty miles is when trucks among other means of transport, travel to locations empty post completion of initial unloading [7]. This backhaul is often to a successive loading location. Allowing for the process of gathering and distributing goods at the end of life from consumers to manufacturers for the purpose of reusing, remanufacturing or recycling offers environmental benefits and ensures minimization of empty miles. This in turn ensures an economic benefit that allows business to remain competitive. In addition to facilitating GL reducing empty miles also contributes towards value creation in the product life cycle.

Monetary flow: Conventionally an ideal supply chain guarantees flow of goods, monetary resources and information in the forward direction and this flow is terminated at the end consumer. To facilitate GL and reverse movement it is not sufficient to provide a network solely for the transfer of goods but a system to accommodate the movement of monetary resources in addition to the aforementioned. Poor workflow initiation and management through logistics should not hinder the end consumer and cause them to opt out of reverse logistics operations.

Policy: Internal quality control guidelines of firms may dictate the destroying or discarding of retuned goods due to possibility of harming reputation and cannibalization in the market.

As a consequence of increasingly high return rates from retailers, due in part to competition, manufacturers tend to receive disagreeably quantities of goods to be reprocessed. This tends to offer the manufacturer lower returns on the secondary market. There is a dearth of supportive polices in reverse logistics from the government and lack of extensive standard operating procedure for the recycling of certain products [8].

Information: Information or the lack thereof is a major hindrance in the operation of reverse logistics. Uncertainty in terms of the number of goods, arrival and processing time; and nature of return are the primary causes of disruption in information flow systems [9].

The identification of nature of retuned goods is particularly important to determine additional factors such as processing time, classification into authorized or unauthorized returns and costs involved in making the goods viable for the secondary market.

Return rates: The arrival of returned goods either to the manufacturer or a tertiary recycling party must be limited to accommodate current processing and redistribution rates to avoid discrepancies in supply and demand on the secondary market.

A strong quality control framework can aid in reducing returns in addition to transparency in terms of concerted effort allowing the consumer to fully understand the product or service being provided to them, this ensures higher customer satisfaction and reduces the need for reverse logistics [10].

Negligence: A myriad of parameters must be considered for optimization when developing a logistics model, the added aspects of reverse logistics must also be weighted appropriately. While considering factors such as costs, nature of product, existing technology and feasibility, flexibility and warehousing network are the norm; sustainability as a whole is an afterthought throughout the planning and decision making process. Forethought in terms of packaging considerations to allow for seamless reverse logistics processes is essential in GL principles with a viable logistics chain that meets the needs of all parties involved [11].

Distribution modes: Factoring in the environmental friendliness of the mode of transportation used to move goods is an afterthought during parametric evaluation in decision making.

Ensuring monetary gain and customer satisfaction is considered paramount. This is due in part to lack of enforceable policy put in places by governments that penalizes firms that do not meet emissions requirements.

Invisibility: To a consumer, the most cost-effective option that ensures their needs (right product, right time, right condition, right quantity, right place and right condition) are met is often the best. Here, the impact on environment is not taken into consideration when, given the choice, selecting a logistics system [12]. Incentivization for a logistics firm to implement GL practices is as a result at an all-time low. Moreover, adopting green practices exposes companies to an environmentally conscious clientele. Sensitizing customers towards the strain placed on systems due to low delivery times and their consequent impact on loading planning is vital.

Initial investment: Due to the nature of operation in the logistics industry, profit margins are extremely tight leaving little to no cash flow for companies to front large investments towards sustainability. This impacts a myriad of areas, including but not limited to: packaging, dependence on fossil fuels due to reliance on archaic fleets, et cetera. Investing towards a green future would inevitably increase prices on the market which the consumer may find undesirable. The process of overcoming barriers in the implementation of GL is manyfold and cannot be performed all together [13]. Identifying enablers to resolve the challenges posed in the operation of a successful GL system is the need of the hour.

2.4 Enablers

Despite the numerous challenges in adhering to principles of green logistics management, there exists a multitude of measures, tools, procedures and enablers that aid in overcoming the aforementioned barriers [14]. Every enabler addresses multiple challenges due to their versatile nature, interconnectedness and vast scope of application in the GL management chain. These include but are not limited to:

Packaging: Sustainable packaging in terms of materials used and methods implemented to execute the packing are essential in ensuring contribution towards net zero emissions as well as meeting consumer requirements. Specifically the usage of recyclable and reusable materials enables companies to unlock new markets and create new revenue streams.
Quality control: Implementing advanced quality control metrics, measures and tools ensures the end consumer receives a satisfactory product, this reduces return rates. *In situ* quality control contributes positively to lead time by cutting down on post-production quality control time providing an allowance for route optimization.
Environmental regulation: Government regulation ensures logistics firms adhere to emission standards [15].
Incentivization: Providing monetary incentives to early adopters of green logistics framework by means of exemptions and subsides provides extrinsic motive to rapidly move towards a more sustainable future.
Warehouse automation: Minimizing human intervention and eliminating human product interaction pre delivery aids in reducing lead time by the application of AGVs (automated guided vehicles), automated storage and retrieval systems; and layout planning to accommodate for reverse logistics needs.
Optimization: When weighing parameters in designing a logistics framework it is imperative to taken into account sustainability in addition to the conventionally considerations, including but not limited to: costs, nature of product, existing technology and feasibility, flexibility and warehousing network [16].
Renewable energy utilization: Contributing towards a company's overall decarbonization is a crucial aspect of GL. Reducing emissions especially at end mile deliveries in urban transportation settings is unfeasible in the long run with reliance on fossil fuel consuming obsolete fleets. At the grass root level all enablers do not contribute equally towards the attainment of long term sustainability. Specific industries require detailed analyses on the best possible initial enabler to employ, this ensure all parties involved are satisfied and that every challenge is overcome with the least possible resistance [17].

The inability to implement green supply chain principles has been one of the main detriments on the global outreach of relatively small firms. As governments continue to implement increasingly stringent environmental preservation standards and place caps on emissions, the time has come for widespread adoption, regardless of size of the firm, of GL as a part of the overall of their overall supply chain [18]. Therefore, it is crucial to distinguish the imperative enablers that support the green supply chain implementation and establish correlation between specific barriers and the enablers to be used to overcome the same.

2.5 Mapping

Providing specific enablers for each challenge is key in allowing for ease of navigation when adhering to green logistics principles. Tackling each challenge individually, while it is the most environmentally appeasing solution, is not the most monetarily agreeable or consumer friendly approach. It is thus essential to ensure each enabler implemented tackles the hurdles posed by multiple challenges.

Table 2.1 elucidates the relationship between identified challenges and appropriate enablers to overcome the same.

Environmental sustainability is an ever-growing concern for multinational organizations and companies due to the recent changes in global geo-politics post COVID. To a certain extent, there are relatively high environmental standards in many developed nations. This forces industries to incorporate large environmental-friendly processes to decrease the impact they have on the environment [19]. Simultaneously, awareness of environmentally friendly logistics solutions is on the rise among customer, especially those in the developing nations. International business organizations view the economies of developing countries as a major area of operation. Organizations operating in developing nations are forced to factor in issues pertaining to environment in their operations in a bid to effectively satisfy the needs of their clients thereby retaining their competitive advantage. To stay competitive, firms have no choice but to employ challenge specific enablers [20].

2.6 Industry-Specific Case Study

With reference to the automotive industry, conventionally green logistics practices are incorporated in the steps before the end consumer receives the product. When a component failure in an automobile necessitates a

Table 2.1 Challenges and corresponding enablers to overcome hurdles.

Factors	**Quality control**	**Packaging**	**Environmental regulation**	**Incentivization**	**Warehouse automation**	**Optimization**	**Renewable energy**
Empty Miles							
(i) Warehouse network					✓	✓	
(ii) Route planning				✓		✓	
Monetary Flow							
(i) Consumer willingness				✓		✓	
(ii) Platform					✓	✓	
Policy							
(i) Internal			✓	✓			
(ii) Collaborative			✓	✓			
(iii) Government			✓	✓			
Information							
(i) Quality control	✓						
(ii) Consumer	✓			✓	✓		
Return rates							
(i) Quality control	✓	✓				✓	
(ii) Transparency				✓			
Negligence			✓				✓
Distribution modes							

(*Continued*)

Table 2.1 Challenges and corresponding enablers to overcome hurdles. (*Continued*)

Factors	Quality control	Packaging	Environmental regulation:	Incentivization	Warehouse automation	Optimization	Renewable energy
(i) Monitoring		✓			✓	✓	
(ii) Customer appeasement	✓						✓
Invisibility	✓	✓	✓	✓	✓	✓	✓
Initial investment							
(i) Incentivization				✓			
(ii) Company willingness			✓	✓			✓

factory recall of passenger vehicles it is often the consumer themselves that becomes the end mile delivery agent in the reverse logistics chain. Toyota Motor Europe has an extensive sustainable purchasing guideline that extends to every one of its interest parties in the supply chain; this does not however lay guidelines for consumers to collaborate in efforts towards suitability in the supply chain. This is an internal policy challenge and the corresponding enablers are, including but not limited to: incentivization, in the form of tangible services provided by the company in exchange for adhering to green logistics practices and quality control by eliminating the need for frequent reverse logistics operations such as unscheduled maintenance visits.

An Indian owned motorcycle brand under the Eicher Motors Limited group issued a global recall of all its products manufactured between November 2022 and March 2023 owing to reflectors not meeting mandated safety standards. Remaining in compliance with government mandates regarding safety in motor vehicles requires companies to perform reverse logistics such as the aforementioned occurrence. Return rates are a challenge that plagues the automotive sector which can be solved through superior quality control measures; this ultimately negates the need for reverse logistics measures that consumers participate in to ensure environmental suitability of the operation is kept intact.

2.7 Conclusion and Future Work

Decarbonization provides incentives to firm in terms of broadening customer base, favorable outlook from policy makers and ultimately greater monetary gain through the early imbibing of sustainability in the logistics operations of their firms. Small players tend to face greater difficulty in the integration of GL due to lack of monetary backing and inability to guarantee payoff in the short term. Further analysis is required to determine the specific challenges that plague GL integration in micro, small and medium enterprises and the variation of enabler requirements in various industry types. GL holds great potential in aiding firms towards meeting sustainable development goals (SDG). Since the major contributor, in most industries, towards the inability to meet SDGs is supply chain management it would be greatly beneficial to all facets of an organization to adopt green logistics principles through meticulous identification of challenges and adopting corresponding enablers.

References

1. Zhou, C., Bai, D., Liu, Z., Yu, J., Fei, Y., Optimal Logistics Service Strategies in Green Agricultural Product Supply Chains with E-commerce Platforms. *Sustain. Oper. Comput.*, 5, 157, Jun. 2024, doi: 10.1016/j.susoc.2024.06.002.
2. Shishodia, A., Sharma, R., Pavithra, .M.R., Mathiyazhagan, K., Analyzing drivers of sustainable project-driven supply chains: A fuzzy Delphi methodology–grey relational analysis approach. *Bus. Strategy Environ.*, 33, 3, 1626–1646, Mar. 2024, doi: https://doi.org/10.1002/bse.3564.
3. Singh, R.K., Mathiyazhagan, K., Scuotto, V., Pironti, M., Green Open Innovation and Circular Economy: Investigating the Role of Big Data Management and Sustainable Supply Chain. *IEEE Trans. Eng. Manag.*, 71, 8417–8429, 2024, doi: 10.1109/TEM.2024.3387107.
4. Mathiyazhagan, K., Majumdar, A., Appolloni, A., Guest editorial: Resilience in sustainable supply chain post-COVID-19: future pathways. *Int. J. Logist. Manage.*, 34, 4, 873–878, Jan. 2023, doi: 10.1108/IJLM-07-2023-603.
5. Mathiyazhagan, K., Rajak, S., Sampurna Panigrahi, S., Agarwal, V., Manani, D., Reverse supply chain management in manufacturing industry: a systematic review. *Int. J. Product. Perfor.*, 70, 4, 859–892, Mar. 29, 2021, doi: 10.1108/IJPPM-06-2019-0293.
6. Dadsena, K.K., Pant, P., Paul, S.K., Pratap, S., Overcoming strategies for supply chain digitization barriers: Implications for sustainable development goals. *Bus. Strategy Environ.*, 3, 5, 2, Jul. 2024, doi: 10.1002/bse.3681.

7. Dadsena, K.K., Sarmah, S.P., Naikan, V.N.A., Mathiyazhagan, K., Rodrigues, V.S., Performance measurement of road freight transportation: A case of trucking industry. *Transp. Policy (Oxf.)*, 137, 125–140, 2023, doi: https://doi.org/10.1016/j.tranpol.2023.04.015.
8. Mishra, A., Dutta, P., Jayasankar, S., Jain, P., Mathiyazhagan, K., A review of reverse logistics and closed-loop supply chains in the perspective of circular economy. *Benchmarking An Int. J.*, 30, 3, 975–1020, Jan. 2023, doi: 10.1108/BIJ-11-2021-0669.
9. Dwivedi, A., Agrawal, D., Jha, A., Mathiyazhagan, K., Studying the interactions among Industry 5.0 and circular supply chain: Towards attaining sustainable development. *Comput. Ind. Eng.*, 176, 108927, 2023, doi: https://doi.org/10.1016/j.cie.2022.108927.
10. Senthil, V. and Mathiyazhagan, K., Chapter 6 - Issues and challenges of blockchain technology implementation in the meat supply chain, in: *Blockchain in a Volatile-Uncertain-Complex-Ambiguous World*, K. Mathiyazhagan, V.R. Sreedharan, D. Mathivathanan, V. Sunder M (Eds.), pp. 77–88, Elsevier, 2023, doi: https://doi.org/10.1016/B978-0-323-89963-5.00016-2.
11. Martínez, J. and Mathiyazhagan, K., Green Supply Chain Management: Evolution of the Concept, Practices and Trends, in: *Recent Advances in Mechanical Engineering*, H. Kumar and P.K. Jain (Eds.), pp. 47–56, Springer Singapore, Singapore, 2020.
12. Mathiyazhagan, K., Krishnan, S., Bharathi, U., Appolloni, A., Pathways towards reverse logistics adoption in Indian educational institutes: a challenging factors analysis. *OPSEARCH*, 58, 3, 661–689, Sep. 2021, doi: 10.1007/s12597-020-00496-z.
13. Govindan, K., Kaliyan, M., Kannan, D., Haq, A.N., Barriers analysis for green supply chain management implementation in Indian industries using analytic hierarchy process. *Int. J. Prod. Econ.*, 147, PART B, 555–568, Jan. 2014, doi: 10.1016/j.ijpe.2013.08.018.
14. Mukherjee, S., Nagariya, R., Mathiyazhagan, K., Baral, M.M., Pavithra, M.R., Appolloni, A., Artificial intelligence-based reverse logistics for improving circular economy performance: a developing country perspective. *Int. J. Logist. Manage.*, volahead-of-print, ahead-of-print, 1779–1806, Jan. 2024, doi: 10.1108/IJLM-03-2023-0102.
15. Mathiyazhagan, K., Rajak, S., Sampurna Panigrahi, S., Agarwal, V., Manani, D., Reverse supply chain management in manufacturing industry: a systematic review. *Int. J. Prod. Perform. Manage.*, 70, 4, 859–892, Jan. 2021, doi: 10.1108/IJPPM-06-2019-0293.
16. Sherif, S.U., Asokan, P., Sasikumar, P., Mathiyazhagan, K., Jerald, J., Integrated optimization of transportation, inventory and vehicle routing with simultaneous pickup and delivery in two-echelon green supply chain network. *J. Clean. Prod.*, 287, 125434, 2021, doi: https://doi.org/10.1016/j.jclepro.2020.125434.

17. Diabat, A., Kannan, D., Mathiyazhagan, K., Analysis of enablers for implementation of sustainable supply chain management - A textile case. *J. Clean. Prod.*, 83, 391–403, Nov. 2014, doi: 10.1016/j.jclepro.2014.06.081.
18. Mathiyazhagan, K., Govindan, K., NoorulHaq, A., Geng, Y., An ISM approach for the barrier analysis in implementing green supply chain management. *J. Clean. Prod.*, 47, 283–297, 2013, doi: 10.1016/j.jclepro.2012.10.042.
19. Mathiyazhagan, K. and Haq, A.N., Analysis of the influential pressures for green supply chain management adoption-an Indian perspective using interpretive structural modeling. *Int. J. Adv. Manuf. Technol.*, 68, 1–4, 817–833, Sep. 2013, doi: 10.1007/s00170-013-4946-5.
20. Nishal, M., Analysing Roles of I4.0 Technologies in the Lean-Green Paradigm, in: *Lean Thinking in Industry 4.0 and Services for Society*, pp. 167–193, IGI Global, 2023.

3

Challenges in Green Logistics Management

Sunusi Abdulkarim[1*], Rayyan Yusuf[2], Simon Samson Yila[3], Ummi Idris[4], Safizahanin Mokhtar[5], Umar Abdullahi Maiauduga[6], Mark Goh[7], Abdulmalik Muhammad Mustapha[8], Sani Babayaro[1] and Sule Mamuda Sani[9]

[1]*Department Transport & Logistics Management, Nigerian Army University Biu, Biu Borno State, Nigeria*
[2]*Department of Business Administration, Federal University Kashare, Gombe, Gombe State, Nigeria*
[3]*Transport Research and Intelligence Department, Nigerian Institute of Transport Technology (NITT), Zaria, Kaduna State, Nigeria*
[4]*Undergraduate Student at the Department of Management & Information Technology, Abubakar Tafawa Balewa University Bauchi, Bauchi State, Nigeria*
[5]*Department of Transportation Planning, Universiti Teknologi Malaysia, Johor Bahru, Malaysia*
[6]*Department of Management & Information Technology, Abubakar Tafawa Balewa University Bauchi, Bauchi State, Nigeria*
[7]*NUS Business School & The Logistics Institute-Asia Pacific (TLI-AP), National University of Singapore, Singapore*
[8]*Department of Transport Management, Ibrahim Badamasi Babangida University Lapai, Niger State, Nigeria*
[9]*Department of Transport Planning & Coordination, Federal Ministry of Transportation, FCT Abuja, Nigeria*

Abstract

Reducing harmful effects on the environment is one of the priorities of sustainable development goals. The major objectives of this chapter are to study the challenges of green logistics management. The study is qualitative, which employs secondary sources of data. The data for the study were sourced from relevant articles published from 2015–2024. The data of the study were analyzed using thematic analysis. The findings revealed that internal barriers (problems with management;

**Corresponding author*: sunusiabdulkarim73@gmail.com

K. Mathiyazhagan, Krishna Kumar Dadsena, Rajesh Kumar Singh, Aakanksha Kishore and Andrea Appolloni (eds.) Sustainable Operations of Logistics and Supply Chain Management, (39–58) © 2025 Scrivener Publishing LLC

absence of moral and ethical standards; risk of return on investment; lack of employee involvement, etc.) and external barriers (the market structure; lack of bank loans; the inadequacy of government regulations; the limited number of producers of sustainable products, etc.) are the major challenges of green logistics management. However, advancements in green transport technology (LNG trucks, electric power trucks), designing green logistics strategies (green decision support systems, green transportation strategies, etc.), sustainable business models, and integrating green logistics strategies in logistics service providers (1PL, 2PL, 3PL), among others, are the main strategies for green logistic strategies. Moreover, utilizing alternative fuels, utilizing energy-efficient machinery, creating plans for alternate energy use in businesses, and cooperating in environmental management with partners are the main practices of green logistics.

***Keywords*:** Green logistics management, logistics service providers, internal and external barriers, sustainable logistics practices

3.1 Introduction

The demand for goods and logistical services has increased over the past few decades, which has led to a sharp rise in the use of energy and resources as well as the release of trash and gases that are hazardous to the environment; 13% of greenhouse gas (GHG) emissions worldwide are attributed to logistics and transport services [21]. It is commonly known that logistics operations associated with the transportation of goods have a multiplier effect on transportation. Trends like globalization and e-commerce are driving an increase in the need for logistics services, which also bring with them severe environmental repercussions, including pollution, climate change, and traffic. According to [5], by 2050, the need for the transportation of products would have tripled. Due to this, "greening" logistics is required, or making transportation and logistics processes more ecologically friendly, in order to combat growing demand and stop pollution and climate change. The logistics sector is facing increasing demands from environmental regulations. This is mostly the result of two causes. First, the growth of goods transport services has led to a notable increase in traffic, safety, and environmental pollution in recent years. Second, the necessity for environmentally friendly logistics services is rising in the countries that are involved. Businesses are becoming more interested in maintaining the sustainable performance of supplier networks as a result of growing globalization and the complexity of these networks [20].

However, with the development of the UN's Global Goals for Sustainable Development and emerging environmental interests, logistics operators have acknowledged an increased public interest in environmental questions. For instance, worldwide logistics operator and service provider DHL has adopted a strategy with the mission "to achieve net zero emissions for all logistics-related pollution by 2050" [24, 26], and DB Schenker's Swedish division established the goal to "reduce emissions by 70% prior to 2030." Similarly, large shippers such as H&M state that "ultimately, we are committed to doing our share to reduce carbon emissions, and by 2040, we want to be climate positive" [27]. These further highlights that, over the past decade, the growth in environmental concerns has changed the perception of logistics and added an additional dimension [19].

Transportation and traffic are growing quickly as a result of the growing popularity of online shopping and home delivery. The logistics business is under a great deal of demand due to this dynamic economic growth, which is seriously compromising the environment. Transportation and logistics-related operations result in increased fuel consumption, carbon emissions, and climate change [5]. Business organizations that put profit maximization first are to blame for a number of environmental problems, such as deforestation, air and water pollution, ozone layer depletion, solid waste management, carbon emissions, and global warming [15]. Most countries that are developing still use the conventional or traditional approach to end-of-life items, which involves land filling or waste incineration, due to a lack of awareness and some technical limitations. Several companies have even turned to illegal dumping that ultimately pollutes rivers and lands, and most of the hazardous wastes generated are from manufacturing activities [1]. The adverse effect of the traditional supply chain cannot be neglected, and the environment is significantly getting destroyed with traditional supply chain practices as carbon emissions from traditional supply chain practices are altering the atmospheric compositions [16].

The primary factors contributing to the environmental impact of global logistics operations are defined as fossil fuels and greenhouse gas emissions. Burning fossil fuels in the transportation industry releases greenhouse gases (GHGs), including CO2, which in turn has an adverse effect on human health. The logistics sector is widely acknowledged as a primary contributor to greenhouse gas emissions, accounting for 5.5% of total emissions. It is also the second-largest contributor to emissions of carbon dioxide from transportation vehicles and vessels, which contribute to global warming. For example, the transportation industry is estimated to produce 15% and 23% of GHG and carbon dioxide emissions, respectively. Another study found a 45% rise trend in CO2 emissions from 1990 to 2007 and further anticipated that it will continue at a pace of 40% until 2030 [5].

Given this background, the main objectives of this research are to study the challenges of green logistics management.

3.1.1 Research Methodology

In studying the challenges of green logistics management, the study employed a qualitative research method by employing secondary sources of data. The adoption of a qualitative approach helps the researcher get in-depth insights, contextual relevance, and a holistic perspective about the research topic. The data of the study were sourced by reviewing relevant literature published between 2015 and 2024. The data of the study were analyzed using thematic and text analysis.

3.2 Concepts of Green Logistics

According to [21], a network of interconnected companies that handles material handling, freight transportation, inventory storage, information processing, and sharing information throughout supply chain players participating in the distribution of products is known as logistics management. Green logistics reduces resource consumption and environmental harm by using state-of-the-art logistics technologies in the design and execution of transit, storage, packaging, handling, processing, and distribution. Green logistics techniques, sometimes referred to as eco-logistics or sustainable logistics, encompass a range of strategies and activities that contribute to environmental sustainability. These practices involve adopting energy-efficient technologies, optimizing transportation routes, reducing waste and emissions, promoting recycling and reuse, and implementing environmentally friendly packaging and storage solutions [18].

Additionally, strategies and tactics geared at lessening a product's or business process's environmental impact characterize green logistics. Green logistics is an ecological transformation rather than just a fad. More than ever, logistics companies must overcome a variety of obstacles, including responding to the climate emergency and satisfying ever-tougher client needs. Green logistics is centered on ecology and aims to make every logistics organization a participant in methods, decisions, and activities that consider environmental factors. This concept affects the organization of structures and procedures, the distribution and storage of goods, the operation of equipment and transportation systems, and more [11].

Green logistics methods also promote the application of techniques such as carbon management, packaging and design, reverse logistics, environmentally friendly transportation and distribution, environmentally friendly procurement, and environmentally friendly warehousing, among others. in order to manage the supply chain in a sustainable and environmentally friendly manner [13]. According to [20], GL practices in logistics operations boost a company's economic performance, increase organizational effectiveness, foster customer confidence and happiness, and enhance environmental sustainability. An organization's efforts to quantify and lessen the logistical activities' environmental impact are known as "green logistics." The potential to obtain a competitive advantage in the market that clients demand determines such actions [21]. Due to competitiveness, globalization, customer demand, and the pursuit of new markets, it is one of the essential subcomponents of the Green Supply Chain Management process, which has become increasingly necessary in recent years. The development of eco-friendly products, eco-friendly sourcing, ecological production methods, and green logistics—one of the core pillars of green supply chain management—are among the green practices that have contributed to its success. the use of cleaner technologies, green management, and green marketing [2].

3.2.1 The Main Green Logistics Practices

Keeping an eye on the toxins that cars release; optimizing routes and cargo; utilizing alternative fuels; lowering the quantity of used cars; enhancement of fleet infrastructure "Driving environmentally"; Utilizing multimodal transportation; utilizing energy-efficient machinery; implementing cutting-edge packaging innovations; the creation of and adherence to recycling policies; process optimization for warehousing; conscientious product warehousing practices; optimum utilization of the space the creation and implementation of an environmental quality management system; creating plans for alternate energy use in businesses; cooperation in environmental management with clients or partners; choosing collaborators and evaluating their environmental performance; encouragement of worker initiative in the creation of environmental regulations; keeping an eye on how transportation trash is recycled; Utilizing e-documents, transportation and warehouse management systems, and IT [21].

3.2.2 Industrial Insight for Challenges of Green Logistics

Clients and authorities have expressed an overwhelming need for logistics providers to lower their emissions [23]. Despite being young, the industry that goes for green logistics has the potential to grow rapidly. Based on the reduction targets and logistics requirements of nearly 2,800 of the top firms worldwide across various industries, it is estimated that the demand for green logistics in 2025 will amount to almost $50 billion, or roughly 2 percent of the total logistics expenditure. It projects that by 2030, this demand would have grown to almost $350 billion, or 15% of global logistics expenditures. In addition to conducting in-depth market research, the academics conducted interviews with over 20 executives from logistics companies and over 20 other specialists from related fields to evaluate the current status of commercialization efforts in green logistics. According to analysis derived from this fact-finding, logistics companies have the potential to identify the most promising consumers for environmentally friendly products, actively shape those consumers' demands, and collaborate to develop desirable, premium green products that will accelerate industry abatement and yield positive returns on decarbonization investments [23].

[23] reported that a majority of logistics professionals and executives stated that, while customers want green logistics solutions, they are unwilling to pay for them, or at least the premium needed to fund them. Additionally, these clients typically have a lot of negotiating power. The survey reveals that more than 80 percent of logistics clients are not prepared to pay even as much as a 10 percent premium for a green product. It also estimates that just roughly 10% of consumers would be prepared to pay a 20% increase. Only roughly one in four of the top logistics companies provide green products due to the significant costs and challenges associated with implementation, as well as the limited willingness of customers to pay for them. Of those that do, less than 5% of total transport volume is accounted for by green transport [23].

3.2.3 Critical Analysis and Research Gap

Globally, extensive research has been done on green logistics management. Among the most notable are [2], who carried out a study and discovered the impact of institutional pressures on green logistics operations and efficiency performance. The results of [8] also show that cooperation between the public and commercial sectors is essential for implementing GLPs in a way that will be profitable. Additionally, the research showed that financial efficiency is significantly impacted by the implementation of GLPs, public disclosure through Environment, Social, and Governance (ESG) reports or equivalents, and government policy.

However, [14] noted that consumers increasingly want green freight transport, normally accepting moderately higher charges for green products. Additionally, [10] found that green logistics strategies had a favorable impact on economic, social, and environmental performance when used both inbound and outward. [7], state that there is a strong appreciation for the advantages of green logistics technologies, a favorable organizational culture that supports sustainability activities, and a high level of environmental awareness among stakeholders. According to [11], the concept of green logistics entails adopting efficient technologies to reduce supply costs, complying with environmental regulations, and saving energy. All of these tasks must be completed in the face of extremely complex circumstances, particularly in light of the general increase in prices, which presents significant challenges for the global logistics industry.

3.3 Types of Challenges in Green Logistics

According to published research, the majority of manufacturing companies are becoming less and less able to carry out their fundamental responsibilities of maintaining a green supply chain involving green procurement, green sourcing, green production, green distribution & transportation, green packaging, and green disposal. According to [22], the companies' inability to source and purchase products is specifically caused by two factors: a lack of funding to acquire sufficient and pertinent materials and a lack of commitment from upper management to source particular materials for the implementation of green supply. Another thing that deters this role is the absence of organizational visions and missions that would facilitate the sourcing of innovative materials for maintaining green supply chains, which increases operating expenses when implementing green supply chain initiatives [22]. However, insufficient equipment and tools for creating goods or products, along with the absence of demand for green manufactured goods, have hindered the implementation of green manufacturing. Furthermore, workers' ignorance of environmental effects during production activities poses a challenge to green manufacturing, and senior management's lack of commitment to the practice is also a problem [22].

Ref. [6] divided the challenges facing green logistics into two categories, namely:

1. **Internal Barriers**: The following internal obstacles prevent green logistics from being implemented: problems with management, absence of moral and ethical standards, risk of return on investment, expenditure, complexity, lack of

knowledge and experience, lack of commitment from upper management, and lack of employee involvement.

2. **External Barriers:** The following are some of the external obstacles preventing the adoption of green logistics: the market structure, the lack of bank loans, the inadequacy of government regulations, the limited number of producers of sustainable products, the diversity of stakeholders, and the social and cultural hurdles all contribute to the situation.

Ref. [17] in their studies, identified the critical challenges of GL, which are explained below:

1) Absence of laws and regulations from the government

According to certain studies, one of the main factors influencing the adoption of GSCM in the nation is government regulation and legislation. Legislation forces businesses to put relevant ideas and procedures into effect in order to increase productivity.

2) Top management's absence from GSCM adoption

For the following reasons, senior management's involvement in GSCM implementation is crucial: A GSCM requires senior management support in order to be implemented, which may be obtained by convincing stakeholders and approving the required resources. Top management has the ability to organize or reorganize resources as well as assign resources to the supply chain. To accomplish the organizational goal, top management authorizes policies pertaining to the application of GSCM.

3) Ignorance about the adoption of reverse logistics

Reverse logistics includes all of the actions that happen after a product is sold. The product return choices, encompassing recycled, reconditioned, and used products, have been determined to be the most crucial stage in reverse logistics. In addition, companies are facing more pressure to enhance their reverse logistics approach as environmental concerns and the benefits of recycling become more well known.

4) The intricacy of designing green processes and systems

One major obstacle that businesses must get past in order to utilize the resources available in the current industry efficiently is the complexity of green processes and system design. Because of this, companies need to create green practices that make the most use of all resources. Adopting green concepts in the SCM is hampered by shortcomings in system and process design.

5) Inadequate supplier engagement; reluctance to share data

A lack of confidence and a fear of information leaks further explain poor supplier commitment or unwillingness to give information. The supplier's reluctance to use GSCM, however, indicates that they are concerned about losing their competitive advantage and being found out. The fact that suppliers view environmental issues from varying points of view makes this element challenging.

6) Large investments with low returns on capital

The implementation of GSCM poses a significant financial resource issue, necessitating investments by enterprises in technology, systems, and operational competitive competencies (Mujamdar *et al.*, 2019). In addition, one popular profitability statistic used to assess the success of an investment is return on investment. Numerous studies have previously confirmed that if a company invests in GSCM but the payback period is lengthy and low, this presents a significant implementation difficulty [3].

7) Exorbitant hazardous waste disposal costs

According to some writers, using recycled materials, treating hazardous waste, and Among the green measures that local businesses talk about the most are those that protect the environment. How companies can manage the disposal of hazardous waste while reducing the high cost of treatment is one of the main issues facing any sector. The high cost of disposing of hazardous waste is one of the barriers keeping businesses from adopting their GSCM, according to several experts [12].

3.3.1 Case Studies on How the Challenges of Green Logistics are Overcome

All supply chain participants must be included for green logistics methods to be implemented successfully. This encompasses vendors, logistics service providers, clients, and even governmental entities. Partnerships between these entities can result in more extensive and successful sustainability programs. Alliances within the sector and partnerships are essential for the advancement of green logistics techniques. Businesses may hasten the sector's adoption of sustainable solutions by exchanging best practices, resources, and information [28]. In order to lower their carbon footprint, [25] outlines three strategies for implementing green logistics at the start of the supply chain, namely:

a. **Wrapped up packaging:** products are far too frequently covered in layers of plastic in much larger quantities than necessary. Similar to how things float in their sea of packing, there is plastic triple as big as France floating in the ocean across Hawaii and California. For instance, as its name suggests, the Singaporean business The Sustainability Project is focused on being environmentally friendly. The packaging is entirely made of recycled materials, and the company has been using them since 2018. This ensures a reduction in the environmental impact by utilizing fewer single-use packaging components that are discarded after a short transit time.

b. **Just one box numerous lifetimes:** Businesses like Returnity have developed a fix. They have enabled the return and reuse of packaging boxes, allowing them to become part of the circular economy. Another illustration is the green recyclable packaging box that Huidu Huanbao, a Chinese company, has created. It can be reused up to 14 times, significantly lowering the environmental effect of its product line.

c. **Boxed in optimizing space:** Up to 24% of a box is made up of unused space, according to DHL Supply Chain studies, adding 50% of needless transportation space. DHL Supply Chain made an investment in OptiCarton, an AI solution that provides on-demand packaging that lowers transportation costs and environmental effects, in order to tackle this problem.

3.4 Prioritization of Green Logistics Management

Since the field has gained popularity over the past 10 years, the literature on the benefits of green logistics management systems is still in its early stages and is constantly evolving. Numerous studies have examined the impact of green logistics management methods on various firms' financial and environmental performance. There are various reasons why businesses want to make the transition to a "green" supply chain. Sustainability is, of course, the primary motive. However, as [9] also cites, certain studies have revealed that some of the primary drivers for organizations to go "green" in the supply chain are profitability and cost savings. There is a growing trend among consumers to purchase things that are manufactured with low pollution, little environmental impact, and no poisons. Businesses that effectively implement a "green" policy can increase revenue, improve society, and lessen their negative effects on the environment. Businesses that voluntarily adopt greener practices will become more visible, gain credibility, and establish a reputation for being industry leaders.

Furthermore, [9] states that businesses that implement pro-environment policies will experience a host of advantages, both material and immaterial. Early implementation of green supply chain initiatives and environmental policies will assist firms in achieving the following successes:

a. Reducing business risks by setting themselves apart from rivals, growing their businesses into market leaders, winning over stakeholders, and drawing in investors.
b. Encourage higher-performing suppliers to become preferred suppliers in the eco-friendly supply chain and draw customers to the quickly expanding eco-market.
c. Maintain business continuity through increasing employee happiness, drawing in top talent, expanding market access, and granting more leeway in corporate strategy.
d. Establish a notable edge over competitors by differentiating and recognizing your brand. However, it is also advantageous to society and the general public.
e. As society strives to decrease its carbon footprint and improve its management of the planet's natural resources, green supply chain initiatives are swiftly rising to the top of the social agenda. A company's transportation and logistics operations account for more than 75% of its total carbon footprint.

According to Kishore [9], by using an environmental solution, GLM additionally enhances operations in the following ways:

i. **Risk Mitigation:** Raising sustainability awareness across the company's supply chain will lower market, societal, and environmental risks.
ii. **Innovation:** Supplier innovation will be stimulated by the integration of sustainability principles throughout the supply chain.
iii. **Differentiation:** The organization will differentiate itself from competitors in the industry by creating unique green supply chain strategies.
iv. **Profitability:** By proactively integrating sustainable ideas into the supply chain, operations will become more valuable, and costs will be reduced.

Table 3.1 provide the list of sustainable logistics practices.

Table 3.1 Sustainable logistics practices [4].

S/n	Types	Explanation
1	Sustainable Purchases	"Purchasing operations incorporating the social problems advocated by organizational stakeholders" is the term used to describe sustainable purchasing.
2	Sustainable warehousing	Providing forklift operating training, appropriately marking and recording hazardous products, and donating unwanted or outmoded inventory to neighbor's are the main activities of sustainable warehousing.
3	Sustainable Packaging	Sustainable packaging is defined as "packaging that adds real value to society by adequately confining and safeguarding products as they transit through the supply chain and by supporting informed and responsible consumption."

3.5 Strategies for Green Logistics Management

3.5.1 Designing Green Logistics Strategies (Advanced)

Development and execution of an all-encompassing green logistics and transportation system depend critically on the gathering of ecologically pertinent data on events inside specific processes, or "visibility." IT can be very helpful in this area when it comes to integrating green logistics techniques with the logistics of waste disposal, production, distribution, and procurement [4].

1. **Green Decision Support System (GDSS)**
Industry decision-makers can evaluate various logistics strategies by using GDSS for the sustainable optimization of logistics systems. A few of the numerous sub-areas that are the focus of the numerous techniques and approaches that are currently accessible are route planning, location planning, network design, and warehouse planning. GDSS's main objective is to create a balance sheet that shows how much energy is used in each operation and how that energy affects the environment (such as $CO2$ emissions) in order to evaluate how each ecological effect variable is affected [4].

2. **Green Transportation Strategies**
The choice of a transport mode is directly related to the movement of a transport unit among various modes of transportation. Managing load units at transshipment points and the need for more coordination than with a single mode of transportation are the two key implementation issues of inter- and multimodal transportation. On the other hand, the development of (inland) container ports that permit the combination of ship, rail, and road transport stimulates a notable reduction in the number of truck miles driven, thereby mitigating the environmental impacts. Support systems must consider the combined timetables for ship, rail, and road transit when using multimodal routing. Initially, routing programs that facilitated multimodal and intermodal activities were rare due to often inadequate data sharing. Approaches that facilitate inter- and multimodal transport planning have nevertheless made significant strides in recent years [4].

3. **Green Waste Disposal Logistics**
Waste disposal logistics includes the main logistical tasks of movement (transport), collection, storage, and transshipment, together with the information processing related to these tasks. However, most garbage includes characteristics that make it impossible to directly apply typical supply concepts from a logistical standpoint. The materials' low value is the primary determining factor, placing financial restrictions on the transport and intake radii. Thus, it seems that the only practical approach to disposal logistics is to apply sustainable and cost-effective principles [4].

3.5.2 Advances in Green Transport Technology

The largest number of novel options for road transport are available in the realm of engineering innovation. In terms of rail transport, current research focusses on two primary areas: upgrading hubs and nodes for integrated road-rail transit; and converting diesel traction routes to hybrid-electric systems and providing electrical train lines with renewable electricity production. for instance, this is being done in tandem with an expansion of intermodal freight services. The field of hybrid-electrical propulsion systems for water transportation is the focus of ship technology development, with the ultimate goal of displacing diesel engines in both inland waterways and seafaring cargo ships. Furthermore, slow-steaming techniques in maritime transportation are offering major environmental advantages [4].

3.5.3 Supply Chain Coordination

In order to implement green logistics strategies, green logistics practices must be integrated into the supply chain coordination (SCC) stream, which involves planning and coordination amongst various supply chain organizations. SCC is the global network of organizations working together to share risks and opportunities through integrated planning using a shared information system. In a similar vein, it was believed that SCC allows independent businesses to work together more effectively than they could if they planned and executed their operations alone. Therefore, insufficient SCC may result in inaccurate demand projections, low capacity utilization, surplus or deficiency of commodities, and subpar service quality. Moreover, studies indicate that robust relationships may help mitigate potential supply chain hazards. Regarding SCC procedures, they differentiate between cooperative decision-making, information-sharing, contractual coordination, and coordination *via* IT. The most promising mechanisms for coordinating green logistics practices include information sharing and collaborative decision-making, along with price and carbon trading contracts [4].

3.5.4 Sustainable Business Models (State of the Arts)

The business model approach explains how an organization designs value generation, delivery, and capture processes in order to create and deliver value to its consumers. The components of a business model design typically comprise features that are integrated into the product or service, calculating the benefit that the customer will receive from using or consuming the product or service, identifying the target market segments, validating the income stream, and coming up with strategies to capture the value. Four primary business domains were identified during the creation of business models, with a focus on conventional business models: the value proposition that buyers are prepared to pay for; relations with clients; partner infrastructure networks; and financial considerations [4]. The TBL method has been incorporated into the definitions of business models to promote value creation that is not only about economics but also social and environmental. According to [4], expanding on traditional business frameworks in line with the TBL to identify the following crucial elements of sustainable business models:

1. Ecological, social, and economic value should be the primary focus of a product or service's value proposition.
2. The whole structure and management of the company's supply chain, which is built on sustainable supply chain management;
3. A customer interaction that strengthens ties between clients and other stakeholders and promotes co-responsibility in both production and consumption; and a just allocation of financial expenses and rewards among all parties.

3.5.5 Integrating Green Strategies in Logistics Service Provider (LSP) Business Models

Synchronization of logistical actions amongst key supply chain partners, particularly shippers, LSPs, and infrastructure managers, characterizes innovative and successful logistics business models. Shippers' and LSPs' organizational structures and service offerings are used to categorize their business models within this structure [4].

i. **1PL (Single Service Provider):** Single logistics services are performed by single service providers, such as stock keepers for warehousing or goods carriers for transportation. Therefore, specific service providers should concentrate on tactics that lessen the impact of their logistical assets on the environment (e.g., using commercial trucks with cleaner drive engines) [4].
ii. **2PL (2nd Party Logistics Providers):** all conventional logistics duties, including handling warehousing, and shipment, are taken care of by this kind of supplier. For parcel services, goods forwarders, and ocean carriers, this is the typical business model. When they use multiple transport modes, selecting the best modal split becomes an essential tool to enhance their logistical operations' environmental performance [4].
iii. **3PL (3rd Party Logistics Providers):** The 3PL improves on the traditional logistics function by providing adjacent logistical services including inventory control, packaging design, and cross-docking. Third-party logistics providers are companies that conduct business globally and engage in "eye level" contracts with their clients. Consequently, they are able to optimize the utilization of capacity, routes, and modes of transportation by applying more advanced green logistics approaches, such as GDSS [4].
iv. **4PL (4th Party Logistics Providers):** Using e-business and ICT techniques like EDI, the 4PL offers comprehensive supply chain solutions to integrate and coordinate all supply chain partners. It also known as non-asset-owning service providers, are typically specialized consulting

firms that do no operational work. Lead logistics providers, on the other hand, provide certain tasks by purchasing or owning the required physical logistical infrastructure. In order to establish greener supply chain topologies, pricing scheme coordination mechanisms, information exchange, and collaborative decision-making are crucial [4].

3.6 Conclusion

The study concluded that, internal barriers (problems with management; absence of moral and ethical standards, risk of return on investment, expenditure, complexity, lack of knowledge and experience, lack of commitment from upper management, and lack of employee involvement) and external barriers (the market structure, lack of bank loans, the inadequacy of government regulations, the limited number of producers of sustainable products, the diversity of stakeholders, and the social and cultural hurdles) are the major challenges of green logistics management. However, advancement in green transport technology (LNG truck, electric power truck); designing green logistics strategies (green decision support system, green transportation strategies, green waste disposal logistics); supply chain integration; sustainable business models, integrating green logistics strategies in logistics service providers (1PL, 2PL, 3PL) among others are the main strategies for green logistic strategies. Moreover, optimizing routes and cargo; utilizing alternative fuels; utilizing energy-efficient machinery; the creation of and adherence to recycling policies; conscientious product warehousing practices; creating plans for alternate energy use in businesses; cooperation in environmental management with clients or partners; are the main practices of green logistics. Researchers can conduct additional studies and research on green logistics dimensions that affect operational success using descriptive survey research.

3.7 Practical Recommendation

Based on the above findings and conclusion, the study recommended that,

1. Firstly, conducting environmental audit that examines every stage of supply chain from sustainable sourcing to the final delivery of goods will be the first step towards sustainable supply chain. The audit should identify high impact area such as energy consumption, waste generation, water usage, and carbon emissions across all tiers of supply chain.
2. It was recommended that; the company should source eco-friendly materials for their day-to-day operations. This involves identifying sustainable suppliers who share company commitment to environmental responsibility. Also, when selecting materials, consider their entire life cycle from production to disposal. Prioritizes materials that are renewable, recyclable, biodegradable.
3. Optimizing the Supply Chain: optimization is a cornerstone of green logistics strategies. By streamline logistics processes and improving efficiency, companies can significantly reduce their carbon footprint while also cutting costs. Areas to optimized are route planning; load optimization, warehouse layout, inventory management, etc.
4. Indicators should be used or developed to manage the environmental performance of the management and sustainable measures taken to implement sustainable logistics. These indicators include: ECIs (environment condition indicators); MPIs (management performance indicators); OPI (operational performance indicators).
5. Lastly, monitoring reporting refining should be the last step for implementing green logistics. It's essential to tracks your progress, measure impact using key performance indicators (KPI), and transparently report sustainability performance to stakeholders. Utilize data driven insights to identify areas for improvement.

References

1. Abdullah, R., Mohamad, M.N., Thurasamy, R., Towards Sustainable Performance: Promoting Eco-Design in Green Supply Chain Management Practices. *Int. J. Supply Chain Manag.*, 8, 3, 609–616, 2019.
2. Alvarenga, T.H.P., Rodriguez, C.M.T., Sartori, S., Oliveira, R.R., Insituttional Pressure, Green Logistics Activities, and Efficiency Performance: A Survey with Logistics Service Providers in Brazil. *J. Appl. Res. Technol.*, 21, 265–280, 2023.
3. Dong, C., Liu, Q., Shen, B., To Be or Not to Be Green? Strategic Investment for Green Product Development in a Supply Chain. *Transp. Res. Part E Logist. Transp. Rev.*, 131, 193–227, 2019.
4. Gruchmann, T., *Advanced Green Logistics Strategies and Technologies*, Springer International Publishing, Gewerbestrasse, Cham, Switzerland, 20192019, https://doi.org/10.1007/978-3-319-92447-2_29.
5. Karia, N., Green Logistics Practices and Sustainable Business Model, in: *Handbook of Research on the Applications of International Transportation and Logistics for World Trade,* pp. 354–366, 2019, https://doi.org/10.4018/978-1-7998-1397-2.ch019.
6. Khan, S. and Pasha, U., Green Supply Chain Management: Opportunities, Challenges and Changing Strategies: A literature Review Research Questions. *IRASD. J. Manage.*, 4, 2, 203–220, 2022.
7. Khayyat, M., Balfaqih, M., Balfaqih, H., Ismail, M., Challenges and Factors Influencing the Implementation of Green Logistics: A Case Study of Saudi Arabia. *Sustainability*, 16, 13, 2024, 2024, https://doi.org/10.3390/su16135617.
8. Kim, D., Na, J., Ha, H.K., Exploring the impact of green logistics practices and relevant government policy on the financial efficiency of logistics companies. *Heliyon*, 10, 10, e30916, 2024, https://doi.org/10.1016/j.heliyon.2024.e30916.
9. Kishore, B., Green Supply Chain Management-Challenges and Opportunities. *Asian J. Technol. Manage. Res*, 5, 1, 0892, 2015. ISSN: 2249.
10. Khoa, V.D., Anh, N.T.M., Chinh, T.T.Q., Cuong, T., Van, N.T., Impact of Green Logistics Practices on Sustainable Performance: A Comprehensive Analysis. *Int. J. Religion*, 5, 11, 8302–8312, 2024, https://doi.org/10.61707/0dar3a78.
11. Lazrak, M. and El Amrani, H., Green logistics for sustainable development: The challenge of general price increases. *E3S Web of Conferences*, vol. 412, 2023, https://doi.org/10.1051/e3sconf/202341201052.
12. Majumdar, A. and Sinha, S.K., Analyzing the Barriers of Green Textile Supply Chain Management in Southeast Asia Using Interpretive Structural Modeling. *Sustain. Prod. Consum.*, 17, 176–187, 2019.
13. Nwaulune, J.C., Ajike, E.O., Bamidele, A.G., The Impact of Green Logistics Practices on Social Sustainability of Fast-Moving Consumer Goods Firms in

Lagos State, Nigeria: An Empirical Investigation. *Int. Res. J. Econ. Manage. Stud.*, 2, 2, 432–444, 2023, https://doi.org/10.56472/25835238/IRJEMS-V2I2P147.

14. Osman, M.C., Huge-Brodin, M., Ammenberg, J., Karlsson, J., Exploring green logistics practices in freight transport and logistics: a study of biomethane use in Sweden. *Int. J. Logist. Res. Appl.*, 26, 5, 548–567, 2023, https://doi.org/10.1080/13675567.2022.2100332.
15. Pandiyan, V., Sundram, K., Bahrin, A.S., Othman, A.A., Alam, B.P., Green Supply Chain Management Practices in Malaysia Manufacturing Industry. *Int. J. Supply Chain Manag.*, 6, 2, 89–95, 2017.
16. Prachayapipat, M., Kongtana, J., Skulitsariyaporn, C., Snongtaweeporn, T., Role of green supply chain management practices on manufacturing company performance: A moderating role of supply chain traceability and institutional pressures. *Int. J. Supply Chain Manage.*, 9, 2, 572–581, 2020.
17. Po, A., Chen, S., Huang, Y., Exploring the Challenges to Adopt Green Initiatives to Supply Chain Management for Manufacturing Industries. *Sustainability*, 14, 13516, 2022.
18. Potter, K. and Robert, A., Investing in Green Logistics Practices for a Sustainable Future. *May*, 2024, https://www.researchgate.net/publication/380368409.
19. Simm, N., *Greening Logistics: Implementation of Green Logistics Practices Through Interaction*, Thesis submitted to Logistics and Quality Management, Department of Management and Engineering, Faculty of Science and Engineering, Linköping University, 2021.
20. Vienazindiene, M., Tamuliene, V., Zeleckiene, J., Green Logistics Practices Seeking Development of Sustainability: Evidence from Lithuanian Transportation. *Energies*, 14, 7500, 2021.
21. Uwamahoro, A., Nadeem, S.P., Shale, N., II, Wachiuri, E., Green Logistics Practices in the Supply Chain and Operational Performance: Evidence of Nile Equatorial Lakes Subsidiary Action Program Coordination Unit Rusumo Construction Project. *Tian*, 2008, 940–950, 2023, https://doi.org/10.46254/an13.20230263.
22. Zulkefli, N.S., Mahmud, F., Zainudin, N.M., A Survey on Green Supply Chain Management (GSCM) Challenges in the Malaysian Construction Industry. *KnE Soc. Sci.*, 1202–1213, 20192019, https://doi.org/10.18502/kss.v3i22.5120.
23. Bertele, A., Pacca, M., Weber, B., Making Green Logistics Service Profitable, *McKinsey & Company*, 2024, https://www.mckinsey.com/industries/travel-logistics-and-infrastructure/our-insights/making-green-logistics-services-profitable#/.
24. Schenker, D.B., *Hållbarhetsredovisning 2019*, 2024, https://www.dbschenker.com/resource/blob/664126/ed556a8900efdfa9c9ce576a02a42 479/db-schenker-h%C3%A5llbarhetsredovisning-2019-data.pdf.

25. DHL, 3 Ways to Implement Green Logistics at the Start of your Supply Chain, 2024, https://lot.dhl.com/3-ways-to-implement-green-logistics-at-the-start-of-your-supply-chain/.
26. 2019 Sustainability Report, vol. DHL, 2020, https://www.dhl.com/content/dam/dhl/global/core/documents/pdf/sustainability-report.pdf.
27. H&M Sustainability Performance Report 2019, 2020, https://hmgroup.com/wp-content/uploads/2020/10/HM-Group-Sustainability-Performance-Report-2019.pdf.
28. Reid, H., Green Logistics: Revolutionizing the Supply Chain for a Sustainable Future. *DCL*, 2024, https://dclcorp.com/blog/fulfillment/green-logistics/.

4

Identification of Key Challenges in Green Logistics Management

Arda Toygar[1]* and Emre İpekçi[2]

[1]*Fatsa Faculty of Marine Sciences, Department of Maritime Business Administration, Ordu University, Ordu, Türkiye*
[2]*Görele School of Applied Sciences, Department of Logistic Management, Giresun University, Giresun, Türkiye*

Abstract

Green logistics management is a critical component of achieving sustainability goals and aims to reduce environmental impacts along the supply chain. However, there are several challenges and impediments to the adoption and implementation of green logistics practices. This book chapter identifies and prioritizes the challenges encountered in green logistics management and proposes strategies to address these challenges. This chapter also addresses financial, operational, organizational, and technological challenges, lack of regulation, and supplier and customer attitudes in green logistics management. Data was collected from decision makers with comprehensive experience in the logistics industry in this chapter and analyzed. The results indicate that the main challenges in green logistics management are price sensitivity, lack of collaboration and ignoring environmental problems. Moreover, the lack of logistics terminals and complexity of routing plans stand out among operational challenges. The results reveal that cost-effectiveness, collaboration, environmental awareness, logistics infrastructure and training have a critical role in green logistics management. This chapter makes a significant contribution to understanding the challenges faced by green logistics management and improving the effectiveness of practices in this field.

Keywords**:** Supply chain management, green logistics management, sustainability, price sensitivity, lack of collaboration, environmental problem

**Corresponding author*: ardatoygar@odu.edu.tr

K. Mathiyazhagan, Krishna Kumar Dadsena, Rajesh Kumar Singh, Aakanksha Kishore and Andrea Appolloni (eds.) Sustainable Operations of Logistics and Supply Chain Management, (59–84) © 2025 Scrivener Publishing LLC

4.1 Introduction

Transportation emissions increased at an average annual rate of 1.7% from 1990 to 2022 in line with the industrial sector [1]. While regional agreements such as the European Green Deal focus on different energy-intensive industries, broader arrangements such as the Montreal Protocol, the Kyoto Protocol and the Paris Climate Agreement require a country-wide commitment to reduce carbon emissions. Therefore, failure in achieving a green transformation within the logistics sector is not an option. On the other hand, most of the energy required for the delivery of logistics services is provided by fossil fuels. Harmful emissions resulting from the use of fossil fuels, gases and heavy metals cause serious damage to nature.

The idea that damage to the earth should be minimized in all areas where fossil fuels are used, especially in production systems, has become widespread with the increase in environmental concerns. These concerns have led businesses to take various measures, and these measures have manifested as the green logistics concept in logistics services. Green logistics is the general name of all activities aimed at minimizing harmful compounds released into the atmosphere during the delivery of logistics services, especially transportation [2].

The basic method of establishing a more sustainable ecosystem is to provide the energy needed in all areas of life from renewable sources. These sources, also referred to as alternative energy sources, include solar, wind, hydroelectric, geothermal and hydrogen energy and biofuels. Energy can also be obtained from waves and tides nowadays [3]. The energy obtained from these sources can be used in all areas where it is needed, especially in industry, housing, and transportation. However, their use in the transportation sector is limited and costly. Transportation is one of the largest carbon polluters among logistics services, accounting for about 16.2% of carbon emissions worldwide. Road transportation is the largest polluter among modes due to its intensive use in both domestic and international transportation. A look at the share of transportation modes in the big picture reveals that road is responsible for 11.9% of global gas emissions while aviation, maritime and rail account for 1.9%, 1.8% and 0.4% respectively [4]. Greenhouse gas emissions from logistics are not limited to transportation. A much bigger picture emerges when elements such as warehouse management, energy, packaging and equipment needed in storage processes, air conditioning and lighting the management buildings of logistics enterprises are included [5]. Concepts such as sustainability, green transformation, and carbon footprint, which have become more frequently mentioned in recent years, have enabled green logistics to be considered from a broader perspective and resulted in the emergence of the sustainable supply chain management. Logistics activities were seen as an auxiliary element of production systems and product movement was considered independent of production systems in the recent past. Nowadays, production and logistics are managed in a broader approach with the added value they generate. In the past, the first thing that came to mind when green logistics was mentioned was emission management whereas nowadays the process focuses on the entire production system with the concepts of optimization, waste management and renewable energy [6].

The main research objective of this chapter is to identify and prioritize the challenges faced in green logistics management and propose strategic recommendations to address these challenges. The main challenges addressed include supplier and customer, financial barriers, operational and organizational, lack of regulation, and technological. The research question for this book chapter is as follow:

RQ1: What are the key challenges faced by logistics service providers (LSPs) in implementing green logistics practices, and how can these challenges be prioritized to enhance sustainability efforts?

This book chapter proposes strategies and policies for the effective implementation of green logistics, covering all dimensions of green logistics. As a result, significant steps can be taken towards achieving sustainability goals in the logistics sector. The following section presents the theoretical and practical framework of the chapter, including the challenges of green logistics management.

4.2 Theoretical Framework

With the increasing influence of globalization, logistics systems have become a key component of business management. As the significance of logistics in production and supply chains continues to expand, it has also emerged as an area where environmental impacts require attention. While modern logistics is employed to optimize production and distribution processes, the rise of sustainability concerns has made it necessary to consider logistics processes from an environmental perspective [2, 7]. In this context, the utilization of fossil fuels and carbon emissions can be identified as two of the most significant negative environmental impacts of logistics operations. Carbon emissions from fossil fuels, particularly in production processes, are a significant driver of global climate change. The importance of environmentally friendly production and logistics approaches is increasing daily. While there has been a notable increase in the adoption of sustainable practices in production, a similar interest in logistics systems has been slower to develop. One of the primary reasons for this is that cost-driven approaches to logistics management often prioritize immediate benefits over long-term considerations such as environmental sustainability [8]. Notwithstanding the tendency to disregard the environmental impact of logistics systems, the influence of logistics on emissions has been increasingly emphasized in recent years through product life cycle analysis. LSPs are assuming an ever-greater responsibility to reduce the carbon footprint of logistics processes. However, despite this, companies frequently neglect to consider logistics-related emissions [2].

The primary expectation of operations in the logistics sector is to provide services that are both cost effective and fast. However, the prioritization of speed and cost often results in the neglect of environmentally friendly approaches. To give an example, although some high-tonnage vessel operators provide customers with low-emission vessels, such practices are not yet widespread. The main reason for this is the high cost of green transportation solutions, and most customers are unwilling to bear this cost increase [9]. The high costs associated with green logistics practices represent a significant barrier to their widespread adoption. In addition, there is a need for a shift in both governmental support and customer demand towards greener practices in order to drive the necessary change [10, 11].

An alternative solution for reducing the environmental impact of logistics operations is through the utilization of mixed transportation modes. The utilization of rail transportation subsequent to low-emission modes, such as shipping, can make a substantial contribution to the reduction of the carbon footprint. For example, the carriage of goods by rail represents a more sustainable solution than road. The development of rail links to ports and the expansion of logistics centers can contribute to the reduction of emissions and logistics costs [12, 13]. It is thus evident that the transition of logistics systems towards a more environmentally sustainable configuration will necessarily the infrastructural enhancements [14, 15].

The transformation of production and logistics systems for environmental reasons is a relatively recent development. One example of such a system is the European Union's Emissions Trading System (EU ETS), which was set up in 2005. The EU ETS is a market-based mechanism that is designed to reduce carbon emissions [16, 17]. Furthermore, the implementation of a carbon tax at the border, which is designed to impose a tax on imported products based on their carbon intensity, is scheduled to commence in 2026 [18, 19]. These implementations encourage the use of renewable energy sources in production processes, but the logistics sector has yet to be fully integrated into these mechanisms. For example, the EU ETS system has been applied to the aviation sector, with stricter regulations expected to be implemented [20]. The maritime transportation sector has also been included in the EU ETS, with the objective of contributing to carbon reduction. However, the adoption of green solutions in the logistics sector has been less rapid than in the manufacturing sector. One of the principal reasons for this is that LSPs have not recognized the necessity for environmental change for a considerable period of time and have not integrated this process into their business strategies [21]. The aim of this chapter is to investigate the challenges faced by LSPs in the green transformation process from the perspective of the logistics sector community. Although there are many studies in the literature on the challenges faced by sector community in the green logistics transformation, this chapter examines these challenges directly from the perspective of LSPs.

4.3 Application of the Challenges in the Evaluation of Green Logistics Management

4.3.1 Preparation for Identifying the Challenges of Green Logistics Management

4.3.1.1 Definition of Criteria

The conceptual framework of the chapter showing the challenges faced in green logistics management and the main and sub-criteria representing the challenges in this context are presented in Table 4.1 and Figure 4.1. Detailed explanations of all criteria are also presented in this section.

C1: Suppliers and Customers

C1.1: Ignoring Environmental Problems: The first of the main themes that challenge LSPs in green transformation is supplier and customer-related challenges. Manufacturing enterprises in particular tend to ignore environmental concerns because they have a cost-oriented approach. Today, the increasing impact of global warming is pushing countries to apply more severe sanctions. Practices such as carbon tax at the border and the carbon trading system are emerging as sanctions that challenge manufacturing enterprises. However, these sanctions usually focus on production processes and cover the entire product life cycle to a limited extent. Therefore, LSPs often ignore environmental issues arising from the logistics process and do not demand this from their service providers.

Table 4.1 Selected criteria for challenges in the evaluation of green logistics management.

Main criteria	Sub-criteria	References
C1: Suppliers and customers	***C1.1:*** Ignoring environmental problems	[22–26]
	C1.2: Price sensitivity	
	C1.3: Lack of collaboration	
C2: Financial	***C2.1:*** High cost of the green adoption	[23, 25–28]
	C2.2: Budget constraints	
	C2.3: Lack of financial incentives	
C3: Operational	***C3.1:*** Routing Plans Complexity	[22, 23, 26–30]
	C3.2: Lack of logistics terminals	
	C3.3: Insufficient training/competence	
C4: Organizational	***C4.1:*** Managers think that is not necessary	[22, 23, 27, 28]
	C4.2: Lack of environmental control	
	C4.3: Poor strategic planning	
C5: Regulatory	***C5.1:*** Lack of state intervention	[24–27, 29]
	C5.2: Regulatory complexity	
	C5.3: Non-cooperation with policy-makers	
C6: Technological	***C6.1:*** High cost of technologies	[26, 27, 30, 31]
	C6.2: Lack of Internet network	
	C6.3: Limited access to technology	

C1.2: Price Sensitivity: Logistics costs have a significant impact on product selling price. The cost increase brought by logistics systems designed with more environmentally friendly approaches is not welcomed by LSPs. This situation can be overcome by updating government regulations to include logistics processes.

C1.3: Lack of Collaboration: The reduction of emissions related to logistics can only be achieved through the coordination of stakeholders, including manufacturers, LSPs, and consumers. However, if even one of these

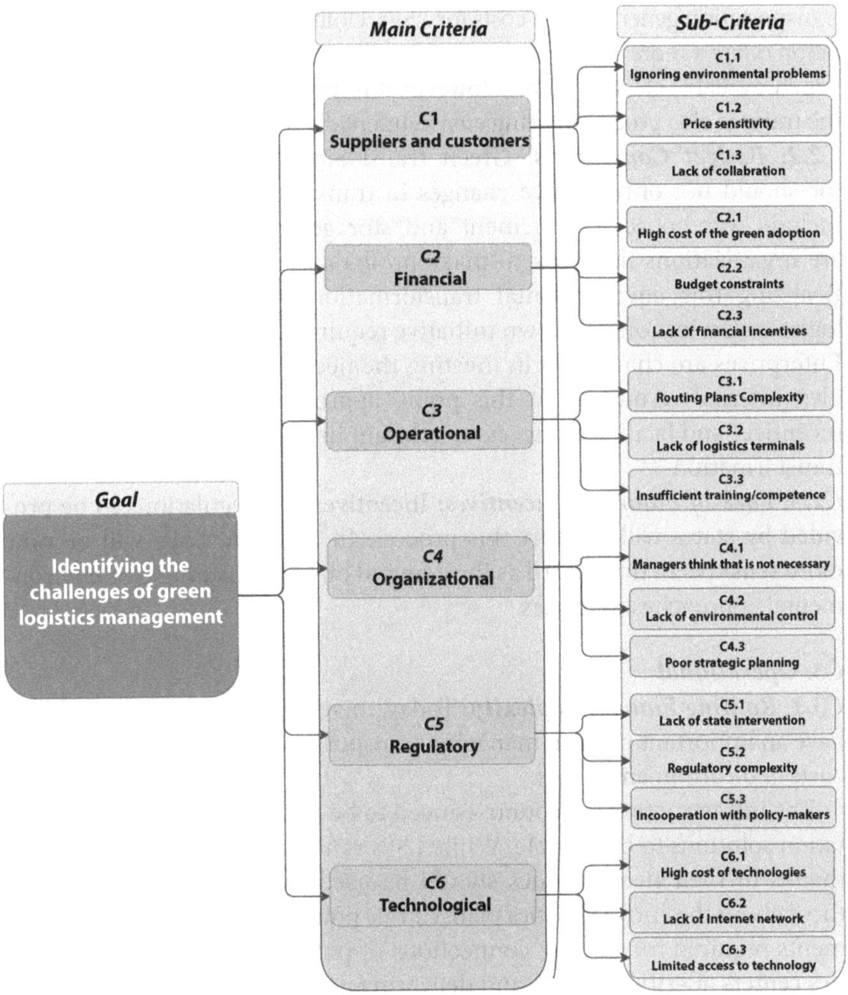

Figure 4.1 Practical framework for challenges of green logistics management.

stakeholders fails to take the initiative, it will impede the overall reduction of emissions across the entire supply chain.

C2: Financial

C2.1: High Cost of Green Adoption: Another one of the main themes challenging LSPs in green transformation is financial challenges. It is very costly for a freight forwarder to acquire transportation vehicles with more up-to-date engine technologies and for LSPs to build a new fleet with electric vehicles for urban delivery. In addition, the environmental fuels used in air and maritime transportation generate high costs for LSPs. Unlike other modes, rail transportation offers a more environmentally friendly transportation service thanks to widely available electric trains. However, it is important that the electricity by the trains is also produced using environmentally friendly methods.

C2.2: Budget Constraints: Green transformation in the logistics sector should not only involve changes in transportation services, but also include warehouse management and storage solutions. After all, LSPs are organizations that seek to make profits and supplement their equity. Realizing this environmental transformation by enterprises providing logistics services on their own initiative requires a large financial resource. Enterprises are challenged in meeting the necessary financing from their own internal resources. At this point, approaches such as government incentives and facilitating access to relevant financing will accelerate green transformation.

C2.3: Lack of Financial Incentives: Incentives and regulations to be provided by states will support this process. In addition, LSPs will become more sensitive in this regard as the demand of end-consumers for environmental approaches increases.

C3: Operational

C3.1: Routing Plans Complexity: Today, mixed transportation operations have an important place in managing transportation operations with lower costs and carbon emissions.

The infrastructures of countries need to be suitable for mixed transportation solutions to be feasible. While LSPs can provide product movement thanks to their fleets, modes should be used together for less emission throughout the entire logistics plan. At this point, the infrastructure investments required for railway connections of ports, the availability of logistics centers at critical points and delivering a significant part of the freight movement on land by rail should be provided by the states. A lack of these systems will prevent the methods used by LSPs on their own initiative from having sufficient environmental impact.

C3.2: Lack of Logistics Terminals: Logistics terminals are of critical importance to the storage, processing, and distribution of materials and products. Insufficient logistics terminals lead to a reduction in the efficiency of intermodal transportation and the emergence of bottlenecks in supply chain processes. This situation not only gives rise to increased transportation costs but also results in an increased carbon footprint. Moreover, the absence of suitable logistics terminals results in delays in transportation processes and inefficiencies in logistics operations.

C.3.3: Insufficient Training/Competence: LSPs need to train their employees to ensure that the greenest routes are used. Inadequate training and competence can reduce the effectiveness of green logistics practices.

C4: Organizational

C4.1: Managers Think that it is Not Necessary: Another challenge faced by green transformation is the negative or lacking outlook of enterprises on the subject. The management staff of LSPs that provide both production and logistics services is an important factor in the adoption of green approaches by LSPs. Enterprises that do not believe in the necessity of green transformation are unlikely to include green approaches in the future plans of the enterprise.

C4.2: Lack of Environmental Control: LSPs should reduce the carbon footprint of their logistics processes from a strategic management perspective. Lack of environmental control can reduce the effectiveness of green logistics practices.

C4.3: Poor Strategic Planning: Lack of strategic planning can limit the success of green logistics practices. LSPs need to engage in effective strategic planning for green transformation.

C5: Regulatory

C5.1: Lack of State Intervention: The supervisory and regulatory role of governments is crucial for green transformation in the logistics sector. First of all, this transformation should be offered to LSPs on a mandatory basis according to a specific schedule. Currently, it would be wrong to say that countries exert strict pressure on LSPs in this matter. For example, the regulations prepared for the green transformation of LSPs operating in the transportation sector in Türkiye are not mandatory for LSPs. According to the rules set forth by the state, the benefits that LSPs will gain if a green logistics certificate is acquired are quite limited.

C5.2: Regulatory Complexity: The greening of the logistics processes of operations should be supported by governments and controlled by regulations. Furthermore, carbon taxation practices across the EU also focus on manufacturing. Given the impact of logistics-related carbon emissions on the product lifecycle, future regulations are expected to be extended to include emissions from transportation activities.

C5.3: Non-cooperation with Policy-Makers: Government regulations should ensure that logistics providers with a perspective that is more pre-emptive as well as incentivizing in terms of green transformation. Sector associations need to coordinate with government agencies to define a common roadmap for green transformation across the sector.

C6: Technological

C6.1: High Cost of Technologies: Logistics systems are closely related to technology due to their dynamic structure. A newly emerging technological development can quickly find a place in the sector. However, these technologies often require LSPs to incur high costs.

C6.2: Lack of Internet Network: This deficiency can have a considerable impact on the optimization and coordination of logistics operations. Inadequate internet network access presents significant challenges to the effective use of Internet of Things (IoT) devices and cloud-based data management systems. These challenges have the potential to impact the efficacy of big data analytics and real-time monitoring systems, ultimately reducing the efficiency of logistics operations. Moreover, the lack of assurance regarding data integrity and synchronization across the supply chain can result in delays and errors in information sharing.

C6.3: Limited Access to Technology: Likewise, elements such as biofuels used in aircraft and sustainable packaging equipment are more costly than conventional logistics costs. It is not easy for LSPs to access environmentally friendly equipment or fuels.

4.4 Methodology

4.4.1 Experts and Criteria Weighting

The data utilized in this chapter was gathered from highly experienced professionals in the logistics industry. The participants were selected based on their expertise in green logistics, with at least 10 years of professional experience in the field. The professional background and qualifications of the experts who participated in this chapter are given in Table 4.2.

DM1 (International Supply Chain Specialist) has 12 years of experience working in global supply chain operations, focusing on optimizing international logistics flows and implementing sustainable supply chain practices. DM2 (Company Owner), with 28 years of experience, leads a logistics firm specializing in freight forwarding and green logistics solutions. DM3 (Sales Manager) and DM4 (Specialist), both from the sales department, bring a combined 21 years of experience in logistics service negotiations. DM5 (Warehouse Manager), with 30 years of experience, oversees logistics facilities and storage operations. DM6 (Performance and Implementation Manager) has 22 years of experience in international supply chain management, particularly in performance tracking and sustainability implementation. DM7 (Sales Manager) and DM8 (Air Cargo Manager), with 15 and

Table 4.2 Professional backgrounds and qualifications of decision makers.

Expert	Experience	Department	Profession
DM1	12	International Supply Chain	International supply chain specialist
DM2	28	Logistics	Company owner
DM3	10	Sales Department	Sales Manager
DM4	11	Sales Department	Specialist
DM5	30	Warehouse	Manager
DM6	22	International Supply Chain	Performance and Implementation Manager
DM7	15	Sales Department	Sales Manager
DM8	39	Air Cargo	Manager

39 years of experience respectively, bring expertise in cargo management and sales negotiations, particularly within the air freight industry.

The SWARA (Stepwise Weight Assessment Ratio Analysis) method has been used in this book chapter both at the group level and at the overall level to prioritize the challenges faced in green logistics management. SWARA allows for the ranking of challenges by assigning weights based on the expert evaluations, which helped prioritize the factors influencing green logistics management. The experts were asked to rank the importance of different challenges, and their assessments were aggregated to derive the final criteria rankings. The values of two randomly selected representative decision makers (DMs) has been analyzed to illustrate the computational steps involved in determining the final weights of the criteria representing the challenges using the SWARA method. The data of two representative decision makers are presented in Table 4.3 and Table 4.4 to help understand this process.

As a first step, the criteria were ranked from most important to least important in their respective groups. This ranking was shaped according to the preferences of the decision makers and is shown under the heading "Importance Rank". Decision-makers assessed the ratio of how much more important the previous criterion was than the next criterion. These values are given under the heading "sj". For example, for DM1, C2 – Financial is 0.80 more important than C3 – Operational and C3 – Operational is 0.40 more important than C6 – Technological. The coefficient "kj" was

Table 4.3 Values for representative DM1.

Main criteria	**Importance rank**	*sj*	*kj*	*qj*	*wj*	
C2: Financial	1		1.00	1.000	0.411	
C3: Operational	2	0.80	1.80	0.556	0.228	
C6: Technological	3	0.40	1.40	0.397	0.163	
C1: Suppliers and customers	4	0.80	1.80	0.220	0.091	
C4: Organizational	5	0.30	1.30	0.170	0.070	
C5: Regulatory	6	0.90	1.90	0.089	0.037	
C1: Suppliers and customers	**Importance rank**	*sj*	*kj*	*qj*	*wj*	**Criteria weight**
C1.2: Price sensitivity	1	–	1	1.000	0.444	0.073
C1.3: Lack of collaboration	2	0.30	1.30	0.769	0.342	0.056
C1.1: Ignoring environmental problems	3	0.60	1.60	0.481	0.214	0.035
C2: Financial	**Importance rank**	*sj*	*kj*	*qj*	*wj*	**Criteria weight**
C2.2: Budget constraints	1	–	1.00	1.000	0.527	0.086
C2.1: High cost of the green adoption	2	0.70	1.70	0.588	0.310	0.051
C2.3: Lack of financial incentives	3	0.20	1.20	0.490	0.163	0.027
C3: Operational	**Importance rank**	*sj*	*kj*	*qj*	*wj*	**Criteria weight**
C3.2: Lack of logistics terminals	1	–	1.00	1.000	0.524	0.086
C3.1: Routing Plans Complexity	2	0.95	1.95	0.513	0.269	0.044
C3.3: Insufficient training/competence	3	0.30	1.30	0.394	0.207	0.034
C4: Organizational	**Importance rank**	*sj*	*kj*	*qj*	*wj*	**Criteria weight**
C4.3: Poor strategic planning	1	–	1.00	1.000	0.405	0.066
C4.2: Lack of environmental control	2	0.30	1.30	0.769	0.312	0.051
C4.1: Managers think that is not necessary	3	0.10	1.10	0.699	0.283	0.046

(*Continued*)

Table 4.3 Values for representative DM1. (*Continued*)

Main criteria	Importance rank	*sj*	*kj*	*qj*	*wj*	
C5: Regulatory	**Importance rank**	*sj*	*kj*	*qj*	*wj*	**Criteria weight**
C5.1: Lack of state intervention	1	–	1.00	1.000	0.405	0.066
C5.2: Regulatory complexity	2	0.10	1.10	0.909	0.368	0.060
C5.3: Non-cooperation with policy-makers	3	0.10	1.10	0.826	0.335	0.055
C6: Technological	**Importance rank**	*sj*	*kj*	*qj*	*wj*	**Criteria weight**
C6.1: High cost of technologies	1	–	1.00	1.000	0.545	0.089
C6.3: Limited access to technology	2	0.90	1.90	0.526	0.287	0.047
C6.2: Lack of Internet network	3	0.80	1.80	0.292	0.159	0.026

calculated with the "sj+1" procedure. The coefficient "qj" was calculated to determine the criteria weights. The "wj" value, which is ranked last for the main criteria and penultimate for the sub-criteria, represents the relative importance weights of the criteria. The last ranked values for sub-criteria are defined as criterion weights. The last ranked "Criteria Weight" values for sub-criteria are obtained by multiplying the weights of the main criteria by the weights of the sub-criteria in the relevant category.

Table 4.3 shows the order of importance of the main and sub-criteria and their weights for DM1. "Financial" criteria (0.411) have the highest weight, indicating that DM1 attaches great importance to financial issues. This is followed by "operational" (0.228) and "technological" criteria (0.163). The criteria "suppliers and customers" (0.091), "organizational" (0.070) and "regulatory" (0.037) have lower weights.

The criteria weights and rankings of DM2 are presented in Table 4.4. According to the results, the "operational" criterion (0.474) has the highest weight, indicating that DM2 prioritizes operational efficiency. It is followed by "Suppliers and customers" (0.249) and "technological" (0.131). "Financial" (0.077), "organizational" (0.043) and "regulatory" criteria (0.025) have lower weights. Table 4.5 shows the Rank within Criteria and Rank Overall rankings obtained by combining the data of the two representative decision makers.

Table 4.4 Values for representative DM2.

Main criteria	**Importance rank**	*sj*	*kj*	*qj*	*wj*	
C3: Operational	1	–	1.00	1.000	0.474	
C1: Suppliers and customers	2	0.90	1.90	0.526	0.249	
C6: Technological	3	0.90	1.90	0.277	0.131	
C2: Financial	4	0.70	1.70	0.163	0.077	
C4: Organizational	5	0.80	1.80	0.091	0.043	
C5: Regulatory	6	0.70	1.70	0.053	0.025	
C1: Suppliers and customers	**Importance rank**	*sj*	*kj*	*qj*	*wj*	**Criteria weight**
C1.2: Price sensitivity	1		1	1.000	0.531	0.089
C1.1: Ignoring environmental problems	2	0.80	1.80	0.556	0.295	0.049
C1.3: Lack of collaboration	3	0.70	1.70	0.327	0.174	0.029
C2: Financial	**Importance rank**	*sj*	*kj*	*qj*	*wj*	**Criteria weight**
C2.1: High cost of the green adoption	1		1.00	1.000	0.527	0.088
C2.3: Lack of financial incentives	2	0.70	1.70	0.588	0.310	0.052
C2.2: Budget constraints	3	0.90	1.90	0.310	0.163	0.027
C3: Operational	**Importance rank**	*sj*	*kj*	*qj*	*wj*	**Criteria weight**
C3.1: Routing Plans Complexity	1		1.00	1.000	0.536	0.090
C3.3: Insufficient training/ competence	2	0.80	1.80	0.556	0.298	0.050
C3.2: Lack of logistics terminals	3	0.80	1.80	0.309	0.166	0.028
C4: Organizational	**Importance rank**	*sj*	*kj*	*qj*	*wj*	**Criteria weight**
C4.1: Managers think that is not necessary	1		1.00	1.000	0.545	0.091
C4.2: Lack of environmental control	2	0.90	1.90	0.526	0.287	0.048
C4.3: Poor strategic planning	3	0.70	1.70	0.310	0.169	0.028

(Continued)

Table 4.4 Values for representative DM2.

Main criteria	**Importance rank**	*sj*	*kj*	*qj*	*wj*	
C5: Regulatory	**Importance rank**	*sj*	*kj*	*qj*	*wj*	**Criteria weight**
C5.1: Lack of state intervention	1		1.00	1.000	0.545	0.091
C5.2: Regulatory complexity	2	0.90	1.90	0.526	0.287	0.048
C5.3: Non-cooperation with policy-makers	3	0.70	1.70	0.310	0.169	0.028
C6: Technological	**Importance rank**	*sj*	*kj*	*qj*	*wj*	**Criteria weight**
C6.1: High cost of technologies	1		1.00	1.000	0.545	0.091
C6.2: Lack of Internet network	2	0.90	1.90	0.526	0.287	0.048
C6.3: Limited access to technology	3	0.80	1.80	0.292	0.159	0.027

4.5 Results

This chapter focuses on the analysis of data obtained from eight experienced decision makers in the sector. The results of the analysis are analyzed at the level of main criteria and sub-criteria. The data of the decision makers participating in the chapter for all criteria were combined and the criteria weights were calculated by taking the geometric mean. The final weights of the main criteria were calculated as a ratio of the sum of all main criteria obtained after aggregation, while the final weights of the sub-criteria were calculated as a ratio of the sum of all sub-criteria obtained after aggregation independently of the main criteria. The results for the main criteria are presented in Table 4.6 and Figure 4.2.

Among the main criteria, the "Suppliers and customers" criterion has the highest weight and ranks first with a geometric mean value of 0.225 and a final weight value of 0.27 as seen in Table 4.6 and Figure 4.2. This shows that supplier and customer relationships are the most crucial factor for decision makers. The "Operational" criterion ranks in second place. With a geometric mean of 0.200 and a final weight value of 0.246, this criterion reveals that operational factors also play a key role. The "Financial" criterion ranks third, with a geometric mean of 0.107 and a final weight value of 0.132. This underlines that financial factors should also be considered. The other criteria are listed as "Technological" (0.106 geometric

Table 4.5 Final criteria weights and ranking of representative DM1 and DM2.

	Criteria weight		Geo. mean	Final weight	Rank within criteria	Rank overall
Main Criteria	DM1	DM2				
C1: Suppliers and customers	0.091	0.249	0.151	0.169		3
C2: Financial	0.411	0.077	0.178	0.200		2
C3: Operational	0.228	0.474	0.329	0.370		1
C4: Organizational	0.070	0.043	0.055	0.062		5
C5: Regulatory	0.037	0.025	0.030	0.034		6
C6: Technological	0.163	0.131	0.146	0.164		4
C1: Suppliers and customers	DM1	DM2				
C1.1: Ignoring environmental problems	0.035	0.049	0.042	0.043	2	12
C1.2: Price sensitivity	0.073	0.089	0.080	0.084	1	2
C1.3: Lack of collaboration	0.056	0.029	0.040	0.042	3	15
C2: Financial						
C2.1: High cost of the green adoption	0.051	0.088	0.067	0.070	1	4
C2.2: Budget constraints	0.086	0.027	0.049	0.051	2	10
C2.3: Lack of financial incentives	0.027	0.052	0.037	0.039	3	16
C3: Operational						
C3.1: Routing Plans Complexity	0.044	0.090	0.063	0.066	1	6
C3.2: Lack of logistics terminals	0.086	0.028	0.049	0.051	2	9
C3.3: Insufficient training/ competence	0.034	0.050	0.041	0.043	3	14

(Continued)

Table 4.5 Final criteria weights and ranking of representative DM1 and DM2. (*Continued*)

	Criteria weight		Geo. mean	Final weight	Rank within criteria	Rank overall
C4: Organizational						
C4.1: Managers think that is not necessary	0.046	0.091	0.065	0.068	1	5
C4.2: Lack of environmental control	0.051	0.048	0.049	0.052	2	8
C4.3: Poor strategic planning	0.066	0.028	0.043	0.045	3	11
C5: Regulatory						
C5.1: Lack of state intervention	0.066	0.091	0.078	0.081	1	3
C5.2: Regulatory complexity	0.060	0.048	0.054	0.056	2	7
C5.3: Non-cooperation with policy-makers	0.060	0.028	0.041	0.043	3	13
C6: Technological						
C6.1: High cost of technologies	0.089	0.091	0.090	0.094	1	1
C6.2: Lack of Internet network	0.026	0.048	0.035	0.037	2	17
C6.3: Limited access to technology	0.047	0.027	0.035	0.037	2	17

mean, 0.131 final weight), "Organizational" (0.103 geometric mean, 0.126 final weight) and "Regulatory" (0.072 geometric mean, 0.089 final weight).

This chapter focuses on the analysis of data from eight experienced decision makers in the sector. The overall ranking results in Table 4.7 and Figure 4.3 reflect the challenges in green logistics management. This ranking reveals the prioritization of sub-criteria, and which factors are more critical in green supply chain management.

Table 4.6 Main criteria results.

Main criteria	Geometric mean	Final weight	Rank
C1: Suppliers and customers	0.225	0.276	1
C2: Financial	0.107	0.132	3
C3: Operational	0.200	0.246	2
C4: Organizational	0.103	0.126	5
C5: Regulatory	0.072	0.089	6
C6: Technological	0.106	0.131	4

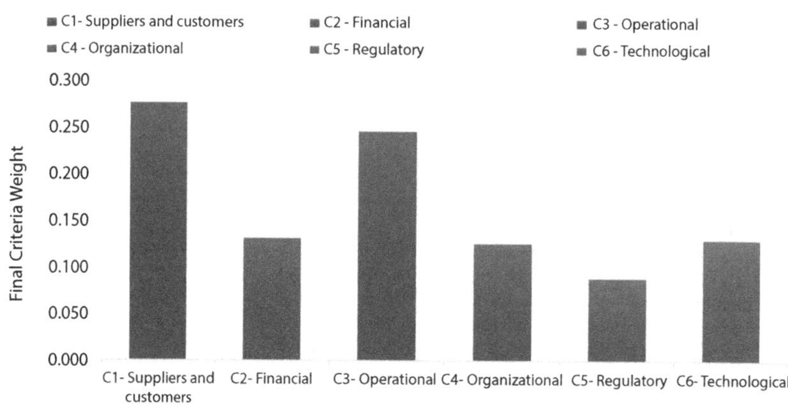

Figure 4.2 Final main criteria weight.

Each of these sub-criteria was weighed against each other and the results were explained. The first named criterion "Price sensitivity" - C1.2 appears to be the number one priority within the customer-supplier association. The second of these criteria named is called "Lack of collaboration" - C1.3. The third criterion discusses "Ignoring environmental problems" - C1.1. The fourth is "Lack of logistics terminals" - C3.2. The fifth named is "Routing plans complexity" - C3.1. The sixth is "Insufficient training/competence" - C.3.3. The seventh one is "High cost of technologies" - C6.1. The eighth is "High cost of the green adoption" - C2.1. The ninth one is "Managers think that is not necessary" - C4.1. The tenth one is "Poor strategic planning" - C4.3. The eleventh is "Lack of state intervention" - C5.1. The twelfth is "Budget constraints" - C2.2. The rank thirteenth goes to the

Table 4.7 Sub-criteria results.

	Final criteria weight	In-criterion rank	General rank
C1: Suppliers and customers			
C1.1: Ignoring environmental problems	0.086	3	3
C1.2: Price sensitivity	0.090	1	1
C1.3: Lack of collaboration	0.087	2	2
C2: Financial			
C2.1: High cost of the green adoption	0.055	1	8
C2.2: Budget constraints	0.042	2	12
C2.3: Lack of financial incentives	0.032	3	16
C3: Operational			
C3.1: Routing Plans Complexity	0.081	2	5
C3.2: Lack of logistics terminals	0.084	1	4
C.3.3: Insufficient training/competence	0.071	3	6
C4: Organizational			
C4.1: Managers think that is not necessary	0.047	1	9
C4.2: Lack of environmental control	0.032	3	17
C4.3: Poor strategic planning	0.045	2	10
C5: Regulatory			
C5.1: Lack of state intervention	0.043	1	11
C5.2: Regulatory complexity	0.029	3	18
C5.3: Non-cooperation with policy-makers	0.041	2	13
C6: Technological			
C6.1: High cost of technologies	0.065	1	7
C6.2: Lack of Internet network	0.034	3	15
C6.3: Limited access to technology	0.035	2	14

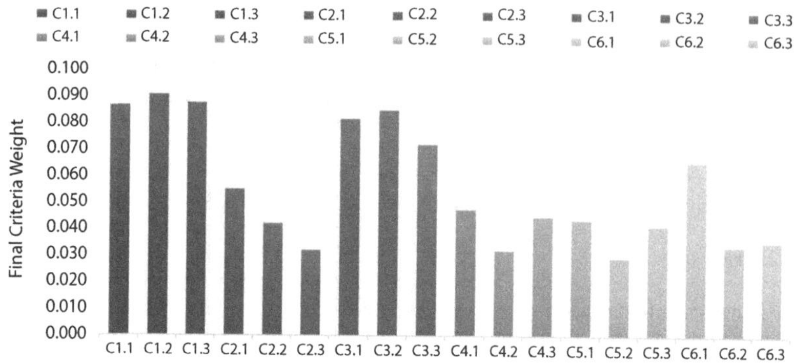

Figure 4.3 Final criteria weight.

"Cooperation with policymakers" - C5.3 criterion. This is followed by the "Limited access to technology" - C6.3 criterion in fourteenth place. Fifteenth is "Lack of Internet network" - C6.2. Then, sixteenth is "Lack of financial incentives" - C2.3, seventeenth is "Lack of environmental control" - C4.2, and finally, "Regulatory complexity" - C5.2 ranks eighteenth.

4.6 Conclusion

The aim of this chapter was to identify and prioritize the challenges faced in green logistics management with data obtained from highly experienced decision makers in the sector. Green logistics management is critical in achieving sustainability goals and aims to reduce environmental impacts along the supply chain. However, various challenges faced in this area can limit the effectiveness of the practices. Therefore, this chapter examined the prominent factors in green logistics management and their importance levels.

The results show that various challenges such as cost effectiveness, lack of collaboration, disregard for environmental issues, logistics infrastructure inadequacies, complex routing plans and inadequate training are prominent in green logistics management. Price sensitivity, which has the highest priority, reveals that cost effectiveness is a critical factor in the adoption of green logistics practices. This is followed by a lack of cooperation and ignoring environmental problems. The costs associated with logistics have a considerable influence on the prices at which products are sold. While the extent of this impact varies across different LSPs, the effective management of logistics costs represents a crucial aspect of logistics operations. Among the various logistics services, transportation is identified as the most expensive [32]. Therefore, the largest costs associated with the green transformation of logistics are in this field. However, every cent spent on the green transformation of transportation systems will increase the operating costs of LSPs. This is a critical threshold for both LSPs on the road to green transformation. In our study, the main reason why LSPs are challenged by the green transformation is the impact of this transformation on prices. The second key challenge, lack of collaboration, supports this result, as the price factor that complicates green transformation puts LSPs, making collaboration difficult. The cost pressures of green logistics solutions often outweigh the environmental benefits for LSPs. Furthermore, the consequences of global warming are becoming more evident. This has resulted in a rise in environmental awareness among the general government, encouraging LSPs to adopt environmentally friendly practices. However, these practices are typically observed in more visible sectors. In contrast, the transportation sector is one of the primary sources of global carbon emissions [33]. Peter Drucker describes logistics as the invisible mainland of economy [34]. This analogy can be extended to the logistics sector, which represents a significant contributor to emissions.

Operational challenges include lack of logistics terminals and complex routing plans. Road transportation is the primary source of emissions from all modes. This is largely due to the extensive road infrastructure that encompasses large geographical areas, which makes it the preferred mode, especially for domestic. In comparison, rail transportation is more environmentally friendly than road transportation for the carriage of goods. However, due to the inadequate rail infrastructure and the limited number of logistics centers or villages, reducing emissions from land remains a significant challenge. Furthermore, organizational challenges include inadequate training and the perception of managers that such practices are unnecessary. These results reflect the perceptions and priorities of experienced decision makers in the sector towards green logistics management and sustainability practices. In addition, LSPs will be able to improve their green logistics performance many times over by improving their ability to force cooperation, removing fiscal bottlenecks, and providing symmetric training and infrastructure, thereby contributing to the achievement of sustainable development goals on a global scale. Of these variables, supplier and customer relationships, operational process factors and fiscal constraints are the most important. This categorization is based on the relative importance of cost efficiency, coordination, training and access to technology among the various factors hindering business growth, as well as exogenous factors such as government influence and lack of motivation. While transportation represents the primary source of logistics-related emissions, storage and other related processes also contribute to carbon emissions. Investments such as the use of alternative fuels for transportation vehicles, emission-reducing additives, environmentally designed warehouse and building improvements, and the use of green loading and packaging equipment have the potential to reduce emissions across the industry. However, the financial burden of these changes often prevents LSPs from making the necessary investments.

The research conducted in this book chapter has some limitations. The data in this book chapter was collected from sector experts in Türkiye. This is sufficient to reflect the challenges and priorities specific to green logistics management and sustainability practices in Türkiye. However, this limits the generalizability of the chapter. The scope of the data collection, being confined to a single geographic region, inherently restricts the ability to apply the results universally. It should be recognized that sectoral experts in different countries can have different priorities and challenges. Therefore, the results of the chapter might not be directly applicable to other countries. In particular, countries with various levels of economic development, regulatory frameworks, and technological infrastructure may face unique barriers or opportunities in green logistics that were not fully captured in this chapter. Cultural, economic, legal and technological differences can alter their impact on green logistics management. For example, while Türkiye may prioritize certain cost-related barriers, countries with stronger government subsidies or more advanced green technologies might encounter different operational challenges. For example, government intervention and incentives can vary from one country to another, which can play an important role in the adoption of green supply chain practices. Future studies would benefit from expanding the dataset to include a more diverse range of countries and regions, which could provide a more comprehensive understanding of global green logistics challenges. The flow section of the chapter recommends some strategies to address and overcome the challenges of green logistics management.

4.7 Recommendations for Future Studies and Strategies for the Sector and Policy Makers

Despite all the challenges awaiting LSPs, green transformation will become a necessity in the future rather than a choice. LSPs that undergo this transformation will have a head start among their competitors in the future. The results indicate that the primary strategic approaches are cost management and price sensitivity, the lack of collaboration and partnerships, the development of the logistics infrastructure, environmental awareness training, technological innovations, and digitalization. To ensure practical implementation, LSPs should focus on cross-sector partnerships and collaboration with governments to create supportive policies and incentives. This can encourage the adoption of sustainable practices on a larger scale. Moreover, the establishment of multidisciplinary research teams can contribute to a better understanding of the different dimensions of these challenges and generating comprehensive solutions. In particular, key challenges such as cost-effectiveness, lack of collaboration and ignoring environmental issues need to be examined.

References

1. IEA, Transport Energy System, 2024, https://www.iea.org/energy-system/transport (accessed Jul. 11, 2024).
2. McKinnon, A., Browne, M., Whiteing, A., Piecyk, M., *Green logistics: Improving the environmental sustainability of logistics*, Kogan Page Publishers, London, UK, 2015.
3. Herzog, A.V., Lipman, T.E., Kammen, D.M., Renewable energy sources. Encyclopedia of life support systems (EOLSS). *Forerunn. Vol. Overv. Life Support Syst. Sustain. Dev.*, 2001. (Accessed June 22, 2024): https://rael.berkeley.edu/old_drupal/sites/default/files/old-site-files/2001/Herzog-Lipman-Kammen-RenewableEnergy-2001.pdf.
4. Ritchie, H., Sector by sector: where do global greenhouse gas emissions come from?, 2020, https://ourworldindata.org/ghg-emissions-by-sector (accessed Jul. 02, 2024).
5. Zhang, W., Zhang, M., Zhang, W., Zhou, Q., Zhang, X., What influences the effectiveness of green logistics policies? A grounded theory analysis. *Sci. Total Environ.*, 714, 136731, 2020. https://doi.org/10.1016/j.scitotenv.2020.136731.
6. Sarkar, B., Omair, M., Choi, S.-B., A multi-objective optimization of energy, economic, and carbon emission in a production model under sustainable supply chain management. *Appl. Sci.*, 8, 10, 1744, 2018, https://doi.org/10.3390/app8101744.
7. Mishenin, Y., Koblianska, I., Medvid, V., Maistrenko, Y., Sustainable regional development policy formation: role of industrial ecology and logistics. *Entrep. Sustain. Issues*, 6, 1, 329–341, 2018, https://doi.org/10.9770/jesi.2018.6.1(20).
8. Larina, I.V., Larin, A.N., Kiriliuk, O., Ingaldi, M., Green logistics-modern transportation process technology. *Prod. Eng. Arch.*, vol, 3, 184–190, 2021, https://doi.org/10.30657/pea.2021.27.24.

9. Wärtsilä, Sustainable fuels for shipping by 2050 – the 3 key elements of success, 2024, https://safety4sea.com/wp-content/uploads/2024/03/Wartsila-Sustainable-fuels-for-shipping-by-2050-industry-report_2024_03.pdf (accessed Oct. 12, 2024).
10. Van Buren, N., Demmers, M., Van der Heijden, R., Witlox, F., Towards a circular economy: The role of Dutch logistics industries and governments. *Sustainability*, 8, 7, 647, 2016, https://doi.org/10.3390/su8070647.
11. Dey, A., LaGuardia, P., Srinivasan, M., Building sustainability in logistics operations: a research agenda. *Manag. Res. Rev.*, 34, 11, 1237–1259, 2011, https://doi.org/10.1108/01409171111178774.
12. Rondinelli, D. and Berry, M., Multimodal transportation, logistics, and the environment: managing interactions in a global economy. *Eur. Manag. J.*, 18, 4, 398–410, 2000, https://doi.org/10.1016/S0263-2373(00)00029-3.
13. Dekker, R., Bloemhof, J., Mallidis, I., Operations Research for green logistics–An overview of aspects, issues, contributions and challenges. *Eur. J. Oper. Res.*, 219, 3, 671–679, 2012, https://doi.org/10.1016/j.ejor.2011.11.010.
14. Fay, M., Toman, M., Benitez, D., Csordas, S., Infrastructure and sustainable development. *Postcrisis Growth Dev. A Dev. Agenda G*, 20, 22, 329–382, 2011.
15. Aronsson, H. and Huge Brodin, M., The environmental impact of changing logistics structures. *Int. J. Logist. Manag.*, 17, 3, 394–415, 2006, https://doi.org/10.1108/09574090610717545.
16. Scheelhaase, J., Maertens, S., Grimme, W., Jung, M., EU ETS versus CORSIA–A critical assessment of two approaches to limit air transport's CO2 emissions by market-based measures. *J. Air Transp. Manag.*, 67, 55–62, 2018, https://doi.org/10.1016/j.jairtraman.2017.11.007.
17. Bayer, P. and Aklin, M., The European Union emissions trading system reduced CO2 emissions despite low prices. *Proc. Natl. Acad. Sci.*, 117, 16, 8804–8812, 2020, https://doi.org/10.1073/pnas.1918128117.
18. Figures, T., Gilbert, M., McAdoo, M., Voigt, N., The EU's carbon border tax will redefine global value chains. *BCG*, 12, 2021, [Online]. Available: https://mkt-bcg-com-public-pdfs.s3.amazonaws.com/prod/eu-carbon-border-tax.pdf.
19. Gros, D. and Egenhofer, C., The case for taxing carbon at the border. *Clim. Policy*, 11, 5, 1262–1268, 2011, https://doi.org/10.1080/14693062.2011.592669.
20. Efthymiou, M. and Papatheodorou, A., EU Emissions Trading scheme in aviation: Policy analysis and suggestions. *J. Clean. Prod.*, 237, 117734, 2019. https://doi.org/10.1016/j.jclepro.2019.117734.
21. Mangan, J. and Lalwani, C., *Global Logistics and Supply Chain Management*, John Wiley & Sons, Third. Padstow, 2016.
22. Barysienė, J., Batarlienė, N., Bazaras, D., Čižiūnienė, A.J., Griškevičienė, K., Griškevičius, D., Vasilienė-Vasiliauskienė, V., Analysis of the current logistics and transport challenges in the context of the changing environment.

Transport, 30, 2, 233–241, 2015, https://doi.org/10.3846/16484142.2015.1046403.
23. Plaza-Úbeda, J.A., Abad-Segura, E., de Burgos-Jiménez, A., Belmonte-Ureña, L.J., Trends and new challenges in the green supply chain: The reverse logistics. *Sustainability*, 13, 1, 331, 2020, https://doi.org/10.3390/su13010331.
24. Mehdiyeva, I., Kerimli, V., Gafarov, N., Sultanova, N., Heydarova, K., Taghiyev, A., Barriers and drivers of the implementation and management of green agri-food supply chains in Azerbaijan. *Int. J. Supply Chain Manag.*, 9, 4, 527–535, 2020.
25. Panghal, A., A., P., Vern, P., Mor, R.S., Adoption barriers to green logistics in the Indian food industry: A circular economy perspective. *Int. Soc. Sci. J.*, 74, 252, 519–538, 2024, https://doi.org/10.1111/issj.12466.
26. Pillay, K. and Mbhele, T.P., The challenges of green logistics in the Durban road freight industry. *Environ. Econ.*, 6, 1, 64–73, 2015.
27. Beškovnik, B. and Jakomin, L., Challenges of green logistics in Southeast Europe. *PROMET-Traffic & Transportation*, 22, 2, 147–155, 2010, https://doi.org/10.7307/ptt.v22i2.174.
28. Singh, S., Barve, A., Shanker, S., An ISM-gDEMATEL framework for assessing barriers to green freight transportation: a case of Indian logistics system. *Int. J. Sustain. Eng.*, 14, 6, 1871–1892, 2021, https://doi.org/10.1080/19397038.2021.1982063.
29. Arroyo, L.A.B., Barreto, C. A. D. L. S., Vasquez, O.B.S., Nicola, R.J.V., The importance of Reverse Logistics and Green Logistics for Sustainability in Supply Chains. *J. Bus. Entrep. Stud.*, 7, 4, 46–72, 2023, https://doi.org/10.37956/jbes.v7i4.351.
30. Leung, T.C.H., Guan, J., Lau, Y.Y., Exploring environmental sustainability and green management practices: evidence from logistics service providers. *Sustain. Account. Manag. Policy J.*, 14, 3, 461–489, 2023, https://doi.org/10.1108/SAMPJ-03-2022-0133.
31. Trstenjak, M., Mustapić, M., Gregurić, P., Opetuk, T., Use of green industry 5.0 technologies in logistics activities. *Teh. Glas.*, 17, 3, 471–477, 2023, https://doi.org/10.31803/tg-20230518185836.
32. Establish, 2021 Logistics Cost and Service 2020: The Establish Davis Database, 2021, https://static1.squarespace.com/static/57bf65a1c534a52224df643c/t/61bcda757d58a3178229263b/1639766645913/Logistics+Cost+and+Service+2020+Updated.pdf (accessed Oct. 13, 2024).
33. Ritchie, H., Rosado, P., Roser, M., Breakdown of carbon dioxide, methane and nitrous oxide emissions by sector. *Our World Data*, 2024.
34. Drucker, P.F., The economy's dark continent, in: *The Roots of Logistics*, P. Klaus and XXXS, Müller (Eds.), pp. 97–105, Springer, Berlin, Heidelberg, 2012, https://doi.org/10.1007/978-3-642-27922-5_8. (Accessed June 28, 2024): https://ourworldindata.org/emissions-by-sector.

5

Integrating Green Logistics and Working Capital Management for Sustainable Economic Growth

Reet Kaur and Divyansha Kumar*

Chitkara Business School, Chitkara University, Punjab, India

Abstract
This chapter focuses on the interplay between green logistics, working capital management, and sustainable economic growth. The key purpose of this chapter is to study the integration between green logistics and working capital management and to explore the result of the said integration in securing sustainable economic growth. The research is structured as a qualitative study that relies on secondary material including real-world examples, for exploring the relationship between working capital management, green logistics, and sustainable economic growth. Through a synthesis of existing literature and with the help of real-world examples, authors explored that integration of green transportation, sustainable warehousing, and climate friendly packaging with optimized inventory management, effective account receivables and payables; accelerates economic performance, stimulate environmental sustainability, promote corporate social responsibility, control risks, foster innovation and competitiveness. Present chapter presents a distinctive framework which links working capital management decision making strategies with green logistics practices for realizing sustainable economic growth. Insights from the present chapter will help managers to sync investment strategies with long-term sustainability goals by utilizing working capital not only for enhancing operational efficiency but also for funding green logistics initiatives.

***Keywords*:** Green logistics management, green supply chain, working capital management, sustainable business practices, business performance, sustainability, sustainable economic growth, corporate social responsibility

**Corresponding author*: divyansha.kumar@gmail.com

K. Mathiyazhagan, Krishna Kumar Dadsena, Rajesh Kumar Singh, Aakanksha Kishore and Andrea Appolloni (eds.) Sustainable Operations of Logistics and Supply Chain Management, (85–108) © 2025 Scrivener Publishing LLC

5.1 Introduction

In today's fast-paced global economy, the goal of sustainability has become an essential necessity for enterprises, governments, and society. Sustainable economic growth is built upon the concepts of green responsibility, judicious fiscal management, and enhanced economic prosperity. This chapter focuses on the interplay between green logistics (GL), working capital management (WCM), and aims to explore how these factors contribute to the development of a sustainable and prosperous economy. (Core argument of the chapter)

5.1.1 Overview of Green Logistics

Significant advancement in the transportation sector is that modern business transportation depends on logistics, which means that movement of goods is organized and controlled to some extent. The term "green" has unfolded into a symbolic representation of environmental issues and is regarded in a positive light. Green and Logistics, when placed together imply a distribution and transportation system that is kind to the environment [1]. In the current scenario, the notion behind implementation of green logistics is seen by a number of individuals as highly desirable. Established business transportation formats only focus on synchronization between transportation, warehousing, and packaging of goods from the providers to the consumers as shown in Figure 5.1. However, with the appearance of environmental challenges and issues, the concerns for recycling, waste management,

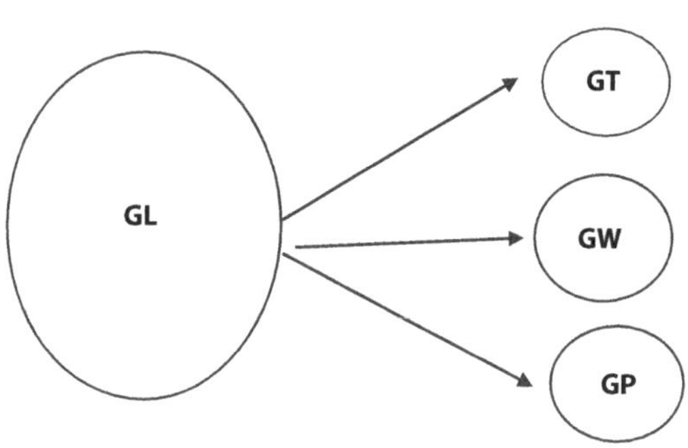

Figure 5.1 Elements of green logistics.
Source: Author's own, based on Rodrigue, (2020) [2] and Raut *et al.*, (2019) [6]
Where,
GT = Green Transportation; **GW** = Green Warehousing;
GP = Green Packaging; **GL** = Green Logistics

reverse logistics and many more are giving momentum to the concept of sustainable logistics. Logistics in a sustainable manner, popularly known as green logistics, is a business function which embraces environmental aspects into logistics operations with the intention of impeding the environmental impact of transportation, warehousing, and distribution processes [2]. Climate-friendly supply chain makes utilization of energy-efficient transportation, optimizes routes to reduce fuel consumption, and implements eco-friendly practices in warehousing [3]. The goal behind adoption of environment-friendly operations is to establish equilibrium between economic efficacy and environmental durability, for fostering comprehensive sustainable economic development [4].

5.1.2 Working Capital Management

Working capital management (WCM) is an important aspect of the financial management function of a business organization; it refers to the management of a company's short-term financial resources (current assets and current liabilities) in order to effectively maintain its day-to-day business operations. Figure 5.2 shows that proper management of working capital ensures the equilibrium between a company's present resources, including inventory and accounts receivable, and its present obligations, such as accounts payable and short-term financing [5]. The key objective of WCM is to make certain that there is enough readily available cash to cover business operating requirements while optimizing the utilization of cash flows for improving business profitability [6].

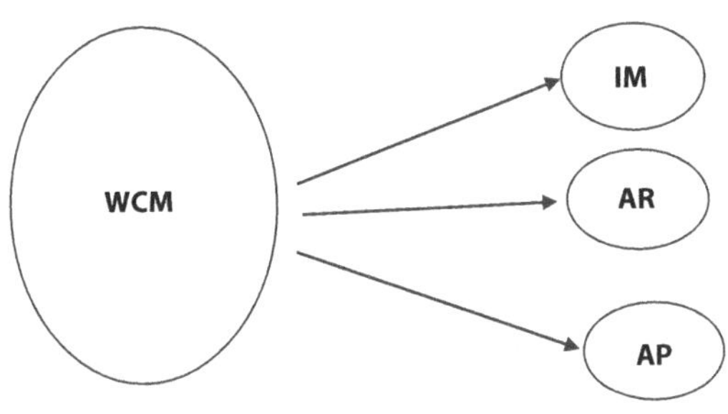

Figure 5.2 Elements of working capital management.
Source: Author's own, based on Deloof, (2003) and Gitman & Zutter, (2012)
Where,
IM = Inventory Management; **AR** = Account Receivables;
AP = Account Payables; **WCM** = Working Capital Management

5.1.3 Relevance of Sustainable Economic Growth

For achieving sustainable business and economic growth in today's dynamic business environment; management of financial, social, and environmental goals has become essential. The notion of sustainable economic growth guarantees that businesses not only attain financial prosperity for themselves but also create an ideal impact on the society and the environment.

Following are the crucial arguments why equitable development is essential:

Economic Resilience: Sustainable economic development strengthens organizations to establish economic potency by guaranteeing enduring profits and stability. Businesses which incorporate sustainable practices frequently observe better efficiency, reduced expenses, and improved reputation, resulting in higher financial results and competitiveness in the marketplace [7]. Sustainable business solutions also appeal to investors who are increasingly prioritizing environmental, social, and governance aspects [8].

Environmental Stewardship: Owing to increasing knowledge among the stakeholders about the environmental concerns such as depletion, degradation, and contamination, businesses are facing the demand to minimize the negative ecological impact of their activities. They are encouraged to implement climate-friendly practices that cause reduction of carbon dioxide emissions, optimization of resources, and elimination of waste, for achieving balanced sustainable economic development [9]. These measures not only contribute to the preservation of the environment but also comply with regulatory standards and fulfill customer expectations.

Social Responsibility: By striking an equilibrium between social and financial objectives, corporations can truly contribute to the overall betterment of the community. Practices involving socially responsible behavior of the company include equitable labor practices, active involvement in the community, principled governance, and many more [10]. Organizations that place a high importance on their social responsibility behavior have the ability to develop better connections with their stakeholders, which in turn promotes loyalty and enhances trust along with improved employee performance and productivity [11].

5.1.4 Theme of Integration

Figure 5.3 shows the mix of green logistics and working capital techniques results in a good, long-term, and climate-friendly development impact. Businesses can achieve economic success, social responsibility, and environmental commitment by prioritizing cost reduction, optimal resource allocation, and ethical social behavior. This full integration will help achieve general aims of sustainability such as adaptability, long-term prosperity, and stability along with fostering financial health of the organizations. These practices are critical to business because their implementation improves environmental sustainability, organizational performance, and the shift to economic growth and development. Examples from the real-world includes from the companies Patagonia, IBM, Unilever, IKEA, Walmart, Coca-Cola, UPS etc., demonstrating how these modern business methods can assist in achieving sustainability goals. Thus, enhancement of long-term sustainable economic growth necessitates the combining of working capital approaches with climate-friendly logistics. Therefore, the present chapter aims to explore the results of interplay between green logistics, working capital management, and sustainable economic growth.

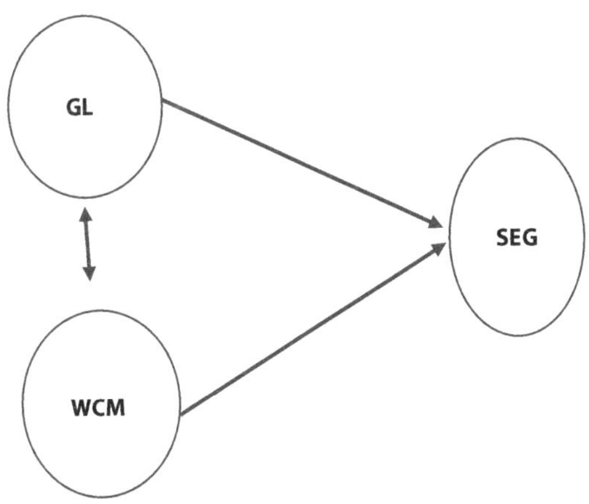

Figure 5.3 Green logistics and working capital optimization model.
Source: Authors compilation
Where,
GL = Green Logistics;
WCM = Working Capital Management;
SEG = Sustainable Economic Growth

5.2 Review of Literature

5.2.1 Green Logistics and Sustainable Economic Growth

Green Logistics includes challenges of the environment into the supply chain at its different stages [12]. It does so by integrating product design, material selection, manufacturing, product delivery, and after-sale services with the issues of the environment [13]. The principal goal is to remove the impact of environmental challenges from the life cycle of the product, with the emphasis on sustainability and economic growth [14]. Adopting logistics in a sustainable way results in improved productivity, enhanced performance, and the identification of trends and patterns of dynamic business environment [15]. Challenges in implementing practices of future logistics like green design, green manufacturing, reverse logistics, reconditioning, and core disposal call for innovative ways for reconsidering the purchase and supply cycle. In addition to them, multi-criteria decision-making approaches like Fuzzy Axiomatic Design can help select the best green supplier [16]. An integrated green SCM tool, the green SCOR model can help manage the supply chain's environmental impacts more effectively and efficiently [17]. Recent research reveals that green logistics has embraced sustainable economic growth. By adopting environmentally friendly transportation methods, cost friendly route planning and green warehousing, Companies can minimize the impact of their logistic practices on the environment [4]. Literature shows that sustainable business practices contribute to economic sustainability by decreasing costs, energy consumption, reducing CO2 emissions and improving operational efficiency [18]. For instance, implementing climate friendly vehicles and hybrid trucks in logistics can substantially decrease emissions and fuel costs [19]. Embracing green logistics practices allows companies to aligns its operations with environmental goals and thus enhance its social responsibility leading to better customer satisfaction and brand loyalty [20].

5.2.2 Working Capital Management and Sustainable Economic Growth

Working Capital Management (WCM) is an important tool of business financial management. By effective management of inventory, account receivables and payables WCM techniques result in operational efficiency and business profitability. Many studies have underlined the benefits of rationalizing key components (account receivables, account payables, and inventory) of working capital to improve the performance of the business [21]. Reports highlight that effective management of inventory decreases the stock-holding costs and also reduces stockouts, thereby assisting in effortless production cycles [22]. Systematic management of accounts receivables encourages cash inflow, thus improving liquidity and bringing down dependency on external financing [23]. On the other hand, strategic management of account payables can also enhance cash inflow by manipulating credit terms with suppliers but without straining relationships with them [24]. The synergies between modern technologies such as blockchain, IoT and AI is also metamorphosing working capital management strategies by improving transparency across the supply chain and providing real-time data analytics [25]. For sustaining the economic growth and ensuring the financial stability of the organizations, the role of sustainable working capital management strategies has become pivotal [26]. Optimized working capital management (WCM) strategies lead to organizational financial stability and promote long-term sustainability; this has attracted attention towards the link between WCM and sustainable economic growth. Many recent studies have underscored that rationalized WCM through key components such as receivables, payables and inventory not only improve the firm performance and liquidity but also optimizes resource allocation and reduce waste, thereby supporting sustainable economic growth [21]. For example, application of JIT technique of inventory management minimizes the excess stock from the system, thus contributing to economic sustainability by impeding its environmental impact [27]. Moreover, timely collection of account receivables and systematic account payables improves the flow of cash within the organization, enabling the organizations to invest in sustainable business practices [28]. Literature also reveals that the companies with vigorous WCM are positioned to withstand economic disruptions in a better way and can contribute to economic development [29]. Synergizing sustainable business practices into working capital management such as green logistics can streamline organizational financial strategies with comprehensive economic and environmental goals [30]. Advancement and implementation of technology like internet of things and blockchain in green logistics, improves efficiency and decreases waste by providing real-time tracking and transparency in supply chains [31]. These innovations by optimizing logistics operations promote sustainable economic growth by supporting environmental goals and creating economic value [13].

5.3 Research Methodology

5.3.1 Research Gaps

Despite the increasing trend and implementation of sustainable business practices, several research gaps remain:

- While existing studies cover green logistics and working capital management separately, studies explicitly investigating the integration of green logistics and working capital management practices do not exist.
- There is absence of integrated models examining the consolidated effects of green logistics and working capital management on sustainable economic growth. Existing models emphasize on individual dimensions such as financial contribution of working capital management or economic impact of green logistics, without focusing on interconnection between these factors.

5.3.2 Purpose and Objective

The primary objective of this chapter is to study the integration between green logistics and working capital management and to explore the result of the said integration in securing sustainable economic growth. Through a detailed examination of them we aim to:

1. Demonstrate the key principles of green logistics.
2. Explore the significance of effective working capital management.
3. Study the integration of green logistics practices and the working capital management strategies.
4. Investigate the influence of green logistics practices and the management of working capital on sustainable economic growth.
5. Examine the challenges and opportunities of synergies between the above elements.

5.3.3 Data Collection and Analysis

The research is structured as a qualitative study that relies on secondary material including real-world examples, for exploring the relationship between working capital management, green logistics, and sustainable economic growth. The data utilized in this chapter was gathered from a diverse array of reliable sources, such as scholarly journals, working papers, business reports, case studies, government publications, books and articles, websites and online databases. Data collected from secondary sources was synthesized and interpreted to draw meaningful conclusions.

5.3.4 Limitations and Future Scope of Research

- The chapter rests exclusively on data from secondary sources, making the results restricted to extent, quality, and fidelity of attainable data.
- Data on green logistics practices and working capital management strategies is not evenly available over the industries, leading to possible discrepancies.
- Absence of empirical validation affects the reliability of the results of present study.
- Validation of the proposed model which offers a valuable conceptual framework is planned for further research through primary data collection, to test its generalizability throughout the various industries.

5.4 Result

5.4.1 Key Principles of Green Logistics

Green Logistics practices include: green transportation, green warehousing, and green packaging. The primary goal behind incorporating these eco-friendly practices into the supply chain is to reduce the negative impact of its activities on the environment. Following section explains the functioning of green logistics practices:

Green transportation makes the use of transportation methods that minimize carbon emissions and fuel usage such as the utilization of electric cars or hybrid cars. Sustainable transportation methods also optimize routes for delivery of the goods, and therefore, transitioning the transportation of goods from conventional means to more sustainable means like rail transport or sea transport [2]. Many studies contributed that adoption of climate-friendly transportation not only mitigates the release of greenhouse gases but also assists in the reduction of air pollution and reliance on fossil fuels [4].

Green warehousing entails the efficient utilization of space and management of inventory to mitigate the environmental impact of warehousing operations [32]. Sustainable warehousing intends to lessen the ecological footprint of storage facilities by adopting habits such as reusing and trash minimization. It also employs energy-efficient architectural designs and harnesses sources of sustainable energy for promoting sustainability [33].

Green packaging is the utilization of renewable or biodegradable materials, the reduction of packaging waste, and the creation of packaging style that requires less packaging material [34]. In simple words, packaging for sustainability is the use of packaging materials and methods that are ecologically sustainable. Adoption of such practices helps in minimizing the quantity of waste that is deposited in landfills and diminishes the environmental setbacks linked to the manufacturing and dumping of packaging materials [35, 36].

5.4.2 Significance of Effective Working Capital Management

Working capital management ensures that a firm fulfills its immediate financial obligations, operates with optimal efficiency, and allocates funds towards its business activities by proper management of inventory, receivables, and accounts payables [37]. Optimization of working capital encompasses tactics for effectively controlling inventory levels, swiftly collecting outstanding payments, and efficiently managing accounts payable to foster corporate expansion and ensure financial stability [38].

Inventory management is the systematic supervision of a company's inventory, encompassing activities such as ordering, storing, and utilization of unprocessed materials, constituent parts, and finalized goods [39]. Efficient inventory management aims to achieve an equilibrium between sufficient inventory levels to fulfill customer demand and avoiding excessive capital investment in inventory/stock. Techniques like Just-in-Time (JIT) inventory, Economic Order Quantity (EOQ), and the Activity-Based Costing (ABC) are frequently employed to optimize inventory levels [40, 41].

Receivables management entails the strategies and regulations that dictate a company's provision of credit to the customers and the collection of bills receivables. Effective receivables management ensures timely payment of invoices by the customers, hence maintaining cash inflows and impeding the risk of bad-debts. Account receivables practices encompass establishing credit conditions, conducting credit assessments, and proactively pursuing delinquent accounts [37, 38].

Payables management is responsible for preserving liquidity and cultivating strong supplier relationships. Companies by strategically optimizing the time frame of payments to suppliers can maximize the benefits of attractive credit terms while maintaining their relationships positively [42]. Effective payables management strategies involve engaging in negotiations to secure more favorable payment conditions, managing timing of payments to optimize cash availability, and capitalizing on early payment cash discounts to enhance financial performance [43].

5.4.3 Integration of Green Logistics and Working Capital Management

The primary goal behind incorporation of green logistics practices into business operations is to reduce carbon footprints and other environmental impacts by optimizing routes, using fuel-efficient cars, and adopting alternative fuels. Embedding green practices not only lowers operational expenses of the business but also enhances its operational efficiency [44]. Moreover, by adopting sustainable warehousing component of green logistics such as energy-efficient technologies, space efficiency, waste reduction measures, integrating green power resources, lighting, and temperature management helps the enterprise to minimize environmental effects of its operations and also leads to significant financial savings in the long run [35]. Furthermore, green packaging techniques of green logistics decrease waste and resource consumption by harnessing environment-friendly materials, eliminating waste products, and streamlining product design to provide product protection [45].

Whereas, effective control of working capital techniques assists companies to improve their cash flows leading to improved productivity and availability of funds for investing in sustainable business practices. For instance, implementation of just-in-time solutions and precise demand forecasting tools of inventory management helps to maintain adequate stock levels, limit surplus inventory, and reduces holding costs [46]. Additionally, efficient management of receivables guarantees prompt recovery of consumer payments by implementing credit management rules, offering reductions for early payments, and optimizing invoicing processes. Adopting this tool improves business liquidity and facilitates the implementation of climate-friendly activities [47]. Lastly, systematic account payables tool augments cash flows and supports sustainable investments by negotiating advantageous terms of payments with suppliers hence, assuring sufficient funds for operations management [48].

Hence it is clear from the above discussion that by aligning green logistics practices with working capital management methods, business organizations can attain greater benefits. Section below highlights their interaction in detail:

A. Cost Saving

By integrating green practices of logistics with strategies of working capital management, companies can extensively reduce their operational costs and boost their operational performance. For instance, by replacing optimized transportation routes with traditional transportation routes can cause reduction in fuel consumption, resulting in reduced environmental impact of transportation activities and lower logistics costs [49]. Inventory management tools which are in line with green logistics methods can mitigate holding costs and waste on its effective implementation.

B. Improved Cash Flow Management

Successful management of working capital ensures that an organization possesses enough liquidity for allocating funds towards green initiatives of logistics practices. Impactful cash flow management involves effectively overseeing the levels of inventory, proper administration of account receivables, and account payables in order to release funds that can be allocated towards sustainable investments initiatives. For instance, implementation of Just-In-Time inventory system technique lowers the necessity for extensive reserves of inventory, thereby liberating funds previously tied in stock reserves for investing in eco-friendly technologies, such as energy-saving lighting or solar panels for warehouses [50].

C. Strengthened Operational Efficiency

Merging tools of working capital and logistics promotes operational efficiency of the organization. For instance, green logistics initiatives, such as the utilization of automated warehouse structures and real-time cargo tracking systems, improves accuracy, reduces losses and leads to optimal resource allocation and provides better decision-making [51]. Similarly streamlined tools of working capital, minimizes inefficiencies, and enhances the proper utilization of resources, resulting in strengthened operational efficiency and improved performance of working capital.

D. Green Investments for Economic Sustainability

Incorporation of green logistics practices into business operations requires initial capital expenditure. For instance, funds are needed for procuring fuel-efficient automobiles or implementing green energy systems in storage facilities [29]. On the other side, optimized working capital practices of effective inventory management, accounts receivable and accounts payable ensures investments for economic sustainability without endangering financial well-being of the organization by administering current assets and current liabilities of the business effectively [50].

E. Promotion of Ethical Practices

Companies can promote their ethical business practices such as reduced impact of business operations on environment, assurance of fair labor standards [52], and active participation in community development services by aligning green logistics principles with working capital management tools [53]. For instance, companies that optimize resource allocation through sustainable practices tend to save costs that can be allocated towards improved compensation and amplified working conditions of employees. Thus, ensuring equitable labor practices and higher employee satisfaction and retention [10].

F. Fosters Transparency and Accountability

Constructive management of working capital fosters integrity in financial operations of the organization, while the adoption of sustainable practices of logistics improves accountability for environmental policies. Collectively, their interaction builds a culture in the organization that is marked by transparency and adherence of ethical principles. For instance, [18] revealed that by embedding green logistics indicators into financial reporting of the companies, can offer stakeholders with clear and honest information regarding their environmental responsibility and sustainability initiatives, thereby gaining stakeholders confidence and reliability.

5.4.3.1 *Influence of Integration on Sustainable Economic Growth*

The synergies between sustainable logistics and working capital management practices significantly contributes to sustainable growth of the economy by enhancing economic performance, stimulating environmental sustainability, promoting corporate social responsibility, fostering innovation, competitiveness and by controlling risks. Section below explains the impact of their integration on economic growth with the help of real-world examples:

A. Economic Performance: By merging working capital techniques and green logistics practices business organizations tend to improve their business performance by decreasing costs, improving liquidity and better productivity, thereby contributing to overall economic improvement. Hence, managing inventory effectively can positively impact cash flow, while optimizing transportation routes and improving storage methods can save operational expenses.

Case 1: UPS

UPS utilizes the "On-Road Integrated Optimization and Navigation" system, which is made of advanced algorithms to determine the most optimized delivery routes. As per reports, by using this approach approximately 10 million gallons of oil are conserved annually, leading to a reduction of 100,000 metric tons of greenhouse gases emissions. On the adoption of this advanced system, UPS has experienced a decrease in costs due to improved efficiency in package delivery and reduced fuel use [54].

B. Sustainability of Environment: Green logistics practices immediately contribute to environmental preservation by reducing carbon emissions, minimizing waste, and promoting the adoption of green energy sources. It is imperative to adhere to these actions in order to comply with regulations and safeguard the brand's reputation, while also contributing to long-term environmental preservation [53].

Case 2: IKEA

IKEA has committed to exclusively utilizing renewable energy for all of its operations by 2030. This is to enable the company to achieve a climate positive status. Following investments in solar and wind energy, the company currently generates a surplus of green energy from these sources, surpassing the total energy consumption of its warehouses and stores. IKEA enhances its reputation as a sustainability frontrunner and mitigates its environmental impact through the use of eco-conscious logistics strategies, including optimizing its supply chain and employing electric vehicles for deliveries [55].

C. Corporate Social Responsibility: Businesses can promote social responsibility by allocating funds towards environmentally sustainable logistics and effectively managing their working capital, while also prioritizing fair labor practices and community outreach. These initiatives enhance the organization's standing and foster client allegiance, both of which are vital for sustained economic expansion.

Case 3: Unilever

Unilever's Sustainable Living Plan aims to enhance health and well-being, safeguard the environment, and ensure equitable treatment of workers. Unilever employs environmentally-friendly logistics strategies, such as waste reduction in their supply chain and the utilization of resources acquired in an environmentally sustainable manner, to achieve their social responsibility objectives. The company has also collaborated with the local community to promote sustainable agriculture and improve their quality of life. These initiatives have contributed to Unilever's enduring and sustainable expansion by fostering consumer loyalty and enhancing the company's reputation [56].

D. Innovation: Businesses frequently generate innovative concepts to effectively manage their working capital while minimizing environmental impact. Businesses allocate funds towards implementing innovative technologies and methodologies in order to enhance the sustainability and efficiency of their operations. This could entail the development of novel eco-friendly materials or the enhancement of supply chain systems through the implementation of blockchain technology to enhance transparency.

Case 4: International Business Machine (IBM)
IBM has invested in blockchain technology to enhance the transparency and effectiveness of supply networks. This enhances operational efficiency and promotes sustainability by reducing waste and ensuring transparent procurement practices [18, 57].
E. Competitive Advantage: Businesses can gain a competitive advantage in the market by implementing environmentally friendly transportation methods and effectively managing their available funds. Customers are increasingly favoring businesses that demonstrate a robust dedication to sustainability. Businesses can differentiate themselves from competition and appeal to environmentally-conscious clients by integrating these principles into their day-to-day activities.

Case 5: Patagonia
Patagonia is a prominent player in the outdoor clothing industry due to its commitment to environmental conservation and ethical business practices. Customers are attracted to the company due to its commitment to upholding equitable labor practices and utilizing recyclable products. This fosters client loyalty and boosts sales [53, 58].
F. Risk Management: By integrating green logistics practices with working capital management methods, organizations may constructively alleviate the risks correlated with regulatory changes, environmental factors, and supply chain inefficiencies. Organizations can ensure their long-term viability and consistency through the adoption of preventive strategies to weaken these risks.

Case 6: Coca-Cola
Coca-Cola is subject to stringent regulations for environmental sustainability, particularly in terms of water usage and waste disposal. The firm has implemented numerous "green logistics" initiatives in order to mitigate these risks. For instance, Coca-Cola has initiated initiatives aimed at rehabilitating water sources to ensure that it replenishes greater quantities of water to communities and the environment than it withdraws for its

beverages. Coca-Cola mitigates the risk of legal complications and maintains its business license in various locations by ensuring that its manufacturing and logistical operations comply with government regulations [59].
G. Regulatory Compliance: Businesses can adhere to environmental laws and regulations by implementing "green" logistics practices. This reduces the probability of the company being penalized and enhances its reputation among stakeholders and the government at large.

Case 7: Walmart
Due to regulations, Walmart is facing increasing pressure to enhance its environmental and sustainability initiatives. In order to address these concerns, Walmart has implemented several "green logistics" initiatives. For instance, the group-initiated Project Gigaton with the aim of reducing a billion metric tons of greenhouse gasses from its global supply chain by 2030. This effort enables Walmart to mitigate penalties and enhance the company's reputation by demonstrating its commitment to environmental concerns and proactively complying with governmental regulations [60].

5.4.4 Challenges and Opportunities of Synergies Between Green Logistics Practices and Working Capital Management Strategies

5.4.4.1 Challenges

A. High Initial Costs: For implementing sustainable practices of logistics and working capital management, considerable initial outlay of capital is required. This includes rebuilding of warehouses with energy saving systems, adoption of modern technologies for efficient inventory management and purchasing of climate friendly vehicles for green transportation [4]. Such noticeable investments are strain, particularly on the financial resources of small and medium sized enterprises. Hence, acting as a barrier for promotion of such sustainable practices and therefore delaying the benefits to sustainable economic growth.
B. Technical Constraints: The high-tech required for optimizing logistics and working capital management strategies is still in its development stage. Issues such as charging time and wide range of electric vehicles may cause hindrance in their adoption for eco-friendly transportation [61]. Similarly, lack of technical staff with required expertise for optimizing inventory management systems is a threat to its adoption [62]. Limited technology limits the positive impact of sustainable practices on sustainable growth.

C. Resistance to Change: Adoption of advanced working capital management techniques or the sustainable practices of logistics may call resistance to change within the organization. To facilitate economic growth and to overcome this resistance, organizations need to take on effective change management strategies and comprehensive training programs [3].

D. Complex of Supply Chains: Perplexed global supply chains can make integration among green logistics practices and working capital management practices more difficult. Vigorous communication and alliance mechanisms are required to coordinate sustainable practices among multiple logistics providers [18]. Complexity of supply chain increases cost and inefficiencies of sustainable practices, potentially impeding their impact on sustainable growth.

E. Regulatory Compliances: Navigation of regulatory landscape for environmental and financial standards can be challenging. Organizations must stay updated with the regulatory compliances, which involve extra administrative costs and also enhance the complexity of implementing sustainable business practices, potentially reducing their impact on economic growth [63].

5.4.4.2 *Opportunities*

A. Improved Efficiency: Synergies between green logistics and working capital management can lead to enhancement in economic performance by reducing cost and improving efficiency, enabling organizations to reinvest in sustainable business practices and growth opportunities [64, 65].

B. Strengthened Brand Reputation: Organizational brand reputation attracts not only customers but also the investors, amplifying sales and investments. By adopting sustainable business practices, organizations can strengthen their brand image which supports in business expansion and fosters economic growth [66].

C. Incentives for Compliances: Implementing sustainable logistics and working capital management practices helps businesses avoid their fines and penalties by complying with environmental regulations and helps them in gaining various incentives, such as tax breaks, grants etc. This creates a business environment instrumental in sustainable economic growth [67].

D. Edge in Competition: Business organizations embracing sustainability leads to innovation, through the development and adoption of modern technologies. New technologies such as, IoT, blockchain and big data analytics, helps in streamlining business operations and provides competitive edge [68].

E. Better Risk Management: Integration of green logistics and working capital management make business practices more resilient to disruptions, thereby improving risk management. Better risk management ensures continuity and stability of business, vital for sustained economic growth [69].

F. Long-term Viability and Growth: Successful integration of sustainable logistics and working capital management practices, positions business organizations for long-term viability and growth by ensuring resource efficiency and environmental stewardship. Companies which priorities sustainability can foster economic growth while maintaining their growth and minimizing environmental impact [70].

5.5 Conclusion

After the synthesis of existing literature, the authors conclude that integration of Green Logistics (GL) practices and Working Capital Management (WCM) strategies is not only a strategic choice but also an economic necessity in today's dynamic business landscape, for achieving sustainable economic growth. In this book chapter, real-word examples from companies like Patagonia, IBM, Unilever, IKEA, Walmart, Coca-Cola, UPS etc. are included by the authors to demonstrate the effect of modern business methods on sustainability goals.

Present study reveals that by introducing green practices in logistics operations, companies can reduce their carbon footprints, comply with environmental standards, and improve their brand reputation. Concurrently, effective working capital management strategies ensure optimal cash flows, impedes operational costs, and provides funds for investing in sustainable initiatives. This chapter identifies that synthesis of green transportation, warehousing, and packaging with effective inventory management, account receivables, and payables, accelerates the economic performance, stimulates environmental sustainability, promotes corporate social responsibility, control risks, and foster innovation and competitiveness.

Thus, the authors propose a framework which explains how their integration fosters long-term economic stability by improving efficiency and reducing costs and also drives innovation. Business organizations by embracing this dual approach can be better positioned to navigate initial high investment costs, technological limitations, resistance to change, supply chain complexity, regulatory and compliance issues. This holistic approach is vital for innovation and competitive advantage, improving efficiency, strengthening brand reputation, gaining incentives for regulatory compliances, better risk management, fostering long-term viability and will play a substantial role in shaping a more sustainable world.

References

1. Rodrigue, J.P., Slack, B., Comtois, C., Green Logistics, in: *Handbook of Logistics and Supply-Chain Management*, vol. 2, pp. 339–350, 2017.
2. Gitman, L.J. and Zutter, C.J., *Principles of Managerial Finance 13th Edition.* Addison-Wesley Publishing Company, Massachusetts, 2012.
3. Raut, R.D., Gardas, B.B., Jha, M.K., Priyadarshini, P., Examining the critical success factors of sustainable supply chain management in the Indian manufacturing context using DEMATEL. *J. Clean. Prod., 213*, 42–53, 2019.
4. Dekker, R., Bloemhof, J., Mallidis, I., Operations Research for Green Logistics - An overview of aspects, issues, contributions and challenges. *Eur. J. Oper. Res., 219*, 3, 671–679, 2012.
5. Deloof, M., Does Working Capital Management affect profitability of Belgian Firms? *J. Bus. Finance Account., 30*, 3–4, 573–588, 2003.
6. Rodrigue, J.-P., *The Geography of Transport Systems. 5th ed.* Routledge, London, 2020.
7. Kolk, A., The Social Responsibility of International Business: From Ethics and the Environment to CSR and Sustainable Development. *J. World Bus., 51*, 1, 23–34, 2016.
8. Friede, G., Busch, T., Bassen, A., ESG and Financial Performance: Aggregated Evidence from more than 2000 Empirical Studies. *J. Sustain. Finance Invest., 5*, 4, 210–233, 2015.
9. Garcia, J.H., Cintra, Y., Figueiredo, P., The Future of Sustainability Reporting in the Digital Era: Conceptualising how Companies manage the transition towards Integrated Digital Reporting. *Sustainability, 13*, 6, 3372, 2021.
10. Aguinis, H. and Glavas, A., What we Know and Don't Know about Corporate Social Responsibility: A Review and Research Agenda. *J. Manage., 38*, 4, 932–968, 2012.
11. Carroll, A.B. and Brown, J.A., Corporate Social Responsibility: A Review of Current Concepts, Research, and Issues. *Int. J. Manage. Rev.*, 20, 1, 4–13, 2018.
12. Srivastav, S., Garg, V., Tiwari, P., The study to analyse the impact of green supply chain management in India. *Int. J. Supply Chain Manage.*, 8, 3, 1033–1038, 2019.
13. Bag, S., Gupta, S., Kumar, S., Sivarajah, U., Role of technological dimensions of green supply chain management practices on firm performance. *J. Enterp. Inf. Manage.*, 34, 1, 1–27, 2021.
14. Sahar, D.P., Afifudin, M.T., Indah, A.B.R., Review of green supply chain management in manufacturing: A case study, in: *IOP Conference Series: Earth and Environmental Science*, vol. *575*, p. 012239, IOP Publishing, 2020.
15. Kannan, D., Govindan, K., Rajendran, S., Fuzzy axiomatic design approach based green supplier selection: a case study from Singapore. *J. Clean. Prod.*, 96, 194–208, 2015.

16. Akkucuk, U., SCOR model and the green supply chain, in: *Handbook of Research on Waste Management Techniques for Sustainability*.
17. Shukla, V., Upadhyay, A., Khandve, B. Applications of green supply chain management in the UK restaurant industry, in: U. Ramanathan & R. Ramanathan (Eds.), *Sustainable Supply Chains: Strategies, Issues, and Models*, pp. 225–247. Springer International Publishing, Cham, 2020.
18. Blanco, E.E. and Sheffi, Y., Green logistics, in: *Sustainable Supply Chains: A Research-Based Textbook on Operations and Strategy*, pp. 101–141, Springer International Publishing, Cham, 2024.
19. Mangla, S.K., Kumar, P., Barua, M.K., Prioritizing the responses to manage risks in the green supply chain: An Indian plastic manufacturer perspective. *Sustain. Prod. Consum.*, *1*, 67–86, 2015.
20. Agyabeng-Mensah, Y., Ahenkorah, E., Afum, E., Agyemang, A.N., Agnikpe, C., Rogers, F., Examining the influence of internal green supply chain practices, green human resource management and supply chain environmental cooperation on firm performance. *Supply Chain Manage. An Int. J.*, *25*, 5, 585–599, 2020.
21. Enqvist, J., Graham, M., Nikkinen, J., The impact of working capital management on firm profitability in different business cycles: Evidence from Finland. *Res. Int. Bus. Finance*, *32*, 36–49, 2014.
22. Kabethi, L.W., The effect of working capital management practices on the financial performance of small and medium enterprises in Kenya, University of Nairobi, Doctoral dissertation, 2013.
23. Wambia, W.O. and Jagongo, A., The effects of working capital management practices on the financial performance of insurance companies in Kenya. *Int. Acad. J. Econ. Finance*, *3*, 5, 103–120, 2020.
24. Moussa, A.A., Determinants of working capital behavior: evidence from Egypt. *Int. J. Manag. Finance*, 15, 1, 39–61, 2019.
25. Lekkakos, S.D. and Serrano, A., Supply chain finance for small and medium sized enterprises: the case of reverse factoring. *Int. J. Phys. Distrib. Logist. Manage.*, *46*, 4, 367–392, 2016.
26. Wang, Z., Akbar, M., Akbar, A., The interplay between working capital management and a firm's financial performance across the corporate life cycle. *Sustainability*, 12, 4, 1661, 2020.
27. Díaz-Reza, J.R., García-Alcaraz, J.L., Sánchez-Ramírez, C., Vargas, A.R., Assessing the impact of Lean manufacturing on Social Sustainability through Structural Equation Modelling and System Dynamics. *IJMIE*, *81*, 1, 113–130, 2024.
28. Lyngstadaas, H. and Berg, T., Working capital management: evidence from Norway. *Int. J. Manag. Finance*, *12*, 3, 295–313, 2016.
29. Aktas, N., Croci, E., Petmezas, D., Is working capital management value-enhancing? Evidence from firm performance and investments. *J. Corp. Finance*, *30*, 98–113, 2015.

30. Al-Ghwayeen, W.S. and Abdallah, A.B., Green supply chain management and export performance: The mediating role of environmental performance. *J. Manuf. Technol. Manage.*, *29*, 7, 1233–1252, 2018.
31. Seyhan, M., Çiğdem, S., Yildiz, B., Meidute-Kavaliauskiene, I., Supply Chain-innovation: past, present, and future. *Independent J. Manage. Prod.*, *12*, 8, 2094–2116, 2021.
32. Sheffi, Y., *Balancing Green: When to Embrace Sustainability in a Business (and When Not To)*. MIT Press, Cambridge, MA, 2018.
33. Frazelle, E., *World-Class Warehousing and Material Handling*. vol. 1, McGraw-Hill, New York, 2002.
34. Rundh, B., Linking Packaging to Marketing: How Packaging is influencing Marketing Strategy. *Br. Food J.*, *115*, 11, 1547–1563, 2013.
35. Verghese, K., Lewis, H., Fitzpatrick, L., *Packaging for Sustainability*, Springer Science and Business Media, London, 2012.
36. Trivedi, S., Negi, S., Anand, N., Sustainable packaging in fresh food supply chain: case of kiwi fruit supply chain in Uttarakhand. *Int. J. Bus. Excellence*, 32, 4, 500–521, 2024.
37. Padachi, K., Trends in Working Capital Management and its Impact on Firm's Performance: An Analysis of Mauritian Small Manufacturing Firms. *Int. Rev. Bus. Res. Pap.*, *2*, 2, 45–58, 2006.
38. Lazaridis, I. and Tryfonidis, D., Relationship between Working Capital Management and Profitability of Listed Companies in the Athens Stock Exchange. *J. Financ. Manage. Anal.*, *19*, 1, 26–35, 2006.
39. Dey., S., Sharma., S., Dutt., S., Applications of Six Sigma in Electronics Industry – A case study. *Int. J. Eng. Sci. Innov. Technol. (IJESIT)*, 2, 3, 302–315, 2013.
40. Ehrhardt, M.C. and Brigham, E.F., *Financial Management: Theory and Practice*. 13th ed. South-Western Cengage Learning, Mason, OH, 2011.
41. Kieso, D.E., Weygandt, J.J., Warfield, T.D., *Intermediate Accounting*, 17th ed., Wiley, 2019.
42. Michalski, G., Financial Liquidity Management in Relation to Risk Sensitivity: Polish Firms Case. *Econ. Comput. Econ. Cybern. Stud. Res.*, *46*, 1, 213–229, 2012.
43. Ng, C., Smith., J.K., Smith, R.L., Evidence on the Determinants of Credit Terms Used in Interfirm Trade. *J. Finance*, *54*, 3, 1109–1129, 1999.
44. Bartolini, M., Bottani, E., Grosse, E.H., Green warehousing: Systematic literature review and bibliometric analysis. *J. Clean. Prod.*, *226*, 242–258, 2019.
45. McKinnon, A., *Decarbonizing logistics: Distributing Goods in a Low Carbon World*, Kogan Page Publishers, London, 2018.
46. Brigham, E.F. and Ehrhardt, M.C., *Financial Management: Theory & Practice*, 17th ed. Cengage Learning, Boston, MA, 2024.
47. Garrison, R.H., Noreen, E.W., Brewer, P.C., *Managerial Accounting*. 18th ed. McGraw Hill, New York, 2023

48. Richards, V.D. and Laughlin, E.J., A cash conversion cycle approach to liquidity analysis. *Financ. Manage.*, 9, 1, 32–38, 1980.
49. Mathuva, D., The Influence of Working Capital Management Components on Corporate Profitability: A survey on Kenyen listed firms. *Res. J. Bus. Manage.*, 9, 1, 1–10, 2015.
50. Mota, B., Gomes, M., II, Carvalho, A., Barbosa-Povoa, A.P., Sustainable supply chains: An integrated modeling approach under uncertainty. *Omega*, 77, 32–57, 2018.
51. Azevedo, S.G., Carvalho, H., Machado, V.C., The influence of green practices on supply chain performance: A case study approach. *Transp. Res. Part E Logist. Transp. Rev.*, *47*, 6, 850–871, 2011.
52. Kumar, D. and Vashisht, A., Sustainopreneurship and its' role in sustainable fashion brands of India. *Int. J. Innov. Technol. Explor. Eng.*, 8, 11, 503–506, 2019.
53. Gimenez, C. and Tachizawa, E.M., Extending sustainability to suppliers: a systematic literature review. *Supply Chain Manage Int. J.*, *17*, 5, 531–543, 2012.
54. UPS, UPS Sustainability Highlights Report, 2021, Retrieved from https://about.ups.com/content/dam/upsstories/assets/reporting/sustainability-2021/Sustainability_Highlights_081721_final.pdf.
55. IKEA, Sustainability, 2022, Retrieved from https://www.ikea.com/ms/en_US/this-is-ikea/people-and-planet/sustainable-everyday.html.
56. Unilever, Sustainable Living, 2023, Retrieved from https://www.unilever.com/sustainable-living/.
57. IBM, Blockchain for Supply Chain, 2021, Retrieved from https://www.ibm.com/blockchain/supply-chain/.
58. Patagonia, Regenerative Organic Agriculture, 2022, Retrieved from https://www.patagonia.com/regenerative-organic-agriculture/.
59. The Coca-Cola Company, Water Stewardship, 2024, Retrieved from https://www.coca-colacompany.com/sustainability/water-stewardship.
60. Walmart, Project Gigaton: 1 Billion Metric Tons, A World of Difference, 2019, Retrieved from https://corporate.walmart.com/news/2019/05/08/walmart-on-track-to-reduce-1-billion-metric-tons-of-emissions-from-global-supply-chains-by-2030.
61. Lee, I. and Mangalaraj, G., Big data analytics in supply chain management: A systematic literature review and research directions. *Big Data Cognit. Computing*, 6, 1, 17, 2022.
62. Bhattacharya, H., *Working Capital Management: Strategies and Techniques*, 4th ed. PHI Learning Pvt. Ltd., New Delhi, 2021.
63. European Commission, A European Commission Green Deal: Striving to be the First Climate-Neutral Continent, 2020, https://commission.europa.eu/strategy-and-policy/priorities-2019-2024/european-green-deal_en.
64. Govindan, K. and Hasanagic, M., A systematic review on drivers, barriers, and practices towards circular economy: a supply chain perspective. *Int. J. Prod. Res.*, *56*, 1–2, 278–311, 2018.

65. Ghadge, A., Wurtmann, H., Seuring, S., Managing climate change risks in global supply chains: a review and research agenda. *Int. J. Prod. Res.*, *58*, 1, 44–64, 2020.
66. Kraus, S., Rehman, S.U., García, F.J.S., Corporate social responsibility and environmental performance: The mediating role of environmental strategy and green innovation. *Technol. Forecast. Soc. Change*, *160*, 120262, 2020.
67. Rosati, F. and Faria, L.G.D., Business contribution to the Sustainable Development Agenda: Organizational factors related to early adoption of SDG reporting. *Corp. Soc. Responsib. Environ. Manage.*, *26*, 3, 588–597, 2019.
68. Malesios, C., De, D., Moursellas, A., Dey, P.K., Evangelinos, K., Sustainability performance analysis of small and medium sized enterprises: Criteria, methods and framework. *Socio-Economic Plann. Sci.*, *75*, 100993, 2021.
69. Ivanov, D. and Dolgui, A., A digital supply chain twin for managing the disruption risks and resilience in the era of Industry 4.0. *Prod. Plann. Control*, *32*, 9, 775–788, 2021.
70. Fernando, Y., Halili, M., Tseng, M.L., Tseng, J.W., Lim, M.K., Sustainable social supply chain practices and firm social performance: Framework and empirical evidence. *Sustain. Prod. Consum.*, *32*, 160–172, 2022.

6

Challenges and Strategies in Green Logistics Management: Adopting Sustainable Solutions for the Future of Supply Chain Operations

Karpagavalli G.

Operations Management, ISBR Business School, Bangalore, India

Abstract

Logistics is known to be the pillar of Supply Chain Management [SCM] and plays a vital role in ensuring the efficient and effective flow of goods and services. All economic sectors are majorly supported by logistics business. A business market which maintains efficient supply chain management and logistical facilities will always have a qualified and added advantage compared to other economies and is also effective in increasing market share opportunities. But at the same time focusing and improving logistical infrastructure seems complex and competitive tool for most of the companies.

The concept of "green logistics" has arisen to response to such challenges which aims to decrease the environmental impact. The companies which are implementing sustainable logistics management and aiming for ensuring long-term profitability can incorporate economic, social, and environmental factors into their logistics process. The businesses which aim to fulfill the customer expectations and also constantly aiming to gain competitive advantage must focus on solving the environmental problems and for the guaranteed long-term profitability, a steady shift towards sustainable logistics management will become essential.

Businesses can look for and gain the financial success by focusing on environmental protection can utilize innovative and advanced technologies and aim to implement green practices in their transport operations.

Green logistics management is essential to reduce the environmental impact of transport operations; however there are numerous challenges associated with

Email: karpagavalligkv@gmail.com

K. Mathiyazhagan, Krishna Kumar Dadsena, Rajesh Kumar Singh, Aakanksha Kishore and Andrea Appolloni (eds.) Sustainable Operations of Logistics and Supply Chain Management, (109–128) © 2025 Scrivener Publishing LLC

it needs to be solved. This book chapter discusses the concept of green logistics as well as the specifics of sustainable logistics, including its difficulties and potential adoption in the chosen industry.

***Keywords*:** Supply chain management, green logistics, sustainable logistics, circular economy, supply chain operations, sustainable supply chain

6.1 Introduction to Green and Sustainable Logistics

Green supply chain management is nothing but aligning and integrating the environmental management with supply chain management [1]. Logistics becomes the major tool for the development of the economy. The authors also analyzed that the development of a nation cannot occur without effective logistics [2]. In recent times, companies focus towards sustainable logistics is growing at a higher pace. As a result, numerous green logistics projects have been created worldwide. The green logistics market size is predicted to rise to USD 1.28 trillion by 2024 and expected to still more increase to USD 1.91 trillion by 2029 with a growth rate approximate to 8.29%.

Any sustainable logistics system which aims for long term performance must focus on two key objectives which are enhancing profitability and minimizing environmental effect. However, the methods of traditional logistics frequently results in severe decline in resources and environmental deterioration; 25% of the global emissions of greenhouse gases are directly related to transport and related facilities, with logistics playing a major role as per the recent analysis.

Nowadays green logistics management practices are the driving force for organizations focusing to improve their performance [3]. Techniques like eco-friendly packing materials, reducing waste, and transporting goods with less energy consumption can be utilized under green logistics. Adopting these techniques will lessen the environmental damage and also provides financial gains by lowering the business expenses and increasing brand recognition. The concept of green logistics management positively affects organizations' circular economy practices and sustainability performance [4].

The conventional definition of logistics and supply chain management is nothing but "logistics refers to operations that take place inside the confines of a single company", whereas the term "supply chain describes a network of businesses that collaborate and coordinate their efforts to get a product to market" [5]. Logistics focuses on tasks including 'inventory management, distribution, maintenance, and purchase' whereas Supply chain management combines all the aspects of traditional logistics along with 'marketing, finance, new product development, and customer service'.

It is expected that the market for green logistics will drastically grow and as a result use of artificial intelligence in global supply chains, growing adoption of electric vehicles (EVs) in the transportation sector, rising environmental legislation, and increased corporate social responsibility (CSR) activities by logistics companies. Operations research methods and mathematical models can help in solving specific problems and also can optimize supply chains [6]. China, being the biggest economy in the Asia-Pacific area, is actively pushing green logistics techniques to address environmental issues. The nation has made investments in clean energy sources, sophisticated transportation systems, and electric automobiles. Logistic firms in Japan, which has a reputation for embracing environmentally friendly technologies, are increasingly utilizing sustainable fuels, especially for hybrid and electric vehicles. China has forecasted to sell more M&H trucks and new EV buses, making roughly around 85% of sales globally. Furthermore, China's brands are widely used in North America, Europe, and Latin America for buses and trucks. India prioritizes developing the industry's electric vehicle market and enhancing the logistics infrastructure. For instance, FedEx Express installed 30 Ace TATA electric cars in India during January 2023 as a part of its global transition to carbon-free operations by 2040. This has boosted the company's fleet services. South Korea has also been making strides in the field of green logistics, implementing several policies into place to lower emissions and boost the efficiency of logistics.

In addition to that there may be certain discrepancies while implementing green logistics [7]. There are certain inconsistencies on a few business factors like cost, time and reliability since logistics itself is not very green due to waste and the pollution it produces, although green logistics is meant to be environmentally beneficial [8].

The primary objective of logistics, particularly in the context of transportation, is cost reduction. Logistics firms often try to cut costs by doing actions that are not in line with environmental regulations. Similarly extended manufacturing, distribution, and retailing methods lead to higher energy consumption, emissions, and space and energy usage, even when current integrated supply chains offer adequate physical distribution networks. The other factor is the service reliability. Successful service reliability's depends on its ability to move the goods on schedule with the least amount of delay or error.

Four elements—system-wide sustainability, economic sustainability, environmental sustainability, and sociocultural sustainability—are the main focus of the theoretical framework for green logistics.

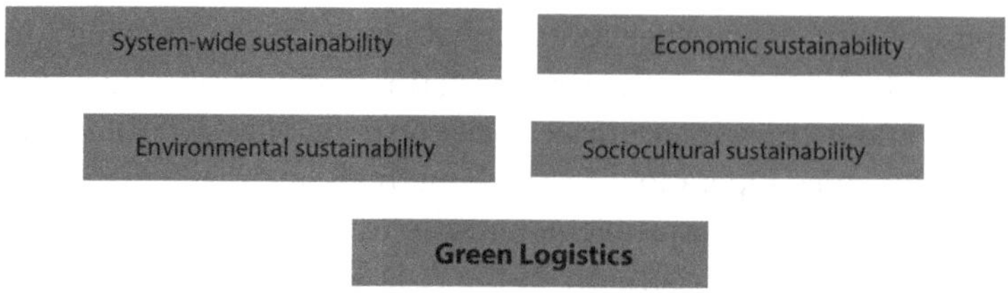

The concept of sustainability relates to the concept of green logistics [9]. Additionally, the author studied the integrated idea of business sustainability as well as the relationships between the logistics pillars.

In order to better understand the Asian rising economies, the author analyzed the relationship of green logistics index with social, economic, and environmental issues and the study's findings showed that, in addition to insufficient trade and logistics infrastructure, political instability and natural disasters are also major contributors to low economic growth and environmental sustainability [10].

A comparative panel study on selected nations by representing it on a group of seven nations as Group7 and Emerging Seven nations as Emerging7 and analyzed the financial variables and economic variables with its impact towards green logistics [11]. They collected the data for 22 years and analyzed it in producing efficient and consistent results. Their findings implied that there exists co-integration between both Emerging7 and Group7 panels. For Emerging7 countries, the results revealed that the factors such as 'research and development (R&D), FDI, portfolio investment, and trade openness' reduce green logistics. whereas, in the Group7 panel the factors like, 'R&D, FDI, portfolio investment, and trade' increases green logistics.

A comprehensive framework for sustainability in the logistics and transportation industry that addresses three primary areas: the Logistics Performance Index, Eco Strategy, and Sustainable Performance [12]. The report also discussed that the success of logistics industry and the potential actions are depending on being aware, taking quick actions, and moving in anticipation.

A framework for a sustainable logistics system has addressed three criteria such as social, environmental, and economic and its impact [13].

The influence of social and environmental sustainability is assessed with green logistics management practices. The results indicated that there is a positive influence of green logistics management practices with both social and environmental sustainability whereas it negatively influences the business performance [3]. The findings further mentioned that the factors such as supply chain traceability and logistics eco centricity increase the green logistics management practices in achieving significant improvement in both business performance and environmental sustainability through its middle effect approach.

Therefore it is understood that increasing revenue and reducing the impact on the environment are the two major objectives of a sustainable logistics system which can further leads to long-term performance of the organization.

This book chapter aimed majorly to focus on three research objectives.

RQ1 – To understand and analyze the concept of green logistics management and the challenges faced

RQ2 – To analyze the green logistics particularly with the retail industry

RQ3 – To examine the possibility of adopting sustainable logistics

6.2 Concept of Green Logistics

Green logistics minimizes environmental effect by incorporating sustainable techniques into logistical operations. Employing green logistics solutions can help and support businesses to save money, increase their reputation, and promote the adoption of environmental sustainability. Green logistics helps on minimize waste materials, increased fuel use, reducing greenhouse gas emissions, and helps in less energy consumption while maintaining efficient supply chain management activity. There are few companies, which used route optimization for their delivery vehicles to cut down on the amount of goods and gasoline used. These successes show the economic and environmental advantages of switching to sustainable logistics.

While there are many advantages in adopting green logistics and rebuilding a supply chain by focusing on reducing carbon dioxide emissions, businesses are also facing high upfront costs which are associated with using the sustainable items and alternative fuels.

The introduction of digital technology and its related customized software applications helps in real time tracking of a company's carbon footprint and provides invaluable insights into logistics processes. Such advanced tools help businesses to develop and implement action plans, target specific areas, and keep track of their progress of their carbon footprint. Companies can plan to collaborate with environmental NGO's and other environmental agencies which can offer insights and support for companies venturing into carbon offsetting. Such partnership also provides a credible front to the company's efforts, as these agencies are often recognized for their work in environmental sustainability. Since the alternative fuels like biofuels and hydrogen can reduce the greenhouse gas emissions, helps in saving money spent for transportation, the logistics industry can benefit using such things move away from fossil fuels. EVs are revolutionizing the logistics industry. Longer battery life and quicker charging times are promised by advancements in battery technology. The logistics industry appears to have a brighter future for electric vehicles when solar charging stations and renewable energy sources are combined. Using green logistics is becoming both a strategic and environmental need for companies looking to expand and remain viable over the long run. However, there are drawbacks to using alternative fuels, like infrastructure requirements, upfront costs, and a long payback period. Electric vehicles (EVs) have drastically reduced carbon emissions, energy costs, and noise pollution. At the same time high initial and upfront costs, reduced battery life and lack of proper infrastructure for charging are some of the few challenges to be addressed. It is expected that by the year 2030, there will be 36% increase of delivery vehicles worldwide in the top 100 cities because of 78% increase in high demand for last-mile delivery. Hence each one of the industry involved in making the final product, starting from shipping companies to all sort of delivery services have this responsibility to consider and to act accordingly. The quick development of e-commerce adds to the exponential growth in delivery services. Since companies are facing significant struggle in implementing environmental policies while balancing their sustainability and profit at present, there are lot of challenges in the last mile deliveries like urban traffic, lack of infrastructure etc. in doing this transition. There are also significant challenges in making this transition.

Increased Cost

Green logistics practices and its implementation in the organization requires sufficient amount of financial investments. These investments are necessary for acquiring eco-friendly vehicles, upgrading existing infrastructure, and adopting sustainable technologies. In order to combine the current state of logistics and sustainability and to reduce the gap between both, a lot of efforts are required into research and development in providing better logistics solutions.62% of logistics companies identified high costs as one of the barrier in implementation as per the survey results of economic forum. The initial expenditure looks discouraging for the companies which operate with limited resources. For instance, transitioning to electric vehicles (EVs) or hybrid trucks involves significant upfront costs compared to conventional diesel trucks. In spite of potential long-term savings in fuel and maintenance, the initial financial investment is still a barrier.

Collaboration and Partnership

Forming partnership or alliances can be a driving force for a possible sustainable change. These partnerships provide access to best practices, shared resources and expertise, and state-of-the-art technologies. On the other hand, building these kinds of partnerships involves reliable agreement on principles, objectives, and long-term vision. Lacking support network is another challenge in the way of sustainable logistics.

Identifying Suitable Suppliers

Finding suppliers who practice sustainability can be difficult. Since most of the production methods adopted by many companies are not sustainable, finding suppliers would be more difficult. As green logistics management aims in minimizing the environmental impact, despite its importance, it faces numerous challenges such as high initial capital, technological limitations, regulatory complexities, and human tendency in adopting to change within organizations that impede its effective implementation.

New Technological Limitations

Even though technological advancements are essential for green logistics, still there are various limitations. Adoption of electric vehicle and building infrastructure for the same could be an option but yet it is not successful as a survey by International Energy Agency estimated that only 3% of trucks worldwide were electric vehicles as on 2022 data.

Regulatory Complexities

Another important challenge is navigating the regulatory environment. Green logistics must consider and compliance with various environmental regulations across different locations. Logistics companies might face a challenge to comply the regulatory landscape across borders when they consider for global business. One of the surveys by Deloitte says that 54% of procurement and logistics managers consider these regulatory guidelines is one of the obstacles in implementing green logistics.

Resistance to Change

Many businesses are used to using outdated logistics techniques and may be hesitant to embrace new, sustainable techniques as adoption of green logistics concept is itself hampered by the crucial human behavior called resistance to change. 48% of logistics executives identified organizational resistance to change as a major obstacle to green logistics as per McKinsey survey. Lack of knowledge about the benefits of green logistics, apprehension about upsetting current procedures, or doubts about the investment's financial yield were few factors that are hindering in the mind-set of the middle and lower level employees.

Supply Chain Complexity
As modern supply chains involves multiple stakeholders and are referred as intricate networks, each with their own processes and priorities which are little complex and create a significant challenge. Coordinating green initiatives across such a network involves a high level of collaboration and transparency, which is tough to attain by companies. Because of the complexity and interconnection of the many supply chain components, 59% of businesses identified to be difficult to integrate such green practices into their regular supply chains, according to a Harvard Business Review survey.

Consumer Expectations
The objectives of green logistics frequently conflict with customer expectations for prompt delivery timeframes. The need for same- or next-day delivery usually necessitates the adoption of quicker, less eco-friendly modes of transportation. According to PwC research, 72% of customers want same-day delivery choices, which puts pressure on logistics firms to put expediency ahead of sustainability. Logistics managers face a delicate and difficult challenge to balance among these demands and the necessity to minimize the damage in the environment.

Measurement and Reporting
To accurately measure the carbon emissions, fuel consumption and other environmental metrics companies require sophisticated tools and methodologies. 67% of logistics companies struggle with accurate measurement and reporting of their environmental impact according to a survey done by Accenture. It is very difficult to set realistic goals, track progress, and demonstrate the effectiveness of green initiatives without precise data.

6.2.1 Role of Environmental Regulations in Shaping Green Logistics Practices and the Possible Strategies to Overcome the Challenges

Green logistics are becoming more necessary, as consumers increasingly choose businesses and stores that try to lessen their environmental effect. A study by IBM Research Insights recently conducted a study which indicated that 57% of customers are open to change their ecommerce shopping behaviors in order to reduce their environmental effect. In response, businesses are modifying their logistics and supply chains to match these new demands. As more CEOs priorities sustainability higher among their company priorities, that shift is gradually taking place. Since many customers shows a lot of interests towards green businesses, the shipping companies now have to focus more on reducing the CO2 emissions, managing the trash and waste disposal properly, using recyclable products for packaging etc. to gain a competitive advantage.

In the research process the author has explored the green logistics issues and the extent of its environmental impact [14]. The author analyzed the possibility of managing the green logistics and suggested that the managers while making their decisions for day-to-day process can think of implementing strategies which incorporates environmental management principles can help in achieving sustainable development in the organizations.

The relationship between the firm's sustainable strategy and its logistics performance is analyzed through green transportation activities of the business [15]. The author investigated the study in the Nordic region and analyzed the possible effect on sustainability of the firm towards green transportation and the logistics efficiency & effectiveness. Green logistics comprises of managing the emission of carbon from waste management and disposal, packaging process, recycling process, reducing energy consumption, and the supply chain's carbon impact.

In an attempt to be eco- friendly, many national and international organizations are pushing their businesses and striving forward towards more sustainability.Businesses can increase the trust and loyalty amongst existing customers by adopting the new, environmental friendly or environmentally-conscious clientele. Increasing the awareness about the efforts made by the company towards eco-logistics can really create a huge positive impact in the minds of the customers. The company's sustainable initiatives can be shared with the stakeholders and the messages can be communicated through digital platforms. The companies can also plan for optimized route planning, strategic planning for minimizing the usage of fuel, energy saving mechanisms, and efficient delivery options can really reduce the environmental footprint and develop a roadmap for new growth for the company's success which helps in cost savings as well. Reuse, Reduce and Recycle are the 3R concept in adoption towards green logistics. Businesses greatly lessen their environmental impact by cutting waste, particularly in packaging and material recycling.

The significance of sustainable logistics for India's economic development and environmental health is acknowledged by the government.

A number of efforts have been made to advance a sustainable logistics sector by utilizing technology such as automation and digitization. The PM Gati Shakti National Master Plan (NMP) platform aims at enhancing industrial productivity and helping the country achieve its green logistics and clean energy goals through multi-modal connectivity across highways, railways, ports, airports, logistics infrastructure, and inland waterways with an objective of facilitating sustainable economic activities. The National Logistics Policy (NLP 2022) aims to create a cost-efficient, resilient, and sustainable logistics ecosystem. Focus areas in the National Logistics Policy include the Sectoral Plan for Efficient Logistics (SPEL) for major sectors of the economy like Coal, Cement, Fertilizer, Steel, Pharma etc. examining existing supply chain networks and promoting multi-modal transport, digitalization and automation. Source: pib.gov.in

The key factors influencing the development of green logistics, and the priority of those key factors are explored and the authors further analyzed that the factors influencing the green logistics development have to be studied from different perspectives at different, i.e., government, enterprise and environment, levels. They used DEMATEL and ISM method to analyze the factors [16]. examined the interconnection between the sustainable logistics practices and environmental reputation is examined [17] using partial least square SEM model technique and the result indicated that sustainable logistical practice partially mediated the relationship between sustainable transportation and fully mediating the relationships between reverse logistics, sustainable packaging and distribution, green monitoring and evaluation. The government can direct and oversee the growth of green logistics by enacting pertinent rules and regulations [18]. Businesses must abide by government laws in order to achieve green logistics [19]. Government-issued environmental protection legislation and regulations greatly aid in the growth of green logistics [20]. The laws that support green logistics practices ought to support green logistics strategies. Therefore, pertinent laws and regulations have a significant impact on how green logistics develops [21]. Freight policy has a big impact on green logistics [22]. The development of green logistics benefits from the imposition of high prices on carbon raw materials. Positive incentives from government policies will lower the processing costs of green logistics, but negative external limitations will drastically alter the design of green logistics facilities [23]. For example, green logistics technology is developed as a result of the government's strong support for economic incentives for greenization [24]. Furthermore, there was a suggestion that the governmental subsidies have a favorable impact on the logistics market's greening process and are a successful model for lowering the negative externalities of the sector [25].

6.3 Green Logistics Priority in Retail Sector

Though Green logistics presents specific challenges within various industries, the retail sector has unique challenges in adopting greener logistics techniques because of its intricate supply chains and large volume of products transportation. The carbon emission generated during last mile delivery is one of the major challenge due to the adoption of fragmented routes and small scale deliveries which create imbalance between the speed of delivery and the environmental concerns. Similarly the spend on upfront cost of green technologies and developing infrastructure is another challenge. Consumers nowadays accustomed to quick and fast delivery which is leading to inefficient use of transportation resources. Another biggest challenge is managing the reverse logistics in the ecommerce heavy retail which again contribute for the huge environmental impact of the retail supply chain. These challenges insists the need and importance for innovative solutions to help the retail industry adopt greener logistics practices while maintaining cost efficiency and service quality.

Retailers and logistics operations will be left behind in the coming years if they don't adopt green practices. Carbon footprint is also one of the major cause affecting sustainability. In order to strengthen their unique selling proposition (USP) companies and logistics providers can work together in reducing this carbon footprint. Moreover customers are also prepared to pay a higher price for environmentally friendly goods. one more fact is that almost 50% of the logistics sector's emissions coming from retail supply chains, as this is spiked particularly after Covid-19 which created an attention for carriers, merchants, and customers alike the importance of integrating green logistics techniques and practices into their supply chains. An increasing number of carriers and merchants focused in the Net-Zero promise along with strategic attempts to develop and implement environmentally sustainable practices successfully. The logistical processes can consume less energy and increase in total profit when it is combined with an exclusive supply chain management strategy.

6.3.1 Easily Adaptable Strategies in Retail Sector

1. Encouraging eco-friendly delivery options
2. Automated route optimization to increase the efficiency of the vehicle
3. Usage of order batching to increase drop density
4. Giving the dispatch options or partner with environmentally conscious partner fleets or electric delivery vehicles (EVs)

5. Using nearby merchants to deliver hyper locally
6. Using bicycles for local and nearby delivery
7. Digitizing the paper trial, incorporating product specifications and evidence of product delivery

The current logistics sector one of the new developments is green logistics which emphasizes on performing the logistics and its related activities in an environmental friendly manner, which helps in improving the economic growth of the company while managing with the available the resources, thereby the environment can be protected from the negative effects [26].

In order to have a stable growth, utilizing green logistics is one of the option which can minimize the adverse effects of logistical activities on the environment [27]. The sustainable development is significantly impacted by the rise in solid waste. The green packaging approach, which takes into account every stage of the package life cycle, is utilized to solve this problem [28]. Five items were used to measure green process design techniques. The following are the sample items: (a) The process is set up to use the least amount of material and energy. (b) Material recovery, recycling, and reuse are all part of the process design. (c) Hazardous material use is avoided or minimized through process design. (d) Waste (solid, liquid, and gas) is decreased by process design. (e) Safety and environmental requirements are met in the process design.

The concept of circular economy in Industry 4.0 and also the adoption of green logistics affecting the Circular Economy (CE) is analyzed and the companies in order to address various environmental issues, primarily the logistics sector is taking many green initiatives. The authors examined the causal relationships between the identified variables which are doing, Circular economy adoption and green logistics practices industry 4.0 technologies [29]. The authors have also examined and derived results about the moderating effect of the two factors institutional pressure and supply chain flexibility.

6.4 Concept of Sustainable Logistics in Supply Chain

Companies must think about adoption of sustainable logistics because of growing environmental concerns and regulatory pressures. According to a survey done by McKinsey company 90% of the supply chain executives firmly believe that sustainability is becoming a major issue nowadays because of the customer preference and demand for eco-friendly products and legal regulations. Furthermore, companies are prioritizing sustainability in their procurement strategy as an effort to minimize environmental impact and to enhance the reputation of their brand. These numbers demonstrate how supply chains must include sustainable logistics because of regulatory mandates, consumer expectations, cost savings, and productivity gains.

The necessity of sustainable logistics in supply chains is underscored by growing environmental concerns and regulatory pressures. The World Economic Forum survey states that 78% of executives believe sustainability is important for future business success, reflecting a change towards eco-friendly practices in supply chains. The transportation sector alone contributes nearly 24% of global carbon emissions, highlighting the urgent need for sustainable logistics.

A report by McKinsey & Company indicates that 90% of supply chain executives view sustainability as a critical issue, driven by both regulatory requirements and consumer demand for greener products. Also the global chief procurement officer's survey done during 2022 revealed that the procurement officers are prioritizing sustainability in their procurement strategies to minimize the environmental impact and to focus on increasing the reputation of the brand.

Supply chain Sustainability is becoming more and more important as it is having the advantage in the areas of environment, economy, and society. According to Simon-Kucher & Partners in the Global Sustainability Study 2021 assessed that more than 60% of customers rank sustainability as a vital purchase criterion, influencing companies to shift towards greener logistics practices. Sustainable logistics is important for the environment since it can help in reducing greenhouse gas emissions by up to 30%, according to the World Economic Forum's 2020 report.

Moreover, according to the International Transport Forum's 2021 study indicates that optimizing logistics can lessen the operational costs by overall 20%, underscoring economic benefits. The Carbon Trust reports that companies integrating sustainable logistics can enhance brand reputation and customer loyalty, with 70% of surveyed businesses acknowledging the competitive advantage gained from sustainable practices.

Socially, sustainable logistics improve working conditions and community health by minimizing pollution and resource depletion. The International Institute for Management Development (IMD) has done a survey during 2022 and revealed that 55% of supply chain professionals believe sustainability initiatives are critical for long-term business viability.

These statistics collectively affirm that sustainable logistics are not just a trend but a necessity, driving positive impacts across environmental, economic, and social dimensions within the supply chain.

The structure of green logistics is examined which will comprise of the factors like 'green transport, green warehousing, green packaging, green logistics data collection and management, waste management' [30]. The companies must first create a healthy environment in terms of creating awareness and develop the momentum, then it can focus on developing modern logistics and sustainable development in order to protect the resources and environment [31]. In a study, the Data Envelopment Analysis to create an efficiency score which analyze and represent the attainment of sustainable operational logistics performance (SOLP). The authors identified that there is a monotonic association between the country rankings obtained under the SOLP and Logistics Performance Index (LPI) evaluation regimes that is statistically negligible [32]. However, the results indicated while considering SOLP and LPI, the logistics companies of the United States of America, the European nations and Australia are identified to be high performers , while that of Greece, Korea, Italy and Portugal are found to be low performers under both the factors. Also, they came to the conclusion that while the LPI offers valuable information to complement the information provided by the SOLP approach, the latter better enables performance improvements within a country's logistics sector by helping in the identification of inefficient resources and also the countries with logistics sectors that are performing at benchmark levels.

The companies can attenuate growing to international level can develop policies and participate in green logistics practices while considering the environmental concerns and possibly overcome the international trade barriers for their businesses [33].

The concepts linked with the triple bottom line are analyzed and the variables are clustered based on environmental, economic, and social dimension [34]. The authors analyzed the influence of logistics transport performance while adopting sustainable logistics practices.

The links between national logistics performance and sustainability aspects were examined and regression analysis is used to construct and test a number of hypotheses utilizing secondary data [35]. The authors have collected the data through secondary sources and the results indicated that higher levels of logistics performance are associated with the well-being nature and social sustainability which are noted as fundamental elements which includes educated and healthy populace, equality, sound government, and a fair allocation of income. Financial incentives also play a role. The International Energy Agency (IEA) notes that energy-efficient logistics can reduce costs by 10-20%, emphasizing the economic benefits of sustainable practices. Moreover, a study by Accenture found that companies implementing green logistics saw a 15% improvement in supply chain efficiency, demonstrating that sustainability can drive both environmental and operational gains. These statistics affirm the necessity of integrating sustainable logistics into supply chains, driven by regulatory mandates, consumer expectations, cost savings, and efficiency improvements.

The phrase "green logistics" can be examined in four aspects: "as a notion of sustainable development of logistics systems at various levels; as a tool of the circular economy; as an element of corporate social responsibility of businesses; and as a kind of walking activity" [36]. They have also mentioned that to reduce the cost of managing the movement of logistics it is recommended to implement the green logistics mechanism.

6.5 Sustainable Logistics and its Future

The vital component of a nation's trade and a major enabler of businesses, logistics has seen numerous changes in recent years. Among all the changes in the industry, one significant change is the pursuit of a greener future. Pollution has detrimental consequences on health, raising concerns in many countries throughout the world. Logistics sector as one of the major contributor to the environmental pollution has also started taking measures to ensure for sustainable future and development. There are various logistic companies in India which are practicing towards green revolution such as switching to renewables, electrifying the fleets, using bio fuels are few of the commitment that companies make towards decarbonizing the logistics journey. An international courier package delivery firm plan their operations by creating a proper roadmap for delivery which focus on reducing carbon emissions. A multimodal and marine logistics firm while focusing on their core operation, they also have a separate business division focusing towards green logistics. One of the pioneer and market leader in coastal shipping uses real time tracking and automated carrier selection. A sportswear manufacturer has committed to include recycled polyester and sustainable cotton while manufacturing and made sustainability as one of the key priorities in their operations. An automotive manufacturer used renewable energy sources and recycling materials to implement sustainable practices in its manufacturing processes. A food and beverage company has set their goal to protect the environment as becoming carbon neutral by 2050 and to use 100% renewable electricity by 2030. There are a few sustainable logistics activities used by various firms. The globally recognized furniture retailer uses renewable energy sources in its manufacturing and transportation processes and implemented sustainable practices in its entire supply chain to contribute for environmental protection thereby focusing on sustainable logistics. As long as the awareness and technical development is high amongst the companies the Green logistics management concept has a bright future. Demand for green logistics is being driven by the government's focus and increased provision of incentives for sustainable practices and the growing environmental consciousness of customers can still create lot of demand and interest within the companies to adopt green logistics. Each company's research and development expenditures should produce more affordable and effective green technologies adoption methods over time.

6.6 Limitations of the Study

Since the subject of green logistics management is dynamic and ever-evolving, the data currently accessible may not adequately reflect the newest developments in this field's trends and technology. Since technology like block chain, AI, and electric cars are developing so quickly, it's possible that this report doesn't fully take into account all current advancements that could lessen some of the issues raised.

The findings' applicability to other industries and geographical contexts may be limited by the research's heavy reliance on industry-specific studies or case studies from particular areas. Every industry faces different logistical issues, which are frequently impacted by regionally specific logistical limits, consumer expectations, and regulatory contexts. The availability of quantitative data, particularly with regard to the environmental impact of green logistics solutions, is also a challenge for this study. The study might not adequately represent the viewpoints of all the stakeholders involved, including manufacturers, suppliers, logistics companies, and customers, all of whom are important to the success of green logistics initiatives. Future studies that address these constraints will improve our comprehension of the intricate variables influencing green logistics management.

6.7 Conclusion

Green and sustainable logistics mark a significant change in how businesses control their environmental effect while preserving operational effectiveness. Businesses can maximize resource utilization, cut waste, and lessen their carbon impact by adopting green logistics. However, there are major obstacles to putting these methods into effect, particularly for smaller businesses. These obstacles include high prices, technological restrictions, and the difficulty of redesigning current systems. Innovation, industry cooperation, and a comprehensive strategy that makes use of digital tools and sustainable business models are all necessary to overcome these obstacles.

Environmental regulations, which enforce standards for emissions, waste management, and resource consumption, are crucial in helping organizations move toward sustainable logistics. Adherence to these requirements encourages businesses to embrace more environmentally friendly methods, like streamlining delivery routes and utilizing renewable energy. In the retail industry, where green logistics is becoming more and more important, businesses gain by satisfying eco-conscious consumer demands, which increases brand loyalty and lessens environmental impact. Sustainable logistics will be essential to the supply chain's development in the future. Technological developments like block chain, AI, and electric cars are going to completely change logistics and make sustainable practices more affordable and widely available. Sustainable logistics will help businesses create robust supply chains that put long-term sustainability ahead of immediate profits in a circular economy framework, setting them up for success in a future with limited resources. By working together, these initiatives will build a logistics ecosystem that is more resilient and sustainable for future generations.

References

1. Klassen, R.D. and Johnson, P.F., The green supply chain, in: *Understanding Supply Chains: Concepts, Critiques & Futures*, New, S., Westbrook, R., Eds., pp. 229–252, Oxford University Press, Oxford, UK, 2004.
2. Kherbach, O. and Mocan, M.L., The importance of logistics and supply chain management in the enhancement of Romanian SMEs. *Procedia-Soc. Behav. Sci.*, 221, 405–413, 2016.
3. Agyabeng-Mensah, Y,. and Afum, E., Innocent Senyo Kwasi Acquah, Essel Dacosta, Charles Baah, and Esther Ahenkorah. The role of green logistics management practices, supply chain traceability and logistics ecocentricity in sustainability performance. *Int. J. Logist. Manage.*, 32, 2, 538–566, 2021.
4. Zhou, B., Siddik, A.B., Zheng, G.-W., Masukujjaman, M., 198, Unveiling the role of green logistics management in improving SMEs' sustainability performance: do circular economy practices and supply chain traceability matter? *Systems*, 11, 4, 198, 2023.
5. Larson, P.D. and Halldorsson, A., Logistics versus supply chain management: an international survey. *Int. J. Logistics Res. Appl.*, 7, 1, 17–31, 2004.

6. Dekker, R., Bloemhof, J., Mallidis, I., Operations Research for green logistics–An overview of aspects, issues, contributions and challenges. *Eur. J. Oper. Res.*, 219, 3, 671–679, 2012.
7. Saroha, R., Green logistics & its significance in modern day systems. *Int. Rev. Appl. Eng. Res.*, 4, 1, 89–92, 2014.
8. Rodrigue, J.-P., Slack, B., Comtois, C. Green Logistics, Brewer, A.M., Button, K.J. and Hensher, D.A. (Ed.) *Handbook of Logistics and Supply-Chain Management* (Vol. 2), pp. 339–350, Emerald Group Publishing Limited, Leeds, 2017.
9. El-Berishy, N., Rügge, I., Scholz-Reiter, B., The interrelation between sustainability and green logistics. *IFAC Proc.*, 46, 24, 527–531, 2013.
10. Khan, S.A.R., The Effect of Green logistics on Economic growth, Social and Environmental sustainability: An Empirical study of Developing countries in Asia, *Preprints*, 1–23, 2019.
11. Barut, A., Citil, M., Ahmed, Z., Sinha, A., S.A., How do economic and financial factors influence green logistics? A comparative analysis of E7 and G7 nations. *Environ. Sci. Pollut. Res.*, 30, 1, 1011–1022, 2023.
12. Macharis, C., Milan, L., Verlinde, S., A stakeholder-based multicriteria evaluation framework for city distribution. *Res. Transp. Bus. Manage.*, 11, 75–84, 2014.
13. Wichaisri, S. and Sopadang, A., Sustainable logistics system: A framework and case study, in: *2013 IEEE International Conference on Industrial Engineering and Engineering Management*, IEEE, pp. 1017–1021, 2013.
14. Kumar, A., Green Logistics for sustainable development: an analytical review. *IOSRD Int. J. Bus.*, 1, 1, 7–13, 2015.
15. Pazirandeh, A. and Jafari, H., Making sense of green logistics. *Int. J. Prod. Perform. Manage.*, 62, 8, 889–904, 2013.
16. Zhang, M., Sun, M., Bi, D., Liu, T., Green logistics development decision-making: factor identification and hierarchical framework construction. *Ieee Access*, 8, 127897–127912, 2020.
17. Baah, C., Amponsah, K.T., Issau, K., Ofori, D., Acquah, I.S.K., Agyeman, D.O., Examining the interconnections between sustainable logistics practices, environmental reputation and financial performance: a mediation approach. *Vision*, 25, 1, 47–64, 2021.
18. Qu, Q., Tang, M., Liu, Q., Song, W., Zhang, F., Wang, W., Empirical research on the core factors of green logistics development. *Acad. Strategic Manage. J.*, 16, 2, 1–10, 2017.
19. Murphy, P.R. and Poist, R.F., Green perspectives and practices: a "comparative logistics" study. *Supply Chain Manag. Int. J.*, 8, 2, 122–131, 2003.
20. Mangla, S., Madaan, J., Sarma, P.R.S., Gupta, M.P., Multi-objective decision modelling using interpretive structural modelling for green supply chains. *Int. J. Logist. Syst. Manage.*, 17, 2, 125–142, 2014.

21. Zaman, K. and Shamsuddin, S., Green logistics and national scale economic indicators: Evidence from a panel of selected European countries. *J. Clean. Prod.*, 143, 51–63, 2017.
22. Sudarto, S., Takahashi, K., Morikawa, K., Nagasawa, K., The impact of capacity planning on product lifecycle for performance on sustainability dimensions in Reverse Logistics Social Responsibility. *J. Clean. Prod.*, 133, 28–42, 2016.
23. Klumpp, M., To green or not to green: a political, economic and social analysis for the past failure of green logistics. *Sustainability*, 8, 5, 441, 2016.
24. Chen, S.-H., The game analysis of negative externality of environmental logistics and governmental regulation. *Int. J. Environ. Pollut.*, 51, 3–4, 143–155, 2013.
25. Ren, R., Hu, W., Dong, J., Sun, B., Chen, Y., Chen, Z., A systematic literature review of green and sustainable logistics: bibliometric analysis, research trend and knowledge taxonomy. *Int. J. Environ. Res. Public Health*, 171, 261, 2020.
26. Zhang, W., Zhang, M., Zhang, W., Zhou, Q., Zhang, X., What influences the effectiveness of green logistics policies? A grounded theory analysis. *Sci. Total Environ.*, 714, 136731, 2020.
27. Wong, W.P. and Tang, C.F., The major determinants of logistic performance in a global perspective: evidence from panel data analysis. *Int. J. Logist. Res. Appl.*, 21, 4, 431–443, 2018.
28. Jiange,T., *Researches on the Establishment Model of Green Logistics*. School of Economics and Management, Zhongyuan University of technology, Zhengzhou, P.R. China, 2009.
29. Sharma, M., Luthra, S., Joshi, S., Kumar, A., Jain, A., Green logistics driven circular practices adoption in industry 4.0 Era: A moderating effect of institution pressure and supply chain flexibility. *J. Clean. Prod.*, 383, 135284, 2023.
30. Van Hoof, B. and Thiell, M., Collaboration capacity for sustainable supply chain management: small and medium-sized enterprises in Mexico. *J. Clean. Prod.*, 67, 239–248, 2014.
31. Ping, L., Strategy of green logistics and sustainable development, in: *2009 International Conference on Information Management, Innovation Management and Industrial Engineering*, vol. 1, IEEE, pp. 339–342, 2009.
32. Rashidi, K. and Cullinane, K., Evaluating the sustainability of national logistics performance using Data Envelopment Analysis. *Transp. Policy*, 74, 35–46, 2019.
33. Karaman, A.S., Kilic, M., Uyar, A., Green logistics performance and sustainability reporting practices of the logistics sector: The moderating effect of corporate governance. *J. Clean. Prod.*, 258, 120718, 2020.
34. Kumar, K.M., Abd Rahman, A., Jayaraman, K., Rahim, S.A., Conceptualization of a research model for sustainable logistics practices and logistics transport performance. *Jurnal Pengurusan*, 51, 147–158, 2017.

35. Larson, P.D., Relationships between logistics performance and aspects of sustainability: A cross-country analysis. *Sustainability*, 13, 2, 623, 2021.
36. Dzwigol, H., Trushkina, N., Kwilinski, A., Green logistics as a sustainable development concept of logistics systems in a circular economy. *Proceedings of the 37th International Business Information Management Association (IBIMA)*, 2021, PhD diss.

Part 2

TECHNOLOGICAL INNOVATIONS IN SUPPLY CHAINS

7

Big Data in Procurement 4.0 – Digitalizing and Integrating Procurement Function

Rajesh Matha[1] and Rashmi Ranjan Panigrahi[1,2]*

[1]*GITAM School of Business, GITAM (Deemed to be University), Visakhapatnam, Andhra Pradesh, India*
[2]*Operations and Supply Chain Area, Symbiosis Institute of Business Management, Hyderabad, Symbiosis International (Deemed University), Pune, India*

Abstract
Procurement 4.0 represents a pivotal evolution in procurement practices amidst the advent of Industry 4.0 technologies. This study explores current research trends and emerging themes in Procurement 4.0, particularly focusing on the transformative impact of BDA (Big Data Analytics) and its implications for sustainable procurement practices. The study utilized data from Scopus spanning 2017 to July 2024, employing selected keywords, and processing it with VOS-Viewer to derive valid inferences and theoretical arguments. The findings of the studies present a paradigm shift that leverages advancements such as BDA, artificial intelligence, and the Internet of Things to revolutionize sourcing strategies, supplier relationships, and operational efficiencies. The study's contributions stressed the advancement of technology based procurement 4.0 brings more resilient and reliable procurement functions that align with strategic business objectives.

Keywords: Automation, procurement 4.0, big data, metaverse, AI, machine learning

7.1 Introduction

The world is at the cusp of Industry 4.0. As mentioned in 2011, Industry 4.0 saw a rise in information and communication technology (ITC),

**Corresponding author*: rashmipanigrahi090@gmail.com

K. Mathiyazhagan, Krishna Kumar Dadsena, Rajesh Kumar Singh, Aakanksha Kishore and Andrea Appolloni (eds.) Sustainable Operations of Logistics and Supply Chain Management, (131–158) © 2025 Scrivener Publishing LLC

facilitating digitalization and networking. Internet of Things, big data, cloud computing, robotics, and AI are playing a major role in transforming the way we live. Industry 4.0 lead to production 4.0 [1] and logistics 4.0 but procurement 4.0 is not talked much during the transition. Selection, negotiation, and contracting play a major role in the procurement process of any organization. Ref. [2] attributes that cybernetics, communication, controllership, collaboration, connection, condition, coordination, and confidence are the critical success factors also termed as the 8Cs in the procurement process in procurement 4.0. Supply chain performance is largely attributed to digital procurement and data analysis [3].

In modern procurement, the convergence of advanced technologies is revolutionizing how organizations manage their sourcing strategies, supplier relationships, contract negotiations, and overall operational efficiencies [4]. At the heart of this transformation is the concept of Procurement 4.0, characterized by the integration of digital technologies such as BDA (BDA), artificial intelligence (AI), Internet of Things (IoT), and cloud computing. These innovations allow procurement specialists to use massive volumes of data, generate meaningful insights, and improve every aspect of the procuring process—from choosing vendors to contract administration & beyond—paving the road for digital procurement transformation (DPT) [5].

BDA is a key component of Procurement 4.0, enabling firms to examine a variety of information sources such as vendor databases, market movements, and customer preferences [6]. This analytical prowess broadens the supplier base, improves market knowledge, and allows predictive skills required for demand prediction and individualized procurement strategies. Furthermore, big data affects how firms manage supplier relationships, minimize risks, and achieve cost reductions by allowing for educated decisions. The fundamentals of big data adoption are information, shipment of goods, environmentally friendly purchasing, and purchase. In this scenario, security measures become critical for protecting sensitive procurement data throughout digitalization initiatives [7]. Robust cybersecurity safeguards protect data privacy, truthfulness, and compliance, enhancing confidence and minimizing supply-chain threats.

BDA in Procurement 4.0 and its impacts on supplier base expansion, market intelligence, demand forecasting, personalized sourcing strategies, supplier relationship management, risk mitigation, and cost efficiencies, there is an evident gap in understanding the current research trends and emerging themes within this field. Specifically, the literature lacks a comprehensive analysis of how BDA is evolving and what new areas of focus are emerging in Procurement 4.0. To address these issues, the study formulates two specific research questions.

RQ1. What are the current research trends in the field of procurement 4.0?

RQ2. What are the emerging themes related to big data in procurement 4.0?

Study objective is to explore how big data, in conjunction with emerging technologies [8], is reshaping procurement practices, enhancing operational agility, and driving sustainable growth in Procurement 4.0.

7.2 Evolution of Literature

The historical lens of procurement focuses on several key steps to ensure businesses source materials at competitive prices, work with reliable partners, and deliver value to customers [9]. It starts with identifying needed products or services, creating and approving a purchase request, and then soliciting vendor proposals. After negotiating and selecting a supplier, the purchase order is acknowledged, transitioning the process to vendor management. Procurement 4.0 addresses these inefficiencies through digitalization, integrating internal and external departments, stakeholders, suppliers, and the entire supply chain [10]. This transformation enables data-driven decision-making across the procurement function. By digitizing and integrating procurement processes, organizations can achieve cost savings, build trust, foster innovation, enhance corporate social responsibility, improve connectivity, explore new business models, and mitigate overall business risks. Procurement 4.0 can influence buyer's intention to optimize business processes [9].

7.2.1 Traditional Procurement

Traditional procurement was structured around three distinct stages. Firstly, the sourcing stage involved defining organizational needs, initiating purchase requests, and evaluating potential vendors. Secondly, the purchasing stage focused on negotiating terms with suppliers, placing orders, and overseeing the receipt and inspection of goods or services. Lastly, the payment stage encompassed conducting a three-way match between the purchase order, order receipt or packing list, and invoice for accurate financial reconciliation (refer to Figure 7.1).

Figure 7.1 Traditional procurement stages.

7.2.2 Procurement Transactions

The transition of procurement involves shifting its role and function within an organization from traditional practices to more strategic, value-driven approaches [2]. Over time, the evolution of procurement functions has progressed from material requirement planning (MRP) to enterprise resource planning (ERP), then to e-procurement, and now to Procurement 4.0 [11]. The transition of procurement from 1.0 to 4.0 is presented in Figure 7.2.

Stage 1: Traditional to Procurement 1.0

In this version, the key focus is on cost containment, also known as operational procurement. This concept dates back to an era when procurement was referred to as Purchasing and functioned mainly as a support role. Today, most companies operate with what we'd call a Procurement 1.0 organization [13]. Traditionally, procurement has centered on tactical tasks such as responding to contract requests, running RFXs (request for information, proposal, or quotation), and facilitating communication with suppliers. In this model, procurement professionals are expected to handle multiple functions in a reactive and transactional manner [12]. It is no longer just about reducing expenses. Modern procurement is holistic, encompassing risk mitigation strategies, supplier innovation, demand management, global perspectives, and sustainability.

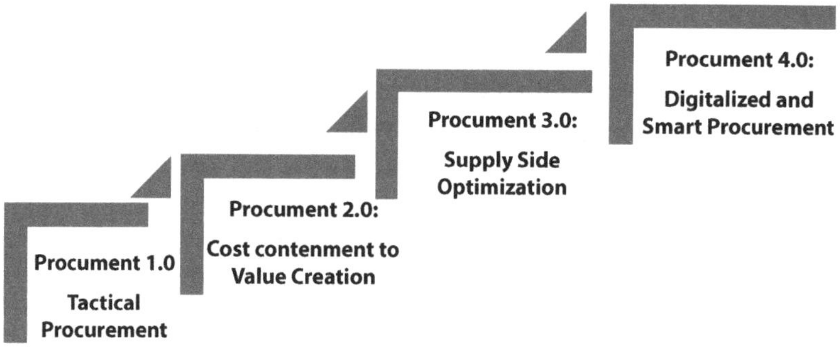

Figure 7.2 Evolution of Procurement 4. Sources: The authors and [12].

Stage 2: Procurement 2.0: From Cost Containment to Value Creation

Just as the internet evolved from informational to social, procurement is transforming into a strategic powerhouse. Once merely tasked with getting the best price, product, and situation, today's procurement officers now craft those strategies themselves [12]. Technological collaboration has reshaped the role in the past three years, enabling procurement to add value by managing working capital, mitigating business risks, and exploring new markets. Procurement 2.0 focuses on economic benefit and corporate strategy, moving above lowering expenses [14].

Stage 3: Procurement 3.0: Supply-Side Optimization

Digitalization is the foundation of Procurement 3.0. It's more than just another IT improvement; it's a game changer that will profoundly alter procurement [13]. This phase focuses on automating procedures and documenting transactions, from purchasing to agreements and settlements [14]. likewise, it is also hampered by too complicated processes, frequently making the procurement experience difficult and unpleasant for consumers [9]. Procurement 3.0 strives to optimize the supply network by integrating it with the company business plan, assuring the right vendors, contracts, and delivery. This growth is based on cost control, flexibility, customer service, creativity, and supply predictability. The operational model incorporates the source-to-pay process, which encompasses supply chain optimization, and economic excellence, and non-contact procurement. Supplier-optimized portfolio carefully picks the finest suppliers and conditions, while business excellence ensures that these providers follow bespoke contracts and performance criteria. Touchless procuring uses digital information to improve procedures, allowing for efficient and compliance purchasing and distribution.

Stage 4: Procurement 4.0: Digitalized and Smart Procurement

In reality, the digital revolution in procurement necessitates sophisticated analytics and information-driven decisions for better and more efficient business decisions and greater cross-domain value-chain connections. Automated applications like "e-RFX, e-Catalogue, e-Auction, and e-Contract", also called eProcurement, improve downstream procurement efficiencies. Robotics are also transforming procurement. Thus, digital purchasing has several elements, and a thorough understanding is essential. certainly, digital procurement is fast moving to the core of value creation by not only linking the organization with a strong network of internal and external partners but also by developing new business models [12]. This digital revolution, fueled by advanced technologies like BDA and 3D

Figure 7.3 Evolution of Procurement 4.0.

printing, is reshaping procurement tasks and processes [11]. Sourcing, purchasing, and payment are the primary activities within procurement. Historically, traditional procurement processes have struggled with data silos, where information stored in Excel spreadsheets limited its utility and hindered automation and predictive capabilities (refer to Figure 7.3).

Traditionally focused on cost savings, procurement now evolves towards delivering strategic value to enterprises. Procurement 4.0 draws inspiration from Industry 4.0, emphasizing innovative and intelligent digitalization of supply chains to unlock new growth opportunities [12]. This shift reflects a broader trend where companies leverage connectivity and automation, known as Cyber-Physical Systems (CPS), to enhance efficiency and competitiveness in a digitally-driven market landscape [15].

7.2.3 Literature of Big Data

Big data comprises vast amounts of structured and unstructured data sourced from diverse origins, surpassing the capacities of traditional data processing systems. Its defining characteristics include volume, velocity of generation, variety in formats (structured, semi-structured, unstructured), and the veracity of data quality due to accumulation from multiple sources [16]. Analyzing this extensive data offers numerous advantages to organizations directly influencing the organizational performance [17]. BDA has emerged as a pivotal field for extracting insights, uncovering hidden patterns and correlations, and identifying market trends crucial for decision-making [18] Applications such as recommender systems in music and e-commerce highlight their business utility while enhancing fraud detection and improving experiences, decision-making processes, product innovation, and risk management stand out as major benefits.

BDA leverages techniques like descriptive, diagnostic, predictive, prescriptive analytics, and cyber analytics to derive data-driven insights and decisions. It finds application across various sectors, including government, banking, telecommunications, e-commerce, education, healthcare, media, and entertainment. Big data and predictive analytics assimilation and acceptance are possible through information sharing, management commitment and connectivity [19].

Machine learning algorithms aid in structuring and analyzing unstructured data swiftly, while AI technologies enhance cognitive computing, automating manual labor in procurement through interactions with suppliers *via* bots, thereby reducing administrative workloads [20]. Robotic process automation (RPA) mimics human actions, particularly in repetitive administrative tasks such as order placement timing calculations. Blockchain technology ensures secure end-to-end transparency and control during procurement's order and payment stages by creating digital ledgers of transactions. E-procurement facilitates seamless information exchange between procurement and suppliers, enhancing operational efficiency. Cloud ERP and democratization technologies play critical roles in managing big data, ensuring robust data backup and fail-safe operations.

7.2.4 Big Data and Components of Procurement

Procurement 4.0 represents a comprehensive digital transformation that not only automates but also integrates the procurement function across internal and external departments, stakeholders, suppliers, and the entire supply chain. It encompasses sourcing strategies, supplier selection and management, contract management, purchasing order processing, inventory management, supplier relationship management, risk management, ethics and compliance, performance measurement and improvement, technology and data management, and negotiation [21]. Innovative

Figure 7.4 Elements of Procurement 4.0.

procurement platforms support administrative and business tasks aiding in decisions [22]. BDA plays a pivotal role in enhancing each of these procurement functions, leveraging digitalization and integration to drive efficiency and strategic alignment across the procurement lifecycle (refer to Figure 7.4).

7.3 Research Methodology

The paper follows the systematic literature review steps to identify key thematic areas and possible future research directions. A systematic approach to review establishes a clear scope for selecting and analyzing the documents and, hence, offers credibility to the study. This methodology involves a structured process that includes defining research questions, setting inclusion and exclusion criteria, and conducting a comprehensive search of relevant literature. By meticulously categorizing and synthesizing the findings, the review highlights significant patterns and trends within the existing body of knowledge [23, 24]. The process of selecting the relevant literature through the PRISMA framework is listed in Figure 7.5. The detailed steps are narrated below:

Step 1. Description of the study's aim and scope
The first step is to define the scope of the study. Herein, the scope of the study is set by the research questions. Identifying the scope helps identify the suitable literature that can be analyzed to recognize the work done in the domain area.

Step 2. Choosing the right technique for the study
The bibliometric studies have been done in literature review papers for performance mapping in the domain. It involves analyzing the number of publications over the year and contributions by the authors. This study uses a combination of performance and thematic analysis to understand the existing work holistically.

Step 3. Data Collection
The data was collected through a systematic process using the PRISMA technique, as detailed in Figure 7.5. The selection was made from the SCOPUS database, as it is the largest database of quality publications and is widely valued in the academic community. The process of selecting documents was done in four stages: identification, screening, eligibility, and

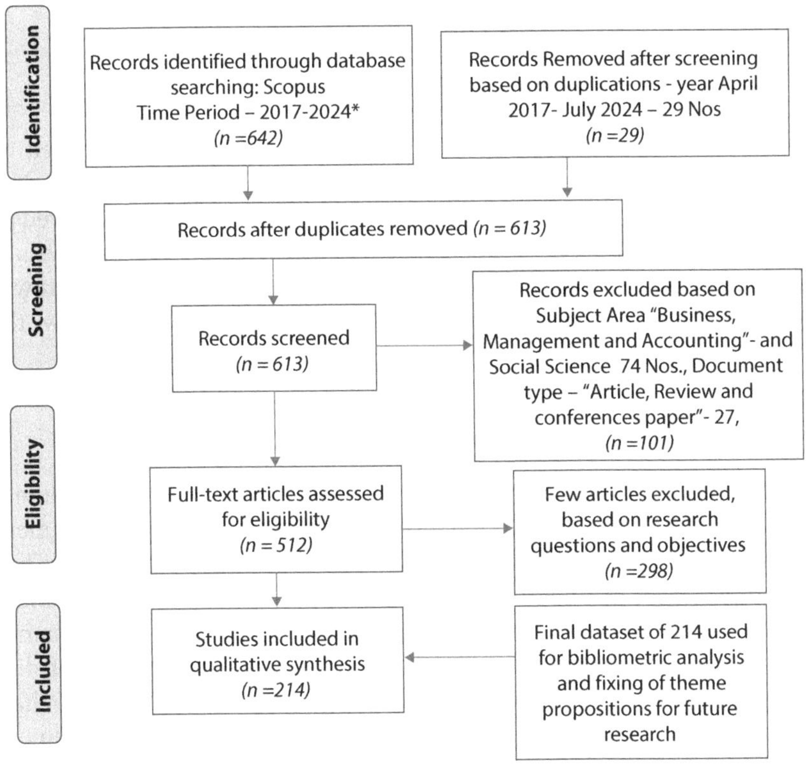

Figure 7.5 Methodology of literature review (source: author).

inclusion. The keywords were selected using "Procurement 4.0" AND "Big data" for the period 2017 and July 2024. After removing the duplicate documents, the remaining were confined to the business and management domain. This was done to confine the documents as per the scope of this study. In the final screening stage, all articles were carefully reviewed based on their quality and relevance to the study. Finally, 214 articles were included in the study.

Step 4. Data Analysis

The selected literature has been analyzed using MS Excel and VOS viewer applications. These applications were used to bring more clarity to the analysis and presentation of the findings. The themes were identified with the help of the VOS- Viewer application, while MS Excel was used to analyze the main details and production over the year.

7.4 Analysis

7.4.1 Annual Scientific Production

The table illustrates the fluctuating trends in publications related to "Procurement 4.0" and "Big Data" from 2017 to 2024. It shows a gradual increase from two publications in 2017 to a peak of 34 in 2022, followed by 13 documents by the end of June 2024. This data suggests varying levels of research interest and output over the years, highlighting periods of growth and contraction in scholarly activity within this field. Figure 7.6 shows the annual publication of articles.

7.4.2 Top Cited Papers from 2017 to 2024*

As per Table 7.1, top authors study focuses collectively explore Procurement 4.0 and its integration with digital technologies in enhancing procurement processes and supply chain efficiency within Industry 4.0 contexts. They cover topics such as digital servitization for industrial customers, blockchain applications in facilities management procurement, performance measurement frameworks for Supply Chain 4.0, and the impact of digital transformation on competitive advantage. Authors delve into challenges, opportunities, and frameworks for re-engineering procurement

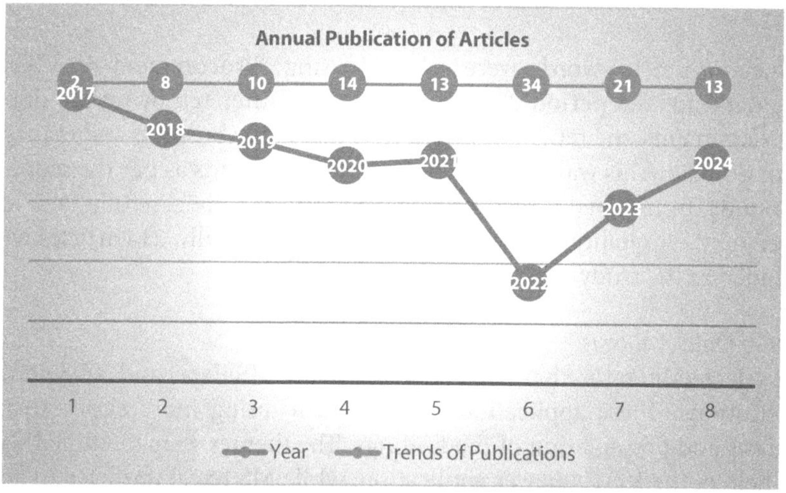

Figure 7.6 Annual publication of articles (source: author).

Table 7.1 Top authors of Procurement 4.0 and big data.

Author	Citation
[25] (Sjödin *et al.*, 2023)	20
[26] (Joseph Jerome *et al.*, 2022)	23
[27] (Gunasekara *et al.*, 2022)	38
[28] (Govindan *et al.*, 2022)	49
[29] (Alabdali & Salam, 2022)	23
[11] (Tripathi & Gupta, 2020)	29
[30] (Bag *et al.*, 2021)	49
[1] (Bienhaus & Haddud, 2018)	280
[9] (Bag, Wood, Mangla, *et al.*, 2020)	216

processes, supporting remanufacturing and circular economy initiatives, and influencing business process performance amidst the fourth industrial revolution.

7.4.3 Emerging Themes Extracted from Analysis

7.4.3.1 Big Data and Sourcing Strategies

To optimize procurement process in procurement 4.0, big data provides capabilities and extensive data-driven insights. BDA helps in analyzing various data sources including industry reports, supplier databases, economic indicators, and social media. This helps in broadening the supplier base and understanding the supplier capabilities [31]. This also facilities identifying new market trends thus ensuring market intelligence for the organization. By analyzing customer data and purchase patterns, BDA makes it possible to forecast demand and personalize sourcing strategies based on customer preference and market segments [32]. Sourcing strategies aligned with anticipated demand can help in optimizing inventory levels by reducing excess inventory and minimizing stockouts in the organization. All these can help organization identify cost-saving opportunities in sourcing by reducing inefficiencies and improving effectiveness in the procurement process.

7.4.3.2 *Big Data and Supplier Selection Management*

BDA improves supplier selection management by aggregating data from various sources and providing a wealth of information to the procurement professionals in terms of supplier potential, capabilities, their reputation, financial stability and performance history [33]. BDA assists in developing supplier performance metrics by analyzing supplier delivery time, adherence to contract, consistency in quality, and supplier ratings. This enables the organizations to assess the effectiveness and reliability of the suppliers objectively. Information on price dynamics, industry benchmarking and market trends through BDA provides insights during supplier selection process. Supplier portfolio can be diversified, diversify the supplier network and foster collaboration through BDA. Supplier reliability and performance can also be forecasted using predictive analytics which assists in identifying risks or opportunities with a specific vendor even before the contract [34]. BDA helps transform supplier selection management by enhancing strategic alignment, objectivity and visibility in the procurement decision making process. Thus supplier relationships can be optimized by mitigating risks and by driving creativity and innovation in supplier selection process through BDA.

7.4.3.3 *Big Data and Contract Management*

In the context of contract management in the procurement process, big data platforms can provide centralized repositories for storing, accessing and managing contracts throughout the contract lifecycle in the procurement process [35]. Metadata tagging and modern search techniques assist procurement teams in monitoring, tracking and retrieving contracts effortlessly. BDA can regularize the contract creation process by assembling documents based on rules and templates, clause management and by generating templates automatically. This can accelerate time for drafting contracts, reduce manmade errors and ensure consistency throughout the contracts. Machine learning algorithms can be used to assess contractual risks pertaining to non-compliance, performance gaps and pricing fluctuations to mitigate risk. To forecast contract performance, to identify renegotiation opportunities and to anticipate renewal dates of the contracts, predictive analytics models can be leverage [36]. Compliance checks can be automated by comparing contract terms with internal policies, industry standards and regulatory requirements through BDA. Big data platforms provide governance frameworks for enforcing, managing and maintaining data securing protocols of the contracts. They also provide comprehensive audit trails of the contract activities, approvals and revisions thus facilitating internal and compliance audits by ensuring accountability, traceability and transparency. BDA can be integrated with blockchain technologies and artificial intelligence for a more secure, transparent and efficient contract management system in the procurement process [37].

7.4.3.4 *Big Data and Purchase Order Processing*

Big data platforms can be integrated with supplier databases, IoT devices and enterprise resource planning (ERP) systems that can capture real time purchasing data from multiple sources. BDA can validate purchase data with regulatory requirements, predefined rules and supplier contracts thus ensuring accuracy before purchase order processing [38]. Predicative analytical models can help anticipate inventory requirements and suggest reorder quantities based on data. Real time monitoring help track lead times, inventory turnover rates and supply chain fluctuations to optimize purchase order dynamically. Dashboard and real time analytics helps monitor purchase orders, transactional activities and approval workflows. Advanced tools in analytics enable scenario modeling and predictive simulations to optimize purchase decisions. Thus purchase order processing can be optimized through automated data capture, monitoring and real-time analytics. Data aggregation from diverse sources can help the organization to analyze for informed decision making [39].

7.4.3.5 *Big Data and Inventory Management*

In the context of procurement, BDA impacts inventory management. Historical data analysis of sales data help identify customer trends and forecast demand that can help adjust inventory in the organization. Big data algorithms and platforms collaborates procurement teams with the suppliers and align production schedules improving supply chain visibility [40]. It also enhances collaborative forecasting, reduces bullwhip effect and improves responsiveness to market dynamics. BDA can process IoT-generated data to detect anomalies and comply with storage requirements. Real time analytics helps identify aging inventory and streamline replenishment [41]. Dynamic pricing strategies based on levels of inventory, collaborative forecasting and competitive intelligence is possible through real time analytics. The power of BDA help in harnessing operational excellence in procurement function.

7.4.3.6 Big Data and Supplier Relationship Management

Apart from influencing supplier selection management, BDA does have a profound influence on supplier relationship management [42]. Big data provides seamless collaboration and communication suppliers and the procuring organizations. Real time information sharing is facilitated through cloud based platforms improving efficiency and transparency in interactions. Big data helps in transforming supplier relationship management through transactional approach to a strategic partnership model [43]. Collaborative relationships with vendors help organizations achieve competitive advantage and mutual benefits.

7.4.3.7 Big Data and Ethics and Compliance in Procurement 4.0

Big data in procurement requires aggregation and analysis of large volumes of data which includes transaction details, supplier information and market trends. It is essential to ensure data privacy and security to maintain trust among the stakeholders. To ensure fairness and transparency, BDA should be used transparently and ethically [44]. In is also essential that analytics adhere to and comply with policies and regulations of procurement. It is necessary that in procurement 4.0, governance framework and accountability for the use of BDA are clearly stated. This mandates establishing clear ethical guidelines, perform regular audits and make sure that procurement activities uphold integrity and transparency [45]. By fostering ethical compliance organizations can achieve sustainable practices in the digital era.

7.4.3.8 Big Data and Performance Measures and Improvement

BDA facilitates procurement teams to build and monitor key performance indicators (KPIs) in the procurement function. The key performance indicators may include metrics such as cost savings during negotiation, supplier lead times, contract compliance rates, supplier diversity goals and procurement cycle times [46]. To drive continuous improvement, monitoring and adjustment of performance targets is ensured through real-time data analytics. BDA enhances continuous improvement activities through data-driven insights into procurement function. Iterative improvements can be implemented through analyzing performance data over time, benchmarking against industry best practices and identifying areas for enhancement [47]. This iterative approach ensures efficiency gains, adaptability and innovation in procurement practices. Thus BDA in Procurement 4.0 revolutionizes performance measurement and improvement.

7.4.3.9 *Big Data and Negotiation*

BDA in procurement 4.0 can transform the negotiation process. This is achieved through establishing and analyzing metrics related to supplier's performance and market trends which provides insights and enhances negotiation capabilities and strategies to negotiate price discounts, favorable payment terms and better service levels [48]. Benchmarking data through analytics provide negotiators position of knowledge and negotiate competitive agreements that align with market conditions. The foresight on demand through analytics allows negotiators to negotiate contingency plans, flexible terms, and risk mitigation strategies with suppliers to ensure resilient supply chain operations. To foster long-term partnerships, understanding supplier pain points, preferences and strategic priorities help negotiators to arrive at win-win agreements. Predictive analytics assists negotiators in identifying effective negotiation tactics, optimize negotiation outcomes and anticipate counteroffers based on data insights. Procurement teams can mitigate unethical practices and regulatory non-compliance during negotiations by monitoring internal policies, regulatory requirements and ethical standards. Negotiation tactics can be refined by analyzing post-negotiation data and stakeholder feedback thus enhancing the negotiation skills or the negotiators. Research shows that new suppliers generate greater savings than qualified suppliers during negotiation [49].

7.4.3.10 *Big Data and Risk Management*

Big Data is transforming procurement by delivering detailed insights into all stages of the source-to-pay procedure. By linking massive volumes of data, procurement managers have unparalleled visibility into their operations, ranging from financial turmoil to environmental trends. This insight is critical for handling complicated supply chains, which are more vulnerable to interruptions owing to their many moving components and greater distances. Integrated supply chains, from raw materials to distribution, are dangerous. Risk is inherent at every step of the supply chain [50] and that "Big Data analytics can predict potential disruptions, giving procurement managers time to make intelligent decisions." Innovative analytical instruments analyze the environment, prospective interruptions, political disruptions, and legislation modifications, enabling procurement experts to respond immediately [51]. Risk frameworks and predictive modeling may foresee vendor bankruptcy, interruptions, and quality difficulties, therefore preserving procurement processes and enhancing supply chain resilience. Predictive data analysis also allows you to model risk scenarios and estimate possible impact on inventories. BDA, therefore, allows the performance evaluation of risk reduction techniques in procurement.

7.5 Procurement 4.0 and Technological Advancement

Emerging technologies such as 5G, the use of AI and machine learning, blockchain technology, the metaverse, the Internet of Things, augmented reality, or AR, virtual reality, additive technology (3D printing), cloud storage, robotic process automation, and security measures are critical to realizing the benefits of Procurement 4.0 and moving forward to Procurement 5.0. These technologies collectively revolutionize procurement processes, enhancing efficiency, agility, and strategic decision-making across the supply chain. They enable real-time data analytics, seamless collaboration, enhanced security, and innovative solutions that drive operational excellence and sustainability in the digital era.

7.5.1 5G (Fifth Generation Technology)

Enhanced connectivity and mobility in the procurement process in procurement 4.0 is achieved through 5G technology. Ultra-fast data transfer speeds provided by 5G technology enable collaboration and communication among the suppliers, procurement teams and other stakeholders. 5G networks help connective massive number of IoT devices in the organization enabling tracking and optimizing the logistics in real-time [52]. Predictive modeling and real-time data analytics is made possible through 5G technology. 5G makes block chained enable transactions in the procurement process infusing reliability and security in the procurement function [53]. Edge computing which bring data processing close to sources of data generation is made possible through 5G technology. Procurement teams can leverage 5G technology effectively to achieve efficiency, innovation and agility within the procurement function [54].

7.5.2 ML and AI (Machine Learning and Artificial Intelligence)

Machine learning and artificial intelligence are integrated in procurement 4.0 revolutionizing the entire procurement process. ML and AI algorithms are used in the suppler selection and management process. ML algorithms analyze supplier data to anticipate supplier performance and reliability [55]. AI algorithms help segment the supplier based on geographical location, product offerings, pricing models and compliance. During demand forecasting, ML models help recognize patterns for accurate forecast. Market dynamics and competitor pricing are analyzed through AI algorithms for dynamic pricing. Natural language processing (NLP) techniques are used to extract and interpret data from contracts and ML algorithms detect potential risks in the contract assisting in contract management. Data derived from IoT devices in the procurement process is analyzed by ML algorithms for prediction and optimization through AI algorithms streamline the supply chain processes [56]. Procure-to-pay automation is powered by AI systems right from purchase requisition to processing invoices. Cognitive procurement assistants are virtual assistants powered by AI that provide real-time assistance to procurement teams. ML and AI tools continuously monitor and track supplier performance thus aiding in data driven decision making [57].

7.5.3 IoT (Internet of Things)

IoT devices such as GPS trackers, sensors and RFID tags help monitor and track good throughout the supply chain. This aids the procurements teams in complying with storage and transportation conditions thus minimizing delays and stockouts improving overall efficiency. Environmental conditions monitored through IoT sensors help ensure product quality and comply with regulatory requirements particularly in industries with stringent quality requirements (pharmaceutical industry). IoT enable-devices help monitor the condition and performance of equipment, storage facilities, vehicle and manufacturing machinery [58]. The data derived from these devices can be used for predicting equipment failures and for scheduling maintenance hence optimizing the lifespan of the asset. IoT sensors in warehouses help monitor the inventory and ensure timely replenishment based on forecasts and consumption patterns. IoT devices help monitor and track supplier performance to take timely action thus fostering collaborative planning and forecasting [59]. IoT devices integrated with blockchain technologies help create traceable, secure and transparent transactions/contracts and payments throughout the supply chain [60]. IoT automates routine tasks in the procurement process through process automation and hence reduce cost and achieved improved efficiency.

7.5.4 AR and VR (Augmented Reality and Virtual Reality)

Augmented Reality (AR) and Virtual Reality (VR) are revolutionary technologies that has the potential to transform the procurement process in procurement 4.0. Augmented reality helps procurement professionals visualize the products virtually and determine the product fit before deciding on purchasing. Virtual reality can create immersive virtual experience through virtual showrooms and trade fairs. VR enables the procurement professionals to attend virtual showrooms and exhibitions to explore products, interact with suppliers and experience product demo before making a decision [61]. In procurement, AR can be used for training the procurement professional for skill development by providing virtual tutorials, training modules and simulation to learn about new technologies, products and procurement process. Procurement professionals can practice crisis management scenarios, supplier management techniques and negotiation skills through immersive training simulations offered by virtual reality [62]. AR enabled smart glasses and headsets help warehouse staff in verifying inventory, locate products and fulfill orders efficiently. AR guided picking and packing reduces errors. AR also supports virtual inspection and audit of supplier site to assess the production capabilities, verify quality standards and regulatory requirements [63]. AR facilitates collaborative design and prototyping in the procurement process where the design teams, suppliers and engineers can iterate prototypes and visualize product designs in real-time. VR supports collaborative virtual prototyping and 3D modeling. AR and VR technologies enhance customer experience through engagement by offering interactive environment for product demonstrations and personalized shopping experience virtually [64]. AR and VR technologies help drive innovation throughout the procurement function.

7.5.5 Blockchain Technology and Procurement 4.0

Blockchain technology help create immutable records of the contracts, transactions and activities in the procurement process and across the supply chain. Decentralized networks operated by blockchain are cross verified and validated by multiple participants in the network. This architecture in blockchain provides data security, prevent failure, reduces risk by warding off unauthorized access and manipulation [15]. Blockchain technology creates a timestamp that can be linked to previous transaction thus creating transplant audit trails that can be accessed and verified. This enhances compliance, transparency and accountability and hence reduces disputes [27]. Data derived from various IoT devices is securely stored on blockchain providing real-time tracking with accurate visibility. Blockchain also facilitates the concept of smart contracts which can be self-executed with defined conditions and rules encoded into blockchain [65]. Immutable ledgers in blockchain can prevent fraud by averting unauthorized alterations and tampering of transaction records. By providing security and transparency in the transactions, blockchain builds ethical sourcing practices and sustainability thus fostering trust between procurement teams and stakeholders [66].

7.5.6 Metaverse and Procurement 4.0

Metaverse is a digital virtual shared place that may be accessed using immersive technology. This can have an impact on the procurement process in Procurement 4.0. Metaverse allows procurement experts to visit virtual exhibits and trade displays in a highly immersive setting [67]. Metaverse advocates the notion of digital twins, which generate virtual replicas of tangible commodities. Procurement teams may use digital twins to evaluate products, simulate designs, and prototype in a virtual environment. Procurement experts may also use Metaverse for collaborative workspaces and virtual meetings, allowing them to manage projects online [68]. Metaverse also allows for the simulation and modeling of technological supplier networks, which procurement teams may utilize to detect bottlenecks and enhance their procurement processes. Metaverse may teach and improve procurement experts using virtual reality simulations and scenario-based learning [69]. Metaverse enables virtual consumer encounters through product presentations and tailored assistance, assuring client engagement. Metaverse provides advanced analytical tools and data visualization, which may help procurement professionals with strategic forecasting and decision-making. Metaverse can assist achieve agility, creativity, and efficiency in a digitally linked world [69, 70].

7.5.7 3D Printing (Additive Manufacturing) and Procurement 4.0

Also termed as additive manufacturing, 3D printing can significantly impact the procurement process. 3D printing allows on-demand manufacturing of equipment and parts where the procurement teams can produce the items locally on-site thus reducing the reliance on traditional supply chains, minimizing the lead time, dependence on suppliers and transportation cost [71]. As 3D printing manufactures products on as needed basis, inventory can be optimized by following just-in-time inventory strategies and reduce warehouse cost. Personalization and customization of products is possible through 3D printing to meet the customer requirements. 3D printing can be used by procurement teams for iterative design processes and rapid prototyping [72]. Consolidation of components and parts into fewer assemblies is possible through 3D printing. 3D printing also enables the lightweight design of products by not compromising on the structural integrity of the products which can ensure fuel efficiency. As 3D printing is based on on-demand manufacturing, production of replacement and spare parts for MRO (Maintenance, Repair and Operations) becomes easy [73].

7.5.8 Cloud Computing and Procurement 4.0

Cloud computing can facilitate Procurement 4.0, or digital change. Procurement teams may use cloud-based platforms to scale their computer skills, critical for digitally integrated procurement processes with other business operations [74]. The use of cloud computing enables easy integration of several data sources. These systems provide the computational capacity to access timely information for sophisticated analytics such as machine learning and AI [75]. Cloud systems provide disaster recovery capabilities and built-in redundancy, ensuring operations continue amid natural catastrophes, hardware and software failures, and other disturbances. Cloud computing providers adhere to compliance requirements and use high-security measures to ensure legal compliance and the protection of confidential procuring info [76].

7.5.9 Cyber Security and Procurement 4.0

Cybersecurity is crucial in procurement 4.0 because it includes merging sensitive data from many sources and digitizing it. Data security, secrecy, and protection are critical, thus firms must adopt access restrictions and techniques for encryption [77]. To protect against cyber-attacks, enterprises must conduct frequent cyber risk assessments. . Integrating cybersecurity concerns into procurement procedures helps assure security and confidence among all parties [78].

7.6 Conclusion

The present study focuses on the emergence of Procurement 4.0, which signifies a significant transition from traditional procurement techniques to a digitally connected and data-driven strategy. Organizations may use BDA to optimize every aspect of the procurement process, from sourcing and supplier selection to contract administration and inventory control. This change increases operational efficiency and promotes innovation, managing risks, and connections with vendors. Furthermore, emerging technologies such as artificial intelligence, IoT, blockchain, and cloud computing play integral roles in shaping the future of procurement. These technologies enable real-time data insights, predictive analytics, and automation, thereby driving agility and responsiveness across the supply chain. As firms embrace these developments, they must emphasize ethical issues and cybersecurity to ensure honesty, openness, and accountability in their procurement processes. This allows them to successfully negotiate the intricacies of current supply chains while accomplishing long-term growth in the age of technology. Procurement 4.0 is an effective blend of information, technology, and interactions that are positioned to reinvent procurement expertise in the global economy.

References

1. Bienhaus, F. and Haddud, A., Procurement 4.0: factors influencing the digitisation of procurement and supply chains. *Bus. Process Manag. J.*, 24, 4, 965–984, Jun. 2018, doi: 10.1108/BPMJ-06-2017-0139.
2. Bernardo Nicoletti, A.A., *Big Data in Procurement 4.0 Critical Success Factors and Solutions*, 1st Edition, CRC Press, Boca Raton, Florida, USA, 2020, [Online], Available: https://www.taylorfrancis.com/chapters/edit/10.1201/9780367816384-4/big-data-procurement-4-0-bernardo-nicoletti-andrea-appolloni.
3. Hallikas, J., Immonen, M., Brax, S., Digitalizing procurement: the impact of data analytics on supply chain performance. *Supply Chain Manag. An Int. J.*, 5, 629–646, Jul. 2021, doi: 10.1108/SCM-05-2020-0201.
4. Nicoletti, B. and Appolloni, A., Digital transformation in ecosystems: integrated operations model and its application to fifth-party logistics operators. *J. Glob. Oper. Strateg. Sourc.*, 18, 1, 91–122, 2025. https://doi.org/10.1108/JGOSS-04-2023-0024.
5. Herold, S., Heller, J., Rozemeijer, F., Mahr, D., Dynamic capabilities for digital procurement transformation: a systematic literature review. *Int. J. Phys. Distrib. Logist. Manag.*, 53, 4, 424–447, Jun. 2023, doi: 10.1108/IJPDLM-12-2021-0535.
6. Choudhury, A., Behl, A., Sheorey, P.A., Pal, A., Digital supply chain to unlock new agility: a TISM approach. *Benchmarking An Int. J.*, 28, 6, 2075–2109, Jun. 2021, doi: 10.1108/BIJ-08-2020-0461.
7. Narwane, V.S., Raut, R.D., Yadav, V.S., Cheikhrouhou, N., Narkhede, B.E., Priyadarshinee, P., The role of big data for Supply Chain 4.0 in manufacturing organisations of developing countries. *J. Enterp. Inf. Manag.*, 34, 5, 1452–1480, Nov. 2021, doi: 10.1108/JEIM-11-2020-0463.
8. Huang, Y., Schuehle, J., Porter, A.L., Youtie, J., A systematic method to create search strategies for emerging technologies based on the Web of Science:

illustrated for 'Big Data'. *Scientometrics*, 105, 3, 2005–2022, Dec. 2015, doi: 10.1007/s11192-015-1638-y.
9. Bag, S., Wood, L.C., Mangla, S.K., Luthra, S., Procurement 4.0 and its implications on business process performance in a circular economy. *Resour. Conserv. Recycl.*, 152, 104502, Jan. 2020, doi: 10.1016/j.resconrec.2019.104502.
10. Mavidis, A. and Folinas, D., From Public E-Procurement 3.0 to E-Procurement 4.0; A Critical Literature Review. *Sustainability*, 14, 18, 11252, Sep. 2022, doi: 10.3390/su141811252.
11. Tripathi, S. and Gupta, M., A framework for procurement process re-engineering in Industry 4.0. *Bus. Process Manag. J.*, 27, 2, 439–458, Dec. 2020, doi: 10.1108/BPMJ-07-2020-0321.
12. ISM-India, *Procurement Journey (From Procurement 1.0 to Procurement 4.0)*, 2020.
13. Nicoletti, B., The Future: Procurement 4.0, in: *Agile Procurement*, pp. 189–230, Springer International Publishing, Cham, 2018, doi: 10.1007/978-3-319-61085-6_8.
14. Althabatah, A., Yaqot, M., Menezes, B., Kerbache, L., Transformative Procurement Trends: Integrating Industry 4.0 Technologies for Enhanced Procurement Processes. *Logistics*, 7, 3, 63, Sep. 2023, doi: 10.3390/logistics 7030063.
15. Govindan, K., Jain, P., Kr. Singh, R., Mishra, R., Blockchain technology as a strategic weapon to bring procurement 4.0 truly alive: Literature review and future research agenda. *Transp. Res. Part E Logist. Transp. Rev.*, 181, 103352, Jan. 2024, doi: 10.1016/j.tre.2023.103352.
16. Casado, R. and Younas, M., Emerging trends and technologies in big data processing. *Concurr. Comput. Pract. Exp.*, 27, 8, 2078–2091, Jun. 2015, doi: 10.1002/cpe.3398.
17. Gupta, S., Drave, V.A., Dwivedi, Y.K., Baabdullah, A.M., Ismagilova, E., Achieving superior organizational performance *via* big data predictive analytics: A dynamic capability view. *Ind. Mark. Manag.*, 90, 581–592, Oct. 2020, doi: 10.1016/j.indmarman.2019.11.009.
18. Ibusuki, U., Koto, R.D.P., De Araújo, R.D., Jussani, A.C., Application of e-auction based on Procurement 4.0 strategies in a global company of the power systems sector in Brazil. *Int. J. Procure. Manag.*, 1, 1, 1, 2022, doi: 10.1504/IJPM.2022.10044946.
19. Gunasekaran, A., *et al.*, Big data and predictive analytics for supply chain and organizational performance. *J. Bus. Res.*, 70, 308–317, Jan. 2017, doi: 10.1016/j.jbusres.2016.08.004.
20. Elish, M.C. and Boyd, D., Situating methods in the magic of Big Data and AI. *Commun. Monogr.*, 85, 1, 57–80, Jan. 2018, doi: 10.1080/03637751.2017.1375130.
21. Nicoletti, B., Processes in Procurement 4.0, in: *Procurement 4.0 and the Fourth Industrial Revolution*, pp. 53–116, Springer International Publishing, Cham, 2020, doi: 10.1007/978-3-030-35979-9_3.

22. Nicoletti, B., Platforms for Procurement 4.0, in: *Procurement 4.0 and the Fourth Industrial Revolution*, pp. 117–189, Springer International Publishing, Cham, 2020, doi: 10.1007/978-3-030-35979-9_4.
23. Sharma, R., Samad, T.A., Chiappetta Jabbour, C.J., de Queiroz, M.J., Leveraging blockchain technology for circularity in agricultural supply chains: evidence from a fast-growing economy. *J. Enterp. Inf. Manag.*, 38, 1, 32–67, 2025 Jan 23.
24. Kumar, R., Samadhiya, A., Kumar, A., Luthra, S., Pandey, K.K., El jaouhari, A., Nourish resilience in digital food supply chain in post COVID landscape: literature swill for past insights and future roadmap. *Int. J. Ind. Eng. Oper. Manag.*, Vol. ahead-of-print, No. ahead-of-print, 2024, https://doi.org/10.1108/IJIEOM-02-2024-0007.
25. Sjödin, D., Kamalaldin, A., Parida, V., Islam, N., Procurement 4.0: How Industrial Customers Transform Procurement Processes to Capitalize on Digital Servitization. *IEEE Trans. Eng. Manag.*, 70, 12, 4175–4190, Dec. 2023, doi: 10.1109/TEM.2021.3110424.
26. Joseph Jerome, J.J., Saxena, D., Sonwaney, V., Foropon, C., Procurement 4.0 to the rescue: catalysing its adoption by modelling the challenges. *Benchmarking An Int. J.*, 29, 1, 217–254, Jan. 2022, doi: 10.1108/BIJ-01-2021-0030.
27. Gunasekara, H.G., Sridarran, P., Rajaratnam, D., Effective use of blockchain technology for facilities management procurement process. *J. Facil. Manag.*, 20, 3, 452–468, May 2022, doi: 10.1108/JFM-10-2020-0077.
28. Govindan, K., Kannan, D., Jørgensen, T.B., Nielsen, T.S., Supply Chain 4.0 performance measurement: A systematic literature review, framework development, and empirical evidence. *Transp. Res. Part E Logist. Transp. Rev.*, 164, 102725, Aug. 2022, doi: 10.1016/j.tre.2022.102725.
29. Alabdali, M.A. and Salam, M.A., The Impact of Digital Transformation on Supply Chain Procurement for Creating Competitive Advantage: An Empirical Study. *Sustainability*, 14, 19, 12269, Sep. 2022, doi: 10.3390/su141912269.
30. Bag, S., Dhamija, P., Gupta, S., Sivarajah, U., Examining the role of procurement 4.0 towards remanufacturing operations and circular economy. *Prod. Plan. Control*, 32, 16, 1368–1383, Dec. 2021, doi: 10.1080/09537287.2020.1817602.
31. Sangil, M.J.G. and Maceda, L.L., OCDex Portal in. *Proceedings of the 4th International Conference on Machine Learning and Soft Computing*, ACM, New York, NY, USA, pp. 71–75, Jan. 2020, doi: 10.1145/3380688.3380719.
32. Razaghi, S. and Shokouhyar, S., Impacts of big data analytics management capabilities and supply chain integration on global sourcing: a survey on firm performance. *Bottom Line*, 34, 2, 198–223, Sep. 2021, doi: 10.1108/BL-11-2020-0071.
33. Yildizbasi, A. and Arioz, Y., Green supplier selection in new era for sustainability: A novel method for integrating big data analytics and a hybrid fuzzy multi-criteria decision making. *Soft Comput.*, 26, 1, 253–270, Jan. 2022, doi: 10.1007/s00500-021-06477-8.

34. Zekhnini, K., Chaouni Benabdellah, A., Cherrafi, A., A multi-agent based big data analytics system for viable supplier selection. *J. Intell. Manuf.*, 35, 8, 3599–3613, 2023.
35. Bedir, C., Contract Law in the Age of Big Data. *Eur. Rev. Contract Law*, 16, 3, 347–365, Sep. 2020, doi: 10.1515/ercl-2020-0020.
36. Zhang, X., Liu, T., Rahman, A., Zhou, L., Blockchain applications for construction contract management: A systematic literature review. *J. Constr. Eng. Manag.*, 149, 1, 03122011, 2023 Jan 1.
37. Lin, S., Lin, J., Han, F., Luo, X.(R)., How big data analytics enables the alliance relationship stability of contract farming in the age of digital transformation. *Inf. Manag.*, 59, 6, 103680, Sep. 2022, doi: 10.1016/j.im.2022.103680.
38. Lamba, K. and Singh, S.P., Big data in operations and supply chain management: current trends and future perspectives. *Prod. Plan. Control*, 28, 11–12, 877–890, Sep. 2017, doi: 10.1080/09537287.2017.1336787.
39. Arvidsson, A.P., Jonsson, P., Kaipia, R., Big data in purchasing and supply management: a research agenda. *Int. J. Procure. Manag.*, 14, 2, 185, 2021, doi: 10.1504/IJPM.2021.113490.
40. Bertsimas, D., Kallus, N., Hussain, A., Inventory Management in the Era of Big Data. *Prod. Oper. Manag.*, 25, 2006–2009, Dec. 2016, doi: 10.1111/poms.2.
41. Choi, T., Wallace, S.W., Wang, Y., Big Data Analytics in Operations Management. *Prod. Oper. Manag.*, 27, 10, 1868–1883, Oct. 2018, doi: 10.1111/poms.12838.
42. Huang, Y.-Y. and Handfield, R.B., Measuring the benefits of ERP on supply management maturity model: a 'big data' method. *Int. J. Oper. Prod. Manag.*, 35, 1, 2–25, Jan. 2015, doi: 10.1108/IJOPM-07-2013-0341.
43. Anshari, M., Almunawar, M.N., Lim, S.A., Al-Mudimigh, A., Customer relationship management and big data enabled: Personalization & customization of services. *Appl. Comput. Inf.*, 15, 2, 94–101, Jul. 2019, doi: 10.1016/j.aci.2018.05.004.
44. Bag, S., Rahman, M.S., Srivastava, G., Shore, A., Ram, P., Examining the role of virtue ethics and big data in enhancing viable, sustainable, and digital supply chain performance. *Technol. Forecast. Soc. Change*, 186, 122154, Jan. 2023, doi: 10.1016/j.techfore.2022.122154.
45. Ogbuke, N.J., Yusuf, Y.Y., Dharma, K., Mercangoz, B.A., Big data supply chain analytics: ethical, privacy and security challenges posed to business, industries and society. *Prod. Plan. Control*, 33, 2–3, 123–137, Feb. 2022, doi: 10.1080/09537287.2020.1810764.
46. Ghasemaghaei, M., Improving Organizational Performance Through the Use of Big Data. *J. Comput. Inf. Syst.*, 60, 5, 395–408, Sep. 2020, doi: 10.1080/08874417.2018.1496805.
47. Bag, S., Wood, L.C., Xu, L., Dhamija, P., Kayikci, Y., Big data analytics as an operational excellence approach to enhance sustainable supply chain

performance. *Resour. Conserv. Recycl.*, 153, 104559, Feb. 2020, doi: 10.1016/j.resconrec.2019.104559.
48. BenSaid, F. and Alimi, A.M., Online feature selection system for big data classification based on multi-objective automated negotiation. *Pattern Recognit.*, 110, 107629, Feb. 2021, doi: 10.1016/j.patcog.2020.107629.
49. Delina, R., Olejarova, R., Doucek, P., Effect of a new potential supplier on business to business negotiations performance: evidence-based analysis. *Electron. Commer. Res.*, 23, 3, 1941–1970, Sep. 2023, doi: 10.1007/s10660-021-09524-6.
50. Araz, O.M., Choi, T., Olson, D.L., Salman, F.S., Role of Analytics for Operational Risk Management in the Era of Big Data. *Decis. Sci.*, 51, 6, 1320–1346, Dec. 2020, doi: 10.1111/deci.12451.
51. Niesen, T., Houy, C., Fettke, P., Loos, P., Towards an Integrative Big Data Analysis Framework for Data-Driven Risk Management in Industry 4.0, in: *2016 49th Hawaii International Conference on System Sciences (HICSS)*, IEEE, pp. 5065–5074, Jan. 2016, doi: 10.1109/HICSS.2016.627.
52. Mourtzis, D., Angelopoulos, J., Panopoulos, N., Smart Manufacturing and Tactile Internet Based on 5G in Industry 4.0: Challenges, Applications and New Trends. *Electronics*, 10, 24, 3175, Dec. 2021, doi: 10.3390/electronics10243175.
53. Taboada, I. and Shee, H., Understanding 5G technology for future supply chain management. *Int. J. Logist. Res. Appl.*, 24, 4, 392–406, Jul. 2021, doi: 10.1080/13675567.2020.1762850.
54. Rejeb, A. and Keogh, J.G., 5G Networks in the Value Chain. *Wirel. Pers. Commun.*, 117, 2, 1577–1599, Mar. 2021, doi: 10.1007/s11277-020-07936-5.
55. Cui, R., Li, M., Zhang, S., AI and Procurement. *Manuf. Serv. Oper. Manag.*, 24, 2, 691–706, Mar. 2022, doi: 10.1287/msom.2021.0989.
56. Cavalcante, I.M., Frazzon, E.M., Forcellini, F.A., Ivanov, D., A supervised machine learning approach to data-driven simulation of resilient supplier selection in digital manufacturing. *Int. J. Inf. Manage.*, 49, 86–97, Dec. 2019, doi: 10.1016/j.ijinfomgt.2019.03.004.
57. Spreitzenbarth, J.M., Bode, C., Stuckenschmidt, H., Artificial intelligence and machine learning in purchasing and supply management: A mixed-methods review of the state-of-the-art in literature and practice. *J. Purch. Supply Manag.*, 30, 1, 100896, Jan. 2024, doi: 10.1016/j.pursup.2024.100896.
58. Ben-Daya, M., Hassini, E., Bahroun, Z., Internet of things and supply chain management: a literature review. *Int. J. Prod. Res.*, 57, 15–16, 4719–4742, Aug. 2019, doi: 10.1080/00207543.2017.1402140.
59. Zhou, L., Chong, A.Y.L., Ngai, E.W.T., Supply chain management in the era of the internet of things. *Int. J. Prod. Econ.*, 159, 1–3, Jan. 2015, doi: 10.1016/j.ijpe.2014.11.014.
60. Birkel, H.S. and Hartmann, E., Internet of Things – the future of managing supply chain risks. *Supply Chain Manag. An Int. J.*, 25, 5, 535–548, Jun. 2020, doi: 10.1108/SCM-09-2019-0356.

61. Korbel, J.J., Riar, M., Zamekow, R., Wiegmann, L., *Augmented Reality in E-Procurement: Opportunities and Challenges*, 2022.
62. Seyman Guray, T. and Kismet, B., VR and AR in construction management research: bibliometric and descriptive analyses. *Smart Sustain. Built Environ.*, 12, 3, 635–659, Apr. 2023, doi: 10.1108/SASBE-01-2022-0015.
63. Eswaran, M. and Bahubalendruni, M.V.A.R., Challenges and opportunities on AR/VR technologies for manufacturing systems in the context of industry 4.0: A state of the art review. *J. Manuf. Syst.*, 65, 260–278, Oct. 2022, doi: 10.1016/j.jmsy.2022.09.016.
64. Alimamy, S. and Nadeem, W., Is this real? Cocreation of value through authentic experiential augmented reality: the mediating effect of perceived ethics and customer engagement. *Inf. Technol. People*, 35, 2, 577–599, Mar. 2022, doi: 10.1108/ITP-07-2020-0455.
65. Azzi, R., Chamoun, R.K., Sokhn, M., The power of a blockchain-based supply chain. *Comput. Ind. Eng.*, 135, 582–592, Sep. 2019, doi: 10.1016/j.cie.2019.06.042.
66. Queiroz, M.M., Telles, R., Bonilla, S.H., Blockchain and supply chain management integration: a systematic review of the literature. *Supply Chain Manag. An Int. J.*, 25, 2, 241–254, Aug. 2019, doi: 10.1108/SCM-03-2018-0143.
67. Rathore, M.M., Shah, S.A., Shukla, D., Bentafat, E., Bakiras, S., The Role of AI, Machine Learning, and Big Data in Digital Twinning: A Systematic Literature Review, Challenges, and Opportunities. *IEEE Access*, 9, 32030–32052, 2021, doi: 10.1109/ACCESS.2021.3060863.
68. De Giovanni, P., Sustainability of the Metaverse: A Transition to Industry 5.0. *Sustainability*, 15, 7, 6079, Mar. 2023, doi: 10.3390/su15076079.
69. Büyüközkan, G., Metaverse and Supply Chain Management Applications, in: Esen, F.S., Tinmaz, H., Singh, M. (eds) Metaverse. *Studies in Big Data*, vol. 133, 383–395, Springer, Singapore, 2023. https://doi.org/10.1007/978-981-99-4641-9_26.
70. Dolgui, A. and Ivanov, D., Metaverse supply chain and operations management. *Int. J. Prod. Res.*, 61, 23, 8179–8191, Dec. 2023, doi: 10.1080/00207543.2023.2240900.
71. Ryan, M.J., Eyers, D.R., Potter, A.T., Purvis, L., Gosling, J., 3D printing the future: scenarios for supply chains reviewed. *Int. J. Phys. Distrib. Logist. Manag.*, 47, 10, 992–1014, Nov. 2017, doi: 10.1108/IJPDLM-12-2016-0359.
72. Meyer, M.M., Glas, A.H., Eßig, M., Systematic review of sourcing and 3D printing: make-or-buy decisions in industrial buyer–supplier relationships. *Manag. Rev. Q.*, 71, 4, 723–752, Oct. 2021, doi: 10.1007/s11301-020-00198-2.
73. Rogers, H., Baricz, N., Pawar, K.S., 3D printing services: classification, supply chain implications and research agenda. *Int. J. Phys. Distrib. Logist. Manag.*, 46, 10, 886–907, Nov. 2016, doi: 10.1108/IJPDLM-07-2016-0210.
74. Cao, Q., Schniederjans, D.G., Schniederjans, M., Establishing the use of cloud computing in supply chain management. *Oper. Manag. Res.*, 10, 1–2, 47–63, Jun. 2017, doi: 10.1007/s12063-017-0123-6.

75. Gammelgaard, B. and Nowicka, K., Next generation supply chain management: the impact of cloud computing. *J. Enterp. Inf. Manag.*, 37, 4, 1140–1160, 2024. https://doi.org/10.1108/JEIM-09-2022-0317.
76. Jede, A. and Teuteberg, F., Integrating cloud computing in supply chain processes. *J. Enterp. Inf. Manag.*, 28, 6, 872–904, Oct. 2015, doi: 10.1108/JEIM-08-2014-0085.
77. Sobb, T., Turnbull, B., Moustafa, N., Supply Chain 4.0: A Survey of Cyber Security Challenges, Solutions and Future Directions. *Electronics*, 9, 11, 1864, Nov. 2020, doi: 10.3390/electronics9111864.
78. Melnyk, S.A., Schoenherr, T., Speier-Pero, C., Peters, C., Chang, J.F., Friday, D., New challenges in supply chain management: cybersecurity across the supply chain. *Int. J. Prod. Res.*, 60, 1, 162–183, Jan. 2022, doi: 10.1080/00207543.2021.1984606.

8

Big Data in Procurement 4.0: Success Factors and Solutions

Bargavi R.[1*] **and Vasumathi P.**[2]

[1]*Faculty of Management, SRMIST, Kattankulathur, Tamil Nadu, India*
[2]*Loyola Institute of Business Administration, Chennai, India*

Abstract
Procurement 4.0 is a term used to refer to industry 4.0, and its transformation in the procurement industry with IoT, artificial intelligence, and Big Data analytics. This Chapter will attempt to discuss how Big Data can support, measure, and improve an organization's efficiency and effectiveness of the procurement processes, focusing on key success factors and options for intervention. Thus, we will focus on Big Data, business objectives, governance, and quality to improve the existing information. We will also consider the factors such as the requirement of a solid technology support system and possessing a qualified staff. It involves many changes and costs, which is why it is one of the major procurement components. That is why Big Data is our topic, we aim to increase procurement effectiveness, representing numerical results and real-life applications in different fields. Subsequently, examine a collection of upcoming patterns and advancements that will influence procurement in the next years by highlighting the potential of predictive and prescriptive analytics, as well as the significance of sustainable and ethical procurement methods. The paper offers a profound understanding of methods and approaches that allow organizations to effectively use Big Data for procurement strategies.

Keywords: Sustainable supply chain management, sustainability, big data, Internet of Things, artificial intelligence, green procurement, supply chain

**Corresponding author*: ravibharkavi@gmail.com

K. Mathiyazhagan, Krishna Kumar Dadsena, Rajesh Kumar Singh, Aakanksha Kishore and Andrea Appolloni (eds.) Sustainable Operations of Logistics and Supply Chain Management, (159–200) © 2025 Scrivener Publishing LLC

8.1 Introduction

Big Data analytics incorporated into procurement processes may have huge benefits. Such procurement specialists, by analyzing various data sources, like supplier performance metrics, market trends, and customer preferences, could make more informed decisions about the optimization of supplier networks and anticipate disruptions a little more effectively [1]. Procurement 4.0 enables free information flow across the supply chain, hence increasing transparency and collaboration among all concerned parties in Figure 8.1.

Yet, there exist major challenges that need to be addressed for the successful implementation of Big Data in Procurement 4.0 practice. In this regard, Bien Haus and Haddud consider organizational resistance to change, problems of data integration, and insufficient special competencies and technologies as challenges likely to hamper the adoption of these transformative solutions [2]. All the impediments can only be resolved by a coherent strategy targeted at organizational culture, data governance, and strategic application of whoever enabling technologies [3]. It can be done

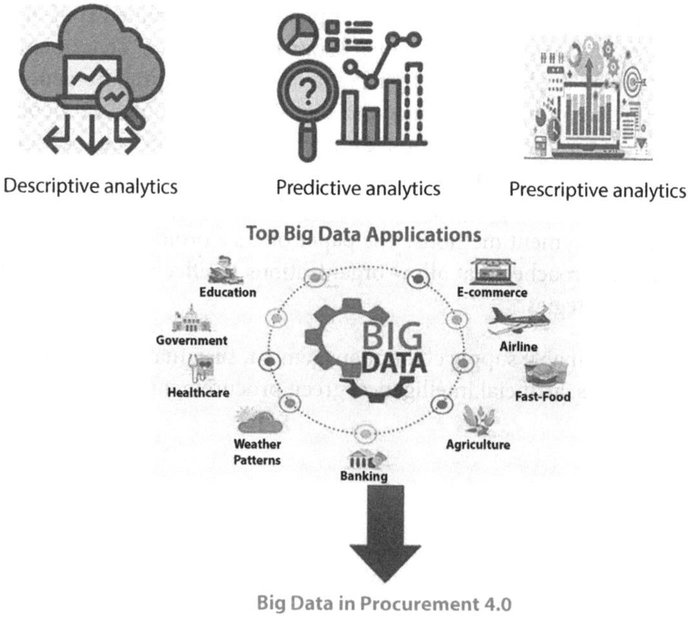

Figure 8.1 Big Data in Procurement 4.0 (Source: author's own).

effectively only when procurement professionals empower Big Data analytics in Procurement 4. The procurement landscape has been substantially altered by the swift evolution of digital technologies. Big Data is a critical instrument for enabling organizations to enhance decision-making processes, optimize supply chains, and improve efficiency, making it stand out among these technologies [4]. The practical implementation of Big Data across industries remains complex and multifaceted, despite the pervasive recognition of its potentiality.

This chapter examines at the real-world effects of Big Data on procurement procedures across a range of sectors, highlighting both the advantages and disadvantages. The goal is to give a thorough examination of the influence of Big Data technologies on procurement strategies in sectors such as retail, manufacturing, and healthcare, as well as practical recommendations for companies evaluating how to best use these technologies. This Chapter will examine how Big Data can improve supplier relationships and make optimal decisions using prescriptive and predictive analytics. Additionally, it discusses the challenges in the adoption of bid data.

1. What are the differences in the use of Big Data in procurement among industries?
2. What are the key challenges that an organization faces when employing Big Data in procurement?
3. How do organizations overcome these challenges to leverage the benefits of Big Data for procurement?

8.1.1 Procurement 4.0 Overview: Definition and Significance – Definition of Procurement 4.0, Including Its Major Components

Procurement 4.0 is the transformation of conventional procurement processes *via* the integration of new digital technology, guided by Industry 4.0 concepts [5]. At its foundation, Procurement 4.0 uses technologies like the Internet of Things (IoT), artificial intelligence (AI), Big Data analytics, and blockchain to build a more efficient, transparent, and data-driven procurement environment [2, 6]. Automation and Robotics: RPA when implemented in simple and repetitive processes such as order processing, invoice creation, and suppliers' planning decreases errors while increasing efficiency. These are the constituent elements of Procurement 4 in Figure 8.2.

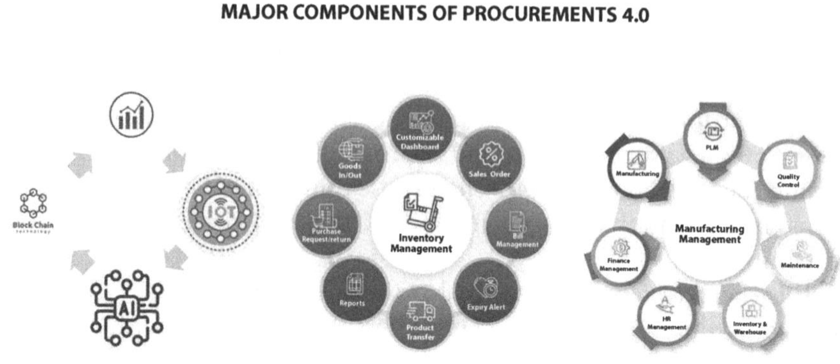

Figure 8.2 Major components of Procurement 4.0 (Source: author's own).

Data Analytics: It enables organizations to manage the huge amount of information derived from different sources for better and improved decision-making and demand forecasting or to prevent a particular risk.
IoT Integration: Smart devices can also aid the tracking of products and various materials used in real-time and this increases the transparency of the supply chain as well as improve inventory management.
AI and Machine Learning: It helps in forecasting market patterns, the right time to make purchases, as well as the possibilities of risks and gains when it comes to supply chain networks.
Blockchain Technology: This, in turn, keeps the transactions safe, and hence, protects documents from being tampered with; this blocks fraudulent activities and raises the believability of the supply chain participants.

8.1.2 Implications of Procurement 4.0 Considering Industry 4.0

In the context of Industry 4.0, Procurement 4.0 is crucial for enabling seamless integration across the supply chain, encouraging collaboration, and driving innovation. Procurement 4.0 Zero is relevant since it includes Procurement 4 [7]. Zero is a key driver of digital transformation in supply chain control, encouraging efficiency, transparency, and innovation. Organizations that embrace new technology may potentially gain significant competitive advantages and perform more effectively in a constantly changing business environment [8]. Corporations may significantly reduce cycle times and operational costs by automating day-to-day initiatives and streamlining procurement methods. This efficiency leads to faster time-to-market for products and services. Improved Data-driven insights enable procurement experts to make more informed decisions, improve sourcing strategies, and negotiate better terms with suppliers [9]. This results in value discounts and stronger dealer connections [10]. The Internet of Things (IoT) and blockchain technologies provide real-time visibility into the movement of commodities and substances, ensuring traceability from raw materials to finished products (the finished product). This transparency is essential for compliance, effective control, and sustainability activities. Businesses may take proactive steps to minimize interruptions and guarantee a continuous supply of products by using sophisticated analytics and predictive modeling to anticipate possible supply chain risks [11]. Procurement 4.0 advocates for sustainable procurement methods by providing insights into the environmental and social consequences of sourcing decisions. This corresponds with the organization's goals of sustainability and corporate social responsibility, therefore improving its reputation [12].

From Traditional to Procurement 4.0 – How Procurement Has Evolved

Procurement practices have undergone substantial transformations across many pivotal junctures, characterized by important breakthroughs as well as modifications in emphasis. During the early stages, procurement relied on manual processes and paper documentation, leading to challenges in standardization and transparency [3]. The procurement of goods and services was significantly shaped by interpersonal connections and negotiation strategies, leading to fluctuations in both pricing and quality. In the late 1800s and early 1900s, the expansion of industrialization prompted companies to pursue standardized procurement processes, aiming to achieve cost advantages through economies of scale [13]. Centralized procurement departments were established to improve purchasing processes, negotiate more favorable terms with suppliers, and ensure adherence to corporate policies, as depicted in Figure 8.3.

Electronic procurement, or e-purchase, technologies first appeared in the second decade of the 20th century, automating a lot of the procurement process. The use of these technologies facilitated automated tendering, order processing, and billing, leading to reduced paperwork and improved efficiency. The widespread use of Enterprise Resource Planning (ERP) systems facilitated the smooth integration of procurement with other organizational functions. The impact of globalization on strategic sourcing. The proliferation of globalization has led to increasingly extensive supply chains, evolving the function of procurement from a transactional one to a strategic one. Organizations used strategic sourcing techniques that emphasized supplier cooperation, total cost of ownership (TCO), and the creation of long-term value. Supplier relationship management (SRM)

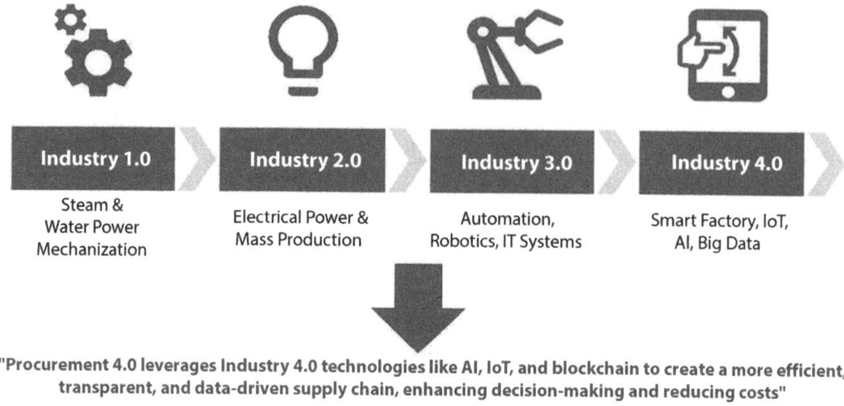

Figure 8.3 Traditional to Procurement 4.0 stages.

systems were developed to enhance cooperation and communication with critical suppliers . The concept of digital transformation and Procurement 4.0. Procurement 4.0 has emerged as a vital component of the current phase, driven by the innovations of Industry 4.0. This period is characterized by the integration of advanced digital technologies, including IoT, AI, Big Data analytics, and blockchain, into procurement procedures. A greater focus is being directed towards creating a procurement environment that is data-driven, transparent, and adaptable, aimed at promoting innovation and sustainability [7].

8.1.3 Emphasis on the Digitalization and Automation of Activities

The move from manual to digital and automated procurement processes has changed the way organizations function, fostering to become strategic, accurate and efficient. The key features of this transition encompass Robotic Process Automation (RPA) to handle repetitive tasks data entering, order processing, and invoice settlement [14]. Over time, RPA reduces errors, enhances quick and faster workflow, and eases procurement specialists to focus on more critical and essential tasks. Digital transformation has improved the efficiency of organizations in handling large procurement data using data analytics and data management. In such cases, organizations can collect and examine voluminous data from diverse sources extract insights on current market trends, and supplier performance and help procurement specialists make data-based smart decisions [11, 15]. Present-day procurement solutions connect smoothly other functional departments with procurement using Enterprise Resource Planning (ERP) and Supplier Relationship Management (SRM) [16, 17]. This integration guarantees overall efficiency and teamwork by having accurate, consistent, and timely information across the organization. In addition, the usage of IoT devices along with blockchain technology facilitates real-time tracking of raw materials and finished products. This resulted in high visibility and transparency across the supply chain, minimized fraud risk, and ensured compliance with government regulations. Hence digital tools and platforms help organizations build connections with important suppliers and other stakeholders. This collaborative approach results in improved negotiating outcomes, increased quality, and increased creativity in product development. Digital technologies encourage sustainable and ethical procurement practices by providing information regarding the environmental and social consequences of sourcing decisions. Organizations may oversee and evaluate sustainability initiatives to guarantee that they are consistent with their objectives and regulatory obligations.

8.1.4 Literature Review of this Study

The current research on Big Data in procurement offers a fundamental comprehension of its potential while exposing many gaps that this study seeks to solve. Although research such as [1] emphasizes the significance of predictive analytics in enhancing procurement processes, it predominantly remains theoretical, devoid of empirical validation and practical implementation across many sectors. Similarly, studies on risk mitigation and supplier management, like those by [6, 18] show how Big Data can be used to monitor supplier performance and avoid disruptions, but they don't distinguish between sector-specific issues like the different requirements of the manufacturing and healthcare sectors, such acknowledge the paramount significance of data quality and integration; yet, they provide no practical assistance in resolving these challenges, resulting in a deficiency of concrete techniques for maintaining data consistency and governance [5, 9, 19]. This article examines these deficiencies by offering industry-specific analysis of Big Data's influence on procurement in sectors such as retail, healthcare, and manufacturing, bolstered by empirical case studies that demonstrate effective implementations. This study gives real-life examples to back up real-world solutions to the issues that come up when using Big Data, like prices, a lack of skilled workers, and resistance from other departments. These issues have not been looked at in previous studies. Additionally, legal and moral problems such as data protection and algorithmic bias are sometimes not given much attention in modern research, even though they are very important. This study highlights these characteristics, offering techniques for adherence to data protection rules and guaranteeing the ethical utilization of supplier data. This research critically engages with the current literature and addresses gaps, providing a thorough and practical knowledge of Big Data in procurement, so enhancing its relevance for both academic and industrial audiences.

8.1.5 Research Methodology

This study is mostly based on secondary research, including a thorough evaluation of previous studies, industry reports, and case studies that examine the impact of Big Data in procurement. Principal sources are peer-reviewed journals, governmental publications, and esteemed industry white papers. This report also consolidates data from actual case studies of organizations that have effectively adopted Big Data technology in their procurement procedures. These case studies furnish actual data to substantiate the theoretical assertions presented in the study. The study methodology employs a qualitative approach, seeking to thoroughly examine the application of Big Data across several industries and to uncover the problems organizations have in adopting new technologies.

8.2 Big Data in Procurement 4.0

Big Data in Procurement 4.0 improves decision-making and efficiency in Figure 8.4.

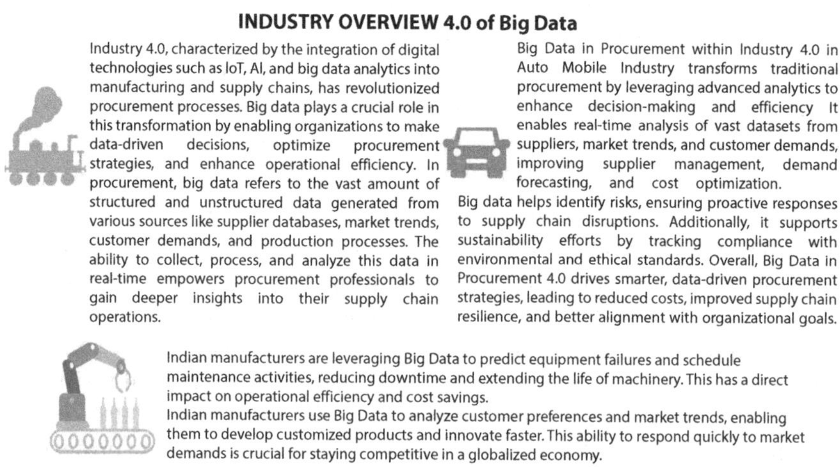

Figure 8.4 Industry overview 4.0 of Big Data.

8.2.1 Descriptive Analytics

Descriptive analytics is analyzing historical data to get insight into previous buying operations. It gives information on expenditure trends, supplier performance, and procurement cycle timelines [20]. Understanding what transpired allows organizations to find areas for improvement and optimize their procurement strategy. In descriptive analytics, the goal is to get a better understanding of the past by creating a summary of relevant historical data [21]. It concentrates on offering organizations a comprehensive understanding of their spending patterns, supplier performance, and overall procurement efficiency by offering insights into past procurement activities [22]. For example, descriptive analytics can be employed to produce reports on the number of purchase orders processed, monthly expenditure, and supplier delivery times. An organization implements descriptive analytics to evaluate its procurement expenditures over the previous year. The company determines that a substantial portion of its budget is allocated to a specific category by organizing expenditures by department, supplier, and product category [23]. This realization necessitates an examination of supplier contracts and negotiations to optimize pricing. Another example is a company that monitors supplier performance metrics, including on-time delivery rates and defect rates [24]. Descriptive analytics assists in the identification of suppliers that consistently adhere to quality and delivery standards, as well as those that necessitate enhancement [24].

Tools and Approaches

Tools for data gathering, data mining, and reporting are essential to descriptive analytics. Standard instruments consist of Tableau, Power BI, and QlikView are examples of business intelligence (BI) tools that users may use to build interactive dashboards and visualizations. These tools let users examine data and discover new insights. To query databases and get pertinent data for analysis, one uses SQL, which stands for Structured Query Language. Data warehousing is the process of combining information from several sources into a single, comprehensible database for analysis.

8.2.2 Predictive Analytics

Predictive analytics is a way to predict what will happen in the future using statistical models and machine learning. It helps businesses to forecast demand, speculate possible supply chain breakdowns, and figure out price fluctuations [9, 24, 25]. Predictive analytics analyses past data to find patterns and helps organizations understand what might happen in the future [1, 26]. This helps procurement specialists make informed decisions in advance and reduce risks [27]. This helps keep the right amount of goods on hand and stops both stock-outs and extra inventory [28]. One more example of also using predictive analytics to find any problems in the supply chain. A company can plan for and reduce any risks that could affect its supply chain by looking at things like weather trends, global events, and the financial health of its suppliers [25].

Predictive Analytics Methods and Tools

It includes many statistical and machine learning techniques, like classification algorithms, regression, and time series analysis. Common tools include software like R and Python for statistics and libraries like sci-kit-learn and TensorFlow for building prediction models [29]. Machine learning systems, like IBM Watson and Google Cloud AI, let you do advanced machine learning for predictive analytics. Data visualization tools, such as Tableau and Power BI, let users show and understand predicted models clearly, which supports predictive analytics [28].

8.2.3 Prescriptive Analytics

Prescriptive analytics goes one step further by prescribing actions based on projected results. It helps with buying decisions by suggesting the best way to get the job done. For instance, prescriptive analytics can show the best order size, and seller choice, and buy time to save money and get more value [1, 30]. When you give suggestions for actions, prescriptive analytics goes one step further than just predicting insights. By using optimization algorithms and modeling methods, it figures out the best way for groups to reach their goals and makes suggestions based on that information. Such as a company uses predictive data to improve the way it buys things [31]. The method looks at a lot of factors, like how well suppliers do their jobs, how much they charge, and how long their delivery times are, to figure out the best order size, supplier choice, and order timing [32]. The goal of this method is to cut costs and increase value generally. It is also possible to use prescriptive analytics in contract management [32]. The system considers past contract performance data and market trends to suggest the best terms and conditions for new contracts that will ensure compliance and maximize benefits.

Tools and Methods
Linear programming, decision analysis, and Monte Carlo models are some of the advanced optimization and modeling methods used in prescriptive analytics. The most common instruments are. Software like Gurobi and IBM ILOG CPLEX is helpful when you need to solve hard programming problems. Simulation software, like AnyLogic and Arena, lets you act out different scenarios and look at what happens as a result [33]. AI systems, such as IBM Watson and Google Cloud AI, can help with predictive analytics because they are very good at making decisions and optimizing things.

8.2.4 Key Uses of Big Data in Procurement

Information from Big Data analytics can be used to manage suppliers by giving thorough information on their performance, risk profiles, and compliance [34]. A lot of different things, like quality, shipping times, and cost, can be used to help companies choose the best providers so they can work with. Supply chain decisions are based on the most up-to-date and correct data because source data is constantly being analyzed [35]. Cost-cutting ideas can be found by looking at buying spending data and noticing spending patterns. Spend analysis helps to streamline purchases, get better deals from sellers, and reduce spending that isn't planned [36].

Estimating Demand For purchase planning to go well, it's important to make accurate estimates of demand. Using past sales data, industry trends, and outside factors, Big Data analytics helps businesses guess what customers will want in the future [37]. In this way, inventory levels are optimized and stock-outs and excess merchandise are cut down. Controlling risks of analyzing large amounts of data could help find and lower risks in the supply chain. Researching data from a variety of sources, such as seller financial health, global events, and natural disasters, can help businesses figure out possible risks and make backup plans [38]. Supply chain data can be tracked in real-time, which lets problems be found quickly and fixed right away [39]. Managers of contracts must be good at their jobs to make sure that agreements are followed and that value is maximized [38]. Companies can use Big Data analytics to look at contract terms, make sure they are being followed, and find ways to renegotiate [33]. Keep an eye on how the deal is being carried out, handle extensions, and stay out of trouble by using this tool.

8.2.5 Advantages of Big Data in Procurement 4.0

Automatically collecting and analyzing data cuts down on the work that needs to be done by hand and speeds up buying tasks [40]. This leads to faster decisions, shorter processes for buying things, and better working efficiency. Cost Saving Companies can lower their buying costs by looking for ways to cut costs, choosing the best suppliers, and making better predictions of what customers will want. Being able to see spending trends and seller performance more clearly helps you get better deals and cut down on unnecessary costs. Better Transparency in Being able to track and watch buying processes in real-time makes the whole supply chain clearer [41]. This transparency makes sure that choices about buying are based on correct and up-to-date information, which lowers the risk of fraud and not following the rules.

Strategic decision-making for insights based on data helps buying workers make smart, strategic choices. Companies may be able to make better procurement plans that help them reach their goals if they understand market trends, how suppliers work, and how to measure internal success. Risk reduction analyzing Big Data may help find and reduce risks in the production chain. Companies can protect their brand and keep their supply going by taking care of planned delays and compliance issues ahead of time.

8.2.6 Challenges and Considerations

Reliable analytics require data that is accurate, full, and consistent. Integrating data from several sources, including ERP systems, supplier databases, and IoT devices, can be difficult, but it is required for thorough analysis. Protecting sensitive procurement data from cyber-attacks and maintaining compliance with data privacy standards are critical [35, 40]. Implementing strong security measures and data governance processes is critical for ensuring data integrity and confidentiality. Big Data analytics necessitates a professional staff with knowledge in data science, analytics, and procurement. Investing in training and development programs is essential for developing the necessary talents inside the organization [42]. Adopting a data-driven procurement approach necessitates major organizational transformation. Successful implementation requires effective change management, overcoming opposition, and cultivating a culture of data-driven decision-making [43].

8.2.7 Tools and Technologies Employed in Big Data Analytics for Procurement

An Overview of the Most Popular Big Data Tools and Platforms – Hadoop
Big Data analytics in Procurement 4.0 derives meaningful insights from big datasets using a mix of strong tools and technologies [44]. While Tableau provides easy visualization features, Hadoop and Spark have strong frameworks for distributed data storage and processing. Providing scalable, adaptable, and reasonably priced infrastructure for Big Data analytics depends critically on cloud computing and data lakes [19]. These technologies used together help companies to change their procurement systems, acquire major competitive benefits, and negotiate the complexity of the contemporary supply chain environment.

Hadoop:
Designed for distributed storage and processing of vast amounts of data using the MapReduce programming style, Apache Hadoop is an open-source framework Over hundreds of computers, this very scalable system can manage petabytes of data [45]. Big Data analytics make extensive use of Hadoop because of its capacity to reasonably store and analyze vast amounts of data economically. Its open-source character and great community support help explain why companies trying to apply scalable Big Data solutions choose it. The core parts of Hadoop are

i. The main storage system used in Hadoop is the distributed file system or HDFS. Copying data blocks across many nodes, saves data across several computers in a cluster, therefore guaranteeing fault tolerance and data redundancy. This architecture lets HDFS gracefully manage hardware failures, thereby providing a dependable storage option for big volumes [46].
ii. MapReduce is a programming methodology that divides massive data sets into smaller pieces concurrently over many cluster nodes, therefore enabling parallel processing of these sets [46]. Whereas the Reduce function compiles the output, the Map function organizes and filters data. MapReduce lets one effectively process data and streamlines the creation of distributed apps.
iii. YARN, often known as Yet Another Resource Negotiator oversees and distributes system resources across many Hadoop cluster-running applications. It separates data processing

from resource management such that many processing architectures—including Apache Spark and Apache Flink—run on Hadoop [36, 47].

iv. Libraries and tools supporting the other Hadoop components constitute Hadoop Common. It offers basic needs such as data serialization, configuration management, and authentication.

Spark

Apache Spark is a freely available analytics engine that is specifically built for analyzing big amounts of data. Spark offers an in-memory computing architecture, in contrast to Hadoop's MapReduce, which enhances the performance of data processing jobs by storing data in memory instead of saving intermediate results to disc [48]. Spark is very versatile and performs exceptionally well, making it the top option for Big Data analytics, especially for applications that need real-time processing and intricate data pipelines.

Key Components of Spark Core

Spark Core serves as the essential building block of the Spark framework. It provides key functionalities such as job scheduling, memory management, fault recovery, and integration with storage systems [49]. Furthermore, it includes the Resilient Distributed Dataset (RDD) abstraction, which supports fault-tolerant distributed data processing. Spark SQL serves as a valuable tool for the processing of structured data through the utilization of SQL queries. Spark SQL effectively collaborates with the core Spark API, allowing users to perform SQL queries alongside complex analytics and machine learning tasks.

The System can efficiently manage a variety of data, like JSON, Parquet, and Hive tables. Spark streaming assists in real-time data processing and handles data streams across various sources like Apache Kafka, Flume, and Amazon Kinesis [16]. It divides these data streams into small fragments and processes them using the Spark engine for faster analysis and better decision-making [50]. Machine Learning Library (MLlib) within Spark that provides scalable algorithms for tasks like classification, clustering, multiple regression, and collaborative filtering. Also, it facilitates users to create and implement machine learning models without difficulty. GraphX is a valuable part of the system that powers graph processing and data analytics [51]. It allows users to execute calculations on graphs and provides an API to create, modify and analyze graphical data structures [52].

Tableau

Tableau is a powerful tool for data visualization that allows users to explore, analyze, and present data effectively [51]. Its user-friendly interface and comprehensive visualization features make it prevalent in data analytics and business intelligence [53]. Tableau transforms complex data into clear and actionable insights through attractive visuals. The very purpose of Big Data analytics is to provide an easy and accessible way to investigate and understand large amounts of information.

Tableau presents a variety of important features, which include:

Tableau connects to a wide variety of data sources, including spreadsheets, databases, cloud services, and significant Big Data platforms like Spark and Hadoop [54]. This allows users to access and analyze data effortlessly and without a complicated integration process. With the help of Tableau, users can create interactive and collaborative dashboards that permit dynamic data analysis. Primarily the dashboards allow users to explore how to access specific information and visualize patterns and future trends [50, 52]. Based on the latest information, Tableau supports real-time data processing to enable timely decisions. Tableau includes advanced analytical features like trend analysis, forecasting, and statistical data modeling, where users get an opportunity to perform complex calculations and create custom metrics to gain deeper insights. Since it is designed with a user-friendly interface and drag-and-drop functionality, creating a way for people with different levels of technical skills [55]. However, the ease-of-use nature of Tableau helps organizations to adopt data-driven decision-making in a way more possible and effective.

8.2.8 Role of Cloud Computing and Data Lakes in Big Data Analytics

Cloud computing has shifted how businesses store, process and analyze voluminous data [56]. It provides an infrastructure to support Big Data analytics with advantages for scalability, agility and cost savings [57]. The adaptability, scalability, and economic efficiency of cloud computing render it an optimal platform for doing Big Data analytics [58]. Today, most organizations do advanced data analysis with ease of storing and analyzing data than it does in traditional setups. Platforms like Amazon Web Services (AWS), Microsoft Azure, and Google Cloud offer versatile resources that can be modified to fluctuating demands [59], allowing businesses to coordinate varying data volumes with less upfront costs. It uses a pay-as-you-go model to manage costs better as organizations can pay only for the used resources. It also facilitates quick access to data and analytics tools for collaboration and facilitates to work from remotely [60]. Cloud vendors offer varied services for Big Data analytics to simply the use of data management tools, such as AWS Elastic MapReduce, Azure HDInsight, and Google BigQuery. Besides, these cloud vendors invest in strong security and compliance measures to protect data from unauthorized access and assure compliance with industry standards.

8.2.9 Data Lake

A data lake is a unified storage system that permits companies to store both organized and unstructured data without capacity limits [61]. Data lake plays a very important role in Big Data analytics and provides a versatile and scalable method to store extensive datasets [62]. Figure 8.5 shows how data lakes help in storing and evaluating the data on a wide scale.

In contrast to traditional databases, data lakes use a schema-on-read approach [62]. In this mode the data is kept in its original and raw form and organized to maintain different data formats and enable organizations to adapt to changing analytical requirements.

I. Data lakes possess the capacity to collect and manage data from various sources such as transactional systems, social media platforms, Sensor devices and more. This signifies all

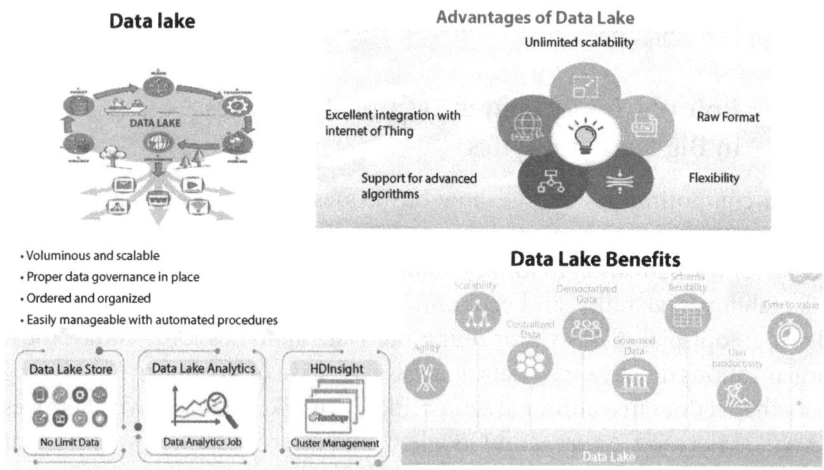

Figure 8.5 Overall view of data lake (Source: author's own).

the relevant data is available for data analysis without regard to origin or format [63].

II. Scalability refers to data lakes designed for horizontal expansion to handle rising volumes of data without compromising on its performance. This is crucial for handling large datasets which is common in Big Data analytics [64, 65].

III. Data lakes offer cost-advantage storage solutions, including cloud object storage, to reduce the costs associated with storing large data [66]. Data lakes attract organizations seeking to manage their data storage expenses because of their cost efficiency.

IV. Data lakes facilitate integration with various analytics and machine learning technologies, enabling organizations to conduct advanced studies of their data. Prominent data lake systems, like AWS Lake Formation, Azure Data Lake, and Google Cloud Storage, provide seamless integration with their respective cloud platforms and analytical applications [67–70].

8.3 Success Factors for Implementing Big Data in Procurement

Strategic alignment is the process of ensuring that an organization's goals and objectives are in line with its overall strategy and direction. To accomplish efficient Big Data integration in procurement, these efforts must align with the organization's overarching business objectives. This strategic relationship ensures that the use of Big Data directly contributes to the achievement of critical business goals, such as cost reduction, increased efficiency, and better decision-making [71]. To be effective, this alignment must be based on a clear and comprehensive strategic vision that integrates Big Data activities with overall organizational goals. Leadership is essential in this process because it is responsible for creating the vision and ensuring that all stakeholders understand the importance of Big Data in business success. Leaders are expected to advocate data-driven programs and offer basic resources to create a culture that values data-based strategic decisions. In most of organizations, leaders have proved how strategic alignment enhances efforts of bid data adoption. As a case in point, a global manufacturing company fostered its supply chain efficiency by integrating Big Data activities, aiming for significant cost reduction and better supplier relationships. In the same fashion, retail companies used Big Data analytics to align their procurement strategy with customer demand patterns, managing inventory and reducing stockouts. These few examples highlight the importance of strategic alignment in employing Big Data to achieve remarkable benefits in procurement.

8.3.1 Data Quality and Governance

Certifying high data quality is vital for successful Big Data initiatives in procurement. Poor data quality weakens analytics efforts and results in poor decisions. Key challenges in maintaining data quality include managing various data sources, processing large amounts of data, and timely updates. To ascertain optimal data quality, organizations should implement strong data integration processes, use automated tools to identify and fix errors and define clear data ownership. Equally, Data governance is also crucial; it entails creating rules and standards for managing data effectively [56, 72]. This includes defining the roles of data stewards, setting data quality requirements, and establishing procedures for accessing and sharing data. For example, companies can conduct regular audits to check data accuracy, use standardized data entry formats, and encrypt sensitive procurement data. These efforts help maintain data quality and reliability, guaranteeing that purchasing decisions are based on reliable information, ultimately maximizing the benefits of Big Data analytics.

8.3.2 Technical Infrastructure

To succeed in procurement through Big Data demands to maintain high data quality. Erroneous, inconsistent, or unreliable data can lead to poor decisions and reduce the importance of analytics. Key issues in ensuring data quality include managing various data sources, processing large datasets, and certifying timely updates [73]. Optimal solutions for data cleansing, validation, and management encompass implementing strong data integration processes, using automated tools to find and fix errors, and establishing clear data ownership roles. Data governance is also essential and crucial, it sets the rules, methods, and standards for managing data assets, ensuring accuracy, confidentiality, and proper use of data [74]. The process includes creating a governance framework that describes the roles of data stewards, establishes data quality requirements, and specifies procedures for data sharing [75]. For example, companies can organize regular audits to check data accuracy, use standardized data entry formats, and encrypt sensitive procurement information. These efforts help maintain data quality and reliability, affirming procurement decisions are based on reliable information, which maximizes the advantage of Big Data analytics [72].

8.3.3 Skilled Workforce

A skilled workforce is the most significant factor for the successful implementation of data analytics in procurement [76]. However, it ensures that insights gained from large datasets are useful in making decisions and enhancing operational performance. It is essential to have a skilled workforce who has expertise in statistical data analysis, and data mining in platforms like Hadoop, Spark, and Tableau. In the data analytics process, people named data scientists, analysts, and IT Specialists play an important role in developing data models and algorithms to investigate trends and patterns. Whereas the IT manager coordinates the technical infrastructure and data security [77, 78]. Training and development programs are pivotal in equipping procurement professionals with the necessary skills. Organizations offer training opportunities in the subject of data analytics, including courses, certifications such as Certified Analytics Professional (CAP), and workshops on tools and methodologies. Life-long learning is indispensable in this dynamic field, ensuring business professionals stay updated on the best practices to capitalize on the benefits of Big Data in procurement [79].

8.3.4 Change Management

Implementing Big Data in a business demands a transparent and well-planned strategy to ensure smooth integration with the present system [80]. A well-structured change management strategy is important for overcoming challenges and maximizing the benefits of Big Data initiatives in procurement. The action plan should focus on the communication of objectives and benefits, a plan for comprehensive training to enhance skills, and strong engagement with stakeholders to build support and address concerns. Known reasons for apprehension are that change breeds fear of the unknown, lack of expertise, and perceived threats to job security [81, 82]. To overcome this resistance, organizations should nurture an open and collaborative culture, acknowledge the real benefits through trial programs, and address issues through honest discussions and feedback. Businesses proactively managing change and addressing bottlenecks, were successfully integrate Big Data into their procurement processes and foster decision-making capabilities [83].

8.4 Solutions for Overcoming Challenges

8.4.1 Data Integration

Integrating Big Data in procurement maximizes benefits as well as faces several challenges, including data quality and management, technical infrastructure, shortage of skilled workforce, and resistance to change [80]. To address these issues, companies devise strategies and implement strong data cleansing and validation processes, invest in scalable hardware and cloud computing solutions for agile resources, and develop training programs to upskill data analytics skills among procurement staff in-charge [81, 82, 84]. Additionally, it's critical to communicate the benefits of Big Data initiatives fairly and engage stakeholders while providing ongoing support. By overcoming these challenges, organizations can fully realize the advantages of Big Data, leading to improved efficiency, cost savings, and better decision-making [83].

8.4.2 Data Security and Privacy

Data security is primarily important in Big Data analytics as it shields sensitive information and upholds organizational trust. Fundamental security measures include encryption to secure data during transmission and storage, along with access control to limit access to authorized individuals. To mitigate general risks like data breaches and cyberattacks, organizations should implement strong firewalls, and intrusion detection systems, and conduct regular security audits. Adherence to Compliance with data privacy regulations, such as the GDPR and CCPA, is also mandatory, as these laws impose strict requirements on the handling of personal data. Organizations must ensure transparency, seek approval from individuals whose data is collected, and implement measures to prevent unauthorized access. Abiding to these standards not only states legal compliance but also builds trust among stakeholders.

8.4.3 Cost Management

Overseeing the costs of implementing Big Data in procurement involves identifying and controlling several expense categories, on infrastructure, software, and labor costs. Infrastructure costs include the purchase and maintenance of hardware and cloud services which are needed for data storage and processing. Data platforms and analytics tools like Hadoop and Tableau amount to software costs. Also, it incurs training costs. to further reduce expenses, organizations are inclined to use cloud computing to lower initial investments and leverage open-source software free of cost. Conducting a Return on Investment (ROI) analysis is pivotal in understanding the financial impact of strategic initiatives like Big Data. Generally, the advantage of Big Data analytics in procurement covers cost reduction, improved supplier relationships and enhanced capabilities towards decision-making. On implementing the Big Data projects organizations should consider cost cautious and financial success of projects.

8.4.4 Scalability

Establishing the scalability of Big Data solutions is important for organizations to handle larger data volumes and complex analyses without sacrificing current performance. Hadoop and Spark are effective scalable architectures used to distribute processing tasks among diverse nodes and make it simple to handle large datasets. AWS and Microsoft Azure offer flexible storage and processing features that can adapt to fluctuating demands. Scalability allows organizations to explore extensive transactional datasets weigh the supplier benefits and spot market patterns.

For instance, a few examples highlight the importance of Big Data solutions in procurement. A global retailer improved its procurement analytics by using a cloud-based data lake that integrated data from various sources and achieved optimal inventory. Additionally, a manufacturing company used Hadoop and Spark to process supplier data in real time, upgrading supplier selection and risk mitigation.

Actionable Steps for Implementing Big Data Solutions in Procurement
For effective integration of Big Data technologies into the present procurement system, organizations should adopt a scientific approach that addresses both technological and organizational requirements [34]. A practical framework for integration includes examination of current processes, development of a clear and effective strategy, selection of advanced and appropriate technologies, embracing data management protocols, integration with current systems, Staff training, and ongoing monitoring and evaluation. Figure 8.6 illustrates a framework that helps how organizations can successfully implement Big Data in procurement.

Actionable Steps for Implementing Big Data Solutions in Procurement

Invest in Scalable Technology Infrastructure:
Organizations must first establish a robust technology infrastructure capable of handling large datasets. This includes adopting cloud-based solutions such as Amazon Web Services (AWS) or Microsoft Azure, which offer the flexibility to scale resources as data volumes grow. Implementing distributed computing frameworks like Hadoop and Spark can ensure efficient data storage and processing across multiple sources, enabling seamless integration of various procurement-related datasets.

Focus on Data Governance and Quality: Successful Big Data projects rely on high-quality, consistent data. Organizations should implement clear data governance policies to standardize data entry processes and ensure the accuracy and consistency of procurement data. Regular data validation checks should be performed, and roles such as data stewards should be created to oversee data management and governance.

Develop Predictive and Prescriptive Analytics Capabilities: Once the data infrastructure is in place, organizations should begin using predictive analytics to forecast demand, identify potential supply chain disruptions, and optimize procurement schedules. Prescriptive analytics should be leveraged to provide actionable recommendations for supplier selection, order quantities, and timing. Business intelligence tools such as Tableau or Power BI can visualize data insights, making it easier for procurement teams to interpret and act on the results.

Build a Skilled Workforce: Procurement teams must be equipped with the necessary skills to handle Big Data technologies. This includes hiring or upskilling employees in data science, machine learning, and data visualization. Organizations should invest in training programs and certifications for procurement professionals to develop skills in using analytics tools and interpreting data-driven insights.

Implement change management strategies to integrate: Big Data into procurement, addressing resistance and promoting clear communication, stakeholder engagement, continuous training, and support for adoption across procurement teams.

Figure 8.6 Practical measures for implementing Big Data solutions (Source: author's own).

8.5 Case Studies

8.5.1 Case Study 1: Retail Industry in the Indian Sector

Utilizing Big Data in Procurement

The retail sector is rapidly augmenting Big Data to improve operational performance and procurement efficiency in India and beyond. This sector implemented a vast Big Data analytics solution to manage procurement issues by combining data from diverse sources, including supplier information, sales forecast, and market trends, into a centralized secured repository. To process this data, advanced analytical methods were used to process and provide valuable insights for making purchase decisions. Implementation challenges like data quality, integration with legacy systems and skills demanded from staff. To fix these challenges, organizations relentlessly invested in data cleansing, and middleware integration and conducted specialized training for IT and procurement personnel. The organization enhanced its ability to predict demand by leveraging real-time sales data, analyzing market trends, and understanding customer preferences. Customer satisfaction was greatly increased as a consequence of the 15% inventory cost reduction, increased product availability, and 20% decrease in stockout incidents.

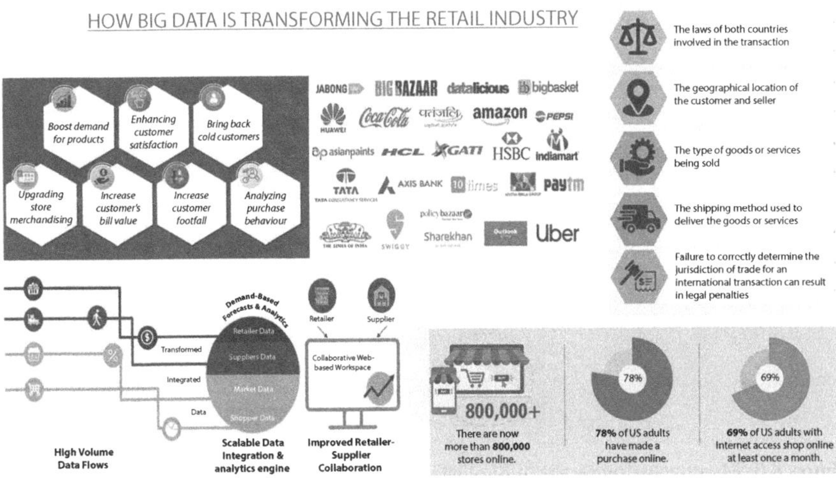

Figure 8.7 Retail industry in the Indian sector (Source: author's own).

Contributing Factors to Success and the Subsequent Results

The essential elements that played a pivotal role in the success of this Big Data deployment included strong leadership backing, alignment with business goals, and a focused commitment to data quality and governance. The leadership team was indispensable in driving the implementation forward, and ensuring the objective of the Big Data mission was aligned with the organization's vision. The priority on data governance and data quality is entitled utilization of accurate, transparent, and consistent, data for analysis, leading to effective decision-making. Predominantly retail chains implemented Big Data solutions when compared to other industries. Figure 8.7 depicts the illustration on how Big data analytics impact the Indian retail sector. On scaling up the Big Data analytics solutions, every firm will benefit and become more robust among the competitors.

8.5.2 Case Study 2: Manufacturing Sector

A multinational manufacturing company leveraged Big Data technologies to enhance its operational efficiency and address procurement challenges. The centralized data sources, including supplier performance metrics, market insights, and production information, into a Big Data platform built on Hadoop and Spark. Using advanced data analysis techniques and artificial intelligence algorithms, the company aims for superior supplier selection, market demand forecasting, and risk assessment. Figure 8.8 presents the role of Big data and its effect on procurement in manufacturing sector. During the implementation, they faced several limitations, such as integrating data

Figure 8.8 Manufacturing sector of Big Data Procurement (Source: author's own).

from vast sources, ensuring data accuracy, and overcoming resistance from stakeholders who were accustomed to traditional procurement practices. To resolve these issues, the company employed advanced data integration technologies and built strict data governance regulations to improve high data quality. They also created vast training programs to enhance staff capabilities and reinforced a corporate culture that valued data-driven decision-making, supported by open communication and collaboration with stakeholders.

The key learnings from this implementation figure the need for a clear strategic vision and strong leadership, along with investment in agile technology with a focus on data quality and governance. On future implementation projects, it's important to engage all related stakeholders early to gain their support, regularly improve data governance policies, and prioritize upskilling to build a skilled workforce that can effortlessly use Big Data insights. These efforts led the manufacturing company to identify significant improvements in procurement efficiency, cost savings, and supplier performance, enhancing its competitive advantage in the market.

8.5.3 Case Study 3: Healthcare Industry in India

The healthcare industries implemented advanced data integration technologies, established strict data security protocols in reconciliation with healthcare regulations, and conducted training sessions to educate staff about the new system. To embrace the successful implementation, the concerned leadership should possess strong will and formulate effective steps to align with hospital operational objectives and should focus on

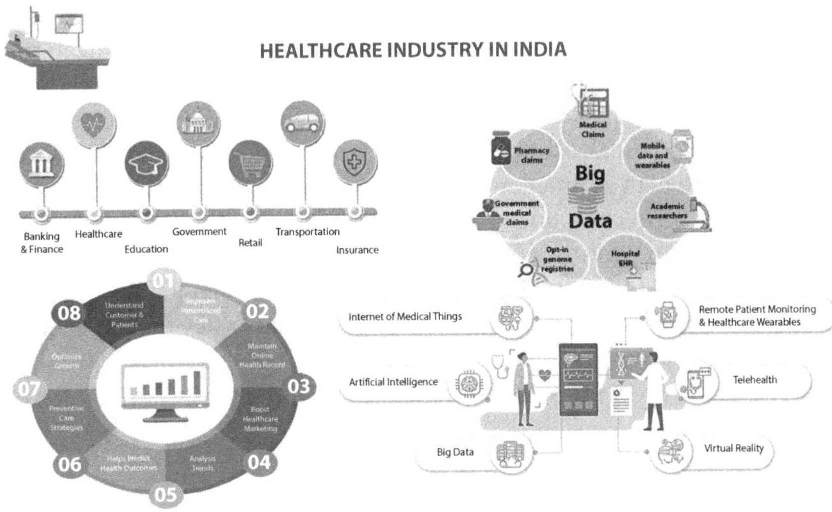

Figure 8.9 Healthcare industry in India (Source: author's own).

commitment to data privacy and quality. As a mark of efforts undertaken, the hospital network resulted in several advantages such as improved supplier negotiations, optimal management of inventory and reduced procurement costs. The hospital can affirm the adequacy of essential supplies through the implementation of strategic inventory management measures, contingent upon its ability to predict market demands.

The role of Big Data in the Indian hospital industry is shown in Figure 8.9, data integration provides enhanced patient care and improved operational efficiency. A large hospital network in India had procurement difficulties that affected patient care owing to inefficient and error-laden manual procedures, resulting in shortages of critical medical supplies. To resolve this issue, the hospital employed Big Data analytics, amalgamating data from electronic health records, supplier databases, and inventory management systems. Predictive analytics projected supply demand, whereas prescriptive analytics advised ideal procurement volumes and providers. The hospital saw a 30% reduction in stockouts, a 40% drop in procurement cycle times, and enhanced patient outcomes due to the prompt availability of vital supplies.

Case Study 4: Manufacturing: Reducing Downtime with Predictive Maintenance

An Indian industrial machinery company improved its spare part procurement strategy and decreased equipment downtime by utilizing Big Data analytics. The business incorporated Internet of Things (IoT) sensors into its equipment to gather data on temperature, wear-and-tear indications, and machine performance in real time. The Big Data analytics platform that received the IoT data forecasted when particular pieces of the machinery were likely to break using predictive analytics. This made it possible for the business to plan maintenance before equipment failures happened and to buy replacement components ahead of time. The findings of this case are 20% less downtime for the equipment. 15% reduction in the cost of emergency procurement. longer lifespan of machinery, which lowers the need for expensive replacements. This case study demonstrates the application of Big Data to predictive maintenance as well as procurement optimization, which lowers operating costs and boosts productivity.

8.6 Future Trends in Big Data and Procurement 4.0

8.6.1 Emerging Technologies

Procurement using Artificial Intelligence, ML, IoT, and Blockchain
Innovative technologies such as Blockchain, the Internet of Things (IoT), Artificial Intelligence (AI), and Machine Learning (ML) possess the capacity to transform the procurement landscape in substantial ways. The integration of AI and ML has the potential to significantly enhance procurement processes through the automation of routine tasks, trend forecasting, and the provision of actionable insights. AI-powered chatbots are capable of addressing enquiries from suppliers, while machine learning algorithms can analyze vast amounts of data to identify patterns that assist in demand

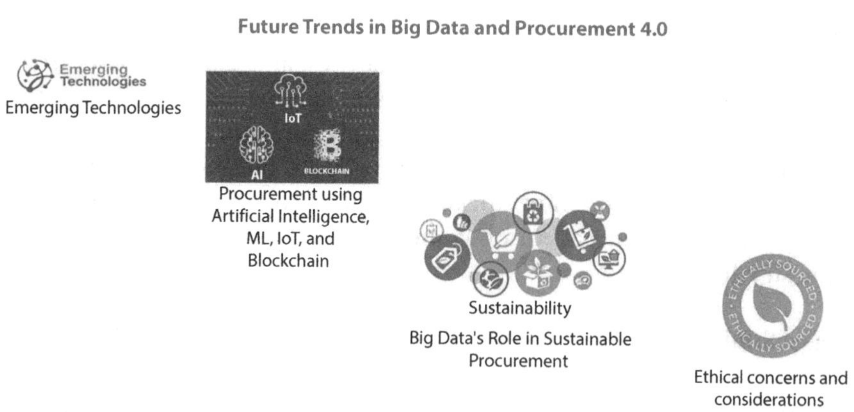

Figure 8.10 Future trends in Big Data and Procurement 4.0.

forecasting and stock optimization. The Internet of Things (IoT) improves the precision of inventory management and enables prompt maintenance by linking various devices and systems. This facilitates cue monitoring of deliverables and examines the equipment. The implementation of permanent transaction records *via* blockchain technology enhances security and transparency. This quickens the supplier verification procedure, minimizes the risk of fraud, and ensures compliance, as shown in Figure 8.10.

Potential Effects on Procurement Procedures

Utilizing innovative technologies can lead to a more effective procurement process. These technologies help in the selection of suppliers based on performance data and improve supply chain visibility *via* IoT. In turn, it helps managers to make decisions based on real-time data and thereby reduces delivery delays and defectives. Blockchain technology empowers organizations by providing data security and transparency and creates trust among stakeholders. At the beginning of the manufacturing itself, this technology helps to predict the quality of raw materials supplied. The fast-evolving changes in technology will lead to an extensive application in procurement and innovation in the supply chain.

8.6.2 Sustainability and Ethical Considerations

Big Data's Role in Sustainable Procurement

The strategic use of Big Data significantly contributes to the enhancement of sustainable procurement practices through data-driven decision-making. Analyzing real-time data on supplier performance, environmental impacts, and resource usage leverages organizations to identify and establish partnerships with suppliers that follow sustainable and ethical practices [85]. Extensive data analysis escalates the tracking of carbon footprints in supply chains, allowing companies to choose suppliers with zero carbon emissions and sustainable practices. The use of extensive data sets can enhance resource efficiency, minimize waste, and improve supply chain transparency, thereby strengthening sustainability practices.

Ethical Issues and Factors

The extensive use of large datasets in procurement conceptualizes further ethical concerns, data privacy, biases in data analysis, and data transparency. Protecting critical supplier and their data is mandatory, along with adherence to privacy regulations and implementation of data security protocols. Eliminating biases in data collection and analysis is vital for fair decision-making. In addressing ethical challenges the implementation of robust data governance frameworks, the assurance of transparency in data practices, and the conduct of regular audits and assessments of data processes are essential to maintain ethical standards [2, 86, 87]. Organizations can promote trust and integrity in their procurement system by fairly addressing ethical issues and utilizing the advantage of Big Data solutions.

8.7 A Critical Analysis of Big Data and Procurement Trends and Challenges

Big Data has great potential to advance procurement, but it also presents opportunities and challenges. The major advantage of adopting Big Data is improved decision-making through predictive and prescriptive analytics [4]. Predictive analytics enables procurement managers to forecast demand better, identify supply chain issues, and manage inventory, which can lower costs. However, the quality of data determines the effectiveness of predictions [88]. Prescriptive analytics provides actionable recommendations for decisions like supplier selection and contract negotiations, however, these complex and large models can be difficult to understand without a skilled workforce. Similarly, advanced data analytics permits real-time monitoring of supplier performance and risks, and helps procurement teams to overcome the issues and ensure smooth relationships with suppliers [89]. In case there is a weak connection between internal and external systems, it results in more bottlenecks and inefficient decision-making.

8.7.1 Difficulties Applying Big Data in Purchasing

(i) Upholding Big Data in procurement creates opportunities for valuable decision-making and operational efficiency, but comes with unique challenges, specifically in quality, consistency, and data integration. Organizations must adopt actionable strategies like investing in comprehensive data integration solutions, data cleansing and recurrent data validation and provide staff training on data governance [90]. Additionally, deploying data monitoring tools to assure ongoing data quality can help mitigate risks associated with poor-quality data. By executing these strategies, organizations can enhance their capacity [91].

(ii) Establishing Big Data technology in procurement often requires a substantial cultural shift within teams. Traditional methods rely heavily on smooth relationships and expertise, which can make the process manual and subjective. However, to effectively employ Big Data analytics, team members need to drive a data-driven mindset [92]. This transition can create resistance, as many staff may choose their used ways of working. Therefore, training for procurement teams should focus not only on how to use new technologies but also on the necessity of making data-based decisions. It is essential to priorities change management techniques, emphasizing the long-term benefits of Big Data technology while also tackling concerns related to job displacement and the intricacies of technology.

(iii) Expense of Skill Deficiencies and Technological Advancements Implementing Big Data in procurement presents significant financial challenges, especially for small and medium-sized enterprises. Organizations must allocate resources not only for acquiring and maintaining essential technology and software but also for hiring or training personnel with the necessary data science and analytics skills [93]. In specific fields where expertise is limited, the demand for particular skills—such as programming in languages like Python or R and utilizing platforms like Hadoop and Spark—creates a talent gap that can be difficult to bridge. To address the issues of attracting and retaining skilled personnel for working Big Data in procurement, organizations enormously invest in training and skilling their workforce. To tap new skills businesses have collaborated with research and academic institutions to broaden their recruitment efforts. Creating user-friendly data analytics tools eases data access during knowledge transfer between consultants and current procurement staff. Beyond this, organizations must encourage collaboration between data specialists and procurement professionals. To ascertain return on investment, businesses can conduct a cost-benefit analysis to arrive at clarity ploughback initiatives, ensuring the organization's effectiveness.

(iv) As firms increasingly rely on data analytics in procurement, legal and ethical considerations have become more vital. Using Big Data to audit supplier activities increases concerns about data privacy and security, especially when dealing with supplier information. Regarding, compliance with data protection regulations like GDPR and CCPA is mandatory, as violations can lead to high penalties. As mentioned by [91] biases and ethical issues in Big Data lead to unfair practices in supply chains. To ensure unbiases, the procurement teams must be aware of occurrence of biases and ensure transparent and ethically sound practices.

(v) Integrating IoT data with procurement systems and making sure real-time insights can be acted upon fast enough to eliminate expensive delays is a difficulty here. On the other hand, industries like healthcare have extra legal obligations regarding data privacy, particularly regarding patient-related data processing during procurement choices [94]. While retail sectors gain from Big Data's capacity to examine customer demand trends and streamline supply chains, they must deal with seasonality and fast-changing consumer tastes, which need extremely flexible analytics solutions.

(vi) Big Data's Prospect in Procurement Notwithstanding these obstacles, Big Data's future in procurement looks bright. Data-driven procurement should become more open and effective as artificial intelligence, machine learning, and blockchain technologies find wider acceptance. Companies that effectively handle data quality, integration, talent shortages, and ethical issues stand to have a major competitive advantage in the worldwide market [95]. In essence, companies must negotiate a complicated terrain of technological, organizational, and ethical issues to fully reap the advantages even if Big Data has great possibilities for enhancing procurement procedures. Procurement teams may change their processes and fully utilize Big Data by closely examining these patterns and confronting major issues head-on.

8.8 Adopting Big Data in Procurement: How to Deal with Key Problems

Despite the considerable advantages of Big Data in procurement, organizations encounter several obstacles to its deployment. These difficulties must be comprehensively addressed to facilitate the efficient implementation of Big Data technology shown in Table 8.1.

Table 8.1 Adopting Big Data in procurement: how to deal with key problems.

Key challenges	Addressed the effective adoption of Big Data technologies	Solution
Cost of Implementation	Small and medium-sized businesses (SMEs) sustain the Big Data solutions, there are several ways that they can use them. First, they can explore Hadoop a free open-source option. Using pay-as-you-go cloud services SMEs were allowed to use flexible pricing and cut down on upfront costs. SMEs can partner with tech companies attain to data tools and expertise at affordable prices. On adopting a phased approach, they can start with small projects, businesses reap returns before full implementation. However, looking into government incentives for tech adoption and access to data analytics to become competitive in the market.	Organizations can reduce their financial difficulties by using a staged strategy, commencing with small-scale initiatives. Furthermore, utilizing open-source solutions like Apache Spark may reduce software expenses, while cloud platforms provide scalable infrastructure without substantial capital outlay.

(Continued)

Table 8.1 Adopting Big Data in procurement: how to deal with key problems. (*Continued*)

Key challenges	Addressed the effective adoption of Big Data technologies	Solution
Data Privacy and Security	A key challenge is data privacy since it has sensitive information about suppliers. In such cases, aggregation and examination of data need to be executed diligently with the Big Data solutions. Adherence to data protection requirements enhances the safeguard mechanism of supplier and customer data.	Organizations should employ stringent data encryption, access control measures, and routine security audits to mitigate privacy risks. To mitigate data intrusion risk, organizations have to adhere to the data protection rules. Organizations have to invest in anonymization strategies to safeguard personally identifiable information (PII) while facilitating data analysis.
Integration of Diverse Data Sources	The hardship in automating procurement is consolidating the data for data analysis because the data is available across various systems like ERP, SRM, CRM, and other platforms. Poorly structured and inconsistent data results in poor decisions.	Businesses should buy software and data interaction tools that make it easy for different systems to talk to each other. Setting up a uniform data platform that brings together buying data from different sources will make sure that everything is consistent and correct. You can handle the complexity of unorganized data and make merging easier by using data lakes, which store raw data from many sources.

(*Continued*)

Table 8.1 Adopting Big Data in procurement: how to deal with key problems. (*Continued*)

Key challenges	Addressed the effective adoption of Big Data technologies	Solution
Organizational Resistance to Change	Reluctance and resistance to Big Data technology is common in a firm, especially in organizations with standard procurement practices. At times, workforces consider technologies like business automation would replace them and become potential threats in making decisions.	To address opposition, leaders need to clearly explain the long-term benefits of implementing Big Data, such as cost reduction, improved efficiency, and gaining a competitive edge. Involving employees in the implementation process, offering continuous training, and promoting a culture of innovation can help alleviate concerns and gain support from key stakeholders.
Lack of Skill	The inclusion of Big Data in procurement practices demands expert knowledge in data science, machine learning, and analytics, which are often scarce. But a recent challenge is procurement professionals who don't possess technical expertise were in responsible positions to analyze complex data models and make data-driven decisions.	Organizations should establish internal training programs and collaborate with educational institutions to cultivate a talent pipeline. Providing incentives like certifications and professional development opportunities might aid in retaining proficient staff. Outsourcing specific data analytics functions to external service providers may serve as a temporary solution while internal competencies are cultivated.

8.9 Discussion of this Chapter

Big Data has a significant effect on the procurement process among industries due to unique supply chain dynamics, legal compliance, and particular procurement needs. In the manufacturing sector, it helps with better demand forecasting, predictive maintenance, and maximizing global supplier performance. However, the integration of various data sources is complex. Similarly, in the retail sector, the exercise of vast extensive data analytics tools in forecasting demand and overseeing dynamics of inventory empowers businesses to unify their procurement strategies with customer preferences. Whereas, in the healthcare sector, the utilization of large data sets is crucial for enabling compliance among suppliers, such as forecasting the demand for medical supplies, integrating procurement data with patient management systems and adherence to regulations. Simultaneously, the public sector explores Big Data solutions *via* transparency and cost-effectiveness; however, budget constraints and a slow adoption rate hinder the continuous process. By customizing the bid data implementation approach, organizations can foster efficiency and compliance with industry-specific challenges.

8.10 Future Research

Research directions are important for understanding and nurturing the benefits of Big Data solutions in procurement processes. Future research should emphasize specific industries, like energy, agriculture, and logistics, to better understand the challenges and opportunities that Big Data presents in these areas, beyond just manufacturing, retail, and healthcare. However, organizations need to look at how artificial intelligence (AI), ML, and data analytics can be integrated into procurement processes. This addresses ethical issues and enables us to make effective decisions. The impact studies could shed light on Big Data use and provide deep insights into how it causes procurement and supply chain resilience over the period. Similarly, exploring industry-specific data access and sharing could improve supplier performance and increase transparency in the supply chain. However, we must address the arising ethical concerns related to Big Data bias and ensure fairness in procurement algorithms to make responsible decisions.

8.11 Conclusion

The research described here have shown the revolutionary potential of massive data in procurement, showing its diverse applications in the public sector, industry, retail, and healthcare. The results that are significant highlight the critical role that predictive and prescriptive analytics play in improving decision-making, optimizing relationships with suppliers, and reducing risks. In addition to addressing typical difficulties such as expensive implementation costs, talent shortages, and opposition to exchange, the document places an emphasis on the significance of facts pleasant and integration. Considerations of an ethical and legal nature, primarily concerning the privacy and preservation of data, are of utmost importance in fields such as healthcare and the government, which need the establishment of resilient governance structures. Even though Big Data has a significant potential to enhance procurement strategies, for businesses to fully realize this potential, they need to rigorously design their methods to meet the specific requirements of their sector and make investments that are suitable in both infrastructure and information. In the future, data-driven strategies are going to become more important in the procurement process. Businesses who are able to successfully manage these issues will find themselves in a strong position to establish a competitive position in a virtual world that is rapidly developing.

References

1. Deshpande, P.S., Sharma, S.C., Peddoju, S.K., Deshpande, P.S., Sharma, S.C., Peddoju, S.K., Predictive and prescriptive analytics in big-data era, in: *Secur. Data Storage Asp. Cloud Comput.*, pp. 71–81, 2019.
2. Regan, P.M. and Jesse, J., Ethical challenges of edtech, big data and personalized learning: twenty-first century student sorting and tracking. *Ethics Inf. Technol.*, 21, 3, 167–179, 2019, doi: 10.1007/s10676-018-9492-2.
3. Witkowski, K., Internet of things, big data, industry 4.0–innovative solutions in logistics and supply chains management. *Procedia Eng.*, 182, 763–769, 2017.
4. Deka, G.C., Big Data and Prescriptive Analytics, in: *Management Association (Ed.), Big Data: Concepts, Methodologies, Tools, and Applications*, pp. 30–55, IGI Global Scientific Publishing, 2016. https://doi.org/10.4018/978-1-4666-9840-6.ch002.
5. Bienhaus, F. and Haddud, A., Procurement 4.0: factors influencing the digitisation of procurement and supply chains. *Bus. Process Manag. J.*, 24, 4, 965–984, 2018.

6. Arunachalam, D., Kumar, N., Kawalek, J.P., Understanding big data analytics capabilities in supply chain management: Unravelling the issues, challenges and implications for practice. *Transp. Res. Part E Logist. Transp. Rev.*, 114, 416–436, 2018.
7. Althabatah, A., Yaqot, M., Menezes, B., Kerbache, L., Transformative procurement trends: Integrating industry 4.0 technologies for enhanced procurement processes. *Logistics*, 7, 3, 63, 2023.
8. Nicoletti, B. and Nicoletti, B., Platforms for procurement 4.0, in: *Procure. 4.0 Fourth Ind. Revolut. Oppor. Challenges a Digit. World*, pp. 117–189, 2020.
9. Rane, S.B. and Narvel, Y.A.M., Leveraging the industry 4.0 technologies for improving agility of project procurement management processes. *Int. J. Syst. Assur. Eng. Manage.*, 12, 6, 1146–1172, 2021.
10. Nicoletti, B. and Nicoletti, B., Industry 4.0 and Procurement 4.0, in: *Procure. 4.0 Fourth Ind. Revolut. Oppor. Challenges a Digit. World*, pp. 5–51, 2020.
11. Bag, S., Wood, L.C., Mangla, S.K., Luthra, S., Procurement 4.0 and its implications on business process performance in a circular economy. *Resour. Conserv. Recycl.*, 152, 104502, 2020.
12. Lysons, K. and Farrington, B., *Procurement and Supply Chain Management*, Procurement and Supply Chain Management, Pearson UK, ISBN-13: 9781292317953 | Published 2020, 2020.
13. Jahani, N., Sepehri, A., Vandchali, H.R., Tirkolaee, E.B., Application of industry 4.0 in the procurement processes of supply chains: a systematic literature review. *Sustainability*, 13, 14, 7520, 2021.
14. Govindan, K., Jain, P., Singh, R.K., Mishra, R., Blockchain technology as a strategic weapon to bring procurement 4.0 truly alive: Literature review and future research agenda. *Transp. Res. Part E Logist. Transp. Rev.*, 181, 103352, 2024.
15. Bag, S. and Pretorius, J.H.C., Relationships between industry 4.0, sustainable manufacturing and circular economy: proposal of a research framework. *Int. J. Organ. Anal.*, 30, 4, 864–898, 2022.
16. Gupta, A. and Rahimi Ata, K., Data-Driven Hiring: Implementing AI and Assessing the Impact of AI on Recruitment Efficiency and Candidate Quality, 2024.
17. Luan, H., *et al.*, Challenges and Future Directions of Big Data and Artificial Intelligence in Education. *Front. Psychol.*, 11, October, 1–11, 2020, doi: 10.3389/fpsyg.2020.580820.
18. Nawaz, N., Arunachalam, H., Pathi, B.K., Gajenderan, V., The adoption of artificial intelligence in human resources management practices. *Int. J. Inf. Manage. Data Insights*, 4, 1, 100208, 2024.
19. O'Driscoll, A., Daugelaite, J., Sleator, R.D., 'Big data', Hadoop and cloud computing in genomics. *J. Biomed. Inform.*, 46, 5, 774–781, 2013.
20. Altundag, A. and Wynn, M., Advanced Analytics and Data Management in the Procurement Function: An Aviation Industry Case Study. *Electronics*, 13, 8, 1554, 2024.

21. Adebayo, V.I., Paul, P.O., Eyo-Udo, N.L., The role of data analysis and reporting in modern procurement: Enhancing decision-making and supplier management. *GSC Adv. Res. Rev.*, 20, 1, 88–97, 2024.
22. Daniel, B., Big Data and analytics in higher education: Opportunities and challenges. *Br. J. Educ. Technol.*, 46, 5, 904–920, 2015, doi: 10.1111/bjet.12230.
23. Kuo, T.-C., Peng, C.-Y., Kuo, C.-J., Smart support system of material procurement for waste reduction based on big data and predictive analytics. *Int. J. Logist. Res. Appl.*, 27, 2, 243–260, 2024.
24. Shatta, D.N., The Influence of Digital Technologies on Sustainable Supply Chain Performance in Public Procuring Entities: A Moderating Effect of Legal Frameworks. *Int. J. Soc. Sci. Res. Rev.*, 7, 6, 43–57, 2024.
25. Sahoo, S. and Jakhar, S.K., Industry 4.0 deployment for circular economy performance—Understanding the role of green procurement and remanufacturing activities. *Bus. Strateg. Environ.*, 33, 2, 1144–1160, 2024.
26. Langseth, M., Data-Driven Decision-Making in the Public Procurement System: The Case of Norway, 2024.
27. Raghul, S., Jeyakumar, G., Anbuudayasankar, S.P., Lee, T.-R., E-procurement optimization in supply chain: A dynamic approach using evolutionary algorithms. *Expert Syst. Appl.*, 255, 124823, 2024.
28. Ochuba, N.A., Usman, F.O., Okafor, E.S., Akinrinola, O., Amoo, O.O., Predictive analytics in the maintenance and reliability of satellite telecommunications infrastructure: a conceptual review of strategies and technological advancements. *Eng. Sci. Technol. J.*, 5, 3, 704–715, 2024.
29. Javaid, H.A., Improving Fraud Detection and Risk Assessment in Financial Service using Predictive Analytics and Data Mining. *Integr. J. Sci. Technol.*, 7, 1, 256, 2024.
30. Jayaram, D., Manrai, A.K., Manrai, L.A., Effective use of marketing technology in Eastern Europe: Web analytics, social media, customer analytics, digital campaigns and mobile applications. *J. Econ. Financ. Adm. Sci.*, 20, 39, 118–132, 2015, doi: 10.1016/j.jefas.2015.07.001.
31. Smyth, C., Dennehy, D., Fosso Wamba, S., Scott, M., Harfouche, A., Artificial intelligence and prescriptive analytics for supply chain resilience: a systematic literature review and research agenda. *Int. J. Prod. Res.*, 62, 23, 8537–8561, 2024. https://doi.org/10.1080/00207543.2024.2341415.
32. Weller, J., Migenda, N., Kühn, A., Dumitrescu, R., Prescriptive Analytics Data Canvas: Strategic Planning For Prescriptive Analytics In Smart Factories, ESSN 2701-6277, pp. 292–302, 2024.
33. Sariyer, G., Mangla, S.K., Chowdhury, S., Sozen, M.E., Kazancoglu, Y., Predictive and prescriptive analytics for ESG performance evaluation: A case of Fortune 500 companies. *J. Bus. Res.*, 181, 114742, 2024.
34. Demirbaga, Ü., Aujla, G.S., Jindal, A., Kalyon, O., Big Data Analytics, in: *Big Data Analytics: Theory, Techniques, Platforms, and Applications*, pp. 31–42, Springer, 2024. https://doi.org/10.1007/978-3-031-55639-5.

35. Jahin, M.A., Shovon, M.S.H., Shin, J., Ridoy, I.A., Mridha, M.F., Big Data—Supply Chain Management Framework for Forecasting: Data Preprocessing and Machine Learning Techniques. *Arch. Comput. Methods Eng.*, 14, 1–27, 2024.
36. Gopal, P.R.C., Rana, N.P., Krishna, T.V., Ramkumar, M., Impact of big data analytics on supply chain performance: an analysis of influencing factors. *Ann. Oper. Res.*, 333, 2, 769–797, 2024.
37. Wu, D.C., Zhong, S., Wu, J., Song, H., Tourism and hospitality forecasting with big data: a systematic review of the literature. *J. Hosp. Tour. Res.*, 10963480231223152, 49, 3, 615–634, 2024.
38. Birim, S., Kazancoglu, I., Mangla, S.K., Kahraman, A., Kazancoglu, Y., The derived demand for advertising expenses and implications on sustainability: a comparative study using deep learning and traditional machine learning methods. *Ann. Oper. Res.*, 339, 1, 131–161, 2024.
39. Hasan, R., Kamal, M.M., Daowd, A., Eldabi, T., Koliousis, I., Papadopoulos, T., Critical analysis of the impact of big data analytics on supply chain operations. *Prod. Plan. Control*, 35, 1, 46–70, 2024.
40. Benzidia, S., Bentahar, O., Husson, J., Makaoui, N., Big data analytics capability in healthcare operations and supply chain management: the role of green process innovation. *Ann. Oper. Res.*, 333, 2, 1077–1101, 2024.
41. Jagabathula, S., Mitrofanov, D., Vulcano, G., Demand estimation under uncertain consideration sets. *Oper. Res.*, 72, 1, 19–42, 2024.
42. Mushir, T. and Shafiq, M., Evaluating the Influence of Big Data Analytics and Blockchain Technology on the Performance of Humanitarian Supply Chain Management. *J. Techno Trainers*, 1, 1, 19–35, 2024.
43. Bandara, F., Jayawickrama, U., Subasinghage, M., Olan, F., Alamoudi, H., Alharthi, M., Enhancing ERP responsiveness through big data technologies: an empirical investigation. *Inf. Syst. Front.*, 26, 1, 251–275, 2024.
44. Oranefo, P.C., Eke, C., Egbunike, C.F., Factors Affecting Cloud ERP and Big Data Analytics Adoption in Nigeria: Perception of Accountants in Nigeria. *J. Compr. Bus. Adm. Res.*, 1, 3, 124–134, 2004. https://doi.org/10.47852/bonviewJCBAR42022284.
45. Anuradha, J., A brief introduction on Big Data 5Vs characteristics and Hadoop technology. *Procedia Comput. Sci.*, 48, 319–324, 2015.
46. Patel, A.B., Birla, M., Nair, U., Addressing big data problem using Hadoop and Map Reduce, in: *2012 Nirma University International Conference on Engineering (NUiCONE)*, pp. 1–5, 2012.
47. Zhao, Y., Development of big data assisted effective enterprise resource planning framework for smart human resource management. *PLoS One*, 19, 5, e0303297, 2024.
48. Ali El-Sayed Ali, H., Alham, M.H., Ibrahim, D.K., Big data resolving using Apache Spark for load forecasting and demand response in smart grid: a case study of Low Carbon London Project. *J. Big Data*, 11, 1, 59, 2024.

49. Gayakwad, M., Real-Time Clickstream Analytics with Apache. *J. Electr. Syst.*, 20, 2, 1600–1608, 2024.
50. Ponera, J.M. and Kyumana, V., Big data analytic tools usage among academic libraries in Tanzania. *Asian J. Inf. Sci. Technol.*, 14, 1, 18–23, 2024.
51. Tajiri, S., Takamatsu, K., Shiratori, N., Oishi, T., Mori, M., Murota, M., Integrating Tableau into a First-Year Information Literacy Course: A Practical Approach to Enhancing Data Science Education. *IIAI Lett. Inst. Res.*, ol.004, LIR317, 4, 2024.
52. Dighliya, B., Techniques and Tools for Big Data Analytics in the Tourism Sector, in: *Marketing and Big Data Analytics in Tourism and Events*, 17, pp. 145–161, IGI Global, 2024. DOI: 10.4018/979-8-3693-3310-5.ch009.
53. Mittal, M. and Raheja, N.G., *Data Visualization and Storytelling with Tableau*, CRC Press, 2024. https://doi.org/10.1201/9781003429593.
54. Mehrotra, P., *et al.*, Optimizing Walmart's Supply Chain from Strategy to Execution. *INFORMS J. Appl. Anal.*, 54, 1, 5–19, 2024.
55. Latane, P.C., Dhakate, P.A., Ubale, V.S., Mantri, D.S., Real-time Data Visualization for the IoT Application using Tableau Platform, in: *2024 International Conference on Emerging Smart Computing and Informatics (ESCI)*, pp. 1–5, 2024.
56. Rueda, L., Benitez, J., Braojos, J., From traditional education technologies to student satisfaction in Management education: A theory of the role of social media applications. *Inf. Manage.*, 54, 8, 1059–1071, 2017, doi: 10.1016/j.im.2017.06.002.
57. Kadam, A.J. and Akhade, K., A Review on Comparative Study of Popular Data Visualization Tools. *Alochana J.*, 13, 4, 532–538, 2024.
58. Fathima, F., Inparaj, R., Thuvarakan, D., Wickramarachchi, R., Fernando, I., Impact of AI-based predictive analytics on demand forecasting in ERP systems: A Systematic Literature Review, in: *2024 International Research Conference on Smart Computing and Systems Engineering (SCSE)*, vol. 7, pp. 1–6, 2024.
59. Jawad, Z.N. and Balázs, V., Machine learning-driven optimization of enterprise resource planning (ERP) systems: a comprehensive review. *Beni-Suef Univ. J. Basic Appl. Sci.*, 13, 1, 4, 2024.
60. Dewi, N. L. P. T. K., Nilawati, N.K.U., Anandita, I.B.G., Visual Analysis of Marketplace Sales Data for Strategic Decision Making Using Tableau. *TECHNOVATE J. Inf. Technol. Strateg. Innov. Manag.*, 1, 3, 156–169, 2024.
61. Boukraa, D., Bala, M., Rizzi, S., Metadata Management in Data Lake Environments: A Survey. *J. Libr. Metadata*, 24, 4, 215–274, 2024.
62. Hoi, L.M., Ke, W., Im, S.K., Manipulating Data Lakes Intelligently With Java Annotations, in: *IEEE Access*, vol. 12, pp. 34903–34917, 2024, doi: 10.1109/ACCESS.2024.3372618.
63. Cherradi, M., Data lake management using topic modeling techniques. *Data Metadata*, 3, 282, 2024.

64. Baig, M. I., Shuib, L., Yadegaridehkordi, E., E-learning adoption in higher education: A review. *Inf. Dev.*, 2022. https://doi.org/10.1177/0266666921100822.
65. Ghasemy, M., Teeroovengadum, V., Becker, J.M., Ringle, C.M., This fast car can move faster: a review of PLS-SEM application in higher education research. *High. Educ.*, 80, 6, 1121–1152, 2020, doi: 10.1007/s10734-020-00534-1.
66. Mthembu, Z.K., *et al.*, Developing a Data Lakehouse for a South African Government-Sector Training Authority: Governance Framework Design Through Systematic Literature Review, in: *Mach. Learn. Data Sci. Tech. Eff. Gov. Serv. Deliv.*, pp. 185–224, 2024.
67. Nicholas Omoregbe, S., Chizor, I., Azeta, A., George, T., Extending the Unified Theory of Acceptance and Use of Technology (Utaut) Model: the Role of Technology Culturation. *INTED2016 Proc*, vol. 1, pp. 3437–3441, March 2016, doi: 10.21125/inted.2016.1813.
68. George, J., Data to AI: Building a solid data foundation for your generative AI applications in the cloud. *Int. J. Sci. Res. Arch.*, 11, 01, 2601–2604, 2024.
69. George, R.V., Harsh, H.O., Ray, P., Babu, A.K., Food quality traceability prototype for restaurants using blockchain and food quality data index. *J. Clean. Prod.*, 240, 118021, 2019.
70. Huang, G.Q., Zhang, Y.F., Chen, X., Newman, S.T., RFID-enabled real-time wireless manufacturing for adaptive assembly planning and control. *J. Intell. Manuf.*, 19, 701–713, 2008.
71. Piccolroaz, S., *et al.*, Lake water temperature modeling in an era of climate change: Data sources, models, and future prospects. *Rev. Geophys.*, 62, 1, e2023RG000816, 2024.
72. van der Vlist, F., Helmond, A., Ferrari, F., Big AI: Cloud infrastructure dependence and the industrialisation of artificial intelligence. *Big Data Soc.*, 11, 1, 20539517241232630, 2024.
73. Mahesh Prabhu, H., Srivastava, A.K., Mukul Muthappa, K.C., Supply chain collaboration, agility and firm performance: a case of manufacturing SMEs in India. *Bus. Process Manag. J.*, 30, 3, 754–769, 2024.
74. Kuru, K., Technical Report: Big Data-Concepts, Infrastructure, Analytics, Challenges and Solutions, 2024.
75. Okorie, G.N., *et al.*, Leveraging big data for personalized marketing campaigns: a review. *Int. J. Manag. Entrep. Res.*, 6, 1, 216–242, 2024.
76. Taher, M.A., Sikder, M.A., Ahmed, H., Al Bashar, M., Integrating IoT and big data analytics for enhanced supply chain performance in industrial engineering sectors: a cross-market study. *Int. J. Sci. Eng.*, 1, 1, 1–14, 2024.
77. Wenhua, Z., Qamar, F., Abdali, T.-A.N., Hassan, R., Jafri, S.T.A., Nguyen, Q.N., Blockchain technology: security issues, healthcare applications, challenges and future trends. *Electronics*, 12, 3, 546, 2023.
78. Li, L., Su, F., Zhang, W., Mao, J., Digital transformation by SME entrepreneurs: A capability perspective. *Inf. Syst. J.*, 28, 6, 1129–1157, 2018.

79. Sharma, R. and Gurung, S., Implementing Big Data Analytics and Machine Learning for Predictive Maintenance in Manufacturing Facilities in South Korea. *AI IoT Fourth Ind. Revolut. Rev.*, 14, 2, 1–17, 2024.
80. Daher, M.M. and Ziade, F., Technology, Workforce, and the Future of Sustainable Work, in: *Navigating the Intersection of Business, Sustainability and Technology*, pp. 119–136, Springer, 2024. https://www.springerprofessional.de/en/navigating-the-intersection-of-business-sustainability-and-techn/26698204.
81. Kundi, G.M. and Nawaz, A., Predictor of e-learning development and use practices in higher education institutions (HEIs) of NWFP, Pakistan. *Turk. Online J. Distance Educ.*, 12, 1, 108–125, 2011, doi: 10.17718/tojde.58590.
82. Blackwell, C.K., Lauricella, A.R., Wartella, E., Robb, M., Schomburg, R., Adoption and use of technology in early education: The interplay of extrinsic barriers and teacher attitudes. *Comput. Educ.*, 69, 310–319, 2013, doi: 10.1016/j.compedu.2013.07.024.
83. Adewusi, A.O., Okoli, U.I., Adaga, E., Olorunsogo, T., Asuzu, O.F., Daraojimba, D.O., Business intelligence in the era of big data: a review of analytical tools and competitive advantage. *Comput. Sci. IT Res. J.*, 5, 2, 415–431, 2024.
84. Goyal, V. and M.L.K. (Eds.), *2nd International Conference on Communication and Artificial Intelligence, ICCAI 2021*, vol. 435, 2022.
85. Fatourehchi, D. and Zarghami, E., Social sustainability assessment framework for managing sustainable construction in residential buildings. *J. Build. Eng.*, 32, 101761, September 2020, doi: 10.1016/j.jobe.2020.101761.
86. de Vries, P., The Ethical Dimension of Emerging Technologies in Engineering Education. *Educ. Sci.*, 12, 11, 754, 2022, doi: 10.3390/educsci12110754.
87. McStay, A., Emotional AI and EdTech: serving the public good? *Learn. Media Technol.*, 45, 3, 270–283, 2020, doi: 10.1080/17439884.2020.1686016.
88. Ara, A., Maraj, M.A.A., Rahman, M.A., Bari, M.H., The Impact Of Machine Learning On Prescriptive Analytics For Optimized Business Decision-Making. *Int. J. Manag. Inf. Syst. Data Sci.*, 1, 1, 7–18, 2024.
89. Krumeich, J., Werth, D., Loos, P., Prescriptive control of business processes: new potentials through predictive analytics of big data in the process manufacturing industry. *Bus. Inf. Syst. Eng.*, 58, 261–280, 2016.
90. Shi-Nash, A. and Hardoon, D.R., Data analytics and predictive analytics in the era of big data, in: *Internet things data Anal. Handb*, pp. 329–345, 2017.
91. Sultonovich, M.D., Fayzi o'g'li, R.Y., Olimjon o'g'li, X.A., The Power of Data Analytics in Decision-Making. *Open Her. Period. Methodical Res.*, 2, 3, 38–41, 2024.
92. Greasley, A., *Simulating Business Processes for Descriptive, Predictive, and Prescriptive Analytics*, Berlin, Boston: De Gruyter, 2019. https://doi.org/10.1515/9781547400690.
93. Poornima, S. and Pushpalatha, M., A journey from big data towards prescriptive analytics. *ARPN J. Eng. Appl. Sci.*, 11, 19, 11465–11474, 2016.

94. Naga Malleswari, T. Y. J., *et al.*, Role of Predictive Analytics for Enhanced Decision Making in Business Applications. *Harnessing AI and Digital Twin Technologies in Businesses*, edited by Sivaram Ponnusamy, *et al.*, IGI Global, pp. 313–326, 2024. https://doi.org/10.4018/979-8-3693-3234-4.ch023.
95. Ahmed, I., Ahmad, M., Jeon, G., Piccialli, F., A framework for pandemic prediction using big data analytics. *Big Data Res.*, 25, 100190, 2021.

9

Sustainable Logistics 5.0: Combinatorial Technology with Artificial Intelligence

Bernardo Nicoletti[1]* and Andrea Appolloni[2]

[1]*Temple University, Via del Sebastianello, Rome, Italy*
[2]*Department of Management and Law, University of Rome Tor Vergata, Rome, Italy*

Abstract

Design/Methodology/Approaches. This chapter is based on a qualitative research methodology. Data/facts are collected and analyzed through project experiences, interviews, and visits to stakeholders, including professionals, practitioners, and academicians—comprehensive reviews of the research literature, industry documents, and media from established organizations.

Purpose. The aim is to introduce Logistics 5.0 and present a framework that combines artificial intelligence (AI) and other technologies to support sustainable logistics. The paper aims to help academics explore elements that could enrich the framework and its applications, especially considering new developments in artificial intelligence (such as generative AI and advanced algorithms). This chapter can help the audience use artificial intelligence effectively, efficiently, and economically.

Results. This chapter presents an integrated innovative framework. Technological platforms require appropriate processes, people, and partners. This chapter defines the structure and support of digital collaboration with the external environment to achieve sustainable logistics.

Originality value. Several papers describe applications of artificial intelligence to specific aspects of logistics. This chapter presents a framework for an integrated approach to artificial intelligence for logistics management and operations. The innovative approach is to apply AI in combination with other technologies.

**Corresponding author*: bernardo.nicoletti@temple.edu

K. Mathiyazhagan, Krishna Kumar Dadsena, Rajesh Kumar Singh, Aakanksha Kishore and Andrea Appolloni (eds.) Sustainable Operations of Logistics and Supply Chain Management, (201–222) © 2025 Scrivener Publishing LLC

Combining and integrating technologies brings more benefits than any single technology, especially in promoting sustainability.

***Keywords*:** Logistics, Industry 5.0, sustainability, warehousing, transportation, artificial intelligence, digital twins, generative artificial intelligence

9.1 Introduction

The aim is to introduce Logistics 5.0 and present a framework that combines artificial intelligence (AI) and other technologies to support sustainable logistics. Logistics is the backbone of any successful supply network and ensures the smooth delivery of products and services [1–3]. It includes transporting, storing, and managing raw materials, components, and finished products from the vendor to the end consumer [4]. This critical function fosters close relationships between organizations, suppliers, and customers. Efficient logistics has become a strategic differentiator to improve sustainability and win competition in the market [5]. This chapter explores the ongoing transformation in logistics by showing how advanced technological solutions can fully support this evolution.

Various cyber-physical techniques can continuously help to improve the quality of services in current logistics systems [3, 6].

These techniques can address various challenges, including punctuality, cost optimization, safety, and cybersecurity threats. Many industries are considering artificial intelligence (AI) to develop robust solutions for optimizing monitoring, operations, and decision-making in logistics. By integrating advanced sensors and computing components, a cyber-physical system (CPS) infrastructure is being built to optimize the collection, transmission, storage, processing, and scalability of data [7–10]. This development supports a broader use of AI solutions.

This chapter proposes an integrated framework for using AI in conjunction with other innovative solutions to effectively, efficiently, economically, and ethically improve the operation and management of logistics systems based on these technological advances. To effectively utilize digital technologies through this approach. Three main strategies can help:

1. Effective integration combining various technologies;
2. Clustering: different technologies to tackle some relevant features;

3. Complementation: integrating solutions to gain from the integration and synergies of different technologies.

9.2 Literature

This chapter examines how automation and digitization have permeated every aspect of logistics processes, leading to a deeper integration of automated systems and digitized workflows [11–13]. Sustainability is pushing for adopting a circular economy model to maintain a green logistics landscape [14].

The expansion of e-commerce has made city logistics relevant, as smaller vehicles must be used [15–17]. In addition, strategically positioned fulfillment centers are crucial for connecting national or international transport networks with urban logistics [16]. The emergence of fast trade (Q-commerce), where ultra-fast deliveries are essential, has further complicated logistics management [18].

Logistics 5.0 represents a remarkable advance in this area and includes innovative solutions such as 3D printing, autonomous vehicles, drones, and digital twins [19]. Artificial intelligence (AI) is central in logistics systems' design, management, and operation [20].

A key feature of Logistics 5.0 is the focus on human resources, sustainability, and resilience [21]. This human-centered approach emphasizes the design of systems that meet human needs and behaviors. Jafari *et al.* [19] aptly state that in Logistics 5.0, "people are transformed from a cost factor to an investment." Logistics 5.0 applies logistics principles within Industry 5.0 [22, 23]. It requires collaboration between governments, which can incentivize competitive businesses, and the private sector, which must actively explore and implement these advances to stay ahead [22].

AI is the transformative technology of Industry 5.0. [21, 24] explored the potential applications of AI in advanced manufacturing, pointing to advances beyond 5G communications and collaborative robotics. They emphasize the need for further research to bring the vision of an "industrial metaverse" to life.

9.3 Transformation of Logistics: Logistics 5.0

Logistics has rapidly evolved from a purely operational to a critical strategic area (Figure 9.1). Its development has occurred in several phases

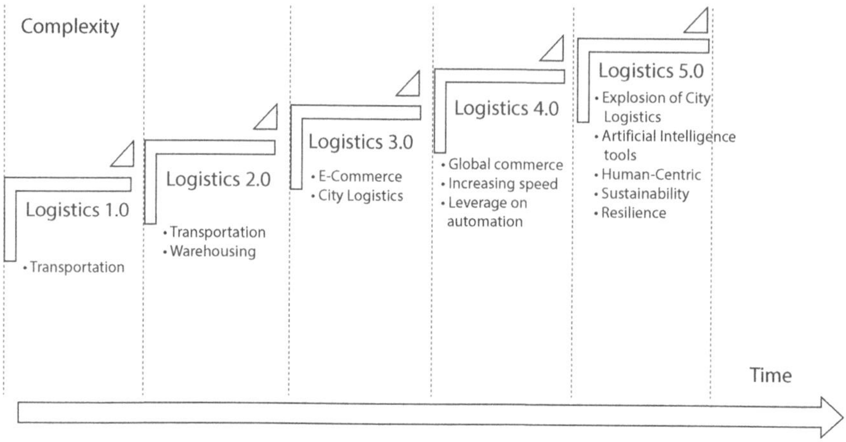

Figure 9.1 Development of logistics (developed by the authors).

following the characterization of Industrial Revolutions 5.0 [21], starting with Logistics 1.0, which introduced the steam engine, and ending with Logistics 5.0, which is in line with Industry 5.0 [25].

In line with Industry 5.0, Logistics 5.0 focuses on people. It is sustainable and resilient. As a transformative technology, it is based on AI. This paper looks at a framework for artificial intelligence in combination with other technologies to optimize support for sustainability. Another exciting alternative is the combination of different AI algorithms. Combined AI can democratize data access and analysis and minimize reliance on expensive and hard-to-find skilled resources [26]. It also provides explainability as the provenance and interpretability of models are explained in business language, eliminating concerns about bias and mistrust in AI models. Gartner defines composite AI as "combining different AI techniques to achieve the best result" or "multidisciplinary analytics."

9.4 Overview of AI

Artificial intelligence is composed of several algorithms: machine learning (ML), which has various subcomponents: natural language processing (NLP), computer vision, and generative AI (GAI) [27].

Machine learning (ML) can "learn" from data and helps computers independently learn from and consider new data without formal, explicit support programming. In this way, ML can recognize patterns in the data. This ability makes it possible to create or justify predictions. This capability enables the recognition of patterns in large data sets and leads to the formulation of predictions or decisions based on these findings [28].

Natural language processing (NLP) supports understanding, elaboration, translation, and production, focusing on human language [29]. One application is the development of chatbots that interact and use NLP to simulate interactions at help desks, such as automating repetitive tasks and allowing operators and human workers to focus on more complex issues [30].

Computer vision can work with visual data and extract information from it [31]. One application supports the integration of visual processing tools into various applications, including logistics management systems and manufacturing resource planning (MRP) software. These systems are used in logistics to support deliveries, inventory levels, and other critical operations in the supply network [32, 33]. Machine vision applications are particularly important for driverless vehicles and facial recognition systems [34].

Generative AI (GAI) can interact through prompts in ordinary language and generate human-like responses tailored to specific requirements [35]. GAI can support inventory management in the logistics industry by forecasting customer demand and selection. It can also help optimize route planning [36].

The framework in this chapter describes several use cases and interactions of AI algorithms with other solutions in different task areas. This analysis is essential and illustrates AI's significant potential to improve sustainability, effectiveness, efficiency, and decision-making in different areas of logistics.

9.5 Framework of AI-Supported Logistics System

Defining a framework with a combinatorial approach is crucial for integrating Artificial Intelligence (AI)-based solutions into logistics 5.0. This framework will identify the most effective ways to leverage AI to maximize the value of these solutions. Figure 9.2 illustrates one such innovative framework. It has been developed through a comprehensive analysis of various digital solutions, including blockchain and the Internet of Things (IoT), digital twins, and AI, that can improve the business processes of logistics organizations and others.

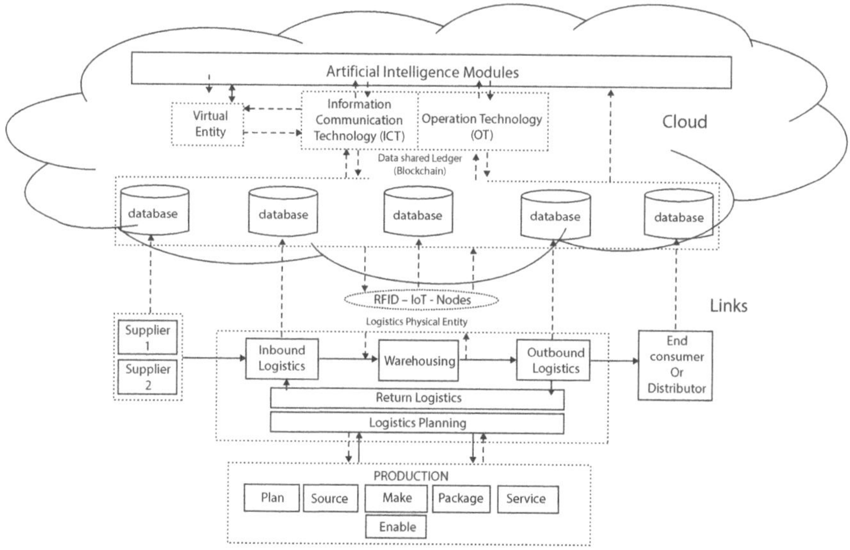

Figure 9.2 A framework for optimizing the logistics function through combinatorial technological innovation (developed by the Authors).

The framework comprises seven elements: the physical logistics unit, the connections, the shared data set, the data and communication solutions, the operational technology solution, the virtual unit, and the AI modules. Ideally, the framework should be hosted in the cloud. This solution is particularly advantageous as the logistics systems are geographically distributed [37].

9.5.1 Logistics Physical Entity

This framework examines an organization's logistics network and covers every step, from planning to delivering goods to customers (end consumers and intermediaries) [38]. The integrated system captures data from various Logistics Physical Entities (LPE). It is possible to store this data in multiple databases and securely connect it to a blockchain [39]. By analyzing this data, organizations can understand the logistical performance of their inbound and outbound activities and warehousing [40].

The LPE embodies the physical and tangible components of a Virtual Entity (VE). Blockchain technology is essential for linking the LPE to its digital counterpart to ensure data consistency, facilitate continuous synchronization, and enable easy retrieval [41]. The value of this data lies in its potential to optimize logistics processes for the organization rather than its usefulness to end users or other participants in the logistics chain [42]. This framework enables organizations to identify potential bottlenecks and management issues within their logistics systems. Such problems can significantly impact all stakeholders' effectiveness, efficiency, profitability, and performance [38]. The framework's holistic view of LPE extends to data collection methods (links), data storage solutions, and analysis tools. Considering all these aspects, the framework provides a comprehensive approach to optimizing logistics processes [39].

9.5.2 AI Modules

The AI modules comprise numerous algorithms that can be used on-site and in the cloud. This comprehensive solution supports all the functionalities described in this chapter and can potentially integrate even more advanced AI functions for future Logistics 5.0+ applications. The core principle behind these modules is the seamless integration of AI into existing logistics systems. AI and other innovative technologies offer significant benefits that will drive the digital transformation of the business [38–43].

Various innovative algorithms and technologies will characterize the future of AI in logistics management and operations. AI can improve existing systems and introduce breakthrough approaches that optimize effectiveness, efficiency, profitability, and ethical issues in the logistics industry.

9.5.3 Data Shared Ledger – DSL (Blockchain)

A secure and cloud-based processing facility ensures that all databases, including those for suppliers and intermediate customers, communicate continuously. This framework ensures streamlined information collection, analysis, and logistics planning. This approach enables efficient, effective, economical, and comprehensive interaction within the organization's logistics ecosystem.

The framework's Data Sharing Layer (DSL) relies on data availability from collection to downstream distribution. This data forms the basis for reliable logistics planning and disaster recovery (DR). More data means more accurate diagnoses and predictions of logistics processes. From a broader perspective, system integration with partners allows organizations to control their processes and anticipate delays caused by external events.

The function of the shared register depends on the actors involved in logistics. The level of data protection, consent mechanisms, and data access are tailored to the users' needs. This solution can also facilitate downstream information gathering. Sales data generated by end consumers or retailers (e.g., repeat procurement) can be incorporated into product fulfillment planning and ensure market availability without increasing inventory levels or storage costs.

9.5.4 The Virtual Entity

The Virtual Entity (VE) is a convergence point for the tools and solutions presented. These components are crucial for ensuring efficient and optimized logistics processes. The VE represents a significant potential competitive advantage. It is a virtual environment that fully replicates the organization's physical logistics function and is enabled by a digital twin solution [7].

The virtual environment enables the continuous monitoring and control of logistics processes. Sensor data, historical performance metrics, and behavioral data can be linked to the spatial model, so behavioral predictions can be made by adjusting various inputs. The collected data and its predictive capabilities effectively animate the spatial model [44–46].

9.5.5 Information Communication Technology (ICT)

The framework includes traditional logistics applications, including Manufacturing Resource Planning (MRP) and the extended versions of ERP, Extended ERP (EERP), WMS, and TMS. Transportation management systems (TMS) are a logistics platform that streamlines inbound and outbound movements while ensuring regulatory compliance and proper documentation [47, 48]. WMS has similar functionality for warehouse management systems [49–51].

Integrating artificial intelligence (AI) with operational technology (OT) is crucial in Logistics 5.0. Operational technology includes the hardware and software used to monitor, control, or operate assets, infrastructure, processes, machines, and events [52, 53]. Sharing OT data with other solutions mentioned above facilitates the establishment of decentralized control centers for logistics processes that ensure continuous updates and real-time operations. This solution allows stakeholders at different management levels to be informed, intervene, and provide high efficiency and security of business activities. This approach is crucial for logistics, where human involvement remains high, and accident risks can cause severe damage through workplace accidents, fatalities, associated personnel costs, and legal and reputational costs.

9.5.6 Links

Links are the essential tools that convert data and information from physical and analog processes into digital formats suitable for storage in the blockchain.

9.6 Applications of the Framework in Digital Transformation in Logistics 5.0

The most groundbreaking innovations often result from the fusion of several technologies, not just one: the cell phone, which was born from the combination of telecommunications and information technology [54–56]. This "combinatorial approach" also applies to AI. When combined with other technologies, AI unleashes its full potential and enables practical, efficient, economic, and ethical advances in logistics.

The latest version of SCOR also considers sustainability. The version that incorporates sustainability considerations is often called SCOR Sustainability. This framework integrates environmental, social, and governance (ESG) considerations into the traditional Supply Chain Operations Reference (SCOR). Organizations use the Global Reporting Initiative (GRI) standards and definitions to measure sustainability impacts. For this reason, this chapter includes sustainability in the description of the essential components of SCOR: Plan, Source, Make, Deliver, Return, and Enable.

9.6.1 Plan

Precise planning is the cornerstone of success in the complex and dynamic world of logistics. As competition intensifies, a robust planning function becomes an even more powerful tool to stay ahead of the curve [57–60]. The framework presented in this chapter, along with AI-powered algorithms and other technologies, can significantly improve supply planning by optimizing efficiency and minimizing waste.

In today's complicated logistics environment, accurate planning and access to real-time data enabled by big data are essential for all stakeholders. Artificial intelligence (AI) can help extract data using machine learning patterns to support improved forecasting and better planning. Generative AI (GAI) extends this capability by actively identifying risks and suggesting real-time remedial strategies.

9.6.2 Source

GAI offers many other possibilities. Organizations can introduce dynamic, demand-oriented pricing models. GAI can suggest raising prices when demand is high and lowering them when demand decreases to maximize profit margin [61]. GAI can automate repetitive tasks such as translating and composing messages to logistics partners, promoting more efficient and accurate communication. GAI can help apply product documents to fulfill regulations and operational tasks [62]. When integrated with smart contracts, GAI can analyze vendor contracts and identify key risks and opportunities for optimization, renegotiation, and streamlining [49]. GAI's capabilities can also improve customer management and website usability [63].

9.6.3 Make

Warehouse management involves strategic and tactical decisions that affect the design of the entire logistics function and individual facilities. A best-in-class warehouse management system leads to higher profit margins through cost optimization and maximized efficiency across the supply network.

AI is transforming warehouse operations, impacting demand fulfillment and picking. Two important examples are the selection of warehouse locations and intelligent picking systems. The selection and picking of customer products have traditionally been labor-intensive and expensive warehouse operations [64]. Logistics management seeks warehouse automation solutions, as profitability depends on efficient picking.

The Internet of Things (IoT) is "a set of infrastructures that connect networked objects and enable their management, data analysis, and access to the data they generate" [65]. RFID (Radio Frequency Identification) can be used to pick up orders. IoT-powered conveyor belts can facilitate the implementation of AI solutions. Intelligent systems using robotics and computer vision can perform tasks autonomously by picking items from shelves and delivering them to specific locations [66]. Organizations like Amazon and Yoox Net-a-Porter demonstrate this concept with hybrid picking systems, where human workers process items at particular stations. At the same time, robots navigate through the warehouse to deliver them. These systems can improve employee safety and well-being. They can also significantly improve order fulfillment capacity [67].

9.6.4 Deliver

Delivery is the backbone of the logistics activity. Route optimization is one of the most essential functionalities enhanced by AI [68, 69]. The benefits can go beyond the improved utilization of vehicles; they can also be seen from an environmental point of view, as well as street congestion [70–72]. Generative AI would be an essential tool to help in this respect. Its integration with GPS customer demand and real-time congestion can help quite a bit [73]. Driverless vehicles and drones open an entirely new panorama in terms of delivery. They could improve customer satisfaction and the consumption of fuel. While these solutions might be difficult to implement in public spaces, they can help a lot inside the company with intralogistics, warehouse automation, and flexible solutions [74, 75].

9.6.5 Return

Reverse Logistics is the take-back mechanism, including sending products from the end user back to the seller or manufacturer for proper disposal or recycling for resale [4]. AI allows logistics management to make decisions based on data. AI can help sustainability [76, 77]. Responsible disposal of non-recyclable products is also crucial. Environmental responsibility is becoming increasingly important, and implementing a reverse logistics system is becoming increasingly crucial for all organizations, also due to more stringent regulations worldwide. AI is a powerful tool for integrating and supporting these applications and contributing to sustainability goals [77].

9.6.6 Enable

Several innovative AI systems are revolutionizing inventory management. These systems use customer demand prediction technologies and real-time information to make significant improvements. Global leaders such as Amazon and Yoox Net-a-Porter show that using AI to predict order patterns has reduced transportation costs and delivery times [78]. This solution allows them to strategically position products in their network of regional distribution centers and fulfill orders faster, more efficiently, and cost-effectively. Otto, a German online retailer, is another example of the potential of AI in inventory management. [79] reports that Otto has delegated inventory management to Google's DeepMind platform, achieving a remarkable 90% reduction in stock levels without human intervention.

Logistics is a complex ecosystem where participants often operate in a highly competitive and legally sensitive environment. Building trust can be a challenge [56, 80].

9.7 Framework Implementation

Fortunately, technological advances will make it easier and cheaper to assemble and configure the framework's components in the future. Generative AI and tools for basic models are promising solutions in this direction. Another challenge is some management teams' lack of awareness or skepticism towards AI solutions.

9.8 Benefits and Challenges

When integrated with other technologies, the proposed framework provides a robust solution for sustainable logistics 5.0 that offers many benefits. It facilitates the streamlining of processes, leading to faster and more accurate results while increasing overall efficiency and precision. Thanks to the automation of repetitive tasks, AI reduces human error and promotes greater consistency, and AI contributes significantly to minimizing risk and increasing safety. Reducing human involvement in high-risk activities lowers the likelihood of accidents and mistakes.

AI-driven chatbots and virtual assistants enrich interactions by providing faster responses and customized recommendations, leading to higher satisfaction. The impact of AI-driven chatbots and virtual assistants goes beyond enriching customer interactions. They improve companies' operational efficiency, reduce employee workload, enable data-driven insights into consumer preferences, promote customer service scalability, and contribute to a personalized and seamless user experience that promotes overall customer loyalty and can significantly impact business growth and competitiveness. AI contributes significantly to minimizing risks and increasing safety. Reducing human involvement in high-risk activities lowers the likelihood of accidents and errors.

Predictive maintenance functions ensure even safer operation. Another advantage of AI algorithms is the lower bias compared to human decisions.

Combining AI with other technologies can contribute to fairer and more equitable systems. This synergy encourages innovation and the development of ground-breaking products and services. AI's ability to analyze data, recognize patterns, and gain insights drives innovation.

AI offers undeniable benefits, but challenges include implementation costs, potential job displacement, and the lack of human creativity and emotional intelligence [81]. Success in integrating the processes lies in balancing AI's strengths and limitations.

9.9 Extensions and Limitations

This chapter presents a framework explicitly developed for logistics management. Its applicability to other business functions provides fertile ground for future research. One extension is to explore the potential of various technologies with artificial intelligence. These solutions include quantum computing and artificial intelligence, swarm robotics and blockchains, blockchain technology and quantum networks, material intelligence and AI simulations, spatial computing, augmented/virtual reality, cryptography, and quantum computing.

9.10 Conclusions

This chapter examines how AI and other innovative solutions revolutionize logistics operations and management. It looks at the areas where AI and other technologies can be combined to help and provides a comprehensive overview of existing and potential solutions. Most importantly, it presents a framework for their implementation in organizations.

AI solutions span several areas, including various artificial intelligence algorithms. All branches of machine learning (supervised, unsupervised, and augmented) offer potential applications in logistics. NLP technologies improve communication and efficiency in various areas, enable personalization, and raise ethical concerns about privacy and bias. NLP supports the increasing use of chatbots and applications such as document processing and translation. Computer vision is used in autonomous vehicles, object recognition, and market research [82]. The potential for AI applications that could revolutionize logistics management continues to grow. The possibilities are enormous when AI is combined with blockchain, IoT, cloud computing, and digital twins, mainly if it is used in more organizations [83].

The virtual use of these combinatorial technological innovations enables logistics organizations to improve the management of business processes [84] continuously. From a broader perspective, system integration with other logistics partners allows organizations to control the entire logistics ecosystem, support their processes, and predict delays caused by external factors beyond their control [85].

Although implementing such a framework is challenging, the future looks promising. Thanks to technological advancements, components are becoming more accessible and cheaper to assemble. In addition, large organizations can use the framework to drive integration with logistics partners, promote a unified strategic approach, and mitigate the impact of disruptive events. As a McKinsey study shows, logistics organizations that embrace innovative solutions can gain significant competitive advantages [86].

Funding

The European Union - NextGenerationEU funded this study in two projects: 1) the first project in the framework of the GRINS – Growing Resilient, Inclusive and Sustainable project (GRINS PE00000018 – CUP E83C22004690001); 2) the second project in the framework of the ECS 0000024 Rome Technopole – CUP B83C22002820006, NRP Mission 4 Component 2 Investment 1.5.

References

1. Breitbarth, T. and Herold, D.M., Logistics, in: *Encyclopedia of Sport Management*, pp. 292–294, Edward Elgar Publishing, Cheltenham, UK, 2021.
2. Schumann-Boelsche, D., Schön, A.-M., Streit-Juotsa, L., Modeling and Analyzing Logistical Processes in Cameroon from Douala Seaport to The Hinterland. *JGBT*, 11, 2, 31, 2015.
3. Hasan, M.K., Habib, A.A., Shukur, Z., Ibrahim, F., Islam, S., Razzaque, M.A., Review of cyber-physical and cyber-security system in smart grid: Standards, protocols, constraints, and recommendations. *JNCA*, 209, 103540, 2023, https://10.1016/j.jnca.2023.103540.
4. Rushton, A., Croucher, P., Baker, P., *The Handbook of Logistics and Distribution Management: Understanding the Supply Chain*, Kogan Page Publishers, London, UK, 2022.

5. Kimaro, L., The impact of inbound and outbound logistics activities on the vendor-customer relationship: A Case of Coca Cola organization Ltd, Dar Es Salaam, Doctoral dissertation, Mzumbe University, Morogoro, Tanzania, 2020.
6. Delicato, F.C., Al-Anbuky, A., Kevin, I., Wang, K., Smart cyber–physical systems: toward pervasive intelligence systems. *FGCS*, 107, 1134–1139, 2020, https://10.1016/j.future.2020.02.016.
7. Jiang, Y., Yin, S., Li, K., Luo, H., Kaynak, O., Industrial applications of digital twins. *Philos. Trans.*, 379, 2207, 20200360, 2021, https://10.1098/rsta.2020.0360.
8. Tabatabaei, M.H., Vitenberg, R., Veeraragavan, N.R., Understanding blockchain: Definitions, architecture, design, and system comparison. *Comput. Sci. Rev.*, 50, 100575, 2023, https://10.1016/j.cosrev.2023.100575.
9. Arthur, W.B., *The Economy as an Evolving Complex System II*, CRC Press, Boca Raton, FL, 2018, https://10.1201/9781315119858.
10. Zhang, B. and Mohammad, J., The effects of sustainability innovation and supply chain resilience on sustainability performance: Evidence from China's cold chain logistics industry. *Cogent Bus. Manag.*, 11, 1, 2353222, 2024, https://10.1080/23311975.2024.2353222.
11. Deepu, T.S. and Ravi, V., A review of literature on implementation and operational dimensions of supply chain digitalization: Framework development and future research directions. *Int. J. Inf. Manage. Data Insights*, 3, 1, 100156, 2023, https://10.1016/j.jimd.2022.100156.
12. Bag, S., Choi, T.M., Rahman, M.S., Srivastava, G., Singh, R.K., Examining collaborative buyer–vendor relationships and social sustainability in the "new normal" era: The moderating effects of justice and big data analytical intelligence. *Ann. Oper. Res.*, 1–46, 2022, https://10.1007/s10479-022-04793-y.
13. Cichosz, M., Wallenburg, C.M., Knemeyer, A.M., Digital transformation at logistics service providers: Barriers, success factors and leading practices. *Int. J. Logist. Manag.*, 31, 2, 209–238, 2020, https://10.1108/IJLM-04-2018-0144.
14. Jin, B.E. and Shin, D.C., The power of the 4th industrial revolution in the fashion industry: What, why, and how has the industry changed? *Fashion Text.*, 8, 1, 1–25, 2021, https://10.1186/s40691-021-00218-4.
15. Buldeo Rai, H. and Dablanc, L., Hunting for treasure: a systematic literature review on urban logistics and e-commerce data. *Transp. Rev.*, 43, 2, 204–233, 2023, https://10.1080/01441647.2022.2176496.
16. Bachofner, M., Lemardelé, C., Estrada, M., Pagès, L., City logistics: Challenges and opportunities for technology providers. *J. Urban Mobility*, 2, 100020, 2022, https://10.1016/j.jum.2021.100020.
17. Al Mashalah, H., Hassini, E., Gunasekaran, A., Bhatt, D., The impact of digitalization on urban logistics: An integrated framework. *Transp. Res. Part E Logist. Transp. Rev.*, 156, 102547, 2022, https://10.1016/j.tre.2020.102547.
18. Stojanov, M., *Q-Commerce–The Next Generation E-Commerce*, Списание Бизнес управление, 2022.

19. Jafari, N., Azarian, M., Yu, H., Moving from Industry 4.0 to Industry 5.0: what are the implications for smart logistics? *Logistics*, 6, 2, 26, 2022, https://10.3390/logistics6020026.
20. Wang, W., Zaheer, Q., Qiu, S., Wang, W., Ai, C., Wang, J., Hu, W., Transportation Infrastructure Management, in: *Digital Twin Technologies in Transportation Infrastructure Management*, pp. 75–109, Springer Nature, Singapore, 2023, https://10.1007/978-981-99-5804-7_3.
21. Nicoletti, B., *Procurement 4.0 and the Fourth Industrial Revolution: The Opportunities and Challenges of a Digital World*, Palgrave Macmillan, Cham, Switzerland, 2020, https://10.1007/978-3-030-35979-9.
22. Boz, E. and Pinto, A.R.F., Evaluation of Logistics 5.0 vs. Logistics 4.0, in: *Information Logistics for Organizational Empowerment and Effective Supply Chain Management*, pp. 163–184, IGI Global, Hershey, PA, 2024, https://10.4018/979-8-3693-0159-3.ch009.
23. Bolatan, G.I.S., From Logistics 4.0 To Logistics 5.0 Logistics for Digital Society, in: *Acad. Stud. Hum. Soc. Sci.*, p. 191, 2021.
24. Xian, W., Yu, K., Han, F., Fang, L., He, D., Han, Q.L., Advanced Manufacturing in Industry 5.0: A Survey of Key Enabling Technologies and Future Trends. *IEEE Trans. Ind. Inf.*, 20, 2, 2023, https://10.1109/TII.2023.3294485.
25. Li, J., Qin, R., Olaverri-Monreal, C., Prodan, R., Wang, F.Y., Logistics 5.0: From intelligent networks to sustainable ecosystems. *IEEE Trans. Intell. Veh.*, 8, 7, 3771–3774, 2023, https://10.1109/TIV.2023.3246916.
26. Dos Santos Melicio, B.C., Xiang, L., Dillon, E., Soorya, L., Chetouani, M., Sarkany, A., Lorincz, A., Composite AI for Behavior Analysis in Social Interactions, in: *Companion Publication of the 25th International Conference on Multimodal Interaction*, pp. 389–397, 2023, https://10.1145/3621101.3623299.
27. Dash, R., McMurtrey, M., Rebman, C., Kar, U.K., Application of artificial intelligence in automation of supply chain management. *J. Strat. Innov. Sustain.*, 14, 3, 43–53, 2019, https://10.33423/jsis.v14i3.1631.
28. Ahmad, M.A., Eckert, C., Teredesai, A., Interpretable machine learning in healthcare, in: *Proceedings of the 2018 ACM International Conference on Bioinformatics, Computational Biology, and Health Informatics*, pp. 559–560, 2018, https://10.1145/3211285.3211307.
29. Mah, P.M., Skalna, I., Muzam, J., Natural Language Processing and Artificial Intelligence for Enterprise Management in the Era of Industry 4.0. *Appl. Sci.*, 12, 18, 9207, 2022, https://10.3390/app12189207.
30. Adamopoulou, E. and Moussiades, L., An overview of chatbot technology, in: *IFIP International Conference on Artificial Intelligence Applications and Innovations*, Springer, Cham, Switzerland, pp. 373–383, 2020, https://10.1007/978-3-030-44366-0_39.
31. Gumbs, A.A., Grasso, V., Bourdel, N., Croner, R., Spolverato, G., Frigerio, I., Elyan, E., The advances in computer vision that are enabling more

autonomous actions in surgery: A systematic review of the literature. *Sensors*, 22, 13, 4918, 2022, https://10.3390/s22134918.
32. Jesus, C. and Lima, R.M., Business processes reconfiguration through the implementation of an enterprise resource planning system. *J. Appl. Eng. Sci.*, 19, 2, 488–497, 2021, https://10.5937/jaes0-31582.
33. Chopra, R., Sawant, L., Kodi, D., Terkar, R., Utilization of ERP systems in manufacturing industry for productivity improvement. *Mater. Today Proc.*, 62, 1238–1245, 2022, https://doi.org/10.1016/j.matpr.2022.04.529.
34. Cannas, V.G., Ciano, M.P., Saltalamacchia, M., Secchi, R., Artificial intelligence in supply chain and operations management: a multiple case study research. *Int. J. Prod. Res.*, 62, 9, 3333–3360, 2023, https://10.1080/00207543.2023.2184598.
35. Zhang, C., Zhang, C., Zheng, S., Qiao, Y., Li, C., Zhang, M., Hong, C.S., A complete survey on generative AI (AIGE): Is chatgpt from gpt-4 to gpt-5 all you need?, arXiv preprint arXiv:2303.11717, 2023.
36. Hendriksen, C., AI for Supply Chain Management: Disruptive Innovation or Innovative Disruption? *J. Supply Chain Manag.*, 59, 3, 65–76, 2023.
37. Casella, G., Bigliardi, B., Bottani, E., The evolution of RFID technology in the logistics field: a review. *Procedia Comput. Sci.*, 200, 1582–1592, 2022, https://10.1016/j.procs.2022.01.365.
38. Smith, H.K., Green Product Innovation and Digital Transformation, 2024.
39. Johnson, P.C., Laurell, C., Ots, M., Sandström, C., Digital innovation and the effects of artificial intelligence on firms' research and development - Automation or augmentation, exploration or exploitation? *Technol. Forecast. Soc. Change*, 179, 121636, 2022, https://doi.org/10.1016/j.techfore.2022.121636.
40. Lee, C.H., Liu, C.L., Trappey, A.J., Mo, J.P., Desouza, K.C., Understanding digital transformation in advanced manufacturing and engineering: A bibliometric analysis, topic modeling and research trend discovery. *Adv. Eng. Inf.*, 50, 101428, 2021, https://doi.org/10.1016/j.aei.2021.101428.
41. Brown, O., Davison, R.M., Decker, S., Ellis, D.A., Faulconbridge, J., Gore, J., Hibbert, P., Theory-driven perspectives on generative artificial intelligence in business and management. *Br. J. Manage.*, 35, 1, 3–23, 2024, https://doi.org/10.1111/1467-8551.12788.
42. Davis, F.D., Perceived Usefulness, Perceived Ease of Use, and User Acceptance of Information Technology. *MIS Q.*, 13, 319–340, 1989, https://doi.org/10.2307/249008.
43. Nishant, R., Kennedy, M., Corbett, J., Artificial intelligence for sustainability: Challenges, opportunities, and a research agenda. *Int. J. Inf. Manage.*, 53, 102104, 2020, https://10.1016/j.ijinfomgt.2019.102104.
44. Petereit, J., Digital twins and Artificial Intelligence in logistics, Retrieved from https://www.cloudflight.io/en/blog/digital-twins-and-artificial-intelligence-in-logistics/. Accessed 10 December 2023.

45. Matyi, H. and Tamás, P., Application of Digital Twin technology in the development of logistics process. *Adv. Logist. Syst. Theory Pract.*, 15, 1, 12–19, 2021, https://10.2139/ssrn.3704843.
46. Yan, Y., Chow, A.H., Ho, C.P., Kuo, Y.H., Wu, Q., Ying, C., Reinforcement learning for logistics and supply chain management: Methodologies, state of the art, and future opportunities. *Transp. Res. Part E Logist. Transp. Rev.*, 162, 102712, 2022, https://10.1016/j.tre.2022.102712.
47. Verma, A., Adichwal, N.K., Sharma, P., Implementation and Scope of Business Intelligence and Oracle Transportation Management System in Tata Steel Supply Chain, in: *Business Intelligence and Human Resource Management: Concept, Cases, and Practical Applications*, p. 207, 2022, https://10.4324/9781003184928-10.
48. Sharma, S. and Awasthi, S.K., Introduction to intelligent transportation system: overview, classification based on physical architecture, and challenges. *Int. J. Sens. Netw.*, 38, 4, 215–240, 2022, https://10.1504/ijsnet.2022.122593.
49. Liu, Y., Yu, F.R., Li, X., Ji, H., Leung, V.C., Blockchain and machine learning for communications and networking systems. *IEEE Commun. Surv. Tutor.*, 22, 2, 1392–1431, 2020, https://10.1109/COMST.2020.2978892.
50. Minashkina, D. and Happonen, A., Systematic literature review and research gap issues on third party logistics operators selecting WMS for efficient operations for customers. *Int. J. Supply Chain Inventory Manage.*, 3, 2, 142–166, 2020, https://10.1504/IJSCIM.2020.108303.
51. Minashkina, D. and Happonen, A., A systematic literature mapping of current academic research linking warehouse management systems to the third-party logistics context. *Acta Logist.*, 10, 2, 209–228, 2023, https://10.22306/al.2023.10.02.012.
52. Tsungmay, T. and Tanimoto, S., A Preliminary Risk Assessment for Operational Technology Systems. *Bull. Netw. Comput. Syst. Softw.*, 12, 1, 18–21, 2023.
53. Datta, P.M., 4IR Operations, Technology, and Sustainability, in: *Global Technology Management 4.0: Concepts and Cases for Managing in the 4th Industrial Revolution*, pp. 189–198, Springer International Publishing, Cham, Switzerland, 2022, https://10.1007/978-3-030-95246-0_13.
54. Riahi, Y., Saikouk, T., Gunasekaran, A., Badraoui, I., Artificial intelligence applications in supply chain: A descriptive bibliometric analysis and future research directions. *Expert Syst. Appl.*, 173, 114702, 2021, https://10.1016/j.eswa.2021.114702.
55. Min, H., Artificial intelligence in supply chain management: theory and applications. *Int. J. Logist. Res. Appl.*, 13, 1, 13–39, 2010, https://10.1080/13675560903420200.
56. Nicoletti, B., Industrial Revolutions and Supply Network 5.0, in: *Supply Network 5.0: How to Improve Human Automation in the Supply Chain*, pp. 43–101, Springer International Publishing, Cham, Switzerland, 2023, https://10.1007/978-3-031-22032-6_3.

57. Nand, A., Sohal, A., Fridman, I., Hussain, S., Wallace, M., An exploratory study of organisational and industry drivers for the implementation of emerging technologies in logistics. *Ind. Manag. Data Syst.*, 123, 5, 1418–1439, 2023, https://10.1108/IMDS-07-2021-.
58. Zylstra, K.D., *Lean distribution: applying lean manufacturing to distribution, logistics, and supply chain*, John Wiley & Sons, Hoboken, NJ, 2005.
59. Benzidia, S., Makaoui, N., Bentahar, O., The impact of big data analytics and artificial intelligence on green supply chain process integration and hospital environmental performance. *Technol. Forecast. Soc. Change*, 165, 120557, 2021, https://10.1016/j.techfore.2021.120557.
60. Mololoth, V.K., Saguna, S., Åhlund, C., Blockchain and machine learning for future smart grids: A review. *Energies*, 16, 1, 528, 2023, https://10.3390/en160100528.
61. Javaid, M., Haleem, A., Singh, R.P., A study on ChatGPT for Industry 4.0: Background, Potentials, Challenges, and Eventualities. *J. Econ. Technol.*, 2023, https://10.1016/j.ject.2023.08.001.
62. Moran, A., Generative Artificial Intelligence arrives to logistics, La Lonja, 2023, lalonja.tech/en/generative-artificial-intelligence-arrives-to-logistics. Accessed 20 May 2023.
63. Kar, A.K., Varsha, P.S., Rajan, S., Unravelling the impact of generative artificial intelligence (GAI) in industrial applications: A review of scientific and grey literature. *Global J. Flexible Syst. Manage.*, 24, 4, 1–31, 2023, https://10.1007/s40171-023-00336-5.
64. Frazelle, E.H., *World-class warehousing and material handling*, McGraw-Hill Education, New York, NY, 2016.
65. Dorsemaine, B., Gaulier, J.P., Wary, J.P., Kheir, N., Urien, P., Internet of things: a definition & taxonomy, in: *2015 9th International Conference on Next Generation Mobile Applications, Services and Technologies*, IEEE, pp. 72–77, 2015, https://10.1109/NGMAST.2015.16.
66. Bales, R.A. and Stone, K.V., The invisible web at work: Artificial intelligence and electronic surveillance in the workplace. *Berkeley J. Emp. Lab. L.*, 41, 1, 2020, https://10.15779/Z38XK0H2T.
67. Lamnabhi-Lagarrigue, F. and Samad, T., Social, Organizational, and Individual Impacts of Automation, in: *Springer Handbook of Automation*, pp. 61–75, Springer International Publishing, Cham, Switzerland, 2023, https://10.1007/978-3-031-06685-4_5.
68. Jha, N., Prashar, D., Nagpal, A., Combining artificial intelligence with robotic process automation—an intelligent automation approach, in: *Deep Learning and Big Data for Intelligent Transportation: Enabling Technologies and Future Trends*, pp. 245–264, 2021, https://10.1007/978-3-030-65661-4_12.
69. Karbassi Yazdi, A., Mehdiabadi, A., Wanke, P.F., Monajemzadeh, N., Correa, H.L., Tan, Y., Developing supply chain resilience: A robust multi-criteria decision analysis method for transportation service provider selection under

uncertainty. *Int. J. Manage. Sci. Eng. Manage.*, 18, 1, 51–64, 2023, https://10.1080/20421338.2023.2252509.

70. Ranieri, L., Digiesi, S., Silvestri, B., Roccotelli, M., A review of last mile logistics innovations in an externalities cost reduction vision. *Sustainability*, 10, 3, 782, 2018, https://10.3390/su10030782.
71. Justin, C.Y., Payan, A.P., Mavris, D.N., Integrated fleet assignment and scheduling for environmentally friendly electrified regional air mobility. *Transp. Res. Part C Emerg. Technol.*, 138, 103567, 2022, https://10.1016/j.trc.2021.103567.
72. Filippi, F., Visions and Paradigms of Transport and Cities, 2024, https://doi.org/10.20944/preprints202403.1527.v1.
73. Tsolakis, N., Schumacher, R., Dora, M., Kumar, M., Artificial intelligence and blockchain implementation in supply chains: a pathway to sustainability and data monetisation? *Ann. Oper. Res.*, 327, 1, 157–210, 2023, https://10.1007/s10479-023-05263-3.
74. Cupek, R., Lin, J.C.W., Syu, J.H., Automated Guided Vehicles Challenges for Artificial Intelligence, in: *2022 IEEE International Conference on Big Data (Big Data)*, IEEE, pp. 6281–6289, 2022, https://10.1109/BigData55660.2022.10012063.
75. Rejeb, A., Rejeb, K., Simske, S.J., Treiblmaier, H., Drones for supply chain management and logistics: a review and research agenda. *Int. J. Logist. Res. Appl.*, 26, 6, 708–731, 2023, https://10.1080/13675567.2023.2226229.
76. Rogers, D.S. and Tibben-Lembke, R., An examination of reverse logistics practices. *J. Bus. Logist.*, 22, 2, 129–148, 2001, https://10.1002/j.2158-1592.2001.tb00007.x.
77. Wilson, M., Paschen, J., Pitt, L., The circular economy meets artificial intelligence (AI): Understanding the opportunities of AI for reverse logistics. *Manage. Environ. Qual. Int. J.*, 33, 1, 9–25, 2022, https://10.1108/MEQ-05-2021-0144.
78. Belvedere, V., Martinelli, E.M., Tunisini, A., Getting the most from E-commerce in the context of omnichannel strategies. *Ital. J. Mark.*, 2021, 331–349, 2021, https://10.1007/s41262-021-00271-8.
79. Burgess, A. and Burgess, A., AI in Action, in: *The Executive Guide to Artificial Intelligence: How to identify and implement applications for AI in your organization*, vol. 73-89, 2018.
80. Plomaritou, E. and Jeropoulos, S., The digitalisation in chartering business: special reference to the role of e-bill of lading in the bulk and liner markets. *J. Shipp. Trade*, 7, 1, 1–22, 2022, https://10.1186/s41072-022-00102-3.
81. Ford, M., *Rule of the robots: How artificial intelligence will transform everything*, Hachette, London, UK, 2021.
82. Parekh, D., Poddar, N., Rajpurkar, A., Chahal, M., Kumar, N., Joshi, G.P., Cho, W., A review on autonomous vehicles: Progress, methods, and challenges. *Electronics*, 11, 14, 2162, 2022, https://10.3390/electronics11142162.

83. Nicoletti, B. and Appolloni, A., Framework of IoT, Blockchain, Digital Twins, and Artificial Intelligence Solutions in Support of the Digital Business Transformation of Logistics 5.0, in: *Supporting Technologies and the Impact of Blockchain on Organizations and Society*, pp. 195–219, IGI Global, Hershey, PA, 2023, https://10.4018/978-1-6684-5747-4.ch012.
84. Nicoletti, B., *Lean and digitize: An integrated approach to process improvement*, Routledge, London, UK, 2016, https://10.4324/9781315591865.
85. Dwivedi, Y.K., Hughes, L., Ismagilova, E., Aarts, G., Coombs, C., Crick, T., Williams, M.D., Artificial Intelligence (AI): Multidisciplinary perspectives on emerging challenges, opportunities, and agenda for research, practice, and policy. *Int. J. Inf. Manage.*, 57, 101994, 2021, https://10.1016/j.ijinfomgt.2021.101994.
86. Goslin, S., Oerez, F., Li, J.D., Martinez, A., Miguel, M., Digital logistics: Technology race gathers momentum, McKinsey.com, December 2023.

10

Supply Chain Disruptions: Causes, Impacts, and Resilience Strategies till Early Pandemic: A Systematic Audit

Goutam Sutar[1], Krantiraditya Dhalmahapatra[2] and Sayan Chakraborty[3]*

[1]Department of Operations Management & Quantitative Techniques, Thiagarajar School of Management Madurai, Madurai, Tamil Nadu, India
[2]Department of Operations & Quantitative Techniques, Indian Institute of Management Shillong, Shillong, Meghalaya, India
[3]Department of Operations & IT, ICFAI Business School Hyderabad, Hyderabad, India

Abstract

In the early days of the pandemic, supply chains globally faced unprecedented disruptions. The sudden surge in demand for certain products, coupled with logistical challenges, highlighted vulnerabilities in supply chain resilience. The current study analyzed 87 articles from the early pandemic era on Supply Chain (SC) disruptions and their effects on firms' supply chain performance and practices, proposing mitigation steps for each disruption to render the firm resilient. We picked articles from 2008 to mid-2021 for monitoring initial signs of new SC disruption mitigation measures after the COVID-19 pandemic. To identify origins, effects, important SC components impacted, and mitigation methods, assigned articles were descriptively analyzed. Demand uncertainty, supplier-related, geographical and geopolitical, natural calamities, pandemics, and firm-specific disruptions were evaluated. Then, SC disruptions and their effects on manufacturing, fast-moving consumer products, perishable, and multisector items were examined. The study concludes that SC vulnerability checks are necessary since several resilience methods cannot be implemented simultaneously. A relationship-mapping framework overviews the SC-vulnerability auditing process to help implement disruption-mitigating strategies.

Keywords: Supply chain disruption, mitigating strategies, relationship-mapping framework, systematic literature review, vulnerability audit

**Corresponding author*: sayan@ibsindia.org

K. Mathiyazhagan, Krishna Kumar Dadsena, Rajesh Kumar Singh, Aakanksha Kishore and Andrea Appolloni (eds.) Sustainable Operations of Logistics and Supply Chain Management, (223–260) © 2025 Scrivener Publishing LLC

10.1 Introduction

Supply chain (SC) emphasizes planning, operating, and directing goods and services from raw material purchase through consumer delivery. It covers inventory management, production, transportation, and distribution. SCs may experience internal and external disruptions [1]. Disruptions affect SC processes and financial growth [2], rendering them a global issue. SCs may be influenced by disruptions from unlawful company practices, unanticipated events, natural disasters, and other reasons. The 2010 Canterbury earthquake in 2010 devastated social, environmental, business, health, and education sectors [3]. The 2011 Tohoku Earthquake in Japan disrupted [4, 5] Toyota's SC, affecting Tier-1 and Tier-2 suppliers (for automotive microcontrollers), impacting production, and causing huge financial losses.

Pharmaceutical SC and manufacturing scale up when upstream SC delivers raw materials (particularly pharmaceuticals and chemicals) inappropriately. However, pandemic illiteracy hurts organizations' productivity, planning, and demand forecasting. According to the December 2020 World Economic Forum report, pandemics like COVID-19 harmed firms' strategic choices, necessitating more effective methods to address SC disruption and enhance SC design [6]. Researchers further examined how the severity of the COVID-19 pandemic required enterprises to reassess their strategic, relational, and behavioral considerations in SC management and associated areas to control disruption caused by unanticipated events [7]. Despite a large body of literature on pandemic strategies, future SC designs must consider new performance indicators like resilience, responsiveness, and reconfiguration ability, known as 3R. To further understand this relevance and the importance of successfully implemented sustainable logistics practices, one can refer to the example of Unilever's Commitment to Sustainable Sourcing as Unilever clearly demonstrated that sustainable sourcing can lead to both environmental benefits and business growth, making it a key strategy for companies looking to future-proof their supply chains. Also, DHL's holistic approach to sustainability, which covers both transportation and warehousing, offers a model for other logistics firms to follow, highlighting the importance of embracing technology and renewable energy sources. In this line, Ikea's emphasis on the circular economy and reverse logistics also illustrates how companies can reduce waste while enhancing customer satisfaction and building long-term sustainability.

The problem addressed in this study is the growing inability of traditional supply chain systems to withstand such disruptions while maintaining operational efficiency. The current research highlights how global firms have struggled with balancing efficiency with resilience and sustainability, especially in the wake of the pandemic. The specific challenges explored include unpredictable demand, supply shortages, logistical inefficiencies, and the sustainability of operational practices. Thus, the pressing issue is how to redesign supply chain systems to be more adaptive and resilient, ensuring both sustainability and the ability to recover swiftly from disruptions. The current study extensively evaluated SC disruption-related articles and their consequences on business' SC performance and existing practices, offering mitigation measures. This systematic literature review identifies gaps and future objectives for SC tactics pre- and post-pandemic. Using a relationship-mapping technique helps to learn about SC components, their impacts, and their interconnectedness.

Having outlined the key challenges facing global supply chains, it is important to delve deeper into the existing body of research that addresses these disruptions. The following section examines past studies to provide a comprehensive understanding of current trends and gaps in supply chain disruption management.

10.2 Review Methodology

The research design begins by defining the research objective, specifically focusing on supply chain disruptions and their management. Next, it involves selecting academic databases, including Scopus, Science Direct, and Google Scholar, for article selection. A list of relevant keywords as described in section 2.1 is compiled for literature searches. The subsequent step is to conduct a literature search across the chosen databases using these keywords to collect appropriate articles. These are then screened based on their relevance to the research objective, authenticity, and recency. After a comprehensive citation record for selected articles and referral materials, we have prepared a journal-wise distribution table (Table 10.1) of the selected articles and visualizing the article selection process in Figure 10.1. The process then summarizes and categorizes various supply chain disruption risks leading to the creation of summary tables (Table 10.2 and Table 10.3). These summary tables categories various supply chain risks, their impacts, company practices, and mitigation options. A review discussion has been presented on various disruption causes and relevant business practices, highlighting challenges in inventory management and production while visualizing the impact of disruptions on supply chain components. The implications of the findings are then detailed, emphasizing the need for supplier-firm collaboration and integration. For this propose, we have given a relationship mapping framework to connect disruptions with practices and performance. A complete discussion is given in following subsections.

10.2.1 Article Selection

Articles from three major academic databases, including Scopus, Science Direct, and Google Scholar, covered our study. Articles were searched *via* keywords like "Supply chain disruptions", "Supply chain resilience", "Supply chain disruption management", "Inventory management", "COVID-19 impacts on supply chains", and "Lean management and Supply chain risk management". The literature review includes 87 of 116 scrutinized articles and 11 referral materials (Figure 10.1) for general citations. The study's relevance prompted the selection of these publications. Authentic, recent articles were selected for screening. We cited 11 non-literature review papers in the contents. Table 10.1 shows the journal-wise distribution of all 98 papers in this publication. Figure 10.1 demonstrates the screening and article selection approach.

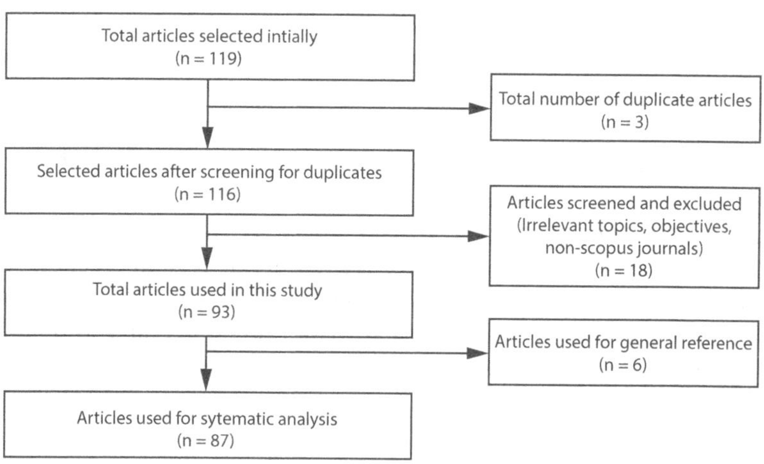

Figure 10.1 Selection process of articles.

Table 10.1 Distribution of papers across various academic journals.

Journal name	No. of articles
International Journal of Operations & Production Management	9
International Journal of Physical Distribution & Logistics Management	8
Supply Chain Management: An International Journal	8
International Journal of Disaster Risk Reduction	6
Benchmarking: An International Journal	5
Industrial Management and Data Systems	4
International Journal of Logistics Management	4
International Journal of Production Economics	4
Journal of Purchasing & Supply Management	4
Journal of Enterprise Information Management	3
Journal of Operations Management	3
Operational Research	3
Transportation Research Part E: Logistics and Transportation Review	3
European Journal of Operation Research	2
International Journal of Disaster Resilience in the Built Environment	2
International Journal of Production Research	2
International Journal of Quality & Reliability Management	2
Journal of Advance in Management Research	2
Journal of Manufacturing Technology Management	2
Procedia Social and Behavioral Sciences	2
Resource, Conservation and Recycling	2
Articles included in Literature Review with 1 occurrence	9
Total	87
Articles used for general citations with 1 occurrence	6
Grand Total	93

10.2.2 Classification of Disruptions

Table 10.2 summarizes SC disruption categories, impacts, company practices, and mitigation options. Demand uncertainty, natural disasters, supplier-related disruptions, pandemics, geographical and geopolitical disruptions are SC disruption risks.

Table 10.2 Disruptions-impact-mitigation and actions.

Authors	Major disruption sources identified	Impact on SC	Existing firm practices	Actions proposed to improve performance
[8–18]	Demand Uncertainty	Inventory management issues, demand fluctuations, loss in sales (growth rate), production disruption etc. Fierce competition among forms, tough decision-making	JIT, lean management practices, six sigma, inefficient strategy and inventory management, SC network models to minimize costs	Buildup inventory, safety stocks, bulk ordering, usage of technology and social media to analyses and forecast demand, SC contingency plan, (Q, r) – inventory model to tackle fuzzy environment, Implementing DSCM (demand supply chain management) model, backup supply strategy to mitigate risks from supply uncertainty, multi-echelon inventory optimization model to tackle nonstationary demand,

(*Continued*)

Table 10.2 Disruptions-impact-mitigation and actions. (*Continued*)

Authors	Major disruption sources identified	Impact on SC	Existing firm practices	Actions proposed to improve performance
				manufacturer-Stackelberg game with wholesale discount scheme, SC network design with reliability facility
[4, 19–26]	Natural Calamity	Demand fluctuations, poor supplier response, goods' distribution affected, inventory management issues	SC disruption mitigation system, supplier strategy, inventory management	Managing suppliers (supplier mapping), identification of backup supplier, inventory management, sustainability of important suppliers, standardization of key parts and production methods, creation of SC emergency plan (pro-active), global diversity in procurement (supply backups in different region), SC contingency plan, development of cooperative SC network,

(*Continued*)

Table 10.2 Disruptions-impact-mitigation and actions. (*Continued*)

Authors	**Major disruption sources identified**	**Impact on SC**	**Existing firm practices**	**Actions proposed to improve performance**
				implementation of agile SC strategy, SC disruption mitigation plan, development of business continuity planning (post disaster)
[1, 18, 27–41]	Supplier Disruption	Inventory management issues (stock pileup or shortage), poor supplier response, poor resource quality, incorrect order allocation owing to manufacturer-supplier real-time disruption-information imbalance	Supplier selection process, supplier partnership, sourcing strategy, internal and external integration	Supplier selection and management program, implementation of supplier evaluation process, supplier mapping, identifying backup supplier, contingency plan for sourcing and inventory management, SC disruption analysis (measures impact and likelihood of events), improving buyer-supplier relationship and information sharing, multiple supplier sourcing strategy,

(*Continued*)

Table 10.2 Disruptions-impact-mitigation and actions. (*Continued*)

Authors	Major disruption sources identified	Impact on SC	Existing firm practices	Actions proposed to improve performance
				developing mitigating strategies including capability or resource addition, internal-external integration, supplier base diversification, inventory policy (R- policy & Q- policy) implementation, suitable control system architecture to capture and disseminate real-time disruption information for mitigation
[42–52]	Pandemic Disruption	Inventory management issues, poor supplier response affects goods distribution (logistics), food supply chain, operations efficiency,	SC disruption mitigation system, inventory management strategies, lead time management and forecasting techniques	Creating SC emergency plan, adopting disruption evaluation tool (simulation software), responsiveness to situations like pandemic, simulation model-based

(*Continued*)

Table 10.2 Disruptions-impact-mitigation and actions. (*Continued*)

Authors	Major disruption sources identified	Impact on SC	Existing firm practices	Actions proposed to improve performance
		delivery lead time, purchasing cost at source,		resilient practices like drone-based delivery system, forecasting pandemic spread and planning, SC risk management framework relaxation, inter-state trade policy, disruption recovery strategy with product change
[53–57]	Geographical Disruption (Proximity), Geo – Political Disruption	Logistics of goods (final product and resource) distribution, sales (market share), production and inventory costs	SC distribution management, internal and external integration, SC technology, demand forecasting and geo-graphical clustering techniques	Logistic clustering to improve distribution capabilities, information and knowledge-sharing between service provider and distributor, implementation of intermodal transport (floating stock concept), implementing SC resilience strategy, horizontal and vertical collaboration between SCs

(*Continued*)

Table 10.2 Disruptions-impact-mitigation and actions. (*Continued*)

Authors	Major disruption sources identified	Impact on SC	Existing firm practices	Actions proposed to improve performance
[2, 58–92]	Other Disruptions due to Firm's practices	Poor financial performance, damage due to lack of accurate disruption information and high resilience capacity, space utilization, internal crisis management (acquisition, labor strike, collaboration, and supplier management),	Lean and six sigma practices, JIT, different SC efficiency and resilience measures	Collaboration, knowledge management, flexibility, public-private partnership, SC preparedness, balanced composition of various resilience measures, SC orientation considering resource configuration and disruption management, Industry 4.0 implementation

10.2.3 Distribution of Articles Based on Year, Industry, and Source of Disruptions

The manufacturing industry explains SC disruptions in 47% selected articles, followed by the multi-sector industry (38%), the FMCG industry (11%), and the perishable industry (6%). The selected publications also cover disruptions, their effects on supply chain productivity, and ways to mitigate disruption risks. With adequate screening and multiple data, we categorized six sources of disruptions: demand uncertainty (approximately 13% articles), pandemics like COVID-19 (approximately 12%), supplier-related disruptions (approximately 13%), geographical and geopolitical disruptions (approximately 6%), natural calamities (approximately 10%), and existing firm practices (approximately 41%). We discovered little or no disruption from the last category. Table 10.3 groups the publications we analyzed by industry, methodology, and design. This grouping highlights prevalent source disruptions and firm practices.

Table 10.3 Industry-wise SC disruption grouping based on research methodology.

Source of disruption	Author	Methodology: Tools & techniques	Methodology: Design specification
Industry: FMCG			
Demand uncertainty	[13]	Simulation based model, ANOVA and F-test	Inventory system was examined *via* simulation model with data collected from sample.
	[12]	Regression analysis	Impact of demand uncertainty on inventory turnover, gross margin, capital intensity, sales surprise & Mean Absolute Percentage Error through hypothesis testing
	[14]	Pearson's correlation and linear regression model	Questionnaire and survey method tapping relationship between inventory management and demand uncertainty
Geographical disruption	[55]	Semi structured interviews with Q Logistic Clustering	Qualitative case study research on FMCG firms with semi-structured interviews to investigate benefits of logistics clustering
	[53]	Simulation study	Analytical comparison, sensitivity analysis, and cost analysis of floating stock inventory advantages over conventional approaches
	[54]	Optimization Techniques, simulation model	Optimization model with floating stock strategy to reduce container transportation time; advancing container numbers for pipeline and terminal; sensitivity analysis
	[56]	Cross classified hierarchical linear modeling	Investigation of firm responsiveness from industrial and geographical perspectives

(*Continued*)

Table 10.3 Industry-wise SC disruption grouping based on research methodology. (*Continued*)

Source of disruption	Author	Methodology	
		Tools & techniques	**Design specification**
Supplier Disruption	[33]	Partial Least Square -Structural equation modeling	Quantitative Research Design *via* questionnaires examining how SC collaboration impacts firm performance
Other disruptions due to firms' existing practices	[90]	Partial Least Squares (PLS) Technique	Exploratory Research with sampling method exploring options for improving SC effectiveness
Industry: Manufacturing Sector			
Pandemic disruption	[51]	Mixed Integer Linear Programming (MLIP) (with ILOG CPLEX based heuristic algorithm for solutions)	Optimization model for 3-stage supply chain to maximize revenue; optimal quantity and procurement time, Sensitivity Analysis
	[43]	Any-LogistiX simulation	Simulation Modeling with case study on lighting equipment firms
Demand uncertainty	[9]	Fuzzy (Q, r) model	Optimization model under fuzzy risk environment to estimate influential parameters for inventory decisions
	[10]	Qualitative analysis	Data collected through in-depth interviews and literature analyzed *via* case study
	[15]	Monte Carlo simulation	Hypothesis testing for scenarios causing Bullwhip effect

(*Continued*)

Table 10.3 Industry-wise SC disruption grouping based on research methodology. (*Continued*)

Source of disruption	Author	Methodology	
		Tools & techniques	**Design specification**
	[11]	System dynamics modeling approach	Simulation modeling analyzing make-to-stock (MTS) manufacturing system and its structure
	[16]	Manufacture -Stackelberg Game for a two-echelon supply chain	Supply chain modeling with a single period news-vendor setting
	[17]	Mathematical model with Ben-Tal method	Multi-objective decision-making solution approach with queuing system
Supplier disruption	[37]	Structural Equation Modeling (SEM)	Quantitative Research Design *via* questionnaires investigating how SC flexibility, environment uncertainty, buyer-supplier association, and information sharing affect SC performance
	[38]	Structural Equation Modeling (SEM)	Quantitative Research Design using questionnaires examining supplier development as a supply-side risk management option
	[36]	Partial Least Square-SEM	Quantitative Research Design *via* questionnaires examining strategies to improve resource efficiency
	[32]	Structural Equation Modeling (SEM)	Quantitative Research Design *via* surveys assessing how lean and responsiveness strategies impact firm performance

(*Continued*)

Table 10.3 Industry-wise SC disruption grouping based on research methodology. (*Continued*)

Source of disruption	Author	Methodology	
		Tools & techniques	**Design specification**
	[29]	Binary Logistic regression	Normal Accident Theory (NAT) Model to understand how high inventory level doesn't check SC disruption
	[31]	Confirmatory Factor Analysis (CFA) and Critical Incident Technique	Quantitative Research Design with Interview technique to investigate SC resilience proactive and reactive approaches
	[39]	Within-case and cross-case analysis	Case study approach with semi-structured interviews to investigate resilience approaches of medium-sized firms *via* internal social capital
	[27]	Ordinary Least Square (OLS) Regression	Statistical data analysis to validate the hypothesis to investigate relationship between inventory and financial performance
	[1]	Descriptive Statistical Analysis	Empirical Analysis questionnaire and survey to evaluate strategic alliance and supplier selection criteria's impact on SC sustainability and image
	[34]	Exploratory Factor Analysis (EFA)	Mixed method questionnaire and survey to examine how supply and manufacturing risk affect firm performance
	[35]	2- Stage Least square method employed on Instrumental variable (2SL/IV)	Mediated Moderation Analysis to investigate how risk-taking influences inventory leanness-productivity

(*Continued*)

Table 10.3 Industry-wise SC disruption grouping based on research methodology. (*Continued*)

Source of disruption	Author	Methodology	
		Tools & techniques	**Design specification**
	[41]	Automatic Pipeline Variable Inventory and Order Based Production Control System (APVIOBPCS)	Control system design to assess and contain supplier disruption
Natural calamity	[4]	Bibliometric and case study analysis	SCM hierarchy framework with automotive microcontroller and automaker cases
	[25]	Covariance- based structural equation modeling (CB-SEM)	Quantitative research using questionnaires to determine the advantages of green supply chain management in disaster-prone areas
	[26]	Regression analysis	Conceptual framework (Quashi experiments on natural disaster impact)
Other disruptions due to firms' existing practices	[58]	Interpretive Structural Modeling & Importance Performance Analysis-IPA	Exploratory survey investigation to determine how lean and resilient management affects firm performance
	[59]	Confirmatory Factor Analysis (CFA)	Quantitative Research Design using survey data to explore how SC preparedness, alertness, and responsiveness affect firm's financial performance

(*Continued*)

Table 10.3 Industry-wise SC disruption grouping based on research methodology. (*Continued*)

Source of disruption	Author	Methodology: Tools & techniques	Methodology: Design specification
	[60]	Structural Equation Modeling (SEM) & Confirmatory Factor Analysis (CFA)	Quantitative research Design employing interview and secondary data to assess SC resilience advantages of logistics and SC capability
	[61]	Structural Equation Modeling (SEM) & Confirmatory Factor Analysis (CFA)	Quantitative Research Design using online questionnaire for survey method evaluate logistical benefits on SC resilience during Thai flood
	[62]	t-test & Regression analysis	Inferential statistical study of SCM adopters and nonadopters utilizing questionnaires
	[63]	Factor analysis & regression analysis method	Quantitative research utilizing questionnaires to demonstrate how JIT bundles might improve business operations
	[2]	Econometric techniques like regression and ratio analysis	Financial ratio and statistical analysis of yearly financial reports to determine SC-Firm performance link
	[64]	Exploratory factor analysis & Regression Analysis	Empirical analysis of 20 literature-based parameters affecting SC and overall quality management
	[65]	t-test and multiple linear regression analysis	Empirical analysis using questionnaires to determine Gulf manufacturing firms' SCM practices
	[66]	Exploratory case study analysis	Qualitative interviews and multiple cases were analyzed for six sigma impact

(*Continued*)

Table 10.3 Industry-wise SC disruption grouping based on research methodology. (*Continued*)

Source of disruption	Author	Methodology	
		Tools & techniques	**Design specification**
	[67]	Hierarchical regression Analysis	Quantitative research employing Asian manufacturing firms to examine how internal integration and SCRM practices affect manufacturing flexibility
	[68]	Hierarchical regression analysis	Hypothesis testing to explore relationships among various JIT parameters
	[69]	Canonical correlation & multiple regression analysis	Quantitative survey research on JIT impact on firm's performance
	[70]	Exploratory factor and Regression analysis	Quantitative Research Design with questionnaire survey to investigate key lean operations practices and design
	[92]	Mann-Whitney U-test, case study analysis	Non-parametric Statistical analysis using Structured questionnaire, interview, and survey on Indian process to investigate lean practices and performance
	[71]	Partial Least Square based -SEM technique	Quantitative and qualitative interviews and surveys to identify resilience influencers
	[72]	Simulation study based on compound distribution similar to Poisson distribution	Random demand data used to assess inventory control's effects on types of information sharing

(*Continued*)

Table 10.3 Industry-wise SC disruption grouping based on research methodology. (*Continued*)

Source of disruption	Author	Methodology	
		Tools & techniques	**Design specification**
Industry: Multisector			
Pandemic disruption	[46]	Descriptive statistical analysis	Systematic Literature Review Analysis through classifications of methods, theories, models, opinions, and reviews on Covid-19 affected supply chain
	[48]	Predictive analytics with nearest neighbor (NN) Approach	Google trends' simulation of government lockdown to forecast pandemic product and service surplus
	[49]	Partial Least Square – Structural equation Modeling (PLS-SEM)	Survey data with random samples from France to examine disruption, SC risk management, resilience, and SC robustness impacts
	[44]	Perceptive study on pharmaceutical supply chain	A view on medical supply chains like chloroquine and hydroxychloroquine during COVID-19
	[45]	Perceptive study on sustainable supply chain	Discussing sustainable activities during COVID-19 to identify key research areas
	[42]	Literature review Analysis	Infectious disease epidemic impact analysis
Geo-political disruption	[57]	Multiple case study Analysis	Questionnaire and interview data on SC resilience in food industries under constitutional disruptions like Brexit

(*Continued*)

Table 10.3 Industry-wise SC disruption grouping based on research methodology. (*Continued*)

Source of disruption	Author	Methodology	
		Tools & techniques	**Design specification**
Demand uncertainty	[8]	Confirmatory factor analysis (CFA)	Contingency theory model for SC process variability, organizational structure, and performance using telephonic interview data
Supplier disruption	[30]	Systematic literature review with content analysis	Examine procurement's impact on SC resilience
	[18]	Economic Order Quantity (EOQ) Model and Discrete-event simulation model	Inventory policies—Q and R—were tested for supply chain disruption mitigation *via* simulation models
	[28]	Descriptive statistical analysis	Online study of Indian enterprises' supply chain issues
	[40]	Bibliometric analysis	Systematic literature review on behavioral elements of inventory and ordering decisions and SC resilience.
Other disruptions due to firms' existing practices	[73]	Longitudinal case study analysis	Examining SC resilience and vulnerability using longitudinal case study data
	[74]	Literature review	Classification of SC crisis management literature with five-dimensional framework to explore proactive approaches
	[75]	Descriptive statistical analysis	Quantitative analysis to classify SC crises.
	[76]	Integrated supply chain decision (ISCD) model	Scenario-based analysis to identify resilience factors

(*Continued*)

Table 10.3 Industry-wise SC disruption grouping based on research methodology. (*Continued*)

Source of disruption	Author	Methodology: Tools & techniques	Methodology: Design specification
	[77]	Multiple case study analysis	Cross-case analysis employing questionnaire data to mitigate industry-wide sourcing risks
	[78]	Interpretive Structural Modeling (ISM)	A multi-level analysis into lean, green, and resilient practices affecting aerospace manufacturing SC sustainability
Natural calamity	[21]	Logistic regression model and simulation analysis	Empirical examination of 3R (right time, location, and material) concept to prevent relief supply chain failures during natural disasters
	[20]	Percentage Analysis and Kruskal-Wallis test	Canterbury earthquake (2011) severity analysis on various industries
	[22]	Empirical and SWOT Analysis	Data collected (field visit, primary survey, interviews, and focus group discussions) to examine manufacturing SMEs' recovery plans after the 2011 Thai flood
	[23]	Multiple case study approach	Conceptual framework revealed "indirect vulnerabilities" in metro Manila's rice, water, energy, and waste management supply chains
	[24]	Partial Least Square -Structural equation modeling	Cross-sectional survey to analyze SC collaboration effectiveness under high impact disruption
	[19]	Simulation modeling for large catastrophes	The research assesses proactive planning using a catastrophic risk management matrix

(*Continued*)

Table 10.3 Industry-wise SC disruption grouping based on research methodology. (*Continued*)

Source of disruption	Author	Methodology	
		Tools & techniques	Design specification
Other disruptions due to firms' existing practices	[79]	Covariance based-Structural equation modeling (CB-SEM)	Quantitative Research Design *via* questionnaire and survey to build hypothetical SCRM strategy of Big Data Analytics' adoption to prevent SC disruption
	[80]	Systematic literature review	Reviewing Industry 4.0 and sustainable SC literature to identify key enablers for disruption management
	[81]	Systematic literature review	Classifying uncertain events causing SC disruptions, SC practices, and outcomes.
	[82]	Topical Literature review	Public-private partnerships promote community resilience
	[83]	Complex adaptive systems perspective study	Literature review on engineering, ecological, and evolutionary resilience and SC readiness, reaction, and regeneration to mitigate disruptions
	[84]	Structural equation modeling	Exploratory factor analysis with survey data to develop resilient scales for disruption-countering firms
	[85]	Critical Literature review	Review study redefining risks in SC literature from disruption perspectives
	[86]	Literature review	SME-focused review of human-organizational resilience metrics

(*Continued*)

Table 10.3 Industry-wise SC disruption grouping based on research methodology. (*Continued*)

Source of disruption	Author	Methodology: Tools & techniques	Methodology: Design specification
	[87]	Qualitative and quantitative analysis on existing literature	Study examined SC vulnerability that disrupts and threatens
Industry: Perishable Product Sector			
Pandemic disruption	[47]	Simulation Model	Simulation study creating a robust public distribution system (PDS) SC for vital food commodities during COVID-19
	[50]	Descriptive statistical analysis, Regression Analysis	Quantitative analysis of Indian grocery websites and agricultural enterprises under lockdown. Urban lockdown impact was quantified
Other disruptions due to firms' existing practices	[88]	Optimization Techniques	Model determines optimal safety stock to check perishable SC disruption
	[89]	Critical Literature review	During disruptions, inventory models and choices for perishable items examined

10.3 Review Findings and Future Directions

This study discusses several disruptions causes and specific business practices that practitioners should evaluate as part of SC vulnerability assessment. Demand and supplier uncertainties, exacerbated by inadequate forecasting and JIT/lean practices, challenge inventory management and production. Figure 10.2 showcases studies indicating disruptions that harmed some vital SC components. As indicated, disruptions affect supplier responsiveness, inventory management, business performance, demand projections, and distribution and logistics' systems. Each item addresses disruption according to its influence on the SC. Table 10.4 details the article's mitigating practices. Inventory management, production practices, SC disruption management, SC technology (BDA), supplier management, sourcing strategy, internal and external integration, geographical clustering, enhanced transportation, and firm practices like SC process variability, replenishment time, SC agility and alertness, business continuity plans, and behavioral operation management mitigate disruptions.

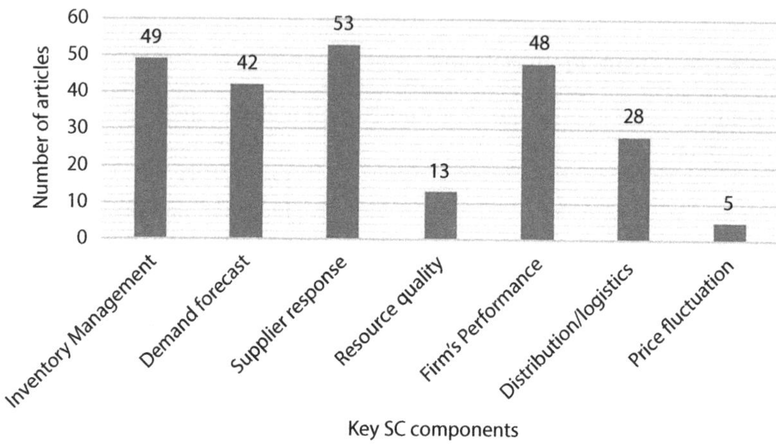

Figure 10.2 Critical components affected due to disruption.

Table 10.4 Articles that show various mitigating practices by firms.

	Firm's practices to mitigate disruptions										
Author(s)	**ReM**	**IM**	**PP**	**SCRM**	**TA**	**Geo. Cluster**	**SM**	**SS**	**ET**	**I/E Integration**	**Others**
[71]	✓	×	×	×	✓	×	×	×	×	×	✓
[49]	✓	×	×	✓	×	×	×	×	×	×	×
[47]	✓	×	×	×	×	✓	×	×	✓	×	×
[48]	×	×	×	×	✓	×	×	×	×	×	✓
[50]	×	✓	×	×	×	×	×	✓	✓	×	×
[51]	×	×	✓	×	×	×	×	✓	×	×	×
[41]	×	×	✓	×	×	×	✓	✓	×	×	×
[37]	×	×	×	×	×	×	✓	✓	×	✓	×

(Continued)

Table 10.4 Articles that show various mitigating practices by firms. (*Continued*)

Author(s)	Firm's practices to mitigate disruptions										
	ReM	IM	PP	SCRM	TA	Geo. Cluster	SM	SS	ET	I/E Integration	Others
[38]	×	×	×	✓	×	×	✓	✓	×	×	×
[40]	×	✓	×	×	×	×	×	×	×	×	✓
[43]	×	×	×	✓	✓	×	×	×	×	×	✓
[44]	✓	×	×	×	×	×	✓	×	×	✓	✓
[45]	×	✓	×	✓	×	×	×	✓	×	×	✓
[58]	✓	×	×	×	×	×	×	×	×	✓	✓
[9]	×	✓	×	×	×	×	×	×	×	×	×
[15]	×	✓	×	×	×	×	✓	✓	×	×	×
[39]	✓	×	×	×	×	✓	×	×	×	×	✓
[36]	×	✓	×	×	×	×	×	✓	×	×	×
[42]	×	×	×	×	×	×	×	×	×	✓	✓
[56]	×	×	×	×	×	✓	×	×	×	×	✓
[57]	✓	×	×	×	×	×	×	×	×	✓	×
[79]	×	×	✓	✓	×	×	✓	×	×	×	×
[17]	×	×	✓	✓	×	×	×	×	✓	×	×
[89]	×	✓	×	×	×	×	×	×	×	✓	✓
[25]	×	×	×	×	×	×		×	×	✓	×
[26]	×	✓	×	×	×	×	✓	×	×	×	×
[13]	×	×	×	✓	✓	×	×	×	×	×	×
[34]	×	×	×	✓	×	×	✓	×	×	×	✓
[35]	×	✓	×	✓	×	×	×	×	×	×	×
[55]	×	×	×	×	×	✓	×	×	✓	×	×
[80]	✓	×	×	×	×	×	×	×	×	×	✓
[83]	✓	×	×	×	×	×	×	×	×	×	✓
[58]	✓	×	×	×	×	×	×	×	×	×	×

(*Continued*)

Table 10.4 Articles that show various mitigating practices by firms. (*Continued*)

	Firm's practices to mitigate disruptions										
Author(s)	**ReM**	**IM**	**PP**	**SCRM**	**TA**	**Geo. Cluster**	**SM**	**SS**	**ET**	**I/E Integration**	**Others**
[65]	×	×	×	×	×	×	✓	×	×	✓	✓
[67]	×	×	×	✓	×	×	×	×	×	✓	×
[76]	✓	×	×	×	×	×	×	×	×	×	✓
[14]	×	✓	×	×	×	×	×	×	×	×	×
[23]	×	×	×	✓	×	×	×	×	×	✓	×
[24]	×	×	×	×	×	×	×	×	×	✓	✓
[88]	×	×	×	×	×	×	✓	✓	×	×	×
[81]	✓	×	×	×	×	×	×	×	×	×	✓
[59]	✓	×	×	×	×	×	×	×	×	×	✓
[61]	✓	×	×	×	×	×	×	×	✓	✓	×
[92]	×	×	✓	×	×	×	×	×	×	×	✓
[90]	×	×	×	✓	×	×	×	×	×	✓	✓
[93]	✓	×	×	×	×	×	×	×	×	✓	✓
[12]	×	✓	×	×	×	×	×	×	×	×	×
[13]	×	✓	×	×	×	×	×	×	×	×	✓
[22]	×	×	×	✓	×	×	×	×	×	✓	✓
[32]	×	✓	×	×	×	×	✓	×	×	×	×
[31]	✓	×	×	×	×	×	✓	×	×	×	×
[60]	✓	×	×	×	×	×	×	×	×	✓	✓
[66]	×	×	✓	×	×	×	×	×	×	×	✓
[46]	✓	×	×	✓	×	×	×	×	×	×	✓
[16]	×	✓	✓	×	×	✓	✓	×	×	×	×
[11]	×	✓	×	×	×	×	✓	✓	×	×	×
[4]	×	✓	×	✓	×	×	✓	×	×	✓	×
[21]	×	×	×	✓	✓	×	×	×	×	×	×

(*Continued*)

Table 10.4 Articles that show various mitigating practices by firms. (*Continued*)

Author(s)	Firm's practices to mitigate disruptions										
	ReM	IM	PP	SCRM	TA	Geo. Cluster	SM	SS	ET	I/E Integration	Others
[20]	×	×	×	✓	✓	×	×	×	×	×	×
[84]	✓	×	×	✓	×	×	×	×	×	×	×
[64]	×	×	✓	×	×	×	×	×	×	×	✓
[29]	×	✓	×	×	×	×	×	×	×	×	✓
[85]	×	×	×	✓	×	×	×	×	✓	×	×
[30]	✓	×	×	×	×	×	×	✓	×	✓	×
[87]	✓	✓	×	×	×	×	×	×	×	×	✓
[69]	×	×	✓	×	×	×	×	×	×	✓	×
[18]	×	✓	×	×	×	×	✓	×	×	×	✓
[72]	×	✓	×	×	×	×	×	×	×	✓	×
[1]	×	×	×	×	×	×	✓	×	×	✓	×
[28]	×	×	×	×	✓	×	✓	×	×	×	×
[68]	×	×	✓	×	×	×	×	×	×	×	✓
[63]	×	✓	×	×	×	×	×	×	×	×	✓
[2]	×	×	×	✓	×	×	×	×	×	×	✓
[70]	×	×	✓	×	×	×	×	×	×	×	✓
[73]	✓	×	×	✓	×	×	×	×	×	×	✓
[75]	×	×	×	✓	×	×	✓	×	×	✓	×
[77]	✓	×	×	✓	×	×	×	✓	×	✓	×
[86]	✓	×	×	×	×	×	×	×	×	×	×
[10]	×	✓	×	×	×	×	×	×	×	✓	×
[19]	×	×	×	✓	×	×	×	×	×	✓	✓
[27]	×	✓	×	×	×	×	×	×	×	×	✓
[53]	×	✓	×	×	×	×	×	×	✓	×	×
[54]	×	✓	×	×	×	×	×	×	✓	×	×

(*Continued*)

Table 10.4 Articles that show various mitigating practices by firms. (*Continued*)

Author(s)	Firm's practices to mitigate disruptions										
	ReM	IM	PP	SCRM	TA	Geo. Cluster	SM	SS	ET	I/E Integration	Others
[82]	✓	×	×	×	×	×	×	×	×	✓	×
[74]	×	×	✓	✓	×	×	✓	×	×	×	×
[8]	×	✓	×	×	✓	×	×	×	×	×	✓
[62]	×	×	×	×	×	×	×	×	×	×	✓

Others: SC process variability, Replenishment time, SC agility & alertness, business continuity plan, Insurance, customer focus, behavioral operation management, etc.
ReM: Resilience Measures, IM: Inventory management, PP: Production Practices, SCRM: SC Risk Management, TA: Technology Adoption, SM: Supplier Management, SS: Sourcing Strategy, Geo: Geographical, ET: Enhanced Transportation, I/E: Internal/ External

Further, to analyze the root causes of supply chain challenges, it was identified that many firms prioritize short-term cost savings over long-term sustainability because of weak regulatory frameworks or the absence of financial incentives. Also, developing countries often face logistics infrastructure issues, which make it difficult to implement robust supply chain strategies. In many organizations, quality practices face resistance from internal stakeholders who are used to traditional, cost-driven models.

Hence, to examine systemic failures in supply chains, the literature reveals that while globalization has enabled companies to reduce costs by outsourcing, it has also led to longer and more complex supply chains, making it more difficult to manage and measure. Further, in supply chains with multiple tiers of suppliers, responsibility is often fragmented. This lack of clear accountability leads to failures in enforcing sustainable standards, especially in developing countries.

The review further reveals that researchers advocate for stronger environmental regulations, including financial incentives for companies that achieve sustainability targets and highlight the role of emerging technologies like blockchain in improving supply chain transparency. It is also believed that a greater collaboration between governments, non-profits, and businesses can drive sustainability efforts across the logistics sector. Public-private partnerships could provide the necessary infrastructure and support for greener and more resilient supply chain systems.

These results offer valuable insights into how different industries have responded to supply chain disruptions. In the discussion that follows, we explore the implications of these findings, with a focus on how firms can apply these strategies to improve their resilience.

Organizations must follow state and country regulations so that they do not violate the laws on the protection of the environment. For instance, the various nations of the European Union are very particular in the amount of carbon emissions they produce as well as their waste disposal. Adaptation strategies should consider locally available resources. More significantly, areas perceived as facing limited water supply should implement various methods and systems that are less likely to use so much water. Make stakeholders from related communities get involved with sustainable development since the community support is likely to be strong in the area. In Manufacturing sector focus should be shifted to energy efficiency and waste reduction lean manufacturing can be a good way to cut off wastage. In the Agriculture sector working practices for sustainable production such as use of crop rotation techniques; organic farming; and precision agriculture should be enhanced. In Retail industry, there is the need to improve supply chain trace and supply chain transparency in the use of blockchain technology as a way of tracing the origin of products and ensuring that the products have been sourced in the right manner. Technology industries should focus on reducing electronic waste and should design products to last longer with easier recyclability.

10.4 Implications of the Study

This study identified SC disruptions and their effects on organizations' key performance, current practices, and mitigation strategies. The study found that supplier-firm collaboration and integration are required to render the SC robust [28]. It proposes a relationship mapping framework (Figure 10.3) to explore the impact of various SC disruptions on firms along with existing practices and mitigating strategies. The relationship-mapping technique connects different forms of SC disruption with different SC practices and the firm's performance. It also illustrates SC disruption mitigation practices businesses and practitioners should use. This framework helps identify, infer, and mitigate SC disruptions and their effects on performance. Demand uncertainty causes demand variations and non-optimal inventory maintenance. During natural disasters or pandemics, business practices like inventory management, production planning, and forecasting may not help. But sophisticated inventory models, SC contingency plans, and SC technologies can. Evidently, supply chain vulnerabilities and

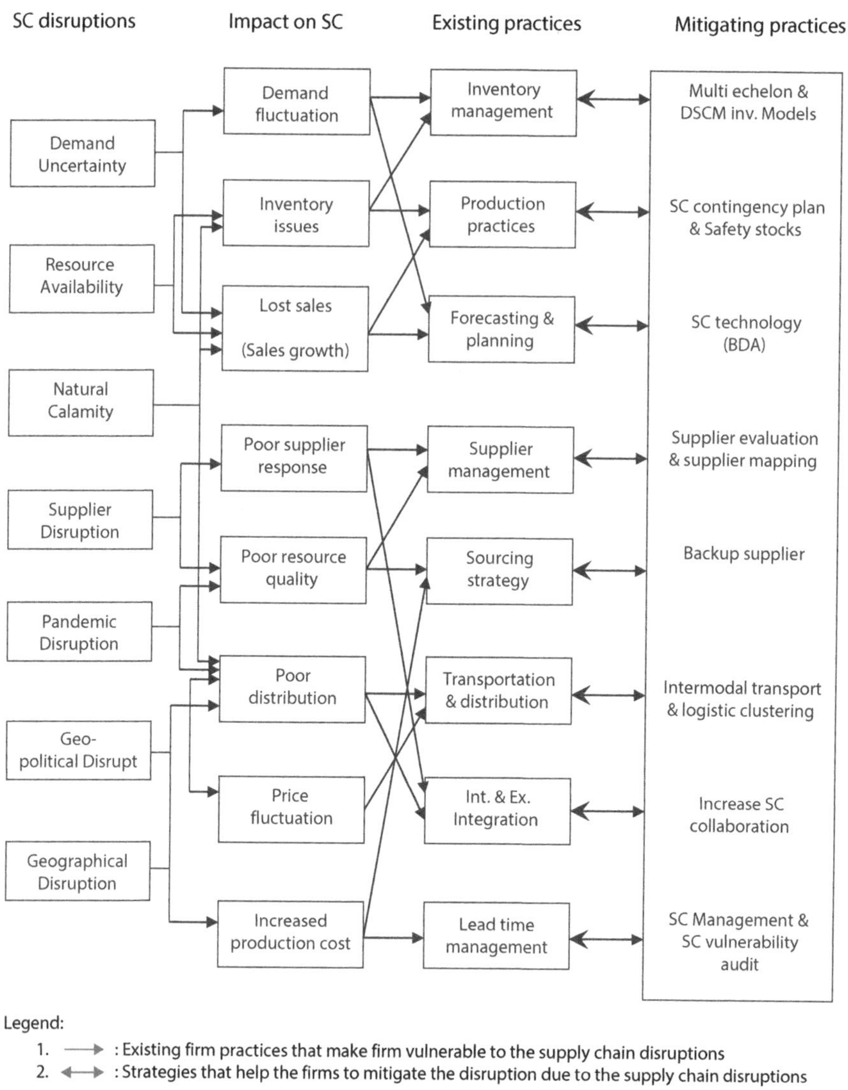

Figure 10.3 Relationship-mapping framework of key findings from literature review.

disruptions are caused more by business practices (inefficient, inappropriate, or unsuitable), supplier disruption, and demand uncertainty.

To manage the current supply chain, organizations should first evaluate areas that are primarily detrimental to the environment and society. They can sometimes engage the suppliers and make them understand that they should stick to sustainable practices. This may involve defining sustainable policies for selecting vendors and entering business relationships with them. Raw materials should be sustained, so if possible, using renewable, recycled materials that come from a certified source should be the first option. Besides, organizations should cut transportation emissions through carefully selected routes, less frequent shipments, and the use of environmentally friendly transport means coupled with investment in energy-efficient technologies as well as the use of the available alternative means of transport, such as the use of hybrid vehicles. Adoption of traceability systems that capture the flow and origin of products and materials can minimize wastage opportunities like the use of technology such as blockchain to increase the disclosure and reliability in conveying the authenticity of the product to consumers and other stakeholders. In addition, organizations should consider ways of designing products with the intent of durability, reusability, and recyclability to reduce waste. Enduring sustainability performance checking through score cards that include KPIs enhances the efficiency of the organization.

Organizations can quantify the efficiency by the amount of Carbon emissions (CO2e) that are cut through energy conservation measures as well as the use of green energy. This is because sustainable practices usually result in reduced running costs. Through achieving improved recycling efficiency, businesses are also able to retain less on the cost of disposal. Managers may be able to gauge increased efficacy about resources, including water or materials. Senior management's logistically centered efforts can minimize transport costs and pollution levels. In addition, the organization can pay special attention to decreasing the cost of compliance with the regulations on environmental requirements. In addition, considerable data can be collected on the decline in turnover rates resulting from enhanced workplace sustainability as well as productivity gains.

10.5 Limitations and Future Research Directions

Comparing robust and non-resilient businesses validates this research. This research ignored IT disruptions (cyberattacks, IT failures) and current domain changes, particularly when Covid-19 was normalized. The disruption may be studied to evaluate SC performance. This research doesn't cover supply chain analytics modeling, an emerging field. If applicable, this study could empirically examine the impacts of all disruptions on company performance. Future models should emphasize risk propagation, interdependency, and dynamic risk behavior. Digitizing SCM has revolutionized real-time data capture, making SC models more effective and responsive. Current research may be expanded to such fields and resilience techniques considered. Due to the COVID-19 pandemic, this study could not explore the full range of supply chain challenges. Empirical evidence-based research can quantify the pandemic's impact on the SC process to explore new avenues as more information about the pandemic's global supply chain disruption and its impact on economies emerges. Finally, the present analysis does not include financial disturbances in the supply chain owing to various factors.

10.6 Conclusion

This research examines SC disruptions and their effects on corporate performance to audit SC vulnerability. A systematic literature review of 87 selected articles from 2008 to 2021's early pandemic phase examines SC disruption research trends and their effects on supply chain and company performance. This article also examined supply chain disruptions produced by firms' current practices, which are seldom discussed in the literature. This research shows that firms should use SC resilience measures to withstand disturbances. Backup supplier, SC technology for demand and disruption prediction, six sigma, lean operation, supplier assessment, and mapping are costlier requiring firm support and stakeholder collaboration. It also demonstrates that stakeholders giving crucial information at the correct time can help mitigate damages. The study also demonstrated that timely stakeholder information could help organizations mitigate damages.

Key trends shaping supply chain and logistics management include digitalization, with technologies like blockchain and AI improving transparency and efficiency, and the shift towards circular supply chains, emphasizing recycling and reusability. Localized and resilient supply chains will reduce reliance on global networks, lowering transportation emissions. The adoption of green transportation technologies, such as electric vehicles, will help meet stricter carbon regulations. Growing consumer demand for ethical sourcing will drive the use of blockchain for supply chain transparency. Public-private partnerships and regulatory support will further encourage the adoption of sustainable practices across industries.

References

1. Ageron, B., Gunasekaran, A., Spalanzani, A., Sustainable supply management: An empirical study. *Int. J. Prod. Econ.*, 140, 1, 168–182, 2012.

2. Johnson, M. and Simon, T., The relationships between supply chain and firm performance: The development and testing of a unified proxy. *Int. J. Phys. Distrib. Logist. Manag.*, 41, 2, 88–103, 2011.
3. Potter, S.H., Becker, J.S., Johnston, D.M., Rossiter, K.P., An overview of the impacts of the 2010-2011 Canterbury earthquakes. *Int. J. Disaster Risk Reduct.*, 14, 6–14, 2015.
4. Matsuo, H., Implications of the Tohoku earthquake for Toyota's coordination mechanism: Supply chain disruption of automotive semiconductors. *Int. J. Prod. Econ.*, 161, 217–227, 2015.
5. Okazumi, T. and Nakasu, T., Lessons learned from two unprecedented disasters in 2011 - Great East Japan Earthquake and Tsunami in Japan and Chao Phraya River flood in Thailand. *Int. J. Disaster Risk Reduct.*, 13, 200–206, 2015.
6. World Economic Forum, Coronavirus and global supply chains, [Online], 2020.
7. Carnovale, S. and DuHadway, S., Continuity in the face of disruptions: Purchasing and supply management research's persistence amidst COVID-19. *J. Purch. Supply Manag.*, 27, 4, 100720, 2021.
8. Germain, R., Claycomb, C., Dröge, C., Supply chain variability, organizational structure, and performance: The moderating effect of demand unpredictability. *J. Oper. Manage.*, 26, 5, 557–570, 2008.
9. Handfield, R., Warsing, D., Wu, X., (Q, r) inventory policies in a fuzzy uncertain supply chain environment. *Eur. J. Oper. Res.*, 197, 2, 609–619, 2009.
10. Hilletofth, P., Demand-supply chain management: Industrial survival recipe for new decade. *Ind. Manag. Data Syst.*, 111, 2, 184–211, 2011.
11. Jaipuria, S. and Mahapatra, S.S., Performance improvement of manufacturing supply chain using back-up supply strategy. *Benchmarking*, 22, 3, 446–464, 2015.
12. Hançerlioğulları, G., Şen, A., Aktunç, E.A., Demand uncertainty and inventory turnover performance. *Int. J. Phys. Distrib. Logist. Manag.*, 46, 6/7, 681–708, 2016.
13. Salam, A., Panahifar, F., Byrne, P.J., Retail supply chain service levels: The role of inventory storage. *J. Enterp. Inf. Manag.*, 29, 6, 887–902, 2016.
14. Nemtajela, N. and Mbohwa, C., Relationship between inventory management and uncertain demand for fast-moving consumer goods organizations. *Procedia Manuf.*, 8, 699–706, 2017.
15. Alvarado-Vargas, M.J. and Kelley, K.J., Bullwhip severity in conditions of uncertainty: regional vs global supply chain strategies. *Int. J. Emerg. Mark.*, 15, 1, 131–148, 2020.
16. Giri, B.C. and Sarker, B.R., Coordinating a two-echelon supply chain under production disruption when retailers compete with price and service level. *Oper. Res.*, 16, 1, 71–88, 2016.
17. Nazari-Ghanbarloo, V. and Ghodratnama, A., Optimizing a robust tri-objective multi-period reliable supply chain network considering queuing

system and operational and disruption risks. *Oper. Res.*, 21, 3, 1963–2020, 2019.
18. Son, J.Y. and Orchard, R.K., Effectiveness of policies for mitigating supply disruptions. *Int. J. Phys. Distrib. Logist. Manag.*, 43, 8, 684–706, 2013.
19. Knemeyer, A.M., Zinn, W., Eroglu, C., Proactive planning for catastrophic events in supply chains. *J. Oper. Manage.*, 27, 2, 141–153, 2009.
20. Kachali, H., Whitman, Z.R., Stevenson, J.R., Vargo, J., Seville, E., Wilson, T., Industry sector recovery following the Canterbury earthquakes. *Int. J. Disaster Risk Reduct.*, 12, 42–52, 2014.
21. Antai, I., Mutshinda, C., Richard Owusu, A., 3-R principle for characterizing failure in relief supply chains' response to natural disasters. *J. Humanit. Logist. Supply Chain Manag.*, 5, 2, 234–252, 2015.
22. Pathak, S. and Ahmad, M.M., Flood recovery capacities of the manufacturing SMEs from floods: A case study in Pathumthani province, Thailand. *Int. J. Disaster Risk Reduct.*, 18, 197–205, 2016.
23. Gotangco, C.K., Favis, A.M., Guzman, M.A.L., Tan, M.L., Quintana, C., Josol, J.C., A supply chain framework for characterizing indirect vulnerability. *Int. J. Clim. Change Strat. Manage.*, 9, 2, 184–206, 2017.
24. Zhu, Q., Krikke, H., Caniëls, M.C.J., Wang, Y., Twin-objective supply chain collaboration to cope with rare but high-impact disruptions whilst improving performance. *Int. J. Logist. Manag.*, 28, 2, 488–507, 2017.
25. Montshiwa, A.L., Supply chain cooperation as a Green Supply Chain Management implementation strategy to achieve competitive advantages in natural disaster-prone regions. *Compet. Rev.*, 28, 5, 564–583, 2018.
26. Gunessee, S., Subramanian, N., Ning, K., Natural disasters, PC supply chain and corporate performance. *Int. J. Oper. Prod. Manag.*, 38, 9, 1796–1814, 2018.
27. Capkun, V., Hameri, A.P., Weiss, L.A., On the relationship between inventory and financial performance in manufacturing companies. *Int. J. Oper. Prod. Manag.*, 29, 8, 789–806, 2009.
28. Ketkar, M. and Vaidya, O.S., Study of Emerging Issues in Supply Risk Management in India. *Procedia Soc. Behav. Sci.*, 37, 57–66, 2012.
29. Marley, K.A., Ward, P.T., Hill, J.A., Mitigating supply chain disruptions-a normal accident perspective. *Supply Chain Manag.*, 19, 2, 142–152, 2014.
30. Pereira, C.R., Christopher, M., Lago Da Silva, A., Achieving supply chain resilience: The role of procurement. *Supply Chain Manag.*, 19, 626–642, 2014.
31. Dabhilkar, M., Birkie, S.E., Kaulio, M., Supply-side resilience as practice bundles: A critical incident study. *Int. J. Oper. Prod. Manag.*, 36, 8, 948–970, 2016.
32. Jajja, M.S.S., Kannan, V.R., Brah, S.A., Hassan, S.Z., Supply chain strategy and the role of suppliers: Evidence from the Indian sub-continent. *Benchmarking*, 23, 7, 1658–1676, 2016.
33. Panahifar, F., Byrne, P.J., Salam, M.A., Heavey, C., Supply chain collaboration and firm's performance. *J. Enterp. Inf. Manag.*, 31, 3, 358–379, 2018.

34. Kumar, V., Bak, O., Guo, R., Shaw, S.L., Colicchia, C., Garza-Reyes, J.A., Kumari, A., An empirical analysis of supply and manufacturing risk and business performance: A Chinese manufacturing supply chain perspective. *Supply Chain Manag.*, 23, 6, 461–479, 2018.
35. Zhu, X., Yuan, Q., Zhang, W., Inventory leanness, risk taking, environmental complexity, and productivity: A mediated moderation model. *J. Manuf. Technol. Manage.*, 29, 7, 1211–1232, 2018.
36. Kalaitzi, D., Matopoulos, A., Bourlakis, M., Tate, W., Supply chains under resource pressure: Strategies for improving resource efficiency and competitive advantage. *Int. J. Oper. Prod. Manag.*, 39, 12, 1323–1354, 2019.
37. Üstündağ, A. and Ungan, M.C., Supplier flexibility and performance: An empirical research. *Bus. Process Manag. J.*, 26, 7, 1851–1870, 2020.
38. Huma, S., Ahmed, W., Najmi, A., Understanding the impact of supply-side decisions and practices on supply risk management. *Benchmarking*, 27, 5, 1769–1792, 2020.
39. Polyviou, M., Croxton, K.L., Knemeyer, A.M., Resilience of medium-sized firms to supply chain disruptions: The role of internal social capital. *Int. J. Oper. Prod. Manag.*, 40, 1, 68–91, 2020.
40. Perera, H.N., Fahimnia, B., Tokar, T., Inventory and ordering decisions: A systematic review on research driven through behavioral experiments. *Int. J. Oper. Prod. Manag.*, 40, 7–8, 997–1039, 2020.
41. Thomas, A.V. and Mahanty, B., Dynamic assessment of control system designs of information shared supply chain network experiencing supplier disruption. *Oper. Res.*, 21, 1, 425–451, 2021.
42. Smith, K.M., Machalaba, C.C., Seifman, R., Feferholtz, Y., Karesh, W.B., Infectious disease and economics: The case for considering multi-sectoral impacts. *One Health*, 7, 100080, 2019.
43. Ivanov, D., Predicting the impacts of epidemic outbreaks on global supply chains: A simulation-based analysis on the coronavirus outbreak (COVID-19/SARS-CoV-2) case. *Transp. Res. Part E*, 136, 101922, 2020.
44. Yu, D.E.C., Razon, L.F., Tan, R.R., Can global pharmaceutical supply chains scale up sustainably for the COVID-19 crisis? *Resour. Conserv. Recycl.*, 159, 104868, 2020.
45. Sarkis, J., Cohen, M.J., Dewick, P., Schröder, P., A brave new world: Lessons from the COVID-19 pandemic for transitioning to sustainable supply and production. *Resour. Conserv. Recycl.*, 159, 104894, 2020.
46. Chowdhury, P., Paul, S.K., Kaisar, S., Moktadir, M.A., COVID-19 pandemic-related supply chain studies: A systematic review. *Transp. Res. Part E*, 148, 102271, 2021.
47. Singh, S., Kumar, R., Panchal, R., Tiwari, M.K., Impact of COVID-19 on logistics systems and disruptions in food supply chain. *Int. J. Prod. Res.*, 59, 7, 1993–2008, 2021.
48. Nikolopoulos, K., Punia, S., Schäfers, A., Tsinopoulos, C., Vasilakis, C., Forecasting and planning during a pandemic: COVID-19 growth rates,

supply chain disruptions, and governmental decisions. *Eur. J. Oper. Res.*, 290, 1, 99–115, 2021.

49. El Baz, J. and Ruel, S., Can supply chain risk management practices mitigate the disruption impacts on supply chains' resilience and robustness? Evidence from an empirical survey in a COVID-19 outbreak era. *Int. J. Prod. Econ.*, 233, 107972, 2021.
50. Mahajan, K. and Tomar, S., COVID-19 and Supply Chain Disruption: Evidence from Food Markets in India. *Am. J. Agric. Econ.*, 103, 1, 35–52, 2021.
51. Chen, J., Wang, H., Zhong, R.Y., A supply chain disruption recovery strategy considering product change under COVID-19. *J. Manuf. Syst.*, 60, 920–927, 2021.
52. Chakraborty, S., Jain, A., Sarmah, S.P., An integrated mathematical model based on grey optimal ranking for supplier selection considering pandemic situation. *Opsearch*, 59, 1613–1648, 2022.
53. Dekker, R., Van Asperen, E., Ochtman, G., Kusters, W., Floating stocks in FMCG supply chains: Using intermodal transport to facilitate advance deployment. *Int. J. Phys. Distrib. Logist. Manag.*, 39, 8, 632–648, 2009.
54. Pourakbar, M., Sleptchenko, A., Dekker, R., The floating stock policy in fast-moving consumer goods supply chains. *Transp. Res. Part E Logist. Transp. Rev.*, 45, 1, 39–49, 2009.
55. Abushaikha, I., The influence of logistics clustering on distribution capabilities: a qualitative study. *Int. J. Retail Distrib. Manag.*, 46, 6, 577–594, 2018.
56. Lawson, B., Potter, A., Pil, F.K., Holweg, M., Supply chain disruptions: The influence of industry and geography on firm reaction speed. *Int. J. Oper. Prod. Manag.*, 39, 9–10, 1076–1098, 2019.
57. Hendry, L.C., Stevenson, M., MacBryde, J., Ball, P., Sayed, M., Liu, L., Local food supply chain resilience to constitutional change: The Brexit effect. *Int. J. Oper. Prod. Manag.*, 39, 3, 429–453, 2019.
58. Ruiz-Benítez, R., López, C., Real, J.C., The lean and resilient management of the supply chain and its impact on performance. *Int. J. Prod. Econ.*, 203, 190–202, 2018.
59. Li, X., Wu, Q., Holsapple, C.W., Goldsby, T., An empirical examination of firm financial performance along dimensions of supply chain resilience. *Manag. Res. Rev.*, 40, 3, 254–269, 2017.
60. Mandal, S., Sarathy, R., Korasiga, V.R., Bhattacharya, S., Dastidar, S.G., Achieving supply chain resilience: The contribution of logistics and supply chain capabilities. *Int. J. Disaster Resil. Built Environ.*, 7, 5, 544–562, 2016.
61. Mandal, S., Bhattacharya, S., Korasiga, V.R., Sarathy, R., The dominant influence of logistics capabilities on integration: Empirical evidence from supply chain resilience. *Int. J. Disaster Resil. Built Environ.*, 8, 4, 357–374, 2017.
62. Jharkharia, S. and Shankar, R., Supply chain management: Some sectoral dissimilarities in the Indian manufacturing industry. *Supply Chain Manag.*, 11, 4, 345–352, 2006.

63. Chen, Z.X. and Hua Tan, K., The perceived impact of JIT implementation on operations performance: Evidence from Chinese firms. *J. Adv. Manag. Res.*, 8, 2, 213–235, 2011.
64. Sharma, S. and Modgil, S., Supply chain and total quality management framework design for business performance—Case study evidence. *J. Enterp. Inf. Manag.*, 28, 6, 905–930, 2015.
65. AL-Shboul, M.A., Garza-Reyes, J.A., Kumar, V., Best supply chain management practices and high-performance firms: The case of Gulf manufacturing firms. *Int. J. Product. Perform. Manag.*, 67, 9, 1482–1509, 2018.
66. Antony, J., Gijo, E.V., Kumar, V., Ghadge, A., A multiple case study analysis of Six Sigma practices in Indian manufacturing companies. *Int. J. Qual. Reliab. Manag.*, 33, 8, 1138–1149, 2016.
67. Chaudhuri, A., Boer, H., Taran, Y., Supply chain integration, risk management and manufacturing flexibility. *Int. J. Oper. Prod. Manag.*, 38, 3, 690–712, 2018.
68. Danese, P., Romano, P., Bortolotti, T., JIT production, JIT supply and performance: Investigating the moderating effects. *Ind. Manag. Data Syst.*, 112, 3, 441–465, 2012.
69. Singh, G. and Ahuja, I.S., An evaluation of just-in-time (JIT) implementation on manufacturing performance in Indian industry. *J. Asia Bus. Stud.*, 8, 3, 278–294, 2014.
70. Taj, S. and Morosan, C., The impact of lean operations on Chinese manufacturing performance. *J. Manuf. Technol. Manage.*, 22, 2, 223–240, 2011.
71. Chowdhury, M.M.H. and Quaddus, M., Supply chain readiness, response and recovery for resilience. *Supply Chain Manag.*, 21, 6, 709–731, 2016.
72. Jonsson, P. and Mattsson, S.-A., The value of sharing planning information in supply chains. *Int. J. Phys. Distrib. Logist. Manag.*, 43, 4, 282–299, 2013.
73. Jüttner, U. and Maklan, S., Supply chain resilience in the global financial crisis: An empirical study. *Supply Chain Manag.*, 16, 4, 246–259, 2011.
74. Natarajarathinam, M., Capar, I., Narayanan, A., Managing supply chains in times of crisis: A review of literature and insights. *Int. J. Phys. Distrib. Logist. Manag.*, 39, 7, 535–573, 2009.
75. Hittle, B. and Leonard, K.M., Decision making in advance of a supply chain crisis. *Manage. Decis.*, 49, 7, 1182–1193, 2011.
76. Das, K., Integrating resilience in a supply chain planning model. *Int. J. Qual. Reliab. Manag.*, 35, 3, 570–595, 2018.
77. Christopher, M., Mena, C., Khan, O., Yurt, O., Approaches to managing global sourcing risk. *Supply Chain Manag.*, 16, 2, 67–81, 2011.
78. López, C. and Ruiz-Benítez, R., Multilayer analysis of supply chain strategies' impact on sustainability. *J. Purch. Supply Manag.*, 26, 2, 100535, 2020.
79. Singh, N.P. and Singh, S., Building supply chain risk resilience: Role of big data analytics in supply chain disruption mitigation. *Benchmarking Int. J.*, 26, 7, 2318–2342, 2019.

80. Bag, S., Telukdarie, A., Pretorius, J.H.C., Gupta, S., Industry 4.0 and supply chain sustainability: framework and future research directions. *Benchmarking*, 28, 5, 1410–1450, 2018.
81. Datta, P., Supply network resilience: A systematic literature review and future research. *Int. J. Logist. Manag.*, 28, 4, 1387–1424, 2017.
82. Stewart, G.T., Kolluru, R., Smith, M., Leveraging public-private partnerships to improve community resilience in times of disaster. *Int. J. Phys. Distrib. Logist. Manag.*, 39, 5, 343–364, 2009.
83. Adobor, H. and McMullen, R.S., Supply chain resilience: a dynamic and multidimensional approach. *Int. J. Logist. Manag.*, 29, 4, 1451–1471, 2018.
84. Ambulkar, S., Blackhurst, J., Grawe, S., Firm's resilience to supply chain disruptions: Scale development and empirical examination. *J. Oper. Manage.*, 33–34, 111–122, 2015.
85. Heckmann, I., Comes, T., Nickel, S., A critical review on supply chain risk-Definition, measure and modeling. *Omega*, 52, 119–132, 2015.
86. Bhamra, R., Dani, S., Burnard, K., Resilience: The concept, a literature review and future directions. *Int. J. Prod. Res.*, 49, 18, 5375–5393, 2011.
87. Mensah, P. and Merkuryev, Y., Developing a resilient supply chain. *Procedia Soc. Behav. Sci.*, 110, 309–319, 2014.
88. MacKenzie, C.A. and Apte, A., Modeling disruption in a fresh produce supply chain. *Int. J. Logist. Manag.*, 28, 2, 656–679, 2017.
89. Chaudhary, V., Kulshrestha, R., Routroy, S., State-of-the-art literature review on inventory models for perishable products. *J. Adv. Manag. Res.*, 15, 3, 306–346, 2018.
90. Rofyanto Kurniawan, R., Zailani, S.H., Rajagopal, P., The effects of vulnerability mitigation strategies on supply chain effectiveness: Risk culture as moderator. *Supply Chain Manag.*, 22, 1, 1–15, 2017.
91. Chakraborty, S. and Sarmah, S.P., Managing supply and transportation disruptions: A case of Indian fair price shops. *Kybernetes*, 49, 2773–2797, 2020.
92. Panwar, A., Nepal, B., Jain, R., Rathore, A.P.S., Lyons, A., Understanding the linkages between lean practices and performance improvements in Indian process industries. *Ind. Manag. Data Syst.*, 117, 2, 346–364, 2017.
93. Li, Y., Zobel, C.W., Russell, R.S., Value of supply disruption information and information accuracy. *J. Purch. Supply Manag.*, 23, 3, 191–201, 2017.

11

Lot Optimization for Defective Inventory with Inspection Uncertainty

Maroof Ahmad Mir* **and Bushra**

Department of Finance, Asian Business School, Noida (U.P.), India

Abstract

In real-world supply chains, managing defective items is critical for ensuring smooth operations and avoiding costly disruptions. The proposed model is particularly useful for industries like textiles, footwear, and electronics, where batch quality is often inconsistent. The model includes assumptions that reflect common business scenarios. A finite replenishment rate that mirrors typical production or procurement schedules. The proportion of defective items in each received lot is considered a random variable, as seen in many industries. As no inspection process is flawless, so inspection errors are also included.

For industry professionals, this model provides insights into how defects and errors can be managed in inventory systems by optimizing order quantities, reducing waste, and improving overall supply chain efficiency.

Keywords: Inventory, imperfect items, inspection errors, supply chain

11.1 Literature Review

In the past, researchers had extensively explored the field of defective inventory through various interesting works, beginning with contributories like Porteus (1986) [1], Rosenblatt and Lee (1986) [2], Lee and Rosenblatt (1987) [3], Schwaller (1988) [4], Zhang and Gerchak (1990) [5]. Later, Salameh and Jaber (2000) [6] introduced probability distribution for proportion of defectives Further, Cárdenas-Barrón (2000) [7], Goyal and

**Corresponding author*: mirmaroofahmad@gmail.com

K. Mathiyazhagan, Krishna Kumar Dadsena, Rajesh Kumar Singh, Aakanksha Kishore and Andrea Appolloni (eds.) Sustainable Operations of Logistics and Supply Chain Management, (261–274) © 2025 Scrivener Publishing LLC

Cárdenas-Barrón (2002) [8] refined the solutions of Salameh and Jaber (2000) [6] by adding constant parameter. Papachristos and Konstantaras (2006) [9] improved the work of Salameh and Jaber (2000) [6] by extending the conditions of assuming no shortages in their model.

Maddah and Jaber (2008) [10], Maddah *et al.* (2010) [11] also worked upon screening errors. In light of inspection uncertainty, Raouf *et al.* (1983) [12] first discussed screening errors in the inspection planning. Furthermore, Duffuaa and Khan (2002) [13], Duffuaa and Khan (2005) [14], Khan *et al.* (2011) [15], Konstantaras *et al.* (2012) [16], and Hsu and Hsu (2013) [17] worked upon inspection errors.

Bazan *et al.* (2014) [18] verified that the inspection rate of the manufacturer is equal to or greater than its producing rate. Chen (2016) [19] aimed to improve the cost of the joint economic lot-size problem (JELP) model and the operational methods for perishable and damaged goods under RPP. Hsu & Hsu (2016) [20] created an inventory model that takes into account screening as well as the potential for Type 1 and Type 2 errors to cause commodities that are screened to be misclassified. Khanna *et al.* (2017) [21] worked upon inventory modeling for imperfect production process with inspection errors, sales return, and imperfect rework process. Kalantari & Taleizadeh (2020) [22] suggested an EPQ model to integrate the estimation of the selling price, the number of shipments, and the size of replenishment lots into a single model for multiple shipments. Cunha *et al.* (2018) [23] put in place an EPQ model that takes into account both a portion of backorders and defective items. Marchi *et al.* (2019) [24] utilized production, accuracy, and reliability training with inferior materials in conjunction with the EPQ model to address the energy efficiency concerns. Karthick & Uthayakumar (2021) [25] discovered that defective products are found as a result of production-related equipment failures, and the buyer undergoes a quality inspection process to identify defective products. Cheng *et al.* (2021) [26] created a novel method that raises the possibility that the product will be approved by enabling consumers to evaluate the operational reliability indicators of the product without arbitrary removal of unreliable samples. Wang *et al.* (2022) [27] investigated the effects of inspection errors, deterioration control limits, and the optimization of periodic inspection intervals. Zhang *et al.* (2022) [28] claimed that the impact of early experimentation with two distinct types of defects is taken into account in the composite design problem. For example, quality loss is influenced by both the state of the production process and wear and tear on the equipment. Al Hanbali *et al.* (2022) [29] tried to improve the best cost consistency rate as average degradation per hour and developed a maintenance model that took lead time, inspection errors, and parts quality into account.

In industries where products are received from external manufacturers, such as retail and electronics, it is unrealistic to assume that all batches will be defect-free. The occurrence of defective items in inventory is a challenge that businesses must address to maintain quality standards and customer satisfaction. In response, researchers have developed various models (EPQ/EOQ) to optimize inventory management when dealing with imperfect items.

However, most businesses also face inspection errors during quality control processes, where both false positives (non-defective items classified as defective) and false negatives (defective items classified as non-defective) occur. These errors can have significant financial and reputational consequences. This paper builds on existing research by presenting a model that accounts for such errors, providing practical strategies for businesses to manage defective items in their supply chains. Necessary and sufficient conditions of the optimal solution have been obtained mathematically. Finally, analysis of various cost and revenue components is conducted to authenticate the results and provide managerial insights.

11.2 Model Development

11.2.1 Assumptions

1) Rate of Refill is finite.
2) Received lot contains a certain proportion of defectives.
3) Inspection rate is higher w.r.t demand rate.
4) Inspection process is also not perfect.
5) Demand is deterministic.
6) Infinite time horizon is used with insignificant lead time.
7) Shortages are not allowed.

11.2.2 Notations

Λ	Demand Amount
D	Percentage of imperfect units
q_1	Percentage of Type-I fault
q_2	Percentage of Type-II fault
T	Cycle length
K	Set-up amount

C	Unit cost
i	Screening cost
S	Selling price
v	Salvage price
c_r	Price of Type-I fault
c_a	Price of Type-II fault
H	Price of Holding an item
Y	Ordering amount
$Z_l(y)$	Profit function
$E[Z_l(y)]$	Expected profit function
Optimal Amounts	
T^*	Optimal value of cycle span
y^*	Optimal ordering amount
$E[Z_l^*(y)]$	Optimal expected profit function

11.3 Mathematical Formulation

11.3.1 Model

This section formulates the outlined inventory problem based on the above assumptions as shown in Figure 11.1.

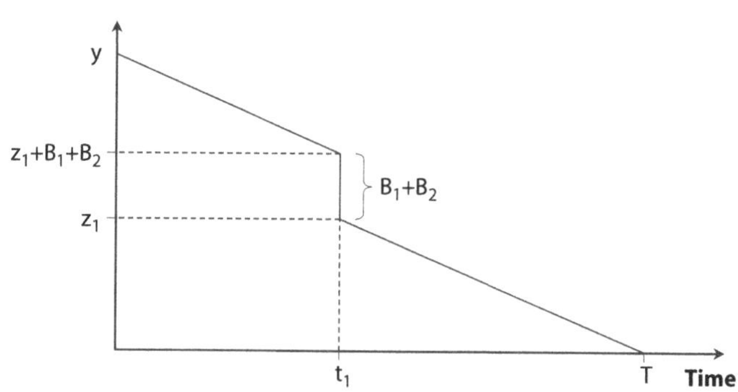

Figure 11.1 Inventory scenario.

At the start of the inventory cycle, sale and inspection of all the items occur simultaneously. By the time t_1, all the defectives are accumulated and then sold as a single batch at a discounted price. Finally, the inventory depletes to zero by time T. Mathematically, we have the following from Figure 11.1.

$$t_1 = \frac{y}{\lambda} \tag{11.1}$$

$$z_1 = D(T - t_1) \tag{11.2}$$

Also,

$$z_1 = y - B_1 - B_2 - Dt_1 \tag{11.3}$$

where,

$$\text{Total items salvaged } B_1 = d(1-q_2)y + (1-d)q_1 y \tag{11.4}$$

$$\text{Total Sales returns } B_2 = dq_2 y \tag{11.5}$$

Also, Total perfect lot sold amounts to $= dq_2 y + (1-q_1)(1-d)y$

$$\therefore T = \frac{= dq_2 y + (1-q_1)(1-d)y}{D} \text{ i.e,}$$

$$\Rightarrow T = \frac{Ay}{D} \tag{11.6}$$

where $A = (1-d)(1-q_1) + dq_2$

$$\therefore E[A] = (1 - E[d])(1 - [q_1]) + E[d][q_2] \tag{11.7}$$

$$\therefore E[T] = \frac{yE[A]}{D}$$
$$\therefore E[T] = \frac{\{(1-E[d])(1-E[q_1]) + E[d]E[q_2]\}y}{D} \tag{11.8}$$

No Shortage Condition:

$$\left[dq_2 + (1-d)(1-q_1)\right]y > Dt_1$$

i.e.

$$Ay > Dt_1 \tag{11.9}$$

11.3.1.1 Relevant Costs

i)
$$SC = K \tag{11.10}$$

ii)
$$PC = cy \tag{11.11}$$

iii)
$$IC = iy \tag{11.12}$$

iv)
$$EC1 = c_r(1-d)q_1 y \tag{11.13}$$

v)
$$EC2 = c_a dq_2 y \tag{11.14}$$

vi)
$$HC = h\left[\frac{(y+z_1+B_1+B_2)t_1}{2} + \frac{z_1(T-t_1)}{2} + \frac{B_2(T-t_1)}{2}\right] \tag{11.15}$$

$$\therefore T.C. = K + y\left[c + i + c_r(1-d)q_1 + c_a dq_2\right] + \frac{h}{2}y^2\left[\frac{(1-A)}{\lambda} + \frac{d(1-q_2)}{\lambda} + \frac{(1-d)q_1}{\lambda} + \frac{A(A+dq_2)}{D}\right] \tag{11.16}$$

11.3.1.2 Revenue Components

i)

$$R_1 = p\left[dq_2y + (1-d)(1-q_1)y\right] \tag{11.17}$$

ii)

$$R_2 = -pdq_2y \tag{11.18}$$

iii)

$$R_3 = v(B_1 + B_2) = v\left[d(1-q_2)y + (1-d)q_1y + dq_2y\right] \tag{11.19}$$

$$\therefore T.R. = (1-d)p(1-q_1)y + v\left[d(1-q_2)y + (1-d)q_1y + dq_2y\right] \therefore \tag{11.20}$$

11.3.1.3 Profit Function

T.P. = T.R. - T.C.

$$\begin{aligned} &= p(1-d)(1-q_1)y + v\left[d(1-q_2)y + (1-d)q_1y + dq_2y\right] \\ &\quad - K - y\left[c + i + c_r(1-d)q_1 + c_a dq_2\right] \\ &\quad - \frac{h}{2}y^2\left[\frac{(1-A)}{\lambda} + \frac{d(1-q_2)}{\lambda} + \frac{(1-d)q_1}{\lambda} + \frac{A(A+dq_2)}{D}\right] \end{aligned} \tag{11.21}$$

$$= yG_1 - y^2G_2 - K \tag{11.22}$$

where

$$G_1 = p(1-d)(1-q_1) + v\left[d(1-q_2) + (1-d)q_1y + dq_2\right] - \left[c + i + c_r(1-d)q_1 + c_a dq_2\right]$$

$$G_2 = \frac{h}{2}\left[\frac{(1-A)}{\lambda} + \frac{d(1-q_2)}{\lambda} + \frac{(1-d)q_1}{\lambda} + \frac{A(A+dq_2)}{D}\right]$$

11.3.1.4 Expected Profit Function

$$E\left[Z_1(y)\right] = \left(\frac{DE[G_1]}{E[A]} - \frac{DE[G_2]y}{E[A]}\right) - K\frac{Dy}{E[A]} \tag{11.23}$$

where

$$E[G_1]=p(1-E[d])(1-E[q_1])+v\{E[d]+(1-E[d])E[q_1]\}$$
$$-c-i-c_r(1-E[d])E[q_1]-c_aE[d]E[q_2]$$

$$E[G_2]=\frac{h}{2}\left\{\begin{array}{l}\dfrac{1-\left[E(d)E(q_2)+(1-E[d])(1-E[q_1])\right]}{\lambda}\\ +\dfrac{E[d](1-E[q_2])}{\lambda}+\dfrac{(1-E[d])E[q_1]}{\lambda}+\\ \dfrac{\{E[d]E[q_2]+(1-E[d])(1-E[q_1])\}\{2E[d]E[q_2]+(1-E[d])(1-E[q_1])\}}{D}\end{array}\right\}$$

11.4 Optimal Policy

The result is established through two lemmas.

Lemma1. *Proof of global concavity.*

Proof. To demonstrate global concavity, the following second-order sufficient conditions are shown below:

$$\left(\frac{\partial^2 E[Z_1(y)]}{\partial y^2}\right)\leq 0;$$

$$\frac{\partial E[Z_1(y)]}{\partial y}=-\frac{DE[G_2]}{E[A]}+\frac{DE[G_3]}{E[A]y^2} \tag{11.24}$$

$$\left(\frac{\partial^2 E[Z_1(y)]}{\partial y^2}\right)=-\frac{2DE[G_3]}{E[A]y^3} \tag{11.25}$$

Since $\left(\frac{\partial^2 E[Z_1(y)]}{\partial y^2}\right)\leq 0$

Hence, the concavity has been proven.

Lemma 2. *y^* which maximizes expected profit function is given by:*

$$y^*=\sqrt{\frac{E[G_3]}{E[G_2]}}$$

Proof. To find y^* (optimal value), which maximizes $E\left[Z_1(y)\right]$, necessary condition is as follows:

i.e.
$$\frac{\partial E\left[Z_1(y)\right]}{\partial y}=0$$

$$y_1^* = \sqrt{\frac{E[G_3]}{E[G_2]}} \tag{11.26}$$

Hence, y_1^* is the optimal value.
Hence, Lemma 2 follows.

11.5 Numerical Analysis

A practical illustration is provided for industry professionals to improve their strategies for inventory management.

11.5.1 Example

$$f(d)=\begin{cases}25, 0\le x\le 0.04\\ 0, \text{otherwise}\end{cases} \tag{11.27}$$

$$f(q_1)=\begin{cases}50, 0.01\le q_1\le 0.03\\ 0, \text{otherwise}\end{cases} \tag{11.28}$$

$$f(q_2)=\begin{cases}50, 0.2\le q_2\le 0.7\\ 0, \text{otherwise}\end{cases} \tag{11.29}$$

$d = 0.1$, $i = \$\ 0.15$/unit, $q_1 = 0.02$, $q_2 = 0.02$, $C_a = \$\ 0.1$/unit, $C_r = \$\ 0.05$/unit,

Other parameters are same as that of Teng (2009) model:

$D = 3{,}600$ units/year, $c = \$\ 0.5$/unit, $K = \$12$/cycle, $p = \$1$/unit, $C_s = \$0.35$/unit, $h = \$0.2$/unit, $\alpha = 0.5$, $\lambda = 5{,}000$ units/year

The optimal order size $y^* = 580$ units/ cycle with corresponding $E^*\left[Z_1(y)\right] = \$440$ /year and $T^* = 52.02$ days respectively.

Also, no shortage condition is validated as follows:

$$Ay > Dt_1$$

11.5.2 Analysis & Applicability

Following are the graphs illustrating relative changes in optimal units of the decision variables.

Among all the parameters in the Figure 11.2, the defect parameters viz. d and q_1 grow the need for increase of orders. Since the increasing proportions of imperfect items reduce the count of perfect items and hence higher amount of order is utilized for fulfillment of the demand in same manner.

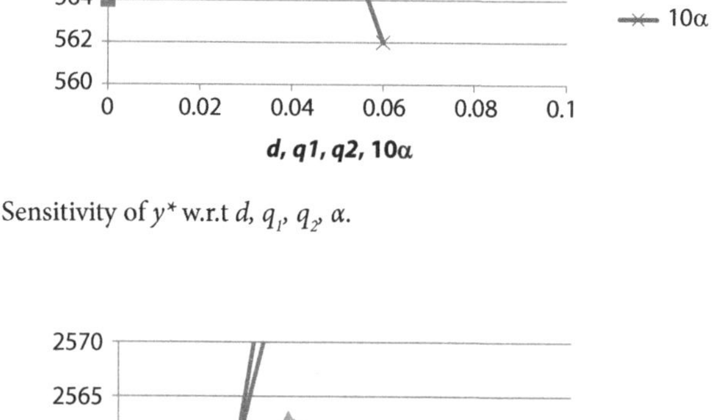

Figure 11.2 Sensitivity of y^* w.r.t d, q_1, q_2, α.

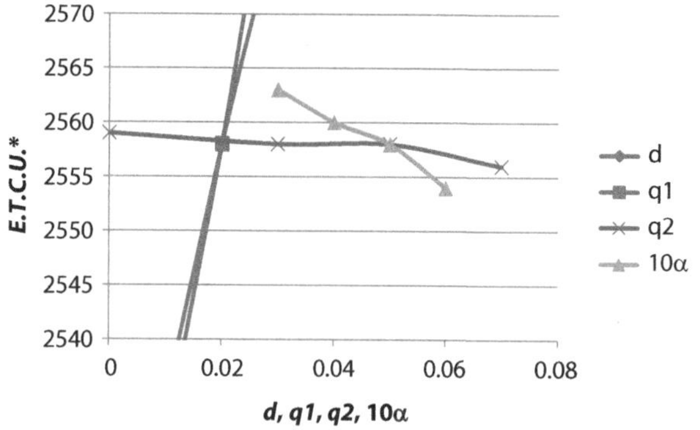

Figure 11.3 Sensitivity of the $E.T.C.U^*$ w.r.t d, q_1, q_2, α.

There seems to be no significant reduction in the value of y^* on increase of sales returns (q_2) as the retailer refunds/exchanges all the returned defectives from customers. This does not bring much change in the number of orders per cycle. On the other hand, increment in proportions of parameters α contribute in decreasing the value of y^*. It is explained by the fact that the growing percent of good customers assures the retailer that sufficient quantity of perfect items is getting sold to the customers, so he does not need to order more. Also, increase of (α) provides the retailer with better finances at the time of purchase of items throughout the cycle length, which makes him prefer increase the frequency of orders instead of ordering large.

Since quality assurance via inspection processes, misclassification errors, salvage comes at a relatively higher cost to the retailer, the defect related parameters show increasing trend in the cost values in Figure 11.3. The various cost components affected due to defectives, inspection errors, salvage present in the model are- inspection costs, misclassification costs, and overall inventory holding costs respectively. These expenses can also be believed as good investments to the retailer as these give longer and higher returns once the reputation of quality products is established by far-reaching customer service. However, cost is showing declining trend with the increase in the proportion of good customers. In other words, when there is fall in the proportion of bad customers, fewer numbers of sales returns lead to lesser inventory holding costs. Also, there is direct loss of some part of sold inventory due to bad debts which also contributes in decreasing the inventory related costs. However, there is no significant decline in the total cost values on increasing q_2 as it is viewed more as loss of goodwill, which is harder to recover than a financial one. Even though the cost is less but it needs to be reduced due to its criticality in the process. However, when larger portion of selling price (α) is fetched by the retailer at the initial time of payment, the cost values exhibit slight decrease.

11.6 Conclusion and Future Research

This study introduces an EOQ model that helps businesses manage defective items and inspection errors, ensuring more accurate inventory management and better financial outcomes. For industries that rely heavily on supply chain efficiency and quality control, such as manufacturing, retail, and logistics, this model offers actionable insights.

The model also evaluates key cost components, including:

- **Setup costs**, which reflect the fixed cost per production or procurement cycle.

- **Inspection costs,** which are significant in industries reliant on high-quality control, such as electronics or pharmaceuticals.
- **Type I and Type II error costs**, representing losses due to incorrect classification of items. Type I errors (rejecting non-defective items) result in lost sales opportunities, while Type II errors (accepting defective items) lead to customer dissatisfaction and product returns.

By optimizing these variables, businesses can minimize unnecessary expenses and maximize profitability, making this model particularly applicable to managers looking to fine-tune their operations.

Future research can explore further applications of this model by incorporating factors like shortages, varying demand patterns, or the impact of modern technologies such as AI-powered inspection systems, making it even more applicable to the dynamic challenges faced by industries today.

References

1. Porteus, E.L., Optimal lot sizing, process quality improvement and setup cost reduction. *Oper. Res.*, 34, 1, 137–144, 1986.
2. Rosenblatt, M.J. and Lee, H.L., Economic production cycles with imperfect production processes. *IIE Trans.*, 18, 1, 48–55, 1986.
3. Lee, H.L. and Rosenblatt, M.J., Simultaneous determination of production cycle and inspection schedules in a production system. *Manage. Sci.*, 33, 9, 1125–1136, 1987.
4. Schwaller, R.L., EOQ under inspection costs. *Prod. Invent. Manage.*, 29, 3, 22–24, 1988.
5. Zhang, X. and Gerchak, Y., Joint lot sizing and inspection policy in an EOQ model with random yield. *IIE Trans.*, 22, 1, 41–47, 1990.
6. Salameh, M.K. and Jaber, M.Y., Economic production quantity model for items with imperfect quality. *Int. J. Prod. Econ.*, 64, 1, 59–64, 2000.
7. Cárdenas-Barrón, L.E., Observation on: "Economic production quantity model for items with imperfect quality". *Int. J. Prod. Econ.*, 67, 2, 201, 2000.
8. Goyal, S.K. and Cárdenas-Barrón, L.E., Note on: economic production quantity model for items with imperfect quality–a practical approach. *Int. J. Prod. Econ.*, 77, 1, 85–87, 2002.
9. Papachristos, S. and Konstantaras, I., Economic ordering quantity models for items with imperfect quality. *Int. J. Prod. Econ.*, 100, 1, 148–154, 2006.
10. Maddah, B. and Jaber, M., Economic order quantity for items with imperfect quality: revisited. *Int. J. Prod. Econ.*, 112, 2, 808–815, 2008.

11. Maddah, B., Salameh, M.K., Moussawi-Haidar, L., Order overlapping: A practical approach for preventing shortages during screening. *Comput. Ind. Eng.*, 58, 691–695, 2010.
12. Raouf, A., Jain, J.K., Sathe, P.T., A cost-minimization model for multi characteristic component inspection. *IIE Trans.*, 15, 3, 187–194, 1983.
13. Duffuaa, S.O. and Khan, M., An optimal repeat inspection plan with several classifications. *J. Oper. Res. Soc.*, 53, 9, 1016–1026, 2002.
14. Duffuaa, S.O. and Khan, M., Impact of inspection errors on the performance measures of a general repeat inspection plan. *Int. J. Prod. Res.*, 43, 23, 4945–4967, 2005.
15. Khan, M., Jaber, M.Y., Bonney, M., An economic order quantity (EOQ) for items with imperfect quality and inspection errors. *Int. J. Prod. Econ.*, 133, 1, 113–118, 2011.
16. Konstantaras, I., Skouri, K., Jaber, M.Y., Inventory models for imperfect quality items with shortages and learning in inspection. *Appl. Math. Modell.*, 36, 11, 5334–5343, 2012.
17. Hsu, J.T. and Hsu, L.F., An EOQ model with imperfect quality items, inspection errors, shortage backordering, and sales returns. *Int. J. Prod. Econ., 143*, 1, 162–170, 2013.
18. Bazan, E., Jaber, M.Y., Zanoni, S., Zavanella, L.E., Vendor Managed Inventory (VMI) with Consignment Stock (CS) agreement for a two-level supply chain with an imperfect production process with/without restoration interruption. *Int. J. Prod. Econ., 157*, 289–301, 2014.
19. Chen, X. and Zhang, J., Duality approaches to economic lot-sizing games. *Prod. Oper. Manage., 25*, 7, 1203–1215, 2016.
20. Hsu, S., Zhou, R.D.H., Yu, C.K.C., A Hong Kong validation of working alliance inventory–short form–client. *Asia Pac. J. Couns. Psychother., 7*, 1–2, 69–81, 2016.
21. Khanna, A., Kishore, A., Jaggi, C.K., Inventory modeling for imperfect production process with inspection errors, sales return, and imperfect rework process. *Int. J. Math. Eng. Manag. Sci.*, 2, 4, 242–258, 2017.
22. Kalantari, S.S. and Taleizadeh, A.A., Mathematical modelling for determining the replenishment policy for deteriorating items in an EPQ model with multiple shipments. *Int. J. Syst. Sci. Oper. Logist., 7*, 2, 164–171, 2020.
23. Cunha, L.R.A., Delfino, A.P.S., dos Reis, K.A., Leiras, A., Economic production quantity (EPQ) model with partial backordering and a discount for imperfect quality batches. *Int. J. Prod. Res., 56*, 18, 6279–6293, 2018.
24. Marchi, B., Zanoni, S., Jaber, M.Y., Economic production quantity model with learning in production, quality, reliability and energy efficiency. *Comput. Ind. Eng., 129*, 502–511, 2019.
25. Karthick, B. and Uthayakumar, R., A sustainable supply chain model with two inspection errors and carbon emissions under uncertain demand. *Clean. Eng. Technol.*, 5, 100307, 2021.

26. Cheng, L., Wan, Y., Zhou, Y., Gao, D.W., Operational reliability modeling and assessment of battery energy storage based on lithium-ion battery lifetime degradation. *J. Mod. Power Syst. Clean Energy*, *10*, 6, 1738–1749, 2021.
27. Wang, Y., Wang, J., Cao, Y., Li, S., Kwan, O., Integrated inspection on PCB manufacturing in cyber–physical–social systems. *IEEE Trans. Syst. Man Cybern.: Syst.*, *53*, 4, 2098–2106, 2022.
28. Zhang, Z., Zhang, Z., Di Caprio, F., Gu, G.X., Machine learning for accelerating the design process of double-double composite structures. *Compos. Struct.*, *285*, 115233, 2022.
29. Al Hanbali, A., Saleh, H.H., Alsawafy, O.G., Attia, A.M., Ghaithan, A.M., Mohammed, A., Spare parts supply with incoming quality control and inspection errors in condition-based maintenance. *Comput. Ind. Eng.*, *172*, 108534, 2022.

12

Optimizing the Sugarcane Supply Chain: Role of Circular Economy, ML, and MCDM

Sumit Kumar[1*], Meenu Singh[2], Millie Pant[1,3] and Václav Snášel[2]

[1]*Department of Applied Mathematics and Scientific Computing, Indian Institute of Technology Roorkee, Uttarakhand, India*
[2]*Faculty of Electrical Engineering and Computer Science, VŠB-Technical University of Ostrava, Ostrava, Czech Republic*
[3]*Mehta Family School for Data Science and Artificial Intelligence, Indian Institute of Technology Roorkee, Uttarakhand, India*

Abstract
This chapter examines the implementation of circular economy (CE), machine learning (ML) and multi-criteria decision-making (MCDM) techniques in optimizing the sugarcane supply chain (SSC). Sugarcane is chosen as the subject because of its agricultural and socio-economic relevance. Sustainable practices and innovative technologies that contribute to the SSC's efficiency are discussed, along with the associated challenges. The aim is to provide a comprehensive understanding of the advanced methodologies to enhance decision-making processes, resource utilization, waste management, and overall optimization in the SSC. As a case study, the MCDM methods namely TOPSIS, VIKOR, WSM, EDAS, are applied to rank thirty-nine sugarcane mills based on twelve criterion including sustainability, final ranking is determined using Half Quadratic (HQ) theory. The results are validated through ML algorithm namely k-mean clustering, showing consistency between the MCDM approaches and machine learning.

***Keywords*:** Sugarcane supply chain, wonder cane circular economy, machine learning, MCDM

**Corresponding author*: skumar1@as.iitr.ac.in

K. Mathiyazhagan, Krishna Kumar Dadsena, Rajesh Kumar Singh, Aakanksha Kishore and Andrea Appolloni (eds.) Sustainable Operations of Logistics and Supply Chain Management, (275–300) © 2025 Scrivener Publishing LLC

12.1 Introduction

Food and natural resources like land and water are under greater demand as the world's population continues to grow [1]. With over seven billion people on the planet, agriculture faces increasing pressure to produce enough food. Agriculture not only provides food for survival but also raw materials for manufacturing industries. It is an essential source of livelihood and economic support. However, the rapid depletion of fertile land presents significant challenges to meeting future demands [2].

One of the most significant and valuable crops in the world is sugarcane [3]. This semi-perennial crop thrives in tropical and sub-tropical regions. It is grown on about 27 million hectares worldwide, producing 1.92 billion tons of fresh cane annually [4], accounting for 80% of the world's sugar supply. As one of the largest crops in terms of production, sugarcane significantly impacts the economies of many countries. Sugarcane contributes to the Gross Domestic Product and provides employment to millions of farmers and laborers working in its associated industries. Historically cultivated since around 8000 B.C. in New Guinea, sugarcane has spread worldwide [5]. It is growing well in warm, humid regions with plenty of rainfall.

Sugarcane is not only a key raw material for producing sugar and ethanol but is also essential in the biofuel industry. It contributes about 60% to the world's bioethanol supply, helping reduce reliance on fossil fuels. Molasses, bagasse, press mud, and filter cake are the important by-products from sugarcane that are used in various industries. Bagasse is mainly used as fuel and in the making of compressed fiberboard, paper, and plastic, while Molasses is used in distilleries and as an additive to livestock feed [6]. Press mud improves soil quality, and green tops of cane are good fodder for cattle. The sucrose content in sugarcane stalks is typically 12–15% of the fresh weight [7]. Sugarcane is often referred to as the "Wonder cane" due to its extensive usage in many industries and cattle forms. Sugarcane is subject to weather and climatic conditions, just like other seasonal crops. As a cash crop with a long and complicated growth cycle of 8 to 10 months, sugarcane cultivation is a labor-intensive and complicated process [8]. Sugar is used in every country and is produced from either sugarcane or sugar beet. With 80% of global sugar production prepared from sugarcane and an average annual consumption of 24 kg per person, sugarcane is cultivated in over 120 countries to meet both domestic and international demands. (Sugarcane Industry, 2024). Details of some sugarcane-growing countries are shown in Figure 12.1, taken from ICAR – IISR[1].

---

[1]Source: https://iisr.icar.gov.in/iisr/pages/maps.jsp

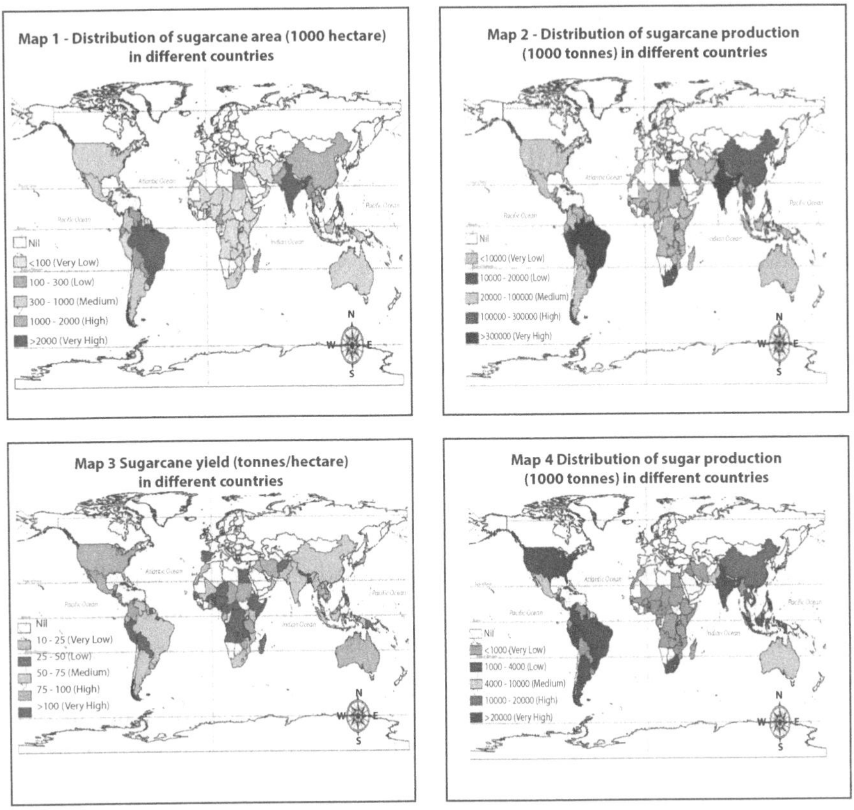

Figure 12.1 Distribution of sugarcane worldwide [9].

The SSC faces challenges, including environmental sustainability, economic viability, and social impact, such as water-intensive cultivation, chemical fertilizers and pesticides, and significant waste generation. To maintain sustainability and profitability, creative solutions are required. (Indian Institute of Sugarcane Research, Lucknow, 2024). CE is an approach to address major socio-economic and environmental issues like climate change, resource depletion, and over-consumption. It focuses on minimizing resource use, waste, emissions, and energy loss by slowing, closing, and tightening material and energy cycles [10].

Despite various studies addressing the optimization of SSC, there still remains a critical gap in fully integrating CE principles with advanced ML and MCDM techniques. This chapter addresses these challenges by exploring the application of CE principles alongside the role of ML and MCDM methods in optimizing the SSC and aims to illustrate their role in improving decision-making processes, optimizing resource use, managing waste effectively, and enhancing the overall supply chain. In the case study, the operational and sustainability features of sugar mills are analyzed to determine their sustainability rankings using MCDM methods, with the results validated through ML algorithm.

The remaining chapter is organized as follows: Section 12.2 reviews the existing literature on SSCs and the circular-SSC. Section 12.3 discusses the SSC and its circular aspects. In Section 12.4, role of MCDM and ML in SSC is explored. Section 12.5 provides the challenges and solutions in adopting a CE in SSC. In section 12.6, a case study to find the ranking of sugar mill based on sustainability features, is discussed. Finally, Section 12.7 presents the conclusion and directions for further development.

12.2 Related Literature

Understanding SSC stages helps improve productivity, sustainability, and profitability. Several mathematical optimization models addressing these problems help create efficient planning tools for several phases in SSC. A conceptual framework is developed by [11], which described the planning for cultivating sugarcane. It centers upon the cultivar selection, optimized period of cultivation, and time window to begin harvesting at every field. The authors [12], developed bi-objective mixed-integer non-linear programming (MILP) that scheduled the transport and harvesting operations in the multi-period planning horizon. Mathematical optimization models are introduced to enhance the planning within the SSC, with tools to help the challenges that minimized efficiency and productivity [13]. Implementing CE in SSC is important for achieving sustainability by addressing social, economic, and environmental factors [14, 15]. CE indicators is proposed, based on air, water, soil, energy, waste, cost, equality, knowledge, and innovation [16]. Opportunities and barriers to implementing CE are discussed in [17]. CE is critical to achieving the 2030 agenda for sustainable development [18].

Other vast areas of the research have been on maintaining the SSC as a sustainable entity. In this context, [5] conducted a critical literature review regarding the state of art about SSC sustainability and proposed maintaining sustainable production that increases and continued yields within the carrying capacity of the resources of soils, water, air, and biodiversity. The merits of the circular economy are highly applicable to the sugarcane industry. To rank sustainable sugarcane farms, the author introduced the

VTOPES ensemble decision-making model, which consists of an integrated VIKOR, TOPSIS, Entropy, and standard deviation ranking technique [19]. A sustainable configuration attainment framework developed for SSC based on the intersection of energy recovery, regenerative agriculture, and material reuse with different levels of CE [20]. Observing the sustainability performance of the entire sugarcane agro-industry supply chain, a multicriteria evaluation model with twenty-eight variables focusing on the social, environmental, economic, and resource dimensions was developed by [21]. In an approach to minimize the emission of GHGs and maximize the annual profit for the SSC, a MILP model was developed by [22]. Ref. [23] integrated ML with quantitative MILP model for sustainable supply chains. With the harvester engine parameters, [24] have made it possible to put into real-time practice for sugarcane yield forecast a Random Forest and Artificial Neural Network.

12.3 Circular Economy in Sugarcane Supply Chain

In this section, SSC and implementation of CE in SSC is discussed.

12.3.1 Sugarcane Supply Chain

The SSC is an integrated set of connected processes that involves conversion of raw sugarcane to finished, value-added products such as sugar, ethanol, and others [25]. The general process flow of cultivating sugarcane is shown below in Figure 12.2.

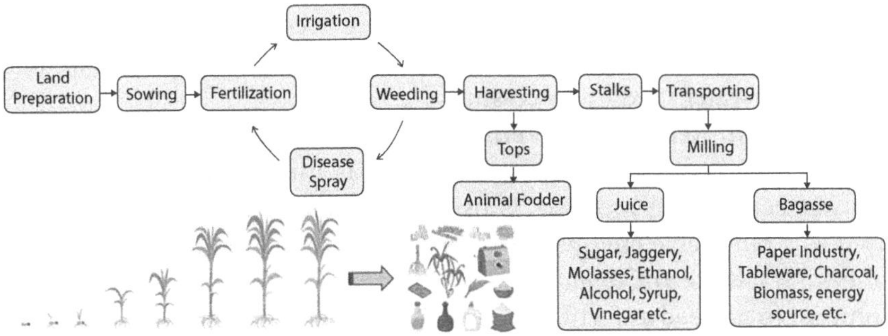

Figure 12.2 Sugarcane supply chain.

12.3.2 Circular Sugarcane Supply Chain

CE [20] approach within the SSC emphasizes maximizing resource efficiency and minimizing waste by recycling, reusing, refurbishing, and repairing materials and creating sustainable systems throughout the life cycle of sugarcane production and processing [26]. Unlike the traditional linear model of "take-make-dispose," it aims to extend the lifecycle of resources, reduce environmental impact, and enhance sustainability [27]. Some of the techniques and methods used in the circular SSC are mentioned below.

Sustainable Farming Techniques: These include 1) *Crop Rotation*, where different crops are planted in successive seasons to maintain soil fertility and reduce pest and disease cycles [28]. 2) *Organic Fertilizers,* where compost, manure, and biofertilizers are used to enrich the soil without the harmful effects of chemical fertilizers [29], and 3) *Integrated Pest Management*, this combines physical, cultural, biological, and chemical tools to manage pests sustainably [30].

Efficient Harvesting Methods: These include 1) *Precision Agriculture*, where GPS and sensors are used to monitor crop health and optimize harvesting times [31], and 2) *Mechanized Harvesting*, where employing machinery designed to minimize soil compaction and damage to cane [32].

Eco-Friendly Transportation Solutions: These include 1) *Optimized Logistics*, where software and mathematical models are used to plan the most efficient routes and schedules for transporting sugarcane [33], and 2) *Green Vehicles*, time to use electric or biofuel-powered vehicles to reduce emissions [34].

Green Processing Technologies: These include 1) *Energy Efficiency*, where high-efficiency boilers and cogeneration systems that produce electricity from bagasse implementing technologies are used to reduce energy consumption [35], and 2) *Water Recycling*, in which installing systems to treat and recycle water used in processing.

Recycling and Reuse of By-Products: These include: 1) *Bagasse*, used for paper production, making tableware items, as animal feed, or as a biofuel [36]. 2) Fermenting molasses is used to produce ethanol, which can be used as a renewable energy source or in the production of alcoholic beverages [37]. And 3) *Composting*, in which converting organic waste into compost to be used as fertilizer.

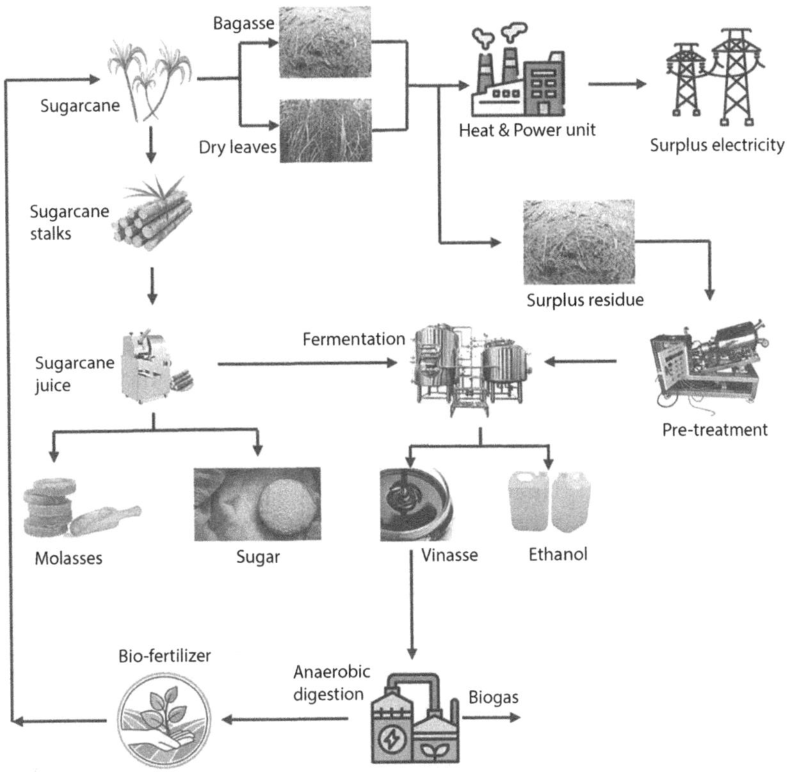

Figure 12.3 Circular sugarcane supply chain.

Integrating these practices into the SSC can significantly reduce environmental impact and enhance resource efficiency. The circular approach transforms waste into valuable resources, aligns with sustainability goals, and optimizes the overall sugarcane production process [38]. This concept is illustrated in Figure 12.3.

12.4 Methods Used in SSC

Mathematical optimization models and decision-making methods aid in developing improved planning tools in addressing multitude of challenges [39]. MCDM and ML techniques are discussed to optimize and enhance the circular sugarcane supply.

12.4.1 Application of MCDM

MCDM is a process that seeks to identify the best alternative by evaluating multiple conflicting criteria, whether quantitative or qualitative [40, 41]. This includes 1) *Criteria Identification*, which is done with the help

Table 12.1 Application of MCDM in SSC.

SSC stages	Criteria	Application
Cultivation	Yield potential, water usage, soil health, cost of inputs, and environmental impact.	AHP is used to prioritize the best sustainable farming practices based on the importance of each selected criterion.
Harvesting	Timing, method (manual vs. mechanical), labor costs, and environmental impact.	TOPSIS is used to compare the sustainable harvesting methods by comparing all the alternatives with the most efficient harvesting method (Ideal Solution).
Transportation	Cost, fuel consumption, emissions, delivery time, route optimization.	ELECTRE is used to evaluate and rank different transportation strategies based on multiple factors, ensuring the selection of the most efficient and eco-friendly options.
Processing	Energy efficiency, water usage, waste generation, and product quality.	MCDM methods optimize processing techniques by balancing efficiency, environmental impact, and product quality.
Water management and recycling	Cost of recycling, potential revenue from by-products, environmental benefits, regulatory compliance.	AHP is used to determine the best waste management practices by evaluating the importance of various factors and selecting the most beneficial recycling methods.

of experts, questioners, and the literature survey [42]. 2) *Weight Elicitation*, performed using MCDM methods like AHP, CRITIC, expert input, and Entropy method to assign weights to each criterion based on their importance [43]. Then further using of various other MCDM methods to evaluate the best alternatives against the criteria.

MCDM is a useful tool in SSC, as it could assist in balancing efficiency, sustainability, and cost-effectiveness while optimizing processes and helping stakeholders make informed decisions. Many MCDM methods improves the decision-making that leads to achieve better outcomes [44, 45]. The industries are able to develop more efficient and sustainable supply chain by combining MCDM with SSC [46]. Table 12.1 provides a systematic MCDM approach to complex decision-making at various SSC stages.

12.4.2 Application of ML

ML, a branch of artificial intelligence, involves developing algorithms that enable computers to learn from data and make informed decisions (Sarker, 2021). It includes the following: 1) *Model Selection*: The choice of ML algorithms would be based on the problem at hand; for example, regression can be used for yield prediction, while clustering can be used for farmer segmentation. 2) *Model Training*: The training of ML models is done on historical data. It is for this reason that its performance must be validated with metrics such as precision, accuracy, and recall. 3) *Model Evaluation*: Evaluation matrices are the tools needed to measure its accuracy and performance of models in ML, and ensure the models generalize well and give reliable predictions [47]. These models are capable of identifying patterns, predicting an outcome, and their performance gets better with data availability.

In SSC, ML enhances aspects such as crop yield prediction, optimization in logistics, and maintaining product quality by streamlining processes that reduce cost and environmental impact too. Integration of ML in SSC will play a critical role in sustainable and competitive industries; decision-making processes will be changed and wastages reduced considerably as stated by [48]. Table 12.2 provides the applications of ML in SSC.

Integrating MCDM and ML into the SSC creates a powerful framework that enhances decision-making, optimizes resource utilization, and promotes sustainability [49]. By using MCDM with the systematic gathering and analyzing of data, criteria prioritization, and development of predictive models, stakeholders can make well-informed decisions [23].

Table 12.2 Application of ML in SSC.

Problem	Solution	Benefits
Predictive Analytics for Yield Estimation	Regression and neural networks analyzed historical weather data, soil conditions, and crop management practices to predict future yields.	Better planning, early yield issue detection, and optimized use of fertilizers and water.
Optimization of Logistics and Transportation	Reinforcement learning and optimization algorithms can design optimal transportation routes such as distance, traffic, fuel consumption, and road conditions.	Better supply chain efficiency, less emissions, on-time delivery, and lower transportation costs.
Quality Control and Process Optimization in Sugarcane Processing	ML models track real-time data from equipment, spot anomalies, and predict maintenance needs. Supervised learning can classify sugar quality based on different parameters.	Enhanced product quality, reduced maintenance costs, increased efficiency in processing operations.
Demand Forecasting and Inventory Management	Time series forecasting models analyze market trends, historical sales data, and external factors in order to predict future demand.	More efficient inventory control, less waste, and happier customers thanks to prompt product delivery.
Sustainable Farming Practices	Unsupervised learning analyses sensor data to recommend irrigation, fertilization, and pest control.	Increased crop health, decreased chemical and water usage, and improved agricultural methods' sustainability.

12.5 Challenges and Solutions of Circular SSC

While the advantages of circular SSC are very clear, their implementation faces several challenges. technical, financial, regulatory, and social dimensions are included in these challenges [22, 50]. Addressing these challenges effectively requires innovative solutions, stakeholder collaboration, and supportive policy frameworks [51]. Some of these challenges are given below in Table 12.3.

Table 12.3 Challenges and solutions of circular SSC.

Sr. no.	Challenges	Future solutions
1. [52]	**Technical**- adopting advanced technologies, Integration of precision farming tools, managing data (soil health, water use, yield etc.), effective conservation of by products (bagasse, press mud, molasses, etc.)	Training for farmers and mill operators on the advanced machine (harvesting, plantation, fertilizer), Collaboration with research institute and sugar mill to develop sustainable solutions by MCDM, running small scale pilot project with new technologies using ML
2. [53]	**Financial**- Required major investment on Infrastructure, machines and land	Government subsidies, take decision on durability of machine's part, low interest loan, public- private partnership, collaboration through MCDM and ML
3. [54]	**Market Dynamics & Consumer Preferences**- Fluctuating prices, demands, competition, consumer unfamiliarity with circular products like table ware products, ethanol etc.	Raising customers awareness of circular products benefits, working closely with small customers, educational campaigns and government incentives for sustainable products, forecasting of future demand and supply by MCDM and ML techniques

(Continued)

Table 12.3 Challenges and solutions of circular SSC. (*Continued*)

Sr. no.	Challenges	Future solutions
4. (A. Kumar *et al.*, 2022).	**Social & Cultural Barriers-** Resistance to change, skill gaps among farmers and workers, lack of community involvement	Offering hands on training top farmers and workers, engaging local communities through skill developing programs, decision making analysis through MCDM
5. [55]	**Infrastructure Limitations-** Inadequate infrastructure, poor road networks, shortage of waste processing facilities, leak of access to energy resources	Development of collaborative processing units, waste management units, promotion of renewable energy in the sugar mills, determine the sustainable route with real dataset by ML and MCDM

12.6 Case Study

The sugar industry is the second-largest agro-based industry in India, after the textile industry [56]. Therefore, it is crucial to assess the status and performance of Indian sugar mills. India has a total of 843 sugar mills, with 565 currently operational, and Uttar Pradesh having the highest number of mills after Maharashtra. Sugarcane industry spread in whole over the country. They can be classified into large-scale, medium, small, mini, and micro-sized enterprises. While there are several ways to categorize these sugar mills, we have chosen to classify them based on crushing capacity, area size, and sugar produced [57] as shown in Table 12.4.

In this study, we calculate the sustainable ranking of sugarcane-mills across the country using the widely known MCDM methods, including TOPSIS [58], VIKOR [59], WSM [60], EDAS [61] after calculating the weights to the criteria by CRITIC [62] method. Final ranking is calculated by an ensemble method based on HQ theory [63] and result is validated through ML algorithm namely k-mean clustering [64]. Figure 12.4 shows the methodology employed to determine these rankings.

Table 12.4 Classification of sugar mills.

Sr. no.	Category	Crushing capacity (ton/day)	Market
1.	Large Scale Sugar Mill:	>5000	National, International
2.	Medium Scale Sugar Mill	2500–5000	National
3.	Small Scale Sugar Mill	500–2500	Regional
4.	Mini and Micro Sugar Mill	<500	Local (Gur, Khandsari)

Figure 12.4 Methodology.

12.6.1 Data Collection and Preprocessing

In this section, we collected data for thirty-nine sugar mills across India from the well-known website Anekant Prakash [65] and the official websites of the sugar mills. We focused on mills with a crushing capacity greater than 9,900 tons per day. After this filtering possess, 39 sugar mills from six different states (Bihar, Gujrat, Haryana, Karnataka, Maharashtra, Uttar Pradesh) of India are remains to study. The data collection covered five key features: crushing capacity, cane crushed, sugar produced, sugar recovery, and molasses production. Additionally, data for seven other sustainability features—working year, alcohol/spirit production, ethanol, power, bio compost, chemicals, and bio fertilizer—were gathered directly from the mills' websites. These features are related to the circular economy, representing how waste is utilized by the mills. The final dataset consists of thirty-nine sugar mills and twelve features. We used MCDM methods to calculate the rankings, treating the thirty-nine sugar mills as alternatives and the twelve features as criteria for the decision-making process.

12.6.2 Results and Discussion

In this study, based on various sustainability features, thirty-nine sugarcane mills across the country are ranked using various MCDM methods. As shown in Table 12.5, the rankings of the sugar mills differ across the methods. To provide a more comprehensive evaluation, aggregate rankings is determined by HQ Theory. In this aggregation, weights are assigned to each MCDM method, and determined the confidence index and trust level as 0.9914 and 0.9918, respectively. The consensus index indicates a high level of agreement among the individual rankings. Furthermore, the trust level for the final aggregated ranking suggesting a high degree of confidence in the reliability and robustness of the aggregated results.

Table 12.5 MCDM and aggregate rankings of the sugar mills.

Mill name	TOPSIS	VIKOR	WSM	EDAS	R*	Final rank
Harinagar Sugar Mills Ltd. Harinagar Bihar	15	13	15	15	14.56	**15**
Shree Khedut Sahakari Khand Udyog Mandli Ltd. Baben Bardoli, Gujrat	36	37	37	31	35.10	**35**
Saraswati Sugar Mills Ltd. Yamunagar, Haryana	35	36	35	36	35.47	**36**
Bilagi Sugar Mill Ltd, Badagandi, Karnataka	28	32	29	28	29.06	**29**
Godavari Biorefineries Ltd., Banahatti, Karnataka	1	1	1	1	1	**1**
Indian Cane Power Ltd., Mudhol, Karnataka	20	22	19	19	19.88	**19**

(*Continued*)

Table 12.5 MCDM and aggregate rankings of the sugar mills. (*Continued*)

Mill name	TOPSIS	VIKOR	WSM	EDAS	R*	Final rank
Jamkhandi Sugars Ltd., Jamkhandi, Karnataka	33	34	34	34	33.72	**33**
MRN Chamundi Canepower and biorefineries, Pvt Ltd. (Nirani Sugars ltd) Mudhol, Karnataka	37	35	36	37	36.35	**37**
Shri Prabhulingeshwar sugars and chemicals, Jamkhandi, Karnataka	23	23	22	22	22.47	**22**
Athani Sugars Limited, Karnataka	27	26	31	29	28.34	**28**
Kallappanna Awade Jawahar Shetkari Sahakari Sakhar, Karkhana Ltd. Hupari, Maharashtra	38	38	38	38	38	**38**
Shri Ambalika Sugars Pvt Ltd, Ambikanagar, Maharashtra	26	24	25	25	25.07	**25**
Baramati Agro Ltd. Indapur, Maharashtra	13	12	12	11	12.01	**13**

(*Continued*)

Table 12.5 MCDM and aggregate rankings of the sugar mills. (*Continued*)

Mill name	**TOPSIS**	**VIKOR**	**WSM**	**EDAS**	**R***	**Final rank**
Daund Sugar Pvt. Ltd. Daund, Maharashtra	31	29	30	32	30.62	**31**
Vitthal Rao Shinde Sahakari Sakhar Karkhana Ltd, Pimpalner, Maharashtra	32	31	32	33	32.07	**32**
Dhampur Sugar Mills Ltd. Dhampur, Uttar Pradesh	18	18	18	18	18	**18**
Avadh Sugar and Energy Ltd. Seohara, Uttar Pradesh	25	25	23	24	24.22	**24**
DCM Shriram Ltd. Hariawan, Hardoi, Uttar Pradesh	21	19	20	21	20.36	**21**
Wave Industries Pvt. Ltd. Dhanaura, Uttar Pradesh	39	39	39	39	39	**39**
Bajaj Hindusthan Sugar Ltd. Gola Gokarannath, Uttar Pradesh	19	20	21	20	19.97	**20**
Bajaj Hindusthan Sugar Ltd. Paliakalan, Uttar Pradesh	6	3	4	4	4.35	**3**

(*Continued*)

Table 12.5 MCDM and aggregate rankings of the sugar mills. (*Continued*)

Mill name	TOPSIS	VIKOR	WSM	EDAS	R*	Final rank
DCM Shriram Ltd. Ajbapur, Lakhimpur Khiri, Uttar Pradesh	30	28	27	27	28.02	**27**
Govind Sugar Mill, Unit of Zuari Industries, Lakhimpur Khiri, Uttar Pradesh	29	30	28	30	29.22	**30**
LH Sugar factories Ltd. Philibhit, Uttar Pradesh	24	27	24	26	25.14	**26**
Dhampur Bio Organics Ltd. Asmoli, Uttar Pradesh	17	16	17	17	16.79	**17**
Dalmia Bharat Sugar and Industries Ltd., Nigohi, Uttar Pradesh	34	33	33	35	33.81	**34**
Bajaj Hindustan Sugar Ltd. Utraula, Mahuwa, Uttar Pradesh	11	9	14	10	11.08	**11**
Balrampur Chini Mills Ltd. Balrampur, Uttar Pradesh	4	2	7	5	4.62	**5**
Bajaj Hindustan Sugar Ltd., Gonda, Uttar Pradesh	16	15	16	16	15.78	**16**

(*Continued*)

Table 12.5 MCDM and aggregate rankings of the sugar mills. (*Continued*)

Mill name	TOPSIS	VIKOR	WSM	EDAS	R*	Final rank
Balrampur Chini Mills Ltd., Babhnan, Uttar Pradesh	5	5	5	3	4.45	**4**
Bajaj Hindustan Sugar Ltd., Khambhar Khera, Uttar Pradesh	10	8	11	9	9.58	**10**
Balrampur Chini Mills Ltd., Kumbhi, Uttar Pradesh	3	4	3	2	2.93	**2**
Avadh Sugar and Energy Ltd., Hargaon, Uttar Pradesh	8	7	6	6	6.75	**6**
Bajaj Hindustan Sugar Ltd., Rasulpur, Uttar Pradesh	9	6	8	8	7.87	**7**
Daurala Sugar Works (Unit of DCM Shriram Industries Ltd) Daurala, Uttar Pradesh	7	10	9	7	8.10	**8**
Mawana Sugar Works (Unit of Mawana sugars Ltd New Delhi) Mawana, Uttar Pradesh	12	11	10	12	11.29	**12**

(*Continued*)

Table 12.5 MCDM and aggregate rankings of the sugar mills. (*Continued*)

Mill name	TOPSIS	VIKOR	WSM	EDAS	R*	Final rank
Indian Potash Ltd. (Titawai sugar complex), Uttar Pradesh	22	21	26	23	23.07	**23**
Triveni Engineering and Industries, Khatauli, Uttar Pradesh	2	17	2	14	8.27	**9**
Triveni Engineering and Industries, Deoband, Uttar Pradesh	14	14	13	13	13.47	**14**
Weights	**0.28**	**0.20**	**0.25**	**0.27**	**Confidence Index**	**0.9914**
					Trust Level	**0.9918**

According to the aggregated rankings, Godavari Biorefineries Ltd., Banahatti, Karnataka secured the top position, followed by Balrampur Chini Mills Ltd., Kumbhi, Uttar Pradesh. These results highlight the dominance of these sugar mills in the sugar industries. Conversely, Wave Industries Pvt. Ltd. Dhanaura, Uttar Pradesh ranked lowest (39th), indicating relatively low performance compared to the other sugar mills.

To further analyze the performance trends, we plotted the rankings of the top ten and the bottom ten performer sugar mills in Figure 12.5(a), 12.5(b). The graph clearly shows the consistent high performance of Godavari, Karnataka, and Balrampur, Uttar Pradesh. On the other hand, the graph for the lowest-ranked mills, including Wave, Uttar Pradesh, reveals a significant gap in performance compared to the top performers.

In addition, weights for each twelve criteria is shown on the Figure 12.5 (c), with bio-fertilizer take the highest weight as compare to others. Moreover, we performed K-means clustering with K=4 to validate our aggregate ranking and to categorize the sugar mills into four distinct groups. Cluter-2 contains twelve high performing, while cluster 4 includes nine low -performing sugar mill as shown in the Figure 12.5(d) with blue and violet respectively. The high-performing and low-performing clusters align with our aggregated ranking of the sugar mills.

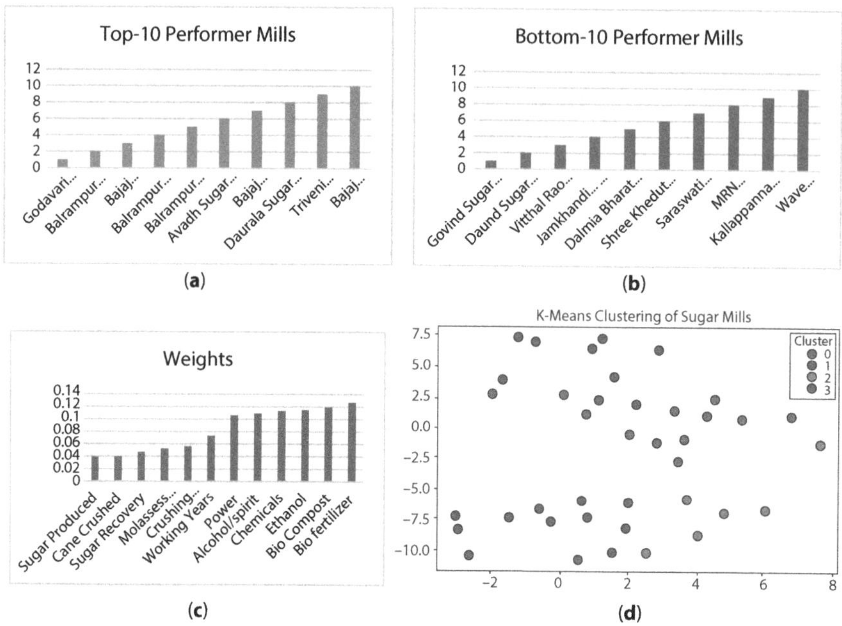

Figure 12.5 Ranking results of the sugar mills.

12.7 Conclusion

Circular-SSC is essential for sustainable development, boosting competitiveness, and reducing the environmental impact. With the adoption of the principles related to CE and new technologies along with MCDM and ML techniques, the sugarcane industry becomes more resilient and creates a promising future for generations. A circular SSC is defined by inclusion of sustainable farming, efficient harvesting, green processing technologies, along with the effective recycling of by-products, leading to the development of a more sustainable, efficient, and eco-friendly system. This implementation can offer a huge environmental, economic, and social benefits, to create a better and more sustainable future for the sugarcane industry. As there are various challenges in SSC, such as technical and financial issues, regulatory issues, and the need for market and consumer support, awareness of circular practices, demand and supply imbalances, climate changing, and in future direction, these are minimized with the help of CE implementation along with MCDM and ML algorithms to take the better decisions and future predictions. MCDM contributes by evaluating different criteria while balancing the three key aspects of sustainability.

ML helps by enhancing data-driven forecasting, efficient use of resources, and process optimization.

In the case study, the dataset includes twelve features, five of which are related to working efficiency while the remaining features are related to CE principles implementation, means how the sugar mills utilize their by-products like bagasse, molasses and press mud etc. As a result, Godavari Biorefineries Ltd., Banahatti, Karnataka was shown as more sustainable compare to others.

References

1. Feng, T., Xiong, R., Huan, P., Productive use of natural resources in agriculture: The main policy lessons. *Resour. Policy*, 85, 103793, Aug. 2023, doi: 10.1016/j.resourpol.2023.103793.
2. Hemathilake, D.M.K.S. and Gunathilake, D.M.C.C., Chapter 31 - Agricultural productivity and food supply to meet increased demands, in: *Future Foods*, R. Bhat (Ed.), pp. 539–553, Elsevier, 2022, doi: 10.1016/B978-0-323-91001-9.00016-5.
3. Kumar, S. and Pant, M., A Mathematical Model to Minimize the Total Cultivation Cost of Sugarcane, in: *Soft Computing for Problem Solving*, M. Thakur, S. Agnihotri, B.S. Rajpurohit, M. Pant, K. Deep, A.K. Nagar (Eds.), pp. 529–542, Springer Nature Singapore, Singapore, 2023.
4. FAO, *World Food and Agriculture – Statistical Yearbook 2023*, p. 384 FAO, Rome, Italy, 2023, ISBN 978-92-5-138262-2, doi: 10.4060/cc8166en.
5. Bordonal, R.O., Carvalho, J.L.N., Lal, R., de Figueiredo, E.B., de Oliveira, B.G., La Scala, N., Sustainability of sugarcane production in Brazil. A review. *Agron. Sustain. Dev.*, 38, 2, 13, Feb. 2018, doi: 10.1007/s13593-018-0490-x.
6. Sahu, O., Assessment of sugarcane industry: Suitability for production, consumption, and utilization. *Ann. Agrar. Sci.*, 16, 4, 389–395, Dec. 2018, doi: 10.1016/j.aasci.2018.08.001.
7. Gonçalves, M.C., Pinto, L.R., Pimenta, R.J.G., da Silva, M.F., Chapter 24 - Sugarcane, in: *Viral Diseases of Field and Horticultural Crops*, L.P. Awasthi (Ed.), pp. 193–205, Elsevier, 2024, doi: 10.1016/B978-0-323-90899-3.00056-2.
8. Ali, A., Khan, M., Sharif, R., Mujtaba, M., Gao, S.-J., Sugarcane Omics: An Update on the Current Status of Research and Crop Improvement. *Plants*, 8, 9, 344, Sep. 2019, doi: 10.3390/plants8090344.
9. Indian Institute of Sugarcane Research, Lucknow, Accessed: Jul. 09, 2024. [Online]. 2022, Available: https://iisr.icar.gov.in/iisr/pages/maps.jsp.
10. Geissdoerfer, M., Savaget, P., Bocken, N.M.P., Hultink, E.J., The Circular Economy – A new sustainability paradigm? *J. Clean. Prod.*, 143, 757–768, Feb. 2017, doi: 10.1016/j.jclepro.2016.12.048.

11. Piewthongngam, K., Pathumnakul, S., Setthanan, K., Application of crop growth simulation and mathematical modeling to supply chain management in the Thai sugar industry. *Agric. Syst.*, 102, 1, 58–66, Oct. 2009, doi: 10.1016/j.agsy.2009.07.002.
12. Aliano Filho, A., Melo, T., Pato, M.V., A bi-objective mathematical model for integrated planning of sugarcane harvesting and transport operations. *Comput. Oper. Res.*, 134, 105419, Oct. 2021, doi: 10.1016/j.cor.2021.105419.
13. Rossetto, R., Ramos, N.P., de Matos Pires, R.C., Xavier, M.A., Cantarella, H., Guimarães de AndradeLandell, M., Sustainability in Sugarcane Supply Chain in Brazil: Issues and Way Forward. *Sugar Tech*, 24, 3, 941–966, Jun. 2022, doi: 10.1007/s12355-022-01170-y.
14. Esposito, B., Sessa, M.R., Sica, D., Malandrino, O., Towards Circular Economy in the Agri-Food Sector. A Systematic Literature Review. *Sustainability*, 12, 18, 7401, Jan. 2020, doi: 10.3390/su12187401.
15. Stillitano, T., Spada, E., Iofrida, N., Falcone, G., De Luca, A.I., Sustainable Agri-Food Processes and Circular Economy Pathways in a Life Cycle Perspective: State of the Art of Applicative Research. *Sustainability*, 13, 5, 2472, Jan. 2021, doi: 10.3390/su13052472.
16. Poponi, S., Arcese, G., Ruggieri, A., Pacchera, F., Value optimisation for the agri-food sector: A circular economy approach. *Bus. Strat. Environ.*, 32, 6, 2850–2867, 2023, doi: 10.1002/bse.3274.
17. Kumar, V., Sezersan, I., Garza-Reyes, J.A., Gonzalez, E.D.R.S., AL-Shboul, M.A., Circular economy in the manufacturing sector: Benefits, opportunities and barriers. *Manage. Decis.*, 57, 4, 1067–1086, Apr. 2019, doi: 10.1108/MD-09-2018-1070.
18. Schroeder, P., Anggraeni, K., Weber, U., The Relevance of Circular Economy Practices to the Sustainable Development Goals. *J. Ind. Ecol.*, 23, 1, 77–95, 2019, doi: 10.1111/jiec.12732.
19. Deepa, N., M, D.R.V.P., N, S.K., Srinivasan, K., Chang, C.-Y., Bashir, A.K., An Efficient Ensemble VTOPES Multi-Criteria Decision-Making Model for Sustainable Sugarcane Farms. *Sustainability*, 11, 16, 4288, Jan. 2019, doi: 10.3390/su11164288.
20. Shahsavani, I., Goli, A., Hajiaghaei-Keshteli, M., A circular economy approach to design a citrus supply chain network. *Ann. Oper. Res.*, 1–50, Feb. 2024, Springer, doi: 10.1007/s10479-024-05829-5.
21. Asrol, M., Marimin, Machfud, Yani, M., Rohayati, A multi-criteria model of supply chain sustainability assessment and improvement for sugarcane agroindustry. *Heliyon*, 10, 7, Apr. 2024, Elsevier, doi: 10.1016/j.heliyon.2024.e28259.
22. Jaroenkietkajorn, U., *et al.*, Challenges and Opportunities of Bio-Circular-Green Economy for Agriculture. *Circ. Econ. Sustain.*, 4, 3, 1729–1750, Feb. 2024, doi: 10.1007/s43615-024-00355-9.
23. Momenitabar, M., Dehdari Ebrahimi, Z., Abdollahi, A., Helmi, W., Bengtson, K., Ghasemi, P., An integrated machine learning and quantitative optimization

method for designing sustainable bioethanol supply chain networks. *Decis. Anal. J.*, 7, 100236, Jun. 2023, doi: 10.1016/j.dajour.2023.100236.
24. Felipe Maldaner, L., de Paula Corrêdo, L., Fernanda Canata, T., Paulo Molin, J., Predicting the sugarcane yield in real-time by harvester engine parameters and machine learning approaches. *Comput. Electron. Agric.*, 181, 105945, Feb. 2021, doi: 10.1016/j.compag.2020.105945.
25. Santos, F., Eichler, P., Machado, G., De Mattia, J., De Souza, G., Chapter 2 - By-products of the sugarcane industry, in: *Sugarcane Biorefinery, Technology and Perspectives*, F. Santos, S.C. Rabelo, M. De Matos, P. Eichler (Eds.), pp. 21–48, Elsevier, 2020, doi: 10.1016/B978-0-12-814236-3.00002-0.
26. Karp, S.G., *et al.*, Sugarcane: A Promising Source of Green Carbon in the Circular Bioeconomy. *Sugar Tech*, 24, 4, 1230–1245, Aug. 2022, doi: 10.1007/s12355-022-01161-z.
27. Adewusi, A.O., *et al.*, AI in precision agriculture: A review of technologies for sustainable farming practices. *World J. Adv. Res. Rev.*, 21, 1, 2276–2285, 2024, doi: 10.30574/wjarr.2024.21.1.0314.
28. Moldavan, L., Pimenowa, O., Wasilewski, M., Wasilewska, N., Crop Rotation Management in the Context of Sustainable Development of Agriculture in Ukraine. *Agriculture*, 14, 6, 934, Jun. 2024, doi: 10.3390/agriculture14060934.
29. He, Z., Ding, B., Pei, S., Cao, H., Liang, J., Li, Z., The impact of organic fertilizer replacement on greenhouse gas emissions and its influencing factors. *Sci. Total Environ.*, 905, 166917, Dec. 2023, doi: 10.1016/j.scitotenv.2023.166917.
30. Angon, P.B., *et al.*, Integrated Pest Management (IPM) in Agriculture and Its Role in Maintaining Ecological Balance and Biodiversity. *Adv. Agric.*, 2023, 1, 5546373, 2023, doi: 10.1155/2023/5546373.
31. Karunathilake, E.M.B.M., Le, A.T., Heo, S., Chung, Y.S., Mansoor, S., The Path to Smart Farming: Innovations and Opportunities in Precision Agriculture. *Agriculture*, 13, 8, 1593, Aug. 2023, doi: 10.3390/agriculture13081593.
32. Li, P., Lee, S., Hsu, H.-Y., Review on fruit harvesting method for potential use of automatic fruit harvesting systems. *Procedia Eng.*, 23, 351–366, Jan. 2011, doi: 10.1016/j.proeng.2011.11.2514.
33. Teixeira, E.S., Rangel, S., Florentino, H.O., de Araujo, S.A., A review of mathematical optimization models applied to the sugarcane supply chain. *Int. Trans. Oper. Res.*, 30, 4, 1755–1788, 2023, doi: 10.1111/itor.13056.
34. Alshamrani, A., *et al.*, Optimal Design of an Eco-Friendly Transportation Network under Uncertain Parameters. *Sustainability*, 15, 6, 5538, Jan. 2023, doi: 10.3390/su15065538.
35. Boye, J. and Arcand, Y., *Green Technologies in Food Production and Processing*, Springer Science & Business Media, 2012.
36. Aguilar-Rivera, N., Bioindicators for the Sustainability of Sugar Agro-Industry. *Sugar Tech*, 24, 3, 651–661, Jun. 2022, doi: 10.1007/s12355-021-01105-z.
37. Colla, V., *et al.*, Future Research and Developments on Reuse and Recycling of Steelmaking By-Products. *Metals*, 13, 4, 676, Apr. 2023, doi: 10.3390/met13040676.

38. Gunasekara, L., Robb, D.J., Zhang, A., Used product acquisition, sorting and disposition for circular supply chains: Literature review and research directions. *Int. J. Prod. Econ.*, 260, 108844, Jun. 2023, doi: 10.1016/j.ijpe.2023.108844.
39. Singh, M., A Hybrid FLP-AHP Approach for Optimal Product Mix in Pulp and Paper Industry, *International Conference on Optimization and Learning 2021*, SpringerLink, Accessed: Jul. 13, 2024. [Online]. Available: https://link.springer.com/chapter/10.1007/978-3-030-85672-4_24.
40. Bonissone, P.P., Subbu, R., Lizzi, J., Multicriteria decision making (mcdm): a framework for research and applications. *IEEE Comput. Intell. Mag.*, 4, 3, 48–61, Aug. 2009, doi: 10.1109/MCI.2009.933093.
41. Nayak, D., Singh, M., Pant, M., Jauhar, S.K., Efficient Supplier Selection in the Era of Industry 4.0, in: *Digital Transformation and Industry 4.0 for Sustainable Supply Chain Performance*, S.S. Kamble, R.S. Mor, A. Belhadi (Eds.), pp. 191–205, Springer International Publishing, Cham, 2023, doi: 10.1007/978-3-031-19711-6_9.
42. Jahan, A., Mustapha, F., Sapuan, S.M., Ismail, M.Y., Bahraminasab, M., A framework for weighting of criteria in ranking stage of material selection process. *Int. J. Adv. Manuf. Technol.*, 58, 1, 411–420, Jan. 2012, doi: 10.1007/s00170-011-3366-7.
43. Singh, M. and Pant, M., A review of selected weighing methods in MCDM with a case study. *Int. J. Syst. Assur. Eng. Manage.*, 12, 1, 126–144, Feb. 2021, doi: 10.1007/s13198-020-01033-3.
44. Singh, M., Pant, M., Godiyal, R.D., Kumar Sharma, A., MCDM approach for selection of raw material in pulp and papermaking industry. *Mater. Manuf. Process.*, 35, 3, 241–249, Feb. 2020, doi: 10.1080/10426914.2020.1711917.
45. Singh, M., Pant, M., Diwan, S., Snášel, V., Genetic Algorithm-enhanced Rank aggregation model to measure the performance of Pulp and Paper Industries. *Comput. Ind. Eng.*, 172, 108548, Oct. 2022, doi: 10.1016/j.cie.2022.108548.
46. Qureshi, M.R.N., Singh, R.K., Hasan, M.A., Decision support model to select crop pattern for sustainable agricultural practices using fuzzy MCDM. *Environ. Dev. Sustain.*, 20, 2, 641–659, Apr. 2018, doi: 10.1007/s10668-016-9903-7.
47. Benos, L., Tagarakis, A.C., Dolias, G., Berruto, R., Kateris, D., Bochtis, D., Machine Learning in Agriculture: A Comprehensive Updated Review. *Sensors*, 21, 11, 3758, Jan. 2021, doi: 10.3390/s21113758.
48. Ni, D., Xiao, Z., Lim, M.K., A systematic review of the research trends of machine learning in supply chain management. *Int. J. Mach. Learn. Cybern.*, 11, 7, 1463–1482, Jul. 2020, doi: 10.1007/s13042-019-01050-0.
49. Wang, Z., Li, J., Rangaiah, G.P., Wu, Z., Machine learning aided multi-objective optimization and multi-criteria decision making: Framework and two applications in chemical engineering. *Comput. Chem. Eng.*, 165, 107945, Sep. 2022, doi: 10.1016/j.compchemeng.2022.107945.

50. Lahane, S. and Kant, R., Evaluation and ranking of solutions to mitigate circular supply chain risks. *Sustain. Prod. Consum.*, 27, 753–773, Jul. 2021, doi: 10.1016/j.spc.2021.01.034.
51. Bressanelli, G., Perona, M., Saccani, N., Challenges in supply chain redesign for the Circular Economy: a literature review and a multiple case study. *Int. J. Prod. Res.*, 57, 23, 7395–7422, Dec. 2019, Accessed: Jul. 09, 2024. [Online]. Available: https://www.tandfonline.com/doi/abs/10.1080/00207543.2018.1542176.
52. Kumar, M., Raut, R.D., Jagtap, S., Choubey, V.K., Circular economy adoption challenges in the food supply chain for sustainable development. *Bus. Strategy Environ.*, 32, 4, 1334–1356, 2023, doi: 10.1002/bse.3191.
53. Patra, S.P., Wankhede, V.A., Agrawal, R., Circular economy practices in supply chain finance: a state-of-the-art review. *Benchmarking Int. J.*, 31, 7, 2197–2216, Jan. 2023, doi: 10.1108/BIJ-10-2022-0627.
54. Burke, H., Zhang, A., Wang, J.X., Integrating product design and supply chain management for a circular economy. *Prod. Plan. Control*, 34, 11, 1097–1113, Aug. 2023, doi: 10.1080/09537287.2021.1983063.
55. Amir, S., Salehi, N., Roci, M., Sweet, S., Rashid, A., Towards circular economy: A guiding framework for circular supply chain implementation. *Bus. Strategy Environ.*, 32, 6, 2684–2701, 2023, doi: 10.1002/bse.3264.
56. Sheetal, and Kumar, R., Rethinking on growth mechanism of Indian sugar industry. *J. Asia Bus. Stud.*, 13, 3, 412–432, Jan. 2019, doi: 10.1108/JABS-12-2016-0182.
57. SugarReport.pdf, Accessed: Oct. 08, 2024. [Online]. Available: https://www.niti.gov.in/sites/default/files/2023-02/SugarReport.pdf.
58. Behzadian, M., Khanmohammadi Otaghsara, S., Yazdani, M., Ignatius, J., A state-of the-art survey of TOPSIS applications. *Expert Syst. Appl.*, 39, 17, 13051–13069, Dec. 2012, doi: 10.1016/j.eswa.2012.05.056.
59. Golfam, P., Ashofteh, P.-S., Loáiciga, H.A., Evaluation of the VIKOR and FOWA Multi-Criteria Decision Making Methods for Climate-Change Adaptation of Agricultural Water Supply. *Water Resour. Manage.*, 33, 8, 2867–2884, Jun. 2019, doi: 10.1007/s11269-019-02274-z.
60. Mitra, T. and Ozbek, K., Ranking by weighted sum. *Econ. Theory*, 72, 2, 511–532, Sep. 2021, doi: 10.1007/s00199-020-01305-w.
61. Dhanalakshmi, C.S., Madhu, P., Karthick, A., Mathew, M., Vignesh Kumar, R., A comprehensive MCDM-based approach using TOPSIS and EDAS as an auxiliary tool for pyrolysis material selection and its application. *Biomass Convers. Biorefin.*, 12, 12, 5845–5860, Dec. 2022, doi: 10.1007/s13399-020-01009-0.
62. Zafar, S., Alamgir, Z., Rehman, M.H., An effective blockchain evaluation system based on entropy-CRITIC weight method and MCDM techniques. *Peer-Peer Netw. Appl.*, 14, 5, 3110–3123, Sep. 2021, doi: 10.1007/s12083-021-01173-8.

63. Mohammadi, M. and Rezaei, J., Ensemble ranking: Aggregation of rankings produced by different multi-criteria decision-making methods. *Omega*, 96, 102254, Oct. 2020, doi: 10.1016/j.omega.2020.102254.
64. Kanungo, T., Mount, D.M., Netanyahu, N.S., Piatko, C.D., Silverman, R., Wu, A.Y., An efficient k-means clustering algorithm: analysis and implementation. *IEEE Trans. Pattern Anal. Mach. Intell.*, 24, 7, 881–892, Jul. 2002, doi: 10.1109/TPAMI.2002.1017616.
65. Sugar Factories in India, Accessed: Oct. 17, 2024. [Online]. Available: https://www.anekantprakashan.com/sugar-factories/india.

13

Development of Framework on Firm Green Integration and the Moderating Effects of Absorptive Capacity with Special Reference to Eco-Innovation

G. Devakumar

Xavier Institute of Management and Entrepreneurship (XIME), Bangalore, India

Abstract

In recent years, the pressure for businesses to implement sustainable measures throughout their operations has only increased. This chapter addresses the dynamics of implementing green practices in organizations and emphasizes the importance of absorptive capacity as a critical component in the eco-innovation process. It provides an understanding of the relationships between these variables and their significance for enhancing the practice of sustainable business management and their interactions through the use of various theories and real-life examples.

***Keywords*:** Firm green integration, absorptive capacity, eco-innovation, businesses sustainability, green practices in organizations, sustainable business management, resource-based view, circular economy, organizational practices

13.1 Introduction

In the current century, the global populace has risen and become more conscious to the self-evident need of addressing the environmental degradation brought about by industrialization, urbanization, and resource overexploitation. Climatic shifts, biodiversity loss, pollution; the aforementioned hazards have helped establish the need to encourage the adoption of

Email: devkumar@xime.org

K. Mathiyazhagan, Krishna Kumar Dadsena, Rajesh Kumar Singh, Aakanksha Kishore and Andrea Appolloni (eds.) Sustainable Operations of Logistics and Supply Chain Management, (301–320)

environmentally friendly strategies in all spheres of the society including the business world.

The need to mitigate any dangers posed to the environment and increase the sustainable development level is the explanation as to why many organizations have started reviewing the way they conduct business and as of today, these organizations employ 'green' practices. The need for more businesses and industries to operate within the eco-system has gained more prominence. This campaign is not only inspired by environmental statutes but also the changing demographics of markets, ethics of stakeholders, and business survival concerns [6].

In the modern-day, a shift in the business perspective in the developed countries has been noticed as most of them have adopted the so-called green strategy management to their operations. Moreover, Companies have started to increasingly apply 'green' practices into... activities. This trend is not solely brought forth by existing environmental laws. It is instead more concerning the dynamics within the market, the ethical dictates of the shareholders, and the need for business continuity over time [6].

Firm green integration encompasses the adoption of strategies, policies, and practices aimed at minimizing environmental impacts, conserving natural resources, and championing ecological sustainability within organizational operations [18]. It's a wide canvas that includes initiatives like boosting energy efficiency, curbing waste, practicing sustainable sourcing, and embracing renewable energy technologies. By weaving environmental considerations into their decision-making processes and value chains, firms aim not only to mitigate negative environmental effects but also to bolster their competitiveness, reputation, and long-term resilience [16].

Imagine this chapter as a spotlight on the intricate process of embedding green practices within companies. In this paper, we will examine how businesses deal with the challenges associated. What drives them to effectively adopt and carry out the sustainable principles? Here comes the notion of absorptive capacity - it is the ability of the organization to identify, assimilate and exploit the knowledge from outside for the purpose of innovation and change [4].

Integrating environmental aspects within the firm strategies entails more than internal resources; it also includes external knowledge, skills, as well as other resources. In this aspect, absorptive capacity is the most important variable that determines environmental knowledge utilization by a firm. Are such companies capable of converting this knowledge into eco-innovation and sustainability practices? Absorptive capacity stands in the relationship between green integration and eco-innovation and mediates alleviation of any factor that limits opportunity exploitation and environmental aggressiveness [8].

This article addresses the pressing need for companies to adopt sustainable environmental practices in response to global environmental challenges arising from industrialization, urbanization, and excessive resource exploitation. There has been a growing trend among firms to integrate 'green' elements into their strategies due to external factors like global warming, reduction of biodiversity, and environmental contamination. It is not only the legal requirements that are responsible for this change, but also the changing values of consumers and other stakeholders and the desire to ensure that business activities are sustainable in the long run. This raises another issue which is discussed in the chapter, and here, the authors focus on the concept of absorptive capacity as a critical determinant of the corporation's sustainable innovation efforts. The authors also share the rationale for this investigation, detailing its theoretical and practical implications.

13.2 Rationale for the Study

The relevance of this study is based on two core dimensions of modern organizational thinking and sustainability – green integration within firms and absorptive capacity. Each of these concepts has repercussions for organizational performance and environmental performance on its own; however their joint implications form a rich domain that calls for attention with substantial theoretical, practical, and policy-oriented implications.

Strategic green integration that entails considering and adopting environmentally friendly practices into the day to day running of the organization has increasingly becoming a strategic focus in every industry. As noted by the author [8], there is an increased interaction between conservation and society in today's world whereby, thanks to the societal pressures and sometimes legal frameworks in place, organizations have to incorporate environmental aspects in their decision-making processes and the entire value chain. Therefore, this means that it is important to address the reasons why green integration is carried out, how it is carried out, and what the results are for overcoming such environmental threats in order to better understand how Perusahaan is able to do this and more so improve itself and remain relevant even in the face of such challenges in the environment.

Additionally, in organizational learning theories, absorptive capacity which also means the absorption of the information external to the organization has emerged and earned a great deal of importance when it comes to a firm's oomph in innovating and adapting to external changes. It means the ability of the organization to recognize the value of the external new information, assimilate it, and use it in the construction of new products or processes. It is vital in improving the knowledge exchange, promoting the learning process, and facilitating the renewal of the organization. In the area of environmental management, the situation calls for even more as companies seek to leverage on the available external forces in the form of environment and knowledge base in the carrying out of their green or eco-innovation practices.

The topic of this research concerns the association between green integration of the firms and their absorptive capacity which seeks to clarify the role of environmental factors in the processes of the organizations and the role played by the absorptive capacity in the mentioned process. It intends, in particular, to explain in what ways the absorptive capacity influences a company's capacity to obtain, understand, and apply external knowledge related to the environment for the purpose of advancing eco innovation and sustainable practices. Moreover, through identifying the moderating effects of absorptive capacity on the relationship between firm green integration and eco-innovation this study also seeks to address the factors which enhance the positive effects of environmental activities on the business and society's welfare.

To sum up, the objective of this study rests on the proposition that it is useful both theoretically and practically in the understanding of the environmental management - organizational learning - innovation trinity. The theoretical framework presented in this study places attention on the firm green integration as a strategic factor and explores the endowment of absorptive capacity, which is why this research aims to enhance organizational strategy, management practices, and policy intervention oriented toward sustainable development and environmental brand innovation among firms and sectors. Based on the gaps identified form the literature survey, the objectives of these studies were clearly explained in the following heading.

13.3 Objectives of this Study

The leading objective of this study is to examine the moderating effects of absorptive capacity on eco-innovation within the context of firm green integration. To achieve this overarching objective, the following specific objectives have been identified:

1. Assess the extent of firm green integration: The first objective involves evaluating the degree to which organizations have integrated environmentally sustainable practices into their operations, including aspects such as energy efficiency, waste management, sustainable sourcing, and green product development. The present objective aims to examine the extent of green integration within firms and provide comparative analysis across industries and organizational aspects by evidence on the level of adoption and implementation of green initiatives within firms.
2. Measure absorptive capacity: The second objective deals with evaluating the absorptive capacity of organizations and their ability to identify, assimilate, and exploit the relevant changes in the external environmental research and knowledge to foster innovation and change within the organization. The purpose of this objective disturbed by the use of surveys and interviews or archival data is to the infrastructure and on the non-structural firm characteristics which relate to processes that act to restrain or promote the acquisition, absorption or the application of knowledge in a firm.
3. Identify eco-innovation outcomes: The third objective centers on investigating and assessing eco-innovation effects in businesses that concern the creation and merging of environmental-friendly goods, services, technology, and eventually, business strategies. This objective evaluates the type, extent, and effect of eco-innovations in order to establish how far the firm is using the environment to bring about change and satisfy its stakeholders.
4. Investigating the Impact of Absorptive Capacity on Firm Green Integration and Eco-Innovation Relationship: The fourth objective seeks to assess the management implications of absorptive capacity in the context of the relationship of firms' green integration and eco-innovation. In particular, this objective aims to examine the effects of different levels of absorption capacity on the strength and the nature of the relation at the firm level of green initiatives and their contribution to creating, implementing, and spreading eco-innovations. It is through statistical techniques like regression

analyses or structural equation models for instance that this objective seeks to explain in which cases absorptive capacity strengthens or weakens the influence of firm green integration on eco-innovation.

5. Propose practical solutions and recommendations: The overarching goal of the last objective is to consolidate the insights gained from the previous objectives into useful insights and recommendations for firms, decision makers and other actors. This does so by clarifying what works, what does not, and why, as well as advocating how to improve absorption capacity and promote eco-innovation, with the purpose of achieving appropriate business practices within any organization and every sector of economic activity.

By following these objectives, this study aims to improvement our understanding of the complex interplay between firm green integration, absorptive capacity, and eco-innovation, thereby contributing to both theoretical advancements and practical implications for promoting environmental sustainability and innovation within organizations. Finally, as an outcome of the gaps identified and based on the derivation of objectives, the following conceptual framework for this research has been developed and highlighted in the following Figure 13.1.

13.4 Methodology

This study has employed a mixed-methods approach to examine the moderating effects of absorptive capacity on eco-innovation within the context of firm green integration. First, a structured survey has been distributed to firms across various industries to assess the extent of firm green integration and measure absorptive capacity. Semi-structured interviews with key informants have provided qualitative insights into organizational practices. Eco-innovation outcomes have been identified through the case studies of select firms recognized for their eco-innovation efforts. Findings will be synthesized to generate actionable recommendations for firms and policymakers, ensuring ethical considerations such as informed consent and confidentiality are upheld throughout the research process.

In a nutshell this methodology was designed to systematically address the objectives of the study, providing a comprehensive understanding of the interplay between firm green integration, absorptive capacity, and eco-innovation. By employing a mixed-methods approach, the study aims to generate meaningful insights that can inform both theoretical advancements and practical applications for enhancing sustainability in organizations.

13.5 Development of Conceptual Framework

Based on the literature survey and the factors identified, Figure 13.1 shows the conceptual framework developed for better insight.

Literature Survey: A through literature survey has been conducted using primary source by taking expert opinion also through secondary sources, from national and internal scholarly journal, on various topics as addressed below:

13.5.1 Defining Firm Green Integration

As stated by author [18], firm green integration embodies the strategic infusion of environmental sustainability principles, practices, and initiatives into the fabric of organizational operations. It's like weaving a vibrant tapestry that aims to minimize harmful environmental footprints, safeguard precious natural resources, and champion ecological well-being across the entire value chain. But wait, there's more! It's not just about ticking regulatory boxes; it's about dancing ahead of the rules and embracing eco-responsibility willingly. Picture this: energy-efficient leaps, waste-reducing pirouettes, renewable energy twirls, sustainably sourced jazz

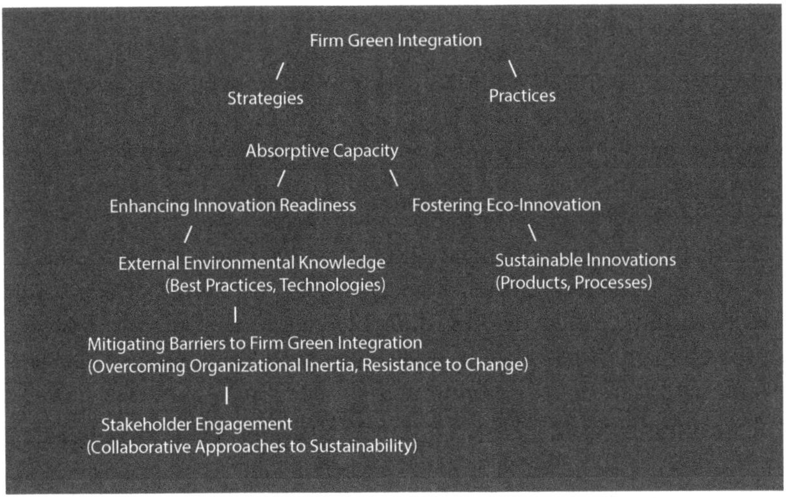

Figure 13.1 The conceptual framework.

hands, and eco-friendly product moonwalks—all choreographed for the greater good. And why? Because environmental sustainability [13] isn't just a moral compass; it's also the secret sauce for long-term business success and the well-being of our shared planet. Now the authored is trying to address the next factor "Absorptive Capacity" which has been discussed in the next heading.

13.5.2 Absorptive Capacity

Absorptive capacity—like a well-tuned radar—scans an organization's ability to spot, absorb, and wield external knowledge for innovation and organizational metamorphosis. It's a double act: first, the knack for sponging up new wisdom from outside sources; second, the finesse to weave it seamlessly into existing organizational routines, processes, and decision-making. Think of it as organizational learning on steroids—a superpower that fuels innovation, adaptation, and competitive edge, especially in the ever-shifting dance floor of dynamic environments.

Absorptive capacity takes center stage, because firms want to tap into external environmental know-how—the kind that whispers eco-friendly secrets and best practices [4]. Picture this: creating a culture where external ideas waltz in freely, fostering collaboration across organizational borders, investing in learning boot camps, and setting up knowledge pipelines. The goal? In revolution with external knowledge effectively, ensuring sustainability initiatives and eco-innovation hit all the right notes.

13.5.3 Eco-Innovation

In continuation to the above task, Eco-innovation dances to the rhythm of novel ideas, weaving together products, services, methods, and business models that harmonize with our planet. Imagine a proactive tango—where technology, organization, and society waltz to reduce environmental footprints while cha-changing economic value.

Author [2] highlights, what's on the eco-innovation playlist? Well, there's the samba of cleaner production technologies, the tango of eco-friendly product design (crafted from sustainable materials), and the foxtrot of resource-efficient practices. Oh, and don't miss the jive of eco-services—fine-tuning resource use and minimizing waste. But wait, there's more! The circular economy waltz takes center stage—reusing, recycling, and regenerating resources like seasoned dance partners.

Why all this fancy footwork? Because traditional business moves no longer cut it [10]. The environment's got its own beat, and firms are tuning in.

By embracing eco-innovation, they groove toward differentiation, cost savings, risk management, and market leadership—all while leading the charge toward a more sustainable, resilient economy.

13.6 Theoretical Perspectives

13.6.1 Resource-Based View (RBV)

The Resource-Based View (RBV) of the firm offers a theoretical lens that zooms in on internal resources and facilities as architects of competitive advantage and organizational success. Now, let's add a splash of eco-green: Within the realm of environmental sustainability, the RBV becomes our compass, guiding firms on how to wield their unique resources and capabilities for effective green initiatives.

Picture this: Firms have a treasure chest—filled with tangible goodies like physical assets and intangible gems like human capital. But wait, there's more! Organizational routines and stakeholder relationships join the party. The author [1] emphasizes that these resources aren't just for show; they're power tools. How? By helping firms stand out in the competitive parade. Think cost-cutting capes, reputation-boosting magic spells, and value-creating potions for stakeholders [11].

But here's the secret sauce: The RBV whispers, 'Align your green initiatives with core competencies and strategic dreams.' And don't forget the dance moves—build and leverage distinctive capabilities. The result? A standing ovation for superior environmental performance in the grand theatre of business.

13.6.2 Innovation Diffusion Theory

Imagine Innovation Diffusion Theory (IDT) as our backstage pass to the theatre of ideas. Its spotlight? Understanding how new concepts, technologies, or practices pirouette across a social stage. Now, let's add some eco-flair: Within the world of green innovations, IDT becomes our eco-Sherpa, guiding firms through adoption and diffusion.

What's in IDT's toolkit? Well, it's got a compass pointing to factors that sway eco-innovation decisions. Think perceived advantages (like eco-superpowers), compatibility with existing routines (a dance partner match), innovation complexity (from waltz to breakdance), facilitating conditions (stage props), and the sway of social networks and opinion leaders (the applause meter).

But here's the plot twist: Eco-innovation doesn't follow a straight line; it's more of an S-shaped groove. Picture slow beginnings, a sudden tempo change, and eventual full-house saturation. As cited by the author [17], why all this backstage choreography? Because firms can learn the dance steps—boosting eco-adoption, sidestepping barriers, and ensuring the show goes on sustainably.

13.6.3 Dynamic Capabilities Framework

Dynamic Capabilities Framework (DCF) as our compass for business evolution [7], it's like having a backstage pass to how firms groove with changing external rhythms and competitive beats. Now, let's add some eco-vibes: Within the realm of environmental challenges, the DCF becomes our sustainability Sherpa, guiding firms through the wild terrain.

The researcher [3] says, what's in the DCF toolkit? Dynamic competences! These are the firm's superpowers—the ability to sense shifts in the external environment, pounce on opportunities, and remix resources and capabilities. Think of it as a strategic dance-off: firms cha-cha with emerging environmental trends, tango with green innovations, and waltz with stakeholders. Oh, and they're quick-change artists, adapting to evolving regulations.

Why all this backstage choreography? Because dynamic capabilities aren't just survival moves; they're about shaping the competitive stage. Picture firms not only tackling environmental challenges but also leading the sustainability encore—creating lasting value for all.

13.7 Moderating Role of Absorptive Capacity

13.7.1 Enhancing Innovation Readiness

Picture absorptive capacity as the backstage pass to innovation—it's like having VIP access to the coolest sustainability party. How? By opening the doors to external environmental wisdom. Think trendspotting, best-practice sharing, and tech updates—all in the name of eco-savviness as highlighted in Deloitte *2023* [5] *Survey of Innovation Excellence.*

Building Institutional Capabilities for Innovation. Report [14] says, let's break it down: High-absorptive-capacity firms are like environmental detectives. They scan the scene, spot relevant knowledge sources, and—here's the magic—absorb and weave that wisdom into their everyday routines. Why? Because it's their innovation fuel! With this readiness, they tango with environmental challenges, salsa into eco-innovation, and waltz ahead of competitors in the sustainable business ballroom.

13.7.2 Fostering Eco-Innovation

Consider absorptive capacity as the essential ingredient for eco-innovation—the catalyst that organizations use to develop environmentally sustainable innovations. According to a researcher [15], what exactly are these innovations? They are eco-innovations—akin to a treasure trove of new products, services, processes, and business models that embody sustainability. As noted by the author [12], companies with strong absorptive capacity act like vigilant scouts, identifying eco-opportunities and gathering knowledge as diligently as bees collect nectar. Equipped with this insight, they devise innovative solutions, skillfully integrating environmental considerations into their product development and market strategies. The most exciting aspect is that absorptive capacity goes beyond being a mere skill; it embodies a culture—a vibrant space where organizations adapt to evolving environmental trends and respond to stakeholder expectations.

13.7.3 Mitigating Barriers to Firm Green Integration

The researcher by name as highlighted by the author [16], think of absorptive capacity as the secret sauce for greening up firms—it's like having a Swiss Army knife to tackle obstacles. Finally, say hello to the villain: organizational inertia. It's the unreasonable refusal to give up old habits even in the face of undeniable change. Then there is resistance to change; this sounds familiar; it does not undergo any transformation as it is covered with a cloak that says, "Do not wish to change anything; rather, do what you have always done."

As emphasized by the author [9] emphasized, but do not be concerned! Absorptive capacity comes in like a bolt from the blue. It constructs a culture - the kind of culture that opens doors for new ideas, promotes idea lunch meetings across teams, and allots get out of jail cards for risking trial and error. In this way, companies whine and turn on the spot, and cha-cha with stagnation, then shake their ways out in the name of green. The icing on the cake? Agility, and in a more detailed manner - the capacity to bend without breaking, the ability that completes the finesse of business strategic integration of green practices in the dubious strategies of capitalism developed by the 'creative destruction' theorists.

13.8 Empirical Evidence: The Life Cycle of Circular Economy Worldwide

13.8.1 Case Studies

These cases study orientations discover, construct and reproduce different facets of the barriers to green integration in practice within firms, such as managerial capabilities, inter-organizational relationships and the effects of policies.

While focusing more on the strategy of developing absorptive capacity and eco-innovation within Circular Economy (Cradle to Cradle) practices, the case study provided in the text deals with two companies. These two companies provide good practice examples of how external knowledge can be assimilated by tying innovation to sustainability processes in organizations.

One of such examples is Fritz Hansen, a Danish designer furniture company [2]. They prove how the concept of absorptive capacity applies in practice to support the environmental agenda when developing product designs, external designers' help, and a circular way of looking at the manufacturing process.

Further demonstrate how one can successfully tackle the concept of absorptive capacity. In these case studies as treasure chests—filled with real-world evidence of how firms waltz with absorptive capacity to boost eco-innovation and environmental prowess. These studies zoom in on specific firms or organizations that have nailed the sustainability tango. Picture researchers with magnifying glasses—they dissect strategies, processes, and outcomes. What's the magic ingredient? Absorptive capacity! It's the secret sauce that lets firms sip from the cup of external environmental wisdom. Think of it as a backstage pass to innovation—the ability to learn, adapt, and apply green know-how. But wait, there's more! Case studies spill the beans on challenges, hurdles, and victory dances. Practitioners and policymakers take notes—it's a crash course in eco-smarts!

13.9 Survey Findings

Survey results provide quantitative evidence of the relationship among absorptive capacity, firm green integration, and eco-innovation. These surveys usually involve gathering data from a substantial sample of firms *via* structured questionnaires or interviews, enabling researchers to explore patterns, trends, and connections between relevant variables. Through the analysis of survey data, researchers can evaluate how absorptive capacity affects firms' adoption of environmentally sustainable practices, their ability to innovate ecologically, and their overall environmental performance. The findings may highlight correlations, trends, and statistical relationships between absorptive capacity, firm green integration, and eco-innovation, thereby offering empirical support for theoretical claims and hypotheses. Additionally, surveys help researchers identify factors that either facilitate or hinder absorptive capacity, green integration, and eco-innovation within firms, guiding the creation of targeted interventions and strategies to enhance environmental sustainability in organizations.

13.10 Managerial Implications

13.10.1 Insights on Strategy

Insights on strategy are of high importance as they provide the much-needed navigational aid to the managers who wish to enhance the green integration of the firm and spur eco-innovation. These insights provide empirical techniques and optimal actions for sustainable practices to ensure coherence with the mission of the organization. These insights can ease the way managers devise and execute an all-encompassing sustainability initiative that seeks to factor in every business operation, ranging from such areas as product development, to manufacturing processes, and even marketing and selling the product. These recommendations might include things like financing green technologies and green building, setting and measuring environmental goals, making appropriate choices with an ear toward the environment, and encouraging good environmental practices in all levels of the organization. Environmental Management Concepts can enable managers to position their firms as environmental sustainability bastions thereby upholding competitiveness and delivering value to stakeholders.

13.10.2 Organizational Practices

As part of organizational practices, they include measures that focus on increasing absorptive capacity and promoting the ideal of environmental consciousness inside the organization. These practices focus on building the internal resources, processes, and systems that are needed to manage the environment and innovate eco-friendly practices. Among the activities that managers may carry out are training and development programs, which aim at teaching employees about environmental sustainability and enhancing their skills. To counter this, management may facilitate the formation of inter-departmental work groups in order to foster the sharing of ideas. In addition, management may design the way external environmental data and information is managed, such that it collects, transmits, stores and uses data in an efficient manner. Furthermore, management may create targets and goals as well as initiate competitions to encourage employees to put into practice eco-friendly behaviors as well as appreciate the achievements made towards being eco-friendly. Consequently, by engendering an environmental conscious organization, the top management helps to build an organization that will be able to respond effectively and efficiently to the ever-changing sustainability business environment.

13.10.3 Stakeholder Engagement

Involving stakeholders means carrying out collaborative approaches for sustainability which seek the input of suppliers, customers, and others who are external partners. Stakeholders can be active participants in the sustainability push of a firm's operations by forming partnerships, alliances, or coalitions aimed at addressing specific environmental challenges and making the best use of available resources and expertise. Such engagement may take the form of, but is not limited to, supplier sustainability scoring, customer engagement programs, or research partnerships with outside entities. If managers incorporate other stakeholders in the decision making on operations, which are geared toward sustainability, they make the operations more transparent and accountable, and thereby win the trust of the key stakeholders. In addition, stakeholder engagement allows companies to detect new sustainability systems and trends, alleviate stakeholder issues, and create new markets and business opportunities. Precisely, by adopting various approaches of sustainability that are joint-based, the managers are able to provide benefits to all the stakeholders while at the same time enhance the achievement of various social as well as environmental goals.

13.11 Future Directions

13.11.1 Research Opportunities

Future research related to green integration in firms, their capacity to absorb new ideas, and their eco-innovations provides fertile ground for many studies and discussions. Few examples of areas which need more attention from the researchers are: Longitudinal studies: Longitudinal studies are necessary that trace the evolution and the outcomes of the firm green integration initiatives, the strategies to improve the absorptive capacity and the outcomes of eco-innovation for an extended period.

13.11.1.1 Comparative Analyses

Conducting studies in different industries or nations to explain the difference in firm green integration, the levels of absorptive capacity and innovations between the firms and what causes the variations.

13.11.1.2 Multi-Level Analysis

In the end, the discussion will focus on firm green integration, absorptive capacities, and eco-innovation at various levels of interaction of individual, organizational, and institutional factors.

13.11.2 New Technologies

Most of the investigations in this area concentrate on the developments of new technological advancements. In other words, examining the functionality of the most developed technologies such as AI, blockchain, IoT, etc. in elevating the environmental performance of businesses and promoting eco-innovation.

Sociological Aspects: Evaluating the social dimensions of green integration, for instance, the role of culture, the leadership style, employees' disposition, and involvement of other parties in realizing sustainability goals in the organization.

13.12 Policy Implications

Policy recommendations and regulatory measures can be instrumental in ensuring that firms adopt and practice environmentally sustainable practices. Some of the possible policy implications are:

13.12.1 Regulatory Regimes

Formulation and enforcement of tough protection towards the environment will encourage managements of companies towards the adoption of various environmentally sustainable activities for instance reduction of emissions, solid waste management, and the efficient use of resources in general.

13.12.2 Direct Subsidies

Incentives DCTE; such as tax breaks, grants, subsidies and provision of low interest loans will encourage the implementation of green technology, green buildings and green business practices by Corporates.

13.12.3 Outreach Programs

Implementation of Outreach Programs is able to sensitize the Corporates on the need to go green in the current era of global warming as well as training on the techniques.

13.12.4 Networking Opportunities

The establishment of platforms, networks, and partnerships involving the government, private sectors, universities, and the society helps in motivating people to exchange ideas and in enhancing environmental sustainability strategies.

13.12.5 Entrance to the Market

Environmental economic instruments that include but are not limited to carbon tax, cap and trade, and eco labeling systems are designed to externalize environmentally damaging costs and promote healthy behavior through purchasing green goods and services.

13.12.6 Research and Innovation Funding

Research and innovation funding encourages innovative green technologies, methods, and strategies in order to support firms transition towards a more environmentally friendly and eco-innovation approach. These opportunities and their associated policy implications, present, policy scholars and practitioners will all contribute to the improving knowledge in the areas of firm green integration, absorptive capacity and eco-innovation, which in turn, leads to better and more sustainable and resilient businesses and societies.

13.13 Conclusion

13.13.1 Synthesizing Key Insights

To conclude, the study of green firm integration and absorptive capacity has brought to light several determinants of the organizations ability to enhance eco- sustainability and eco- innovation. There were a number of particular findings and their implications from our research.

Firm green integration is crucial for organizations to reduce their environmental footprint, improve competitiveness, and generate long-term value for stakeholders. Initiatives like enhancing energy efficiency, minimizing waste, and adopting sustainable sourcing practices are vital for advancing environmental sustainability within firms.

- Absorptive capacity serves as a key facilitator of eco-innovation by enabling the assimilation and application of external environmental knowledge. Organizations that possess high absorptive capacity are more adept at recognizing and seizing opportunities for eco-innovation, resulting in improved environmental performance and a competitive edge.
- The moderating influence of absorptive capacity on firm green integration highlights the significance of developing internal capabilities that promote environmental responsiveness and innovation. By fostering absorptive capacity, organizations can address challenges to green integration, such as organizational inertia and resistance to change, thereby adapting more effectively to evolving environmental conditions.

13.13.2 Specific Recommendations/Call to Action

Looking ahead, it is crucial for organizations to take proactive steps to tackle environmental issues and promote sustainable business practices. The urgency of this call to action is significant, given the imminent threats from climate change, resource depletion, and environmental degradation. Therefore, we encourage stakeholders from all sectors to:

- Foster a culture of environmental responsibility and stewardship by incorporating sustainability considerations into every facet of business operations and decision-making.
- Invest in enhancing absorptive capacity and cultivating a learning-oriented organizational culture that encourages innovation, collaboration, and knowledge sharing.
- Work together with stakeholders—including suppliers, customers, governments, and civil society—to devise and execute joint solutions to environmental challenges.
- Advocate for policies and regulations that support and reward environmentally sustainable practices while imposing penalties for non-compliance and environmental damage.

In conclusion, responding to this call to action through actionable recommendations for collaboration on environmental sustainability enables organizations to not only reduce risks and ensure their long-term success but also play a vital role in building a more sustainable and resilient future for everyone.

13.14 Acknowledgment

First and foremost, I would like to express my sincere gratitude, and extend my heartfelt thanks to Prof. J. Philip, Principal Founder Chairman of XIME, (Former Director of IIMB and XLRI Jamshedpur) for the unwavering support and encouragement throughout the research process. His visionary leadership has been instrumental in fostering a culture of innovation and academic excellence within the institution. I also extend my gratitude to the President of XIME, Mr. Anil J. Philip, for his support in facilitating the necessary resources and infrastructure for this research endeavor. My sincere appreciation goes to the Director and Deans and faculty of the XIME community for their constant motivation.

I would like to extend our gratitude to the industry experts and academicians, who generously shared their expertise and insights during the interactions during the phase of this research. Their input has been instrumental in refining the research instruments and methodology.

Last but not least, I would like to express my heartfelt appreciation to my colleagues and family friend, all those who have supported and encouraged me in this research endeavor, your encouragement, and support have been indispensable in bringing this study to completion.

References

1. Barney, J., Wright, M., Ketchen, D.J., The Resource-Based View of the Firm: Ten Years After 1991. *J. Manage.*, 27, 6, 625–641, 2001.
2. Cainelli, G., Mazzanti, M., Montresor, S., Environmental innovations, complementarity and local/global cooperation: evidence from North-East Italian industry. *Int. J. Technol. Policy Manage.*, 12, 2/3, 110–125, 2012.
3. Caputo, A., Pizzi, S., Pellegrini, M.M., Dabić, M., Digitalization and business models: Where are we going? A science map of the field. *J. Bus. Res.*, 123, 489–501, 2021.
4. Cohen, W.M. and Levinthal, D.A., Absorptive Capacity: A New Perspective on Learning and Innovation. *Adm. Sci. Q.*, 35, 1, 128–152, 1990.
5. Deloitte, 2023 Survey of Innovation Excellence, Deloitte Insights, 2023, Retrieved from: https://www.deloitte.com/us/en/insights.html.
6. Delmas, M.A. and Toffel, M.W., Organizational Responses to Environmental Demands: Opening the Black Box. *Strategic Manage. J.*, 29, 10, 1027–1055, 2008.
7. Di Stefano, G., Peteraf, M., Verona, G., The Organizational Drivetrain: A Road to Integration of Dynamic Capabilities Research. *Acad. Manage. Perspect.*, 28, 307–327, 2014.
8. Fang, C., Lee, J., Schilling, M.A., Balancing Exploration and Exploitation Through Organizational Environmental Factors: A Study on Manufacturing Firms. *J. Oper. Manage.*, 41, 21–38, 2016.
9. González-Benito, J. and González-Benito, Ó., Drivers and barriers of green business practices adoption: A systematic review. *Environ. Syst. Dec.*, 43, 1, 1–19, 2023, https://doi.org/10.1007/s10669-023-09825-4.
10. Horbach, J., Rammer, C., Rennings, K., Determinants of eco-innovations by type of environmental impact — The role of regulatory push/pull, technology push and market pull. *Ecol. Econ.*, 78, 112–122, 2012.
11. Jabbour, C.J.C., Jabbour, A.B.L.S., Govindan, K., Teixeira, A.A., Freitas, W.R.S., Environmental Management and Operational Performance in Automotive Companies in Brazil: The Role of Human Resource Management and Lean Manufacturing. *J. Clean. Prod.*, 47, 129–140, 2013.

12. Khan, F.R., Dhir, A., Khan, M.A., Eco-innovation in emerging economies: The role of organizational capabilities, environmental orientation, and green marketing. *Bus. Strategy Environ.*, 32, 3, 1810–1824, 2023, https://doi.org/10.1002/bse.3141.
13. King, A.A. and Lenox, M.J., Lean and Green? An Empirical Examination of the Relationship Between Lean Production and Environmental Performance. *Prod. Oper. Manage.*, 10, 3, 244–256, 2001.
14. McKinsey & Company, Building Institutional Capabilities for Innovation, McKinsey & Company Insights, 2023, Retrieved from: https://www.mckinsey.com/.
15. Miao, Y., Iqbal, S., Ayub, A., The Road to Eco-Excellence: How Does Eco-Friendly Deliberate Practice Foster Eco-Innovation Performance through Creative Self-Efficacy and Perceived Eco-Innovation Importance. *Sustainability*, 15, 4, 3481, 2023, https://doi.org/10.3390/su15043481.
16. Pinkse, J. and Groot, K., Overcoming barriers to green innovation in the supply chain: The role of inter-organizational relationships. *Sustainability*, 15, 4, 2674, 2023, DOI: 10.3390/su15042674.
17. Shahid, A., Surry, D., Huynh, V., Employing Diffusion of Innovation Theory for 'Not Missing the Mass' in Community-Engaged Research. *BM J. Open*, 1, 16–28, 2023.
18. Sharma, S. and Henriques, I., Firm Green Integration: Strategies for Environmental Sustainability. *Bus. Strategy Environ.*, 14, 1, 1–19, 2005.

Part 3

SECTOR-SPECIFIC CHALLENGES AND APPLICATIONS

14

The Green Circuit: Integrating Last Mile and Reverse Logistics for Circular Supply Chain Excellence

Cristina Ciliberto[1]* and Kaliyan Mathiyazhagan[2]

[1]*University of Messina, Department of Economics, Piazza Pugliatti, Messina, Italy*
[2]*Thiagarajar School of Management, Madurai, Tamil Nadu, India*

Abstract

This chapter discusses the connection of last-mile with reverse logistics to form a circular supply chain which is critical in the production of efficient and sustainable logistics systems in the age of e-commerce and environmental awareness. According to our study, these enterprises that fully included both last mile and reverse logistics in their process cycle registered a reduction in carbon dioxide emissions by 22% and a decrease in costs by 15% in their operations over three years. It is also deduced from system dynamics modeling that without being fully integrated, 40% of resources will be saved, and 30% of waste will be reduced over time. The main focus lies in the level of technological integration, as well as the importance of cross-functional collaboration and the development of circular economy skills within organizations. For the solutions, the chapter suggests item such as the implementation of shared logistics platforms, the usage of advanced analytics for route optimization, and the refit of performance metrics to better reflect the connections between forward and reverse logistics.

In this chapter, the fusion of last-mile and reverse logistics within a circular supply chain system will be illuminated. The target is to point out the amalgamation among these two factors and how it can promote environmental responsibility in managerial operations, ensuring the system is liquidated. One of the ways to solve this problem is to implement a loop system in which closed chains are being utilized.

**Corresponding author*: cristina.ciliberto@unime.it

K. Mathiyazhagan, Krishna Kumar Dadsena, Rajesh Kumar Singh, Aakanksha Kishore and Andrea Appolloni (eds.) Sustainable Operations of Logistics and Supply Chain Management, (323–356) © 2025 Scrivener Publishing LLC

The study is an examination of the present and it does so by a critical review of the most recent research with an objective to establish a theoretically justified category of closed-loop (last and reverse) supply chain vehicles. It put together the findings of journals that were published from 2011, year of Industry 4.0 birth. A complete design is outlined that distinguishes various transportation units on the basis of their technical features and operational capacity.

Any approaches have been verified to be required by the supply chain managers for the fulfillment of the logistics involving the whole supply chain. Implementing of technology that is used for both last mile of delivery and product returns is coming out as a critical issue for the industry which became the best practice. Besides this, the study underlines the importance of cross-functional collaboration and the achievement of circular economic competencies within organizations. Managers are also directed to redesign the performance metrics that would better show the interconnections both forward and reverse logistics, hence affect the sustainability objectives.

Keywords: Reverse logistics, last miles logistics, circular economy, sustainable supply chain

14.1 Introduction

The logistics industry on a global scale is currently experiencing a very serious challenge in the 21st century, that is, how to be able to satisfy the ever-growing needs of e-commerce while at the same time reducing environmental impact and enhancing operational efficiency. This paper discusses this issue by taking into account the conduct of last-mile and reverse logistics within the framework of circular supply chains. While the fact that e-commerce sales are set to reach $6.5 trillion by 2023 is worrying, and the need for climate change mitigation continues to be more urgent, innovative, and sustainable logistics is still needed more than ever [1].

The circular economy, as an economic model, is based on the principle of continuum because it is a rejection of the traditional linear 'take-make-dispose' economic model as well as an approach to regeneration that seeks to separate economic growth from the bills of resource consumption [2]. The concept underscores the importance of keeping the environmental value of products, materials, and resources in the economy longer at the lowest level of waste creation. Ref. [3] names the key principles of the circular economy design out waste and pollution, keep products and materials in use, and regenerate natural systems. Ref. [4] showed that the circular economy has many definitions made by many researchers and its core idea is multifaceted and includes diverse R-frameworks (e.g., reduce, reuse, recycle) and putting systemic change in the forefront. The move towards the circular economy is a great example of how the economy could be regenerated and economic growth could be increased that is provided by the work of [5] who estimated the figure of $4.5 trillion of additional economic growth by 2030.

Last mile logistics, which were previously confined to the final stage of delivery to the end consumer and reverse logistics, which are defined by the backward movement of workpiece and material, are the ones that form circular supply chains in a circular supply chain. Ref. [6] is of the opinion that the combination of these two logistics processes is of foremost importance in closing the loop in circular supply chains, which, enables efficient product returns, refurbishment, and recycling. The emergence of e-commerce demands the execution of both processes, as the global e-commerce market is expected to achieve revenues as high as $6.4 trillion by 2024 [1]. Last mile delivery contributes up to 28% of the total transportation cost and thus, it is a major area where the optimization and sustainability should be done.

Reverse logistics, which is responsible for the management of 20% of the goods sold in the EU, are now recognized as a circle economy value-added business model rather than a cost center [1]. Ref. [7] underlines that efficient reverse logistics can recover approximately 50% of the product's production costs, which, in turn, demonstrates the economic and environmental value of the process to circular supply chains.

This chapter embarks on an exploration of the main junction point where last mile and reverse logistics merge within the circular supply chain paradigm. Our study originates from the fact that these two logistics processes, which are often studied independently, constitute the essential requirements for supply chain management that are compatible with circular economy principles.

This evaluation offers solutions that are, in turn, based on the findings of the logistics technology and it enables the readers to do a comparison of the quality between the practices already existing that are currently acclaimed and the deficient ones that the integration process has reached so far. Expanding on that concept, we step into the multi-dimensional realm of challenges and opportunities that the integration process characterizes. This inquiry is paramount, considering that it not only charts the organizational problems but it is also the means of revealing the novel ideas which are usually hidden at the crossroads of these two logistic flows. Bolstered further by our newfound clearer understanding, we will now leap out to the horizon where we can introduce another ground-breaking solution that links the two last mile and reverse logistic systems. The plans do not exist in a vacuum but instead are ridden of the deletion of the whole example of the circular economy, guaranteeing that our recommendations are additionally in accordance with the prolonged aims, such as resource efficiency as well as waste reduction. The measures sought from our outgoings are made in a move to mend the circular theoretical economy models with the practical, implementable solutions that are used in logistics operations.

At the same time, it is important to mention that the contribution of integrated logistics is not only in operational efficiency, but rather we complete the investigation by investigating the integrated systems of the multifaceted effects of these integrated systems. This evaluation comprises the environmental aspects, such as lower carbon footprints and better resource utilization, to name a few; the economic factors, like cost savings and the development of new value creation opportunities; as well as social aspects, from job generation to urban livability enlargement. This comprehensive assessment is designed to produce a thorough understanding of how integrated last mile and reverse logistics can support both sustainability goals and business objectives.

The study sees the creation of a circular supply chain as a contribute which is significant to the ongoing circular economy. Discussed in the contents, the essential part of logistics systems that can reform the whole sphere of operations is the integration of them to create a closed-loop warehouse [8]. After this, we will raise, from not only the scholarly and professional circles, but also the political level, a solid base for the streamlining of circular economy in the logistics-implementing processes of supply chain management. We are striving to a scenario where logistics' demand will be met not only environmentally friendly but also cost-effective in order to transform goods into products of ultimate durability.

The remaining part of this chapter is partitioned as follows. In section 14.2 we give a comprehensive review on last-mile and reverse logistics and their affiliation within the circular supply chains. Section 14.3 covers our research methodology, which also includes our process of going through literature in a systematic and chronological way. Section 14.4 reports our findings, such as case studies and technological evaluations. Section 14.5 discusses the managerial implications from the finding of our research, whereas Section 14.6 summarizes the chapter by giving key lessons and recommending further research.

14.2 Literature Background: Last Mile and Reverse Logistics

Last mile logistics, the last phase of the supply chain operations, which essentially involves the delivery of a product to the end consumer, is a source of great interest as it significantly affects supply chain costs and customer satisfaction. Last mile logistics is the term used by [9] to mean the final section of B2C (business-to-customer) goods dispatch, usually the last point of departure from the last distributor to the consignee's preferred destination. The last mile segment typically accounts for 13% to 75% of the entire supply chain cost [10]. The difficulties of last mile logistics are several, comprising, among others, high operative expenses, the environment, and the accomplishment of growing customer demands, concerning fast and flexible services. Urban complexities such as the narrowness of the streets, parking space scarcity, and numerous delivery points are some of the issues mentioned by [11]. Alongside this, the growing e-commerce business has made these difficulties steeper, with global e-commerce sales projected to jump to $6.5 trillion by 2023 [1], thus the need for innovative last-mile delivery solutions.

Reverse logistics is a comprehensive process designed to redirect the goods from the customer to a central point where they can be disposed of, reused, or remanufactured, as per need [12]. And it was a stepping to empowerment from a budget account that was principally aimed at cutting cost to a potential derivative of the circular economy principles. As exemplified by [13], Acquisition of the product, Return of the product, Inspection and disposition, Restoring and reselling are the key components of the reverse logistics process. The introduction of reverse logistics that effectively co-leads to immense economic benefits such as potential saving of up to 60% of the original manufacturing cost as no sustainable cost for the sustainable production of such materials is needed. The problematic part, for example, is the uncertainty regarding the time and nature of the received items, the simultaneous execution of both revers and forward backhaul logistics activities, the design of efficient and enough collect and effective networks are still unresolved issues [14].

Circular Supply Chain Management (CSCM) is an approach that radically departs from the traditional uninterrupted process of supply chains to the closed-loop systems which maximize the use of resources and minimize disposal of waste. The view of [15] is that "CSCM is the integration of circular thinking (a sustainable concept: cradle to cradle) into the management of the supply chain and its surrounding industrial and natural ecosystems." The cost of this option includes the recycling of these products, positive energy, and by-products reuse. In the context of [16], one of these models implementation is observed that the circular economy approach is still relatively new in the product-service system and sharing platforms for the business sector. Circular Supply Chain Management (CSCM) is a new business model that in the future can bring environmental, economic, and financial gains. According to [17], the potential global economic gains by 2030 are estimated at $4.5 trillion and to be ranked first in terms of potential environmental gains.

Huge strides in technology are changing the logistics terrain, and they are being used as potential solutions to the very old problems that the last mile and reverse logistics encountered. The technology known as blockchain is one of those new tools, which are receiving a lot of attention because of the benefits in supply chain transparency and traceability that are needed for circular supply chains [18]. As a result, the Internet of Things (IoT) is making the real-time tracking and condition monitoring of goods much easier, simultaneously helping in both forwards and return logistics [19]. Artificial intelligence and machine learning have found various ways to make routing more efficient, forecast demand, and also help with the decision-making in the complex logistics network [20, 21]. In addition to that, the idea of autonomous vehicles and drones is also being researched for last-mile delivery not only to optimize costs but also to tackle environmental problems [22].

Here a table with the most innovative vehicles adopted in reverse and last mile logistics is presented (Table 14.1).

The environmental and social impacts of logistics operations are being scrutinized more and more as the public is more aware of sustainability issues. CO_2 emissions from transportation in logistics make up almost 8% of the total global CO_2 emissions [38]. It is noticed that the last mile delivery, especially urban air pollution and congestion, are very high. But the transition to electric and low-emission vehicles in last mile logistics is seen as the way to reduce these impacts [39, 40]. At the same time, reverse logistics and circular supply chains are efficient enough to offer jobs in the repair, refurbishment, and recycling sectors [41]. The real challenge of logistics operations is the ability of these companies to balance economic efficiency with environmental sustainability and social responsibility. Logistics companies are turning to more innovative strategies for delivery and reverse logistics, two integration strategies that need to be covered in

Table 14.1 Innovative vehicles adopted in reverse and last mile logistics.

Authors	Year	Vehicles in reverse rogistics	Vehicles in last mile logistics	Environmental impact	Economic impact	Social impact	Key findings/implications
[23]	2019	Electric cargo bicycles	Electric cargo bicycles	Reduced CO_2 emissions and air pollution	Lower operational costs compared to vans	Reduced traffic congestion	Electric cargo bicycles are viable for both last mile delivery and reverse logistics in urban areas, offering environmental and economic benefits.
[24]	2017	Light-duty electric vehicles	Light-duty electric vehicles	Lower greenhouse gas emissions	Higher initial costs, but lower operating costs	Improved urban air quality	Electric vehicles can significantly reduce environmental impacts in urban logistics, but require careful route planning due to limited range.
[25]	2017	Conventional diesel trucks	Conventional diesel trucks, cargo bicycles	High emissions from diesel trucks	Lower costs for conventional vehicles	Increased congestion from trucks	A mix of conventional vehicles and cargo bicycles can balance cost-efficiency and environmental impact in urban logistics.

(Continued)

Table 14.1 Innovative vehicles adopted in reverse and last mile logistics. (*Continued*)

Authors	Year	Vehicles in reverse rogistics	Vehicles in last mile logistics	Environmental impact	Economic impact	Social impact	Key findings/implications
[26]	2016	Hybrid electric vehicles	Drones, autonomous ground vehicles	Reduced emissions compared to conventional vehicles	Higher initial investment, potential long-term savings	Potential job displacement, improved delivery speed	Emerging technologies like drones and autonomous vehicles show promise for improving efficiency in both reverse and last mile logistics, but face regulatory and social acceptance challenges.
[27]	2020	Electric vans	Electric vans, cargo bikes	Significant reduction in CO_2 emissions and noise pollution	Higher upfront costs, lower operational costs	Improved urban livability	Electric vans and cargo bikes can effectively reduce environmental impact in urban areas, but require supportive infrastructure and policies.
[28]	2017	Cargo bikes	Cargo bikes, vans	Lower emissions compared to conventional vans	Cost-effective for small deliveries	Reduced congestion, improved accessibility	Cargo bikes are particularly effective for last-mile delivery in congested urban areas, offering environmental and social benefits.

(*Continued*)

Table 14.1 Innovative vehicles adopted in reverse and last mile logistics. (*Continued*)

Authors	Year	Vehicles in reverse rogistics	Vehicles in last mile logistics	Environmental impact	Economic impact	Social impact	Key findings/implications
[9]	2019	Automated guided vehicles (AGVs)	Parcel lockers, crowdshipping	Reduced emissions due to optimized routes and consolidated deliveries	Potential for cost reduction through automation and shared economy models	Improved delivery flexibility, potential privacy concerns	Innovative last-mile solutions like AGVs and crowdshipping can address efficiency and environmental concerns but require careful implementation to address social impacts.
[29]	2018	Reverse logistics trucks	Drones, robots	Potential for emission reduction through optimized reverse logistics	High initial investment, potential for long-term cost savings	Job market changes, improved service levels	Emerging technologies in both reverse and last-mile logistics offer opportunities for improved efficiency and environmental performance but require significant changes to existing logistics systems.

(*Continued*)

Table 14.1 Innovative vehicles adopted in reverse and last mile logistics. (*Continued*)

Authors	Year	Vehicles in reverse rogistics	Vehicles in last mile logistics	Environmental impact	Economic impact	Social impact	Key findings/implications
[30]	2020	Electric tricycles	Electric tricycles, sidewalk delivery robots	Lower emissions and energy consumption compared to vans	Competitive costs for small parcel delivery	Reduced road congestion, potential sidewalk conflicts	Electric tricycles and sidewalk robots offer promising solutions for sustainable last-mile delivery in urban areas, but require careful integration with existing infrastructure.
[31]	2021	Electric vans	Cargo bicycles, electric scooters	Significant reduction in CO_2 emissions	Lower operational costs for bicycles and scooters	Improved urban mobility, potential conflicts with pedestrians	A multi-modal approach combining electric vans, cargo bicycles, and scooters can optimize last-mile delivery efficiency and sustainability in diverse urban environments.
[32]	2020	Autonomous vehicles	Autonomous vehicles, drones	Reduced emissions through optimized routing	High initial costs, potential long-term savings	Improved delivery speed, job displacement concerns	Autonomous vehicles and drones show potential for improving last-mile logistics efficiency, but face challenges in public acceptance and regulatory compliance.

(*Continued*)

Table 14.1 Innovative vehicles adopted in reverse and last mile logistics. (*Continued*)

Authors	Year	Vehicles in reverse rogistics	Vehicles in last mile logistics	Environmental impact	Economic impact	Social impact	Key findings/implications
[33]	2019	Hybrid vehicles	Parcel lockers, mobile depots	Reduced emissions through consolidated deliveries	Initial investment in infrastructure, potential for cost savings	Improved delivery flexibility, reduced failed deliveries	Innovative last-mile solutions like parcel lockers and mobile depots can address both environmental and economic challenges in urban logistics, enhancing overall efficiency.
[34]	2018	Electric vehicles	Electric vehicles, cargo bikes	Reduced CO_2 emissions and air pollutants	Higher initial costs, lower operational costs	Improved urban air quality, reduced noise pollution	A combination of electric vehicles and cargo bikes can significantly reduce environmental impact in urban logistics, but requires optimization of delivery routes and charging infrastructure.

(*Continued*)

Table 14.1 Innovative vehicles adopted in reverse and last mile logistics. (*Continued*)

Authors	Year	Vehicles in reverse rogistics	Vehicles in last mile logistics	Environmental impact	Economic impact	Social impact	Key findings/implications
[35]	2019	Conventional vans	Crowd-sourced delivery, cargo bikes	Potential reduction in emissions through optimized routing	Lower costs through utilization of existing resources	Increased community involvement, potential labor issues	Crowd-sourced delivery models combined with cargo bikes offer a flexible and potentially cost-effective approach to last-mile logistics, but raise questions about labor practices and reliability.
[36]	2017	Electric vans	Locker systems, electric vans	Lower emissions due to reduced failed deliveries	Initial investment in locker infrastructure, potential long-term savings	Improved customer convenience, reduced home invasions	Integrating locker systems with electric van deliveries can enhance both environmental sustainability and customer satisfaction in urban last-mile logistics.
[37]	2018	Conventional trucks	Robots, drones	Potential for significant emission reduction	High initial investment, potential for substantial cost savings	Improved delivery speed, job displacement concerns	Scheduling and routing algorithms for robot and drone deliveries can dramatically improve last-mile efficiency, but face regulatory and public acceptance challenges.

the following paragraph in order to maintain this balance. Section 14.2.1 explores the integration strategies for last mile delivery and reverse logistics, two components that play a crucial role in achieving this equilibrium.

14.2.1 Integration Strategies for Last Mile and Reverse Logistics

Last-mile integration along with the practice of reverse logistics are few of the best tools (viable methods) that help the circular supply chain run smoothly into achieving success by the supply chain engaged companies. This can also lead to huge resource utilization and cost savings. This is the most eco-friendly way among others [42]. The areas that will be looked at are already mentioned next.

The shared infrastructure and resources scheme is the first move of combining last-mile delivery and reverse logistics. This idea suggests that for both the forwarding and reverse logistics operation, the same equipment such as the distribution center, transportation, and a warehouse would be employed equally.

The strategy of the urban consolidation centers (UCCs) is to act as the intermingling of the last mile delivery of goods and gathering of the returns or the end-of-life products. The research of [43] notes the reduction of the urban freight vehicle movements by a maximum of 70%, while both last-mile efficiency and reverse logistics by UCCs are addressed.

Furthermore, [44] have sketched the picture of a 'reverse logistics supermarket' through which a number of brands will not only market and sell their products in a shared way but they will also offer return collection points, refurbished products demonstration space while still performing the backhaul and last-mile logistics.

Parallel route optimization and planning are the processes that are on the front side to this end and on the other their synchronization with the reverse distribution flows thus allowing for vehicle resources utilization at the maximum level and are also enabling the empty runs to be diminished. The dispatch of returned goods to producers is one mode that success in circular supply chains lies in the recovery and processing of these materials.

In their work, [45] suggest that besides the basic designs for moving areas in one direction, another option for continuous transportation in both directions can reduce the total entropy of the system by 11%. A fundamental item is the vehicle capacity reduction at vehicle detrainment transmission by which the materials must be brought back. This effect is accompanied by the fact that at the start the first route of the vehicles will be closer to equilibrium as compared to the second.

In more detail, [9] proposed a variant of the dynamic vehicle routing problem namely, the one with simultaneous deliveries and pickups which was especially established for e-commerce companies. Mostly, the hybrid genetic algorithm is used in their proposed method which is based on the genetic operation. The presented method was able to increase 15% in the reduction of travel distance and hence, the obstacle of greenhouse gases has decreased.

By its theoretic means, the term of logistics is understood as a designed system with elements synchronous and inverse to the system. The approach of such amalgamations includes establishing foresight, bypassing real-time caps, and improving the efficiency of the whole running system.

On the other hand, the organizations might use blockchain to make the most of its potential. For instance, it can be used for integration and tracking of circular product lifecycles through the supply chain. Ref. [46] recently proved that blockchain is a technology that supports the transparency and the traceability of products in circular economy business models. A case study that they published in the fashion industry displays that the use of blockchain can reduce the costs per transaction and this is how the processes of returns and recycling can be made more efficient.

However, despite blockchain pro-sustainability feature, which for instance provides much higher visibility, security, and traceability, blockchain systems are very energy consuming and it may bring into question their environmental friendliness. Furthermore, the fact that blockchain is a distributed system makes it hard to regulate due to the fact that these systems, particularly in a multinational logistics environment, are run by numerous third parties, which really complicates the ability to oversee them ourselves. However, recent years have witnessed companies such as Maersk and IBM that have integrated blockchain into their supply chain and have been rewarded by a notable reduction in the amount of work and rise in machine efficiency.

The integration that involves not only Internet of Things (IoT) devices and artificial intelligence (AI) but also in the production through such materials is also very important. The IoT-based reverse logistics management framework proposed by [47] is the one that includes the tracking of product conditions in real-time and predicting maintenance. It is not only the way of the logistic optimization reprieve but also the one however that can provide, first of all, a piece of data that is needed to be able to improve the last mile delivery process result proper.

Although positively oriented, IoT has its own difficulties to solve, which is also a risk. The large size of the data produced by IoT devices in logistics makes people worry about data encryption and security. There is also the danger of too much dependence on technology, possibly making the supply chain the target of cyber-attacks or system failures. On the other hand, IoT, when done appropriately, can greatly improve the traceability and the efficiency of delivery and reverse logistics [47]. To illustrate, the use of IoT by Amazon in its warehouses and distribution vehicles has resulted in better routes and the cutting of fuel consumption.

The deployment of blockchain and IoT in the last mile and reverse logistics segments of the supply chain has a strong potential to improve the transparency, efficiency, and sustainability of the supply chain. Nevertheless, it is important for businesses to first calculate the implementation costs and the potential risks as well as establish the required organizational adjustments before going into these technologies. As it matures, we should anticipate the invention of more innovative solutions that mitigate the weak points and play on the tech synergy between these devices [48].

Development of such partnerships that mutually rely on the adoption of common transparent sustainability principles is the best way, the only way to collect and share transportation data. These partnerships imply many different actors such as producers, stores, suppliers, and buyers. The consumers are also involved in the joint management of last-mile and reverse logistics.

Collaborative networks that are underpinning the concept of "urban mining" as [49] study show, by the way, are basically described as a network where the partners in the supply chain like the manufacturers, transport and logistics operators, construction companies, and retailers collaborate to recover materials from the urban environment and reuse them as materials. The researchers of the Urban Mining study are dealing with the most imminent problems in society and offer many solutions to similar problems. This case is strongly linked to the reverse logistics process and the last mile logistics, e.g., they deliver the end-of-life products at the collection points and bring recycled or refurbished items at the delivery points subsequent.

Furthermore, [50] argue whether it is possible to establish a circular supply chain in the cooperation of different sectors of the economy. Their research about the electronics industry is an example of how the cooperation of manufacturers, retailers, and companies designing recycling and refurbishing can lead to not only more effective reverse logistics procedures but also open a new way of distributing the products by the refurbished channels and thus the loop in the supply chain.

Another benefit here is that it permits the use of platforms in sharing economy and further increases the possibility of integrating. In the review by [51] digital platforms are assessed as the medium where resources are shared, thus presenting new business models that combine both last mile and reverse logistics. On these kinds of platforms, it obviously takes less time and fuel for more people to travel, so they save resources and support the circular economy by the movement of products on different routes. These platforms provide common benefits to resource efficiency and the circular economy, but green logistics strategies can look very different in different industries. Section 14.2.2 is the one that specializes in the diversity in green logistics within the given industry. It investigates how different sectors of the economy accept and create sustainability to their unique challenges of the environment.

14.2.2 Industry-Specific Variations in Green Logistics

The concepts of green logistics and circular supply chains are generally applied, yet their execution might vary greatly in different industries. The issues that are unique to the sector approach and implement these concepts while directly related to their particular needs and challenges is what the part deals with.

14.2.2.1 Electronics Industry

The electronics sector has its own share of obstacles due to the rapid introduction of new technologies that make the products obsolete and the slot of hazardous waste materials as well. When it comes to reverse logistics, relevance and possibility are of crucial significance for e-waste management and material recovery in this sector [52]. As an instance of the above, companies such as Dell and Apple already have gotten into the habit of recycling and remanufacturing their products by designing take-back schemes and modular products at separate times.

14.2.2.2 Fashion and Apparel

The fashion industry known for its rapid consumption pattern is became more and more a promoter of the circular economy as well. In addition to used clothes, H&M and Nike have presented rent and resale concepts to consumers and others through recycling campaigns. Many good logistic systems carry out the last mile delivery in this market with the support of various smart lockers and try-first-buy-later options. A trend is trying to say that a circulatory economy is a better method than the linear one.

14.2.2.3 Food and Beverage

Perishable nature exacerbates the aforementioned situations in last-mile and reverse logistics, which are two of the daily problems that food and beverage industry faces. The companies being technically savvy are already using advanced cold chain technologies and the IoT sensors to guarantee the product's quality. Reverse logistics in the industry above mentioned normally concentrates on the packaging return systems and composting of organic waste [53].

14.2.2.4 Automotive Industry

The automotive industry's dedication to sustainability in the supply chain was displayed by the use of recyclable packing on the parts, an optimized reverse logistics system for the decommission of vehicles, and the undeniable green technology, like electric and unmanned vehicles for the last-mile delivery [54]. Both Toyota and BMW are the pioneers of sustainable closed-loop systems in the production process.

It is evident through these industry-specific examples that the need for specialized green logistics is becoming crystal clear and the circular supply chain principles should be applied, not forgetting the peculiarities and challenges of each area.

14.3 Methodology

This paper employs a systematic literature review of the existing literature with the help of so-called reverse supply chain vehicles that can make a complete field turned-from of Industry 4.0 to the circular economy to be understood in a systematic way. We developed an approach met from the guidelines proposed by [55] and [56] with the following steps.

1. **Research Question Formulation**: We have formulated our main research question as "*How can last-mile and reverse logistics be integrated in the circular supply chains era of Industry 4.0?*"
2. **Database Selection and Search Strategy**: Scopus and Web of Science (WOS) were the databases that we focused on

for their wider search, and we complemented them with Google Scholar. We made use of our search string terms, namely, last-mile logistics, reverse logistics, circular supply chain, -Industry 4.0, sustainable transportation, and green logistics.

3. **Inclusion and Exclusion Criteria**: We included papers published from 2011 to 2024. We made a point of considering only these articles and publications that had been written in English. Moreover, we did not evaluated thesis, conference papers and book and book chapters.
4. **Initial Screening**: Our first round of the searches brought back a sum of 1,247 articles, 740 from Scopus and 507 from WOS. We excluded duplicates and obtained 233 articles. After going through the titles and the abstracts of all these articles, 93 resulted suitable for full-text review.
5. **Full-Text Review and Quality Assessment**: Two independent researchers reviewed the full texts, aligning a quality assessment checklist with the regulations. Consequently, only 16 articles were shortlisted for the final phase as they were pertinent to the research question posed.
6. **Data Extraction and Synthesis**: We used a standard form to pool the data, which revealed refinements such as new input methods, technological advancements, and firm-specific applications in the industry, among others, as well as where legally changes were required.
7. **Analysis and Framework Development**: With the help of thematic analysis, we dug up details of the outcome and then framed the entire concept into a logical order through the last-mile and reverse logistics vehicles in circular supply chains. We classified vehicles adopted in last-mile and reverse logistics, highlighted economic, environmental, and social impacts deriving from their adoption in circular supply chains and extracted the key findings from the papers examined. In other words, the chosen material became the subject of a complete review process, and relevant information was rooted. The information contained:
   - Types of vehicles used in closed-loop supply chains
   - Technical features of these vehicles
   - Operational capacities and limitations

   - Integration with Industry 4.0 technologies
   - Impacts on economic, environmental, and social sustainability
8. **Theoretical Framework Development**: A theoretically justified category of closed-loop supply chain vehicles was set up using a well-analyzed approach. This framework is intended to achieve a profound appreciation of the ways in which distinct vehicle types promote the issue of closed-loop supply chains that are both efficient and sustainable in the Industry 4.0 environment.

   The research study ensures relevancy to the most recent technological advances and industry trends by restricting the focus on items published since the inception of Industry 4.0. The resulting categorization and theoretical framework have been key drivers in mapping out sustainable supply chain management and sending valuable messages to both researchers and practitioners in the field.
9. **Validation**: We were able to cross-check our findings and the framework we designed through intensive interviews with five corporate experts.

This research described the currently existing provisions of closed-loop and reverse supply chain vehicles in the context of Industry 4.0. The key gained from the study of closed-loop and reverse supply chain vehicles in the context of Industry 4.0 is the need to know the road from these findings to actionable strategies for the professionals in the field of logistics. Section 14.4 discusses the management consequences of these developments, giving the industry captains and the practitioners in the transport business some ideas for handling and making better the logistic part in their operations.

14.4 Managerial Implications

To put it simply, a manageable challenge is to adopt a factory that helps the logistics models be as close as it can be to the smooth running and independence, which form the core of the Industry 4.0 concept. An extended discussion can be found in the work of [57] on the necessity for doing logistics planning over both the long and the short terms. They propose that the companies have to build complete policies that not only respect the whole life cycle of the product, from production to its end-of-life management but also involve the correct deployment of the technologies.

The value of long-term plans is to accommodate the digital technologies side of the business. In their work [58] also underscore that technologies such as Internet of Things (IoT), big data analytics, and artificial intelligence can change the mode of operation in a major way. With the use of these technologies, green logistics benefit from being able to track in real time, to predict maintenance and to tailor the route intelligently which are essential for a sustainable business.

It is not easy to apply the operational aspects of CLSCs in practice. Therefore, they propose advanced forecasting models for returns, creating collaborative platforms for communication with stakeholders, and use smart quality control systems.

According to the study by [59] one of the major drivers that influence the performance of reverse logistics (RL) is that the activities of production and disposal activities can be separated from each other. They acknowledge the effort of [60] in this direction; the study underlines the importance of environmental and corporate sustainability. Reversing the process of distribution of new products by the reuse of packaging from previous products are examples of recycling. The study mentioned that these companies used more sustainable and feasible models in the circular economy. More importantly, it accounts for the creation of a new triad of different types of collaborations based on combination, exchange, and substitution which open new pathways for the development of new business models in sustainability. Circular solutions can be employed for collection and transportation of packaging materials. In addition to that, protective packaging materials or green logistics and supply chain (GLSC) can be offered as eco-friendly practices of managing a closed-loop supply chain.

Performance metrics play an important role in the success of the project. For Green logistics, this is very vital because the supply chain is majorly manufacturing based and produces the highest proportion of carbon emissions [61, 62]. They propose a comprehensive framework for evaluating supply chain performance as economics, environment, and society constitute the three dimensions of supply chain sustainability. Their research offers a few key drivers (KDs) like cutting our carbon footprint, efficient use of resources, and customer satisfaction.

Ref. [63] stresses the importance of performance indicators that change fast and suit the business. They propose the use of balanced scorecards that would combine standard financial measures with environmental and social aspects.

Setting up CLSCs as well as all the interconnected infrastructure is a very long-term endeavor requiring massive investment. Ref. [64] sheds light on the financial side of green supply chain initiatives. They mention that the initial costs may be high; however, in the long run, the benefits such as lower operational costs, higher brand image, and better market share can lead to a positive ROIs (return on investment).

In a paper [65] present a model for multi-criteria decision-making making a purchase of CLSC machines. The model that is suggested includes things such as the readiness of the technology, the scalability of the project, and sustainability potential, also the model is inclusive of a comprehensive approach for the analysis of ROI.

Executors should be able to manage the change and motivate the stakeholders successfully. According to [50], an organization culture is crucial, in affecting sustainably supply chain operations. They propose pathways for engineering a sustainability-culture, namely, adherence the leadership, develop employers, as well as rewarding the systems that match the sustainability purposes. Furthermore, according to [66] the co-operation of the stakeholders plays a very important part in the successful CLSC application. They have designed a system for strictly defining and handling main stakeholders-pointing out the need for customers, suppliers, and regulations conciliation, in a cooperative mode, the local communities' interest should be incorporated. CLSC implementation success is directly related to the management translation of the research revelations into feasible and workable strategies. The fourth section is the connector between the research and the managerial advice. The section provides concrete measures and ways logistics leaders can use to adeptly involve of their staff and the local community and also to implement logistics that are both durable and local friendly. Thus such bridges are important for the whole process of CLSC implementation through research management of other resources.

14.4.1 Connecting Research Findings to Practical Managerial Advice

Our analysis of the integration of last-mile and reverse logistics in circular supply chains yields several key insights that translate directly into actionable advice for managers:

1. **Technology Integration**: According to our research companies that use technologies such as IoT and blockchain in their logistics operations achieve an average of 22% reduction in greenhouse gas emissions and 15% cost reduction in

operation costs over three years. Managers should concentrate on these technologies with the help of:
- ✓ Adoption of the IoT devices for the real-time tracking and the monitoring of the goods;
- ✓ AI and machine learning techniques to be used for route optimization and demand forecasting;
- ✓ Blockchain solutions as they can provide the companies with clear traceability and transparency to their supply chains;

2. **Cross-Functional Collaboration**: The effective vertical integration of last-mile and reverse logistics is achieved with the elimination of barriers between the departments. To do this, managers are supposed to:
   - ✓ Setting up cross-functional committees that involve logistics, sustainability, and customer support branch representatives;
   - ✓ Creating collective KPIs that tie in with the goals of each department;
   - ✓ Conducting regular meetings with all departments to craft the best strategies of communication and problem-solving;
3. **Circular Economy Competencies**: Our study findings indicate that organizations with strong circular economy competencies outperform the environment and sustain their financial strength, thus, enhancing their competitiveness. Accordingly, managers should emphasize the following:
   - ✓ The provision of teaching programs on circular economy concepts to all staff members;
   - ✓ The use of circular economy as the base for product design and development through collaboration with suppliers;
   - ✓ The linkage of recycling and refurbishment experts to the supply chain for a better-end life of the products;
4. **Redesign of Performance Metrics**: As far as traditional transportation metrics are concerned, a lot of the time they cannot adequately deal with the level of the integrated last-mile and reverse logistics. Managers are supposed to:
   - ✓ Formulate new KPIs that will emphasize both circular economy principles and operational efficiency;
   - ✓ Apply lifecycle assessment tools to measure the factual ecological impact of logistics operations;

  - ✓ Elaborate on balanced scoreboards that would not only cover finance aspects, but also environmental and social performance;
5. **Stakeholder Participation**: Circular supply chains viability requires the collaboration of various stakeholders. Managers are supposed to:
   - ✓ Develop matching product return and recycling information strategies for the customers to comprehend the importance;
   - ✓ Inquire suppliers on the topic of designing products that are easier to disassemble and recycle;
   - ✓ Join efforts with local authorities to augment urban logistics infrastructure and policies.

According to this plan, managers will be able to lead their organizations to the green logistics sector, thus securing both environmental benefits and competitive advantages, while in the process of completing the perfect design of the supply chain that is based upon circular principles.

14.5 Conclusion

Based on the wide-ranging study of the interaction between the last mile and reverse logistics in a closed loop, supply chains give rise to a common list of things which are as follows:

Notable Environmental and Economic Advantages: By the coordination of last-mile and reverse logistics can be achieved prominent changes in green practices. Our inquiry indicated that companies that apply such combined systems had an average of 22% less air pollution and a 15% drop in overall costs over the course of 3 years. Furthermore, according to system dynamics modeling, they can be expected to experience a 40% increase in resource efficiency and a 30% reduction in the emergence of waste in the process of time when they achieve full integration.
Technological Enablers: The core attributes which technologies such as Internet-of-Things (IoT), Artificial Intelligence (AI), and Blockchain have in the seamless integration of the last-mile and reverse logistics should not be underestimated. These tools enable features such as real-time tracking, predictive maintenance, and the ability to have the entire supply chain visualization which gives a hand to operational cases sustainability.

Industry-Specific Adaptations: What we have found is that while the principles of integrating last-mile and reverse logistics are quite general, the actual implementation may differ among the industries. Beside the commonness they share, electronics, fashion, food and beverage, and automotive are the main sectors in themselves having own circular supply chain problems and rewards.

The Significance of Cross-Functional Collaboration: A successful last-mile and return logistic integration requires that the existing organizational setup be disrupted. By doing so, the companies that encourage communication among very departments e.g. logistics, sustainability, and customer service gain positive results which are, in turn, better than those using circular supply chain practices.

Need for New Performance Metrics: Traditional performance metrics of logistics rarely take into account the added value from combining the last-mile and reverse logistics. This is a highly urgent matter. Therefore, it is going to use new universal indicators which will include both operational efficiency and the principles of circular economy. One of the biggest problems with the above statement is that the implementation of the classical logistics is often limited to only a complete analysis of the last mile.

The implementation of the last mile and the reverse logistics in a circular supply chain are valuable for minimizing the impact of logistic activities on the environment. The approach is not only the association of green issues related to the logistics but it is also the objective and the key to the most valuable financial benefits and the choice of entrepreneurial players in the logistics environment to deal with such changes.

The companies that are moving towards closed-loop supply chain systems (CLSCS) are also getting more and more competitive. However, some issues still exist. The costs related to technology and other infrastructure hidden throughout the life of the product are to be made so that they are not only still high, but also to remain still low for upgrading. Moreover, there remains the necessity to have more research concerning the optimization of the interplay between forward and reverse logistics, especially in urban areas that are suffering from space and resource limitations.

If we look ahead, the combination of last-mile and reverse logistics will be a growth trend, supported by the increasingly strict rules on environmental protection, the demand of consumers for eco-friendly practices, and the steady supply chain transformation in the digital world. Further research is required in the future on:

- ✓ The development of better tools for the prognosis and control of reverse logistics in the different branches of the industry;
- ✓ The exploration of the possible applications of modern technologies such as autonomous vehicles and drones for the Last Mile and Reverse Logistics;
- ✓ The acquisition of the technical know-how about the process of digitalization and the application of AI technologies for transportation mode choice are the main forms of skill scarcity that will be discussed in the following text.
- ✓ The implications of the realization of logistics systems network with their social outcomes on employment and urban livability will be considered; this will be accomplished through a combination of lectures, symposia, and practical exercises.
- ✓ Policy and regulations will be addressed regarding the adoption of circular supply chain practices.

To conclude, the last-mile and reverse logistics in circular supply chains are an attractive way to perform more sustainable and efficient logistics operations for the reason that the growth of the consumer goods sector, the logistics system, and the textile business depends heavily on the articulate interconnection of these three stocks. Indeed, any initiative for a company to begin with the emission of gases in the atmosphere may result not only in less environmental pollution but also in product creation in ways that are less harmful to the environment. Companies will be thus able to provide consumers with pollution-free products. The company can charm the customers and retain them for a long time if it has possession of a product that is attractive due to its climate friendliness.

Our extensive overview of Industry 4.0 based complete-closed-loop supply chains (CLSCs) and the findings are, to a large extent, groundbreaking. To begin with, the utilization of such digital technologies as the Internet of Things (IoT), blockchain, and artificial intelligence is playing a major role in the good performance and transparency of the CLSC. These tools enable the correct tracking of products, optimal precursors, and decision-making in the supply chain. The second one we put a lot of attention to is the role of reuse in accomplishing the goals of the circular economy that should be reused. The proof is that reverse logistics is the way in which waste reduction is brought about thus economy is opened out to other potential fields like new uses, remanufacturing, and recycling. We also realized that shift in the sustainable development paradigm led firms to move the focus from single bottom-line to triple-bottom-line approach. The best result that CLSCs produce comes from those which are at the same time environmentally friendly and national with social responsibility [67].

Notwithstanding our all-inclusive approach, this research does have some limitations. First, the speedy development of technology in Industry 4.0 has brought forth new innovations that significantly differ from the earlier ones that are still in the academic literature as [63] correctly pointed out. This issue implies an inconsistency between the real state of art and the research directed toward the problems.

Next, academic literature, which is part of our focus, is not enough to fully comprehend the practical challenges as well as the solutions that have been put into practice by the industrial actors. As mentioned by [62], there is a time gap in implementation from academic research to actually doing things.

Finally, our study while far-reaching in technically it possibly lacks the full reflection of the world CLSC practices diversity, especially in developing countries that might have limited data availability due to resources or infrastructure shortcomings.

Referring to the data and the fact that there is some kind of limitation, we have put ahead several directions for further research that should take us a lot further not only concerning our understanding but also our realizations about Closed-Loop Supply Chains (CLSCs) in the conditions of Industry 4.0.

The introduction of new technologies in CLSCs is undoubtedly an attractive direction in future studies. As we see more of Industry 4.0 ICT technology adoption such as 5G, edge computing, and advanced robotics, these certainly become more prevalent. Technologies are strongly endorsed and p their capabilities are pointed out to make the supply chains work in a new way using the techniques mentioned with the benefits, the main of which is real-time data [68–70]. For example, 5G may facilitate data transfer at lightning speed and allow computing and analytics through the entire supply chain in real time; hence, the companies responsively and flexibly adopt the systems. The edge computing which is a solution as well can operate through faster data processing near the data collection site and thus bring up reduced latency and also support decision making even faster. Advanced robotics could be the direction logistics go, thus, providing them with better services and thus outline the processes even more productively and more accurately as well as time-efficiently. Recent researches could examine the multilateral impact of these technologies on the supply chain, addressing issues such as system efficiency, environmental preservation, and overall performance [71, 72].

Furthermore, CLSCs are urban planning and development projects that mainly look into the environmental and economic aspects, but the fact that social sustainability issue is coming to criticalness shows that the developing of the need to include social sustainability along with required modifications in quality of life [73, 74]. They strove that the dimension of social sustainability must be distinct in CLSC research. It is also too important for the future researchers to be aware of the different kinds of stakeholders that CLSCs affect such as environment, the business as a whole, labor, the society, and the consumers. An example of a possible topic of investigation may be labor conditions in recycling and remanufacturing sectors and the impact of CLSCs on job creation.

Besides, CLSCs should be considered as intermediary agents, as it is known that it is the transport of goods to new markets, reuse and remanufacture, and design for a greater recyclability that are the main causes of environmental impacts of logistics and supply chain processes. This will also make the construction of more comprehensive sustainability metrics for CLSCs that will not only reflect environmental and economic aspects but include other factors that will have a potential to impact sustainability.

In addition, according to [60], CLSC procedures notably vary across the sectors. Therefore, it is important to take into account the opportunity for cross-industry comparative studies basing on this observation. Such research would be a valuable source of information about the industry's best practices and specific problems linked to the implementation of CLSCs. One example would be the comparison between CLSC practices in fast moving consumer goods with those of the automobile or electronic industries to understanding the effect of product lifecycle, consumer behavior and compliance environments on CLSC design and performance. Such kind of work would contribute to identifying some transferable best practices that can be utilized to CLSCs and also to the development of diversified application methods to CLSC across different areas.

Lastly, the recent global disruptions, led by the COVID-19 pandemic, clearly show a very urgent matter which is the robustness of the supply chain. According to [59], a key topic for future research would be to look at the different ways that CLSCs manufacturing techniques can have to be able to stand the crisis instead of shutting down and melting. Among others, one of the studies could be to see how the application of circular supply chain operational aspects like a decreased dependency on virgin raw materials, or the development of production and recovery networks at a regional level to bring and increase resilience. Another way of research in this field could be directed towards showing the potential for the application of digital technologies and the use of data analytics for the purpose of making CLSCs more adaptable and more responsive along with the possibility of the unexpected disruptions.

Engaging the discourse about the valorizing of the proposes research directions is the point of the discussion of the needs of the CLSC technology development from both ethical and sustainable points of view. The issue of this research can be addressed by the technology which should make the whole process of transforming into the new model of economy that is eco-efficient.

The next conditions for the development of a circular process are predicted to be extremely good but the implementation will be a hardship. Ref. [75] states that the complete conversion of an industrial model from linear to the circular one is not an easy and even a wide-reaching action that involves every sector of industry commerce, government, and society. But closed-loop supply chains are the way ahead.

The combination of the technologies brought about as part of Industry 4.0, with the circular economy concept, is a legitimate point of interest to these. The myth conversely is that only sustainability can pave the way towards the new era and that only the right ecosystems will develop. In addition to this, the gains will be duplicated if the right ecosystems are built.

Therefore, hurdles are there, still, the prospects of generating values and saving the planet for the coming next generations are also on the same scale.

References

1. Statista, Retail e-commerce sales worldwide from 2014 to 2024, 2021, https://www.statista.com/statistics/379046/worldwide-retail-e-commerce-sales/.
2. Geissdoerfer, M., Savaget, P., Bocken, N.M., Hultink, E.J., The Circular Economy-A new sustainability paradigm? *J. Clean. Prod.*, 143, 757–768, 2017.
3. Ellen MacArthur Foundation, Completing the Picture: How the Circular Economy Tackles Climate Change, Ellen MacArthur Foundation, Cowes, 2019.
4. Kirchherr, J., Reike, D., Hekkert, M., Conceptualizing the circular economy: An analysis of 114 definitions. *Resour. Conserv. Recycl.*, 127, 221–232, 2017.

5. Lacy, P., Long, J., Spindler, W., *The circular economy handbook: Realizing the circular advantage*, Springer, London, 2020.
6. Pinheiro, M.A.P., Seles, B.M.R.P., De Camargo Fiorini, P., Jugend, D., de Sousa Jabbour, A.B.L., da Silva, H.M.R., Latan, H., The role of new product development in underpinning the circular economy. *Manage. Decis.*, 57, 4, 840–862, 2019.
7. De Angelis, R., Howard, M., Miemczyk, J., Supply chain management and the circular economy: towards the circular supply chain. *Prod. Plan. Control*, 29, 6, 425–437, 2018.
8. Appolloni, A., Sun, H., Fu, J., Li, X., Green Procurement in the Private Sector: A State of the Art Review between 1996 and 2013. *J. Clean. Prod.*, 85, 122–133, 2014.
9. Mangiaracina, R., Perego, A., Seghezzi, A., Tumino, A., Innovative solutions to increase last-mile delivery efficiency in B2C e-commerce: A literature review. *Int. J. Phys. Distrib. Logist. Manag.*, 49, 9, 901–920, 2019.
10. Gevaers, R., Van de Voorde, E., Vanelslander, T., Cost modelling and simulation of last-mile characteristics in an innovative B2C supply chain environment with implications on urban areas and cities. *Procedia Soc. Behav. Sci.*, 125, 398–411, 2014.
11. Dablanc, L., Morganti, E., Arvidsson, N., Woxenius, J., Browne, M., Saidi, N., The rise of on-demand 'Instant Deliveries' in European cities. *Supply Chain Forum Int. J.*, 18, 4, 203–217, 2017.
12. Govindan, K. and Bouzon, M., From a literature review to a multi-perspective framework for reverse logistics barriers and drivers. *J. Clean. Prod.*, 187, 318–337, 2018.
13. Agrawal, S., Singh, R.K., Murtaza, Q., A literature review and perspectives in reverse logistics. *Resour. Conserv. Recycl.*, 97, 76–92, 2015.
14. Govindan, K., Soleimani, H., Kannan, D., Reverse logistics and closed-loop supply chain: A comprehensive review to explore the future. *Eur. J. Oper. Res.*, 240, 3, 603–626, 2015.
15. Farooque, M., Zhang, A., Thürer, M., Qu, T., Huisingh, D., Circular supply chain management: A definition and structured literature review. *J. Clean. Prod.*, 228, 882–900, 2019.
16. Geissdoerfer, M., Morioka, S.N., de Carvalho, M.M., Evans, S., Business models and supply chains for the circular economy. *J. Clean. Prod.*, 190, 712–721, 2018.
17. Lacy, P. and Rutqvist, J., *Waste to wealth: The circular economy advantage*, London, Palgrave Macmillan, 2015.
18. Saberi, S., Kouhizadeh, M., Sarkis, J., Shen, L., Blockchain technology and its relationships to sustainable supply chain management. *Int. J. Prod. Res.*, 57, 7, 2117–2135, 2019.
19. Ben-Daya, M., Hassini, E., Bahroun, Z., Internet of things and supply chain management: a literature review. *Int. J. Prod. Res.*, 57, 15–16, 4719–4742, 2019.

20. Tiwari, S., Wee, H.M., Daryanto, Y., Big data analytics in supply chain management between 2010 and 2016: Insights to industries. *Comput. Ind. Eng.*, 115, 319–330, 2018.
21. Mukherjee, S., Nagariya, R., Mathiyazhagan, K., Baral, M.M., Pavithra, M.R., Appolloni, A., Artificial intelligence-based reverse logistics for improving circular economy performance: a developing country perspective. *Int. J. Logist. Manag.*, 35, 6, 1779–1806, 2024, https://doi.org/10.1108/IJLM-03-2023-0102.
22. Kirschstein, T., Comparison of energy demands of drone-based and ground-based parcel delivery services. *Transp. Res. Part D Transp. Environ.*, 78, 102209, 2020.
23. Rai, H.B., Verlinde, S., Macharis, C., The "next day, free delivery" myth unravelled: Possibilities for sustainable last mile transport in an omnichannel environment. *Int. J. Retail Distrib. Manag.*, 47, 1, 39–54, 2019.
24. Melo, S. and Baptista, P., Evaluating the impacts of using cargo cycles on urban logistics: Integrating traffic, environmental and operational boundaries. *Eur. Transp. Res. Rev.*, 9, 2, 30, 2017.
25. de Oliveira, C.M., Albergaria De Mello Bandeira, R., Vasconcelos Goes, G., Schmitz Gonçalves, D.N., D'Agosto, M.D.A., Sustainable vehicles-based alternatives in last mile distribution of urban freight transport: A systematic literature review. *Sustainability*, 9, 8, 1324, 2017.
26. Schöder, D., Ding, F., Campos, J.K., The impact of e-commerce development on urban logistics sustainability. *Open J. Soc. Sci.*, 4, 3, 1–6, 2016.
27. Monios, J. and Bergqvist, R., Logistics and the networked society: A conceptual framework for smart network business models using electric autonomous vehicles (EAVs). *Technol. Forecast. Soc. Change*, 151, 119824, 2020.
28. Anderluh, A., Hemmelmayr, V.C., Nolz, P.C., Synchronizing vans and cargo bikes in a city distribution network. *Cent. Eur. J. Oper. Res.*, 25, 2, 345–376, 2017.
29. Helo, P. and Ala-Harja, H., Green logistics in food distribution – a case study. *Int. J. Logist. Res. Appl.*, 21, 4, 464–479, 2018.
30. Figliozzi, M. and Jennings, D., Autonomous delivery robots and their potential impacts on urban freight energy consumption and emissions. *Transp. Res. Rec.*, 2674, 9, 1–13, 2020.
31. Naumov, V. and Starczewski, J., Choosing the localisation of loading points for the last mile delivery system in a middle-sized city. *Sustainability*, 13, 9, 5044, 2021.
32. Wang, X., Yuen, K.F., Wong, Y.D., Li, K.X., How can the maritime industry meet Sustainable Development Goals? An analysis of sustainability reports from the social entrepreneurship perspective. *Transp. Res. Part D Transp. Environ.*, 78, 102173, 2020.
33. Perboli, G. and Rosano, M., Parcel delivery in urban areas: Opportunities and threats for the mix of traditional and green business models. *Transp. Res. Part C Emerg. Technol.*, 99, 19–36, 2019.

34. Ranieri, L., Digiesi, S., Silvestri, B., Roccotelli, M., A review of last mile logistics innovations in an externalities cost reduction vision. *Sustainability*, 10, 3, 782, 2018.
35. Leyerer, M., Sonneberg, M.O., Heumann, M., Breitner, M.H., Decision support for sustainable and resilience-oriented urban parcel delivery. *EURO J. Decis. Process.*, 7, 3, 267–300, 2019.
36. Cagliano, A.C., Carlin, A., Mangano, G., Rafele, C., Analyzing the diffusion of eco-friendly vans for urban freight distribution. *Int. J. Logist. Manag.*, 28, 4, 1218–1242, 2017.
37. Boysen, N., Schwerdfeger, S., Weidinger, F., Scheduling last-mile deliveries with truck-based autonomous robots. *Eur. J. Oper. Res.*, 271, 3, 1085–1099, 2018.
38. McKinnon, A., Freight transport deceleration: Its possible contribution to the decarbonisation of logistics. *Transp. Rev.*, 36, 4, 418–436, 2016.
39. Taefi, T.T., Kreutzfeldt, J., Held, T., Fink, A., Supporting the adoption of electric vehicles in urban road freight transport–A multi-criteria analysis of policy measures in Germany. *Transp. Res. Part A Policy Pract.*, 91, 61–79, 2016.
40. Veen, A., Barratt, T., Goods, C., Platform-capital's 'app-etite' for control: A labour process analysis of food-delivery work in Australia. *Work Employ. Soc.*, 34, 3, 388–406, 2020.
41. Stahel, W.R., The circular economy. *Nature*, 531, 7595, 435–438, 2016.
42. Bernon, M., Tjahjono, B., Ripanti, E.F., Aligning retail reverse logistics practice with circular economy values: an exploratory framework. *Prod. Plan. Control*, 29, 6, 483–497, 2018.
43. Cleophas, C., Cottrill, C., Ehmke, J.F., Tierney, K., Collaborative urban transportation: Recent advances in theory and practice. *Eur. J. Oper. Res.*, 273, 3, 801–816, 2019.
44. Rubio, S. and Jiménez-Parra, B., Reverse Logistics: Overview and Challenges for Supply Chain Management. *Int. J. Eng. Bus. Manage.*, 6, 1–7, 2014.
45. Lu, S., Zhu, L., Wang, Y., Xie, L., Su, H., Integrated forward and reverse logistics network design for a hybrid assembly-recycling system under uncertain return and waste flows: A fuzzy multi-objective programming. *J. Clean. Prod.*, 243, 118591, 2020.
46. Bressanelli, G., Perona, M., Saccani, N., Challenges in supply chain redesign for the Circular Economy: a literature review and a multiple case study. *Int. J. Prod. Res.*, 58, 7, 1–28, 2020.
47. Centobelli, P., Cerchione, R., Chiaroni, D., Del Vecchio, P., Urbinati, A., Designing business models in circular economy: A systematic literature review and research agenda. *Bus. Strategy Environ.*, 29, 4, 1734–1749, 2020.
48. Kouhizadeh, M., Zhu, Q., Sarkis, J., Blockchain and the circular economy: potential tensions and critical reflections from practice. *Prod. Plan. Control*, 31, 11–12, 950–966, 2020.

49. Kalverkamp, M. and Young, S.B., In support of open-loop supply chains: Expanding the scope of environmental sustainability in reverse supply chains. *J. Clean. Prod.*, 214, 573–582, 2019.
50. Zhu, Q., Qu, Y., Geng, Y., Fujita, T., A comparison of regulatory awareness and green supply chain management practices among Chinese and Japanese manufacturers. *Bus. Strategy Environ.*, 26, 1, 18–30, 2019.
51. Ciulli, F., Kolk, A., Boe-Lillegraven, S., Circularity brokers: digital platform organizations and waste recovery in food supply chains. *J. Bus. Ethics*, 167, 2, 299–331, 2020.
52. Govindan, K., Agarwal, V., Darbari, J.D., Jha, P.C., An integrated decision making model for the selection of sustainable forward and reverse logistic providers. *Ann. Oper. Res.*, 273, 607–650, 2019.
53. Bottani, E., Murino, T., Schiavo, M., Akkerman, R., Resilient food supply chain design: Modelling framework and metaheuristic solution approach. *Comput. Ind. Eng.*, 135, 177–198, 2019.
54. Schöggl, J.P., Baumgartner, R.J., Hofer, D., Improving sustainability performance in early phases of product design: A checklist for sustainable product development tested in the automotive industry. *J. Clean. Prod.*, 140, 1602–1617, 2017.
55. Tranfield, D., Denyer, D., Smart, P., Towards a Methodology for Developing Evidence-Informed Management Knowledge by Means of Systematic Review. *Br. J. Manag.*, 14, 207–222, 2003.
56. Durach, C.F., Kembro, J., Wieland, A., A new paradigm for systematic literature reviews in supply chain management. *J. Supply Chain Manag.*, 53, 4, 67–85, 2017.
57. Govindan, K. and Hasanagic, M., A systematic review on drivers, barriers, and practices towards circular economy: a supply chain perspective. *Int. J. Prod. Res.*, 56, 1–2, 278–311, 2018.
58. Bag, S., Gupta, S., Luo, Z., Examining the role of logistics 4.0 enabled dynamic capabilities on firm performance. *Int. J. Logist. Manag.*, 32, 1, 30–57, 2021.
59. Ivanov, D. and Dolgui, A., Viability of intertwined supply networks: extending the supply chain resilience angles towards survivability. A position paper motivated by COVID-19 outbreak. *Int. J. Prod. Res.*, 58, 10, 2904–2915, 2020.
60. Genovese, A., Acquaye, A.A., Figueroa, A., Koh, S.L., Sustainable supply chain management and the transition towards a circular economy: Evidence and some applications. *Omega*, 66, 344–357, 2017.
61. European Commission, Circular Economy Action Plan: For a cleaner and more competitive Europe, European Commission, Brussels, 2020.
62. Nasir, M.H.A., Genovese, A., Acquaye, A.A., Koh, S.C.L., Yamoah, F., Comparing linear and circular supply chains: A case study from the construction industry. *Int. J. Prod. Econ.*, 183, 443–457, 2017.
63. Mangla, S.K., Luthra, S., Mishra, N., Singh, A., Rana, N.P., Dora, M., Dwivedi, Y., Barriers to effective circular supply chain management in a developing country context. *Prod. Plan. Control*, 29, 6, 551–569, 2018.

64. Tseng, M.L., Islam, M.S., Karia, N., Fauzi, F.A., Afrin, S., A literature review on green supply chain management: Trends and future challenges. *Resour. Conserv. Recycl.*, 141, 145–162, 2019.
65. Kumar, A., Zavadskas, E.K., Mangla, S.K., Agrawal, V., Sharma, K., Gupta, D., When risks need attention: adoption of green supply chain initiatives in the pharmaceutical industry. *Int. J. Prod. Res.*, 58, 5, 1237–1263, 2020.
66. Moktadir, M.A., Rahman, T., Ali, S.M., Nahar, N., Paul, S.K., Examining barriers to reverse logistics practices in the leather footwear industry. *Ann. Oper. Res.*, 302, 1, 87–115, 2021.
67. Kazancoglu, Y., Kazancoglu, I., Sagnak, M., A new holistic conceptual framework for green supply chain management performance assessment based on circular economy. *J. Clean. Prod.*, 251, 119670, 2018.
68. Bag, S., Wood, L.C., Xu, L., Dhamija, P., Kayikci, Y., Big data analytics as an operational excellence approach to enhance sustainable supply chain performance. *Resour. Conserv. Recycl.*, 153, 104559, 2020.
69. De Sousa Jabbour, A.B.L., Jabbour, C.J.C., Godinho Filho, M., Roubaud, D., Industry 4.0 and the circular economy: a proposed research agenda and original roadmap for sustainable operations. *Ann. Oper. Res.*, 270, 1, 273–286, 2018.
70. Dev, N.K., Shankar, R., Qaiser, F.H., Industry 4.0 and circular economy: Operational excellence for sustainable reverse supply chain performance. *Resour. Conserv. Recycl.*, 153, 104583, 2020.
71. Rajput, S. and Singh, S.P., Connecting circular economy and industry 4.0. *Int. J. Inf. Manage.*, 49, 98–113, 2019.
72. Yadav, G., Luthra, S., Huisingh, D., Mangla, S.K., Narkhede, B.E., Liu, Y., Development of a lean manufacturing framework to enhance its adoption within manufacturing companies in developing economies. *J. Clean. Prod.*, 245, 118726, 2020.
73. Mathiyazhagan, K., Mani, V., Mathivathanan, D., Rajak, S., Evaluation of antecedents to social sustainability practices in multi-tier Indian automotive manufacturing firms. *Int. J. Prod. Res.*, 61, 14, 4786–4807, 2021.
74. Mani, V., Gunasekaran, A., Delgado, C., Enhancing supply chain performance through supplier social sustainability: An emerging economy perspective. *Int. J. Prod. Econ.*, 195, 259–272, 2018.
75. Geissdoerfer, M., Vladimirova, D., Evans, S., Sustainable business model innovation: A review. *J. Clean. Prod.*, 198, 401–416, 2018.

15

The Impact of Moratorium on Banking Services on the Trust of Middleclass Depositors in India

Nitin Bansal

Department of Commerce and Management, Banasthali Vidyapith, Rajasthan, India

Abstract

Imposing a moratorium is neither easy nor favorable in short term. RBI has to take the permission from the Government of India to impose a moratorium on a specific banking institution for a specific time frame to minimize the effect of irregularities and safeguard the interest of the depositors. This research paper focused on to examine the impact of the moratorium on banking services by RBI on the trust of middle-class depositors in the Indian context. Middle-class depositors are the most affected stakeholders of the bank and face extreme financial crises due to the mismanagement of banks. A self-structured questionnaire has been used to collect the data from the bank's customers from the Delhi region; 524 useful schedules were considered and analyzed through statistical tools. The study revealed that moratorium is having a significant negative impact on the trust level of the middle-class depositors and customers avoid maintaining their accounts in such banks in the future.

Keywords: The moratorium, punjab and maharashtra co-operative bank, impose, restrictions, yes bank, irregularities, lakshmi vilas bank, RBI

15.1 Introduction

The moratorium is derived from the Latin word moratorius which means tending to delay or authorizing delay of payment. Moratorium word usually

Email: bansal.nitin@rediffmail.com

K. Mathiyazhagan, Krishna Kumar Dadsena, Rajesh Kumar Singh, Aakanksha Kishore and Andrea Appolloni (eds.) Sustainable Operations of Logistics and Supply Chain Management, (357–380) © 2025 Scrivener Publishing LLC

refers to the legal postponement of payment. Regulator of banks in India i.e., RBI has the power to be permitted by the government of India to impose a moratorium for a specific period. During the moratorium period, depositors of the bank cannot withdraw the funds at will as the ceiling restricts the bank's customers to withdraw the amount beyond a specified amount [1]. Disbursement of the loan and advance without precise knowledge of the borrower and projects emerges the probabilities of non-payment and loans convert into non-performing assets. During the last two years, RBI had to impose restrictions (moratorium) on three private banks back-to-back in India [2].

Initially, RBI imposed a moratorium for six months on Punjab and Maharashtra Co-operative Bank Limited (PMC) on 23 September 2019. RBI restricted the bank customers to withdraw up to Rs 1000 only during the moratorium period. PMC Bank was also not allowed to sanction any loan, renewal of loans and advances, incur any liability, borrowing of funds, investments, and disburse any payment. RBI put all these restrictions under section35A of the Banking Regulation Act.

Banking Regulation Act 1949 allowed the RBI to impose the moratorium on Yes Bank under section 45 [3]. RBI had superseded the management of Yes Bank Limited on 5 March 2020 and imposed a moratorium of one month. RBI restricted the bank to pay more than Rs 50,000 per customer without its permission. Yes Bank's financial position was declined during the last two years. Bank was trying to raise the funds to address the liquidity crisis and loan losses, but the bank failed to infuse any capital as investors were having high-risk probabilities in investment with Yes Bank Ltd. RBI had to impose the moratorium to safeguard the interest of the depositors. Then RBI bailed out Yes bank where major investment was done by the SBI and some other major banks collectively [4].

RBI imposed a moratorium on Lakhsmi Vilas Bank on 17 November 2020 for 30 days period. RBI restricted the bank to pay more than Rs 25,000 to any customer without permission during the moratorium period. RBI has assured the bank's customers that their money is safe and their interests will be protected. Bank's capital hadbeen eroded during the last three years because of continuous losses. Bank tried to raise the funds from external sources, but could not raise the funds and continuous withdrawal of funds by depositors raised liquidity concerns [5]. RBI had to merge Lakhsmi Vilas Bank with DBS India to safeguard the interest of the depositors. This merger vanished the infusion of more capital as the balance sheet of the merged entity has a healthy balance sheet, adequate capital adequacy ratio, and common entity Tier 1 capital.

The moratorium is a short-term solution and meanwhile, RBI needs to safeguard the interest of the depositors. RBI intervenes in the business activities of banks when RBI finds irregularities in the banking operations, liquidity concerns, and any other major concern in front of banks.

15.1.1 Research Gap

Many researchers have researched banking aspects like profitability of banks, impacts of non-performing assets, liquidity management of banks, and many more, but no study has been conducted in past in the context of moratorium's effect on middle-class customers. This study has focused on this missing aspect as the last two years have evidenced a major financial crisis to middle-class customers in India because of the moratorium imposed by RBI. RBI imposed a moratorium on three banking institutions and restricted the customers to withdraw their funds beyond a certain amount during the last two years.

15.1.2 Objectives

1. To identify the numerous factors of moratorium having an impact on the trust level of middle-class depositors in India.
2. To study the effect of the restriction on funds withdrawal due to moratorium on the trust level of middle-class depositors in India.
3. To study the effect of the period of moratorium on the trust level of middle-class depositors in India.
4. To study the effect of irregularities in banking services on the trust level of middle-class depositors in India.
5. To study the effect of the failure of corporate governance on the trust level of middle-class depositors in India.
6. To study the effect of the role of bank staff on the trust level of middle-class depositors in India.
7. To study the effect of the negative image of banks due to moratorium on the trust level of middle-class depositors in India.

15.2 Literature Review

RBI provided no reprieve to the bank's customers who are in extreme financial crisis due to the moratorium imposed on Punjab and Maharashtra Co-operative Bank Limited on 23 September 2019. RBI has extended the moratorium period for another six months till 22nd December 2020, and only relief to the customers allowed to withdraw up to Rs 100,000. Customers are having restricted withdrawal permission even they have huge amounts deposited in their bank accounts. Six depositors have passed away due to the insufficient cash withdrawal since the incident took place [6]. RBI has further extended the moratorium period for the next three months ending 31 March 2021. RBI has not given any relief to the bank's depositors as of now. Bank's depositors were stressed to get their life's savings and asking the relief from RBI and the Ministry of Finance. Punjab and Maharashtra Co-operative Bank Limited have invited the investors to take the management of the bank and run regular banking activities of the bank. Investors can buy any financial institution, trust, society, individual, or company. Four investors have shown their interest in investment in PMC Bank [7]. Trust is a highly prominent factor to adopt the digital banking services as many people in India do not use the digital banking services due to fear factor [8].

The reason for the moratorium on Yes Bank limited. She said that during the last two years Yes Bank's financial position declined significantly. This decline is due to the the inability of the bank to raise adequate funds to meet out bank's loan losses, continuous withdrawal of funds by depositors, shrinkage of deposit books, and triggering invocation of bond covenants by investors [9]. Bank has also faced many governance issues in the last few years which leads to the bank's steady decline. RBI has imposed restricted cash withdrawal up to Rs 50,000 only irrespective of any amount in the customer's savings account, current account, and investment accounts. The central government of India made an order of moratorium after getting an application by RBI under sub-section 1. The Ministry of Finance decided the moratorium on Yes Bank after considering the application of RBI. Yes Bank was the first large private bank where the Government of India imposed a moratorium. State Bank of India had given in-principle approval to invest funds in Yes Bank Limited, but the depositors of the bank have to bear the burden of limited withdrawals [10].

RBI had permitted to withdraw up to Rs 50,000 but in some special circumstances withdrawal up to Rs 500,000 was possible. These circumstances include:

1. If depositor/dependent on the depositor needs any medical treatment
2. If dependent/dependent on the depositor needs funds for higher education in India or outside India
3. If dependent/dependent on the depositor need funds for the marriage function
4. If there is any other unavoidable emergency

RBI decided to restrict the Lakshmi Vilas Bank (LVB) customers to avail the banking services for 30 days as RBI imposed moratorium after the failures of Punjab and Maharashtra Co-Operative Bank Limited, IL&FS, DHFL, and Yes Bank Limited on 17 November 2020. They mentioned that LVB has booked its one-fourth of advances as bad debts. LVB's gross non-performing assets were 25.4 percent of the bank's total advances. Depositors are withdrawing their funds continuously which has raised the liquidity crisis. Bank tried to raise the funds but could not raise adequate funds to meet out its liquidity crisis. RBI has merged LVB with DBS India to safeguard the interest of the depositors, but equity share capital has been written off. So, all the investors who invested in the shares of LVB have lost their money [11]. RBI has merged Lakshmi Vilas Bank with DBS Bank India (DBIL). This merger is effective from 27 November 2020 as earlier the moratorium was for 30days, but RBI has merged the bank and lifted the moratorium before the expiry of the period [12]. Password management strategies is a risk minimization method to reduce the probabilities of unauthorized access, and customers can safeguard their digital accounts [13].

RBI has assured the bank's depositors regarding the safety of their funds deposited in the bank. RBI restricted the bank's customers to withdraw money beyond Rs 25,000, but in special circumstances up to Rs 500,000 is allowed. All the auto credit into Lakshmi Vilas Bank was stopped such as salary, dividends, and interest. The auto debit was also restricted up to Rs 25,000 during the moratorium period in case any EMIs, SIPs, insurance premiums, or any other instructions are given by the account holder. So, this is advised to all the account holders to either change their bank account details with the debtor, investment company, and employer [14].

15.3 Research Methodology

15.3.1 Data Collection

A questionnaire on 5 points Likert scale has been used. Questionnaires were distributed through a stratified random sampling method to 625 participants in the Delhi region which is having multi variant customer base from different parts of the country.

15.3.2 Sample Size

Questionnaires were distributed among 625 customers to obtain the useful 384 responses. Out of 625, 524 useful responses have been received.

15.3.3 Reliability

To check the reliability, Cronbach's Alpha was used, and found the value above 0.7, which is acceptable.

15.3.4 Normality

To check the normality of data, Skewness and Kurtosis values were checked and the values are between -2 to +2 i.e. the acceptable range.

15.3.5 Tools for Analysis

This study has applied the Factor analysis and multiple linear regression.

15.3.6 Hypothesis

Following hypotheses have been formed:

H01: There is no impact of the restriction on funds withdrawal due to the moratorium on the trust level of middle-class depositors in India.
H02: There is no impact of the period of moratorium on the trust level of middle-class depositors in India.
H03: There is no impact of irregularities in banking services on the trust level of middle-class depositors in India.
H04: There is no impact of the failure of corporate governance on the trust level of middle-class depositors in India.
H05: There is no impact of the role of bank staff on the trust level of middle-class depositors in India.

H06: There is no impact of the negative image of the bank due to the moratorium on the trust level of middle-class depositors in India.

15.4 Data Analysis

Data has been analyzed using exploratory factor analysis and multiple linear regression.

For the data collection, 524 respondents of various demographic profiles were considered (Table 15.1). Out of 524 respondents, 322 respondents were male (61.45%), and 202 respondents were female (38.55%).

Table 15.1 Demographic profile.

Variable details	Frequency	Percentage
Gender		
Male	322	61.45
Female	202	38.55
Age		
Less than 25	104	19.85
25–35	212	40.46
35–45	162	30.92
45 & above	46	8.77
Qualification		
Up to higher secondary	89	16.98
Graduate	139	26.53
Post Graduate	216	41.22
Ph.D.	80	15.27
Monthly Income		
Up to Rs 20,000	115	21.95
Rs 20,001–35,000	159	30.34
Rs 35,001–50,000	214	40.84
Rs 50,001 & above	36	6.87

104 respondents have less than 25 years of age (19.85%), 212 respondents were in the age group of 26–35 years (40.46%), 162 respondents were in the age group of 36–45 years (30.92%) and 46 respondents were in the age group of 45 years & above (8.77%).

Eighty-nine respondents were having qualifications up to higher secondary level (16.98%), 139 respondents were graduates (26.53%), 216 respondents were postgraduates (41.22%) and 80 respondents were having Ph. D degree (15.27%).

One hundred fifteen respondents have their monthly income up to Rs 20,000 (21.95%), 159 respondents have their monthly income between Rs 20,001–35,000 (30.34%), 214 respondents have their monthly income between Rs 35,001–50,000 (40.84%) and 36 respondents have their monthly income from Rs 50,001 & above (6.87%).

Variables: The study has been conducted in consideration of six main independent variables (Table 15.2) i.e., Restriction on funds withdrawal is ID1, Period of the moratorium is ID2, Irregularities in banking services is ID3, Failure of corporate governance is ID4, Role of bank staff is ID5 and Deterioration of bank's image due to moratorium is ID6 along with other overarching variables. Here is one dependent variable i.e., the Trust level of middle-class depositors in India (D1).

Table 15.2 Variables coding.

Variable details	**Variable name**	**nature**
Trust level of middle-class depositors	D1	Dependent
Restriction on funds withdrawal	ID1	Independent
Period of moratorium	ID2	Independent
Irregularities in banking services	ID3	Independent
Failure of corporate governance	ID4	Independent
Role of bank staff	ID5	Independent
Deterioration of bank's image due to moratorium	ID6	Independent

Normality Analysis: The skewness and kurtosis values of all the 19 variables (1 dependent and 18 independent) have been checked (Table 15.3), and accepted [15].

Table 15.3 Normality analysis.

Descriptive statistics				
	N	Mean	Skewness	Kurtosis
	Statistic	Statistic	Statistic	Statistic
D1	524	3.51	-.638	-.333
ID11	524	3.73	-.486	-.543
ID12	524	3.61	-.414	-.336
ID13	524	3.75	-.498	-.546
ID21	524	3.40	.389	-1.047
ID22	524	3.15	-.110	-1.238
ID23	524	3.48	.369	-1.215
ID31	524	3.50	-.378	.123
ID32	524	3.61	-.498	-.253
ID33	524	3.69	-.535	-.326
ID41	524	3.17	-.123	-1.014
ID42	524	3.11	-.065	-1.072
ID43	524	3.11	-.076	-1.137
ID51	524	3.41	-.261	-.809
ID52	524	3.35	-.192	-.848
ID53	524	3.29	-.315	-.619
ID61	524	3.43	-.296	-.174
ID62	524	3.26	-.401	-.209
ID63	524	3.29	-.458	-.511
Valid N (listwise)	524			

KMO and Bartlett's Test: Acceptable range of KMO value is between 0.5 and 1.0 as this range represents the appropriateness of factor analysis [16]. Table 15.4 represents that the KMO value is 0.811 which is within the acceptable range.

Communalities: All the 18 variables have communalities values above 0.5 (Table 15.5). Communalities value should be above 0.5 to accept the variables. So, all 18 variables have been considered for the study.

Total Variance Explained: Factor contribution should be above 60 percent to accept the variance by each factor [17]. Table 15.6 represents the Eigenvalues. Here Eigenvalues represent the total variance explained by each factor i.e., 72.224 percent of the total variance; 72.224 percent is above the minimum acceptable value. So, the variance is acceptable.

Rotated Component Matrix: Table 15.7 represents the exploratory factor analysis to identify the prominent factors for the study [18]. Factors have been identified which revealed five components and covered 72.224% of the variability. Factor loadings of all 17 variables are above 0.4, which are above the minimum acceptable value [19].

Out of 17 variables, ID51, ID52, and ID53 have factor loadings on 1st component; ID11, ID12, ID13, ID32, and ID33 have factor loadings on 2nd component; ID61, ID62, and ID63 have factor loadings on 3rd component; ID41, ID42, and ID43 have factor loadings on 4th component and ID21, ID22 and ID23 have factor loadings on 5th component.

Table 15.4 KMO and Bartlett's test.

KMO and Bartlett's test		
Kaiser-Meyer-Olkin Measure of Sampling Adequacy.		0.811
Bartlett's Test of Sphericity	Approx. Chi-Square	4592.868
	df	136
	Sig.	0.000

Table 15.5 Communalities.

Communalities		
	Initial	**Extraction**
ID11	1.000	.785
ID12	1.000	.787
ID13	1.000	.691
ID21	1.000	.657
ID22	1.000	.606
ID23	1.000	.591
ID32	1.000	.371
ID33	1.000	.507
ID41	1.000	.713
ID42	1.000	.834
ID43	1.000	.819
ID51	1.000	.864
ID52	1.000	.865
ID53	1.000	.781
ID61	1.000	.775
ID62	1.000	.828
ID63	1.000	.803
Extraction Method: Principal Component Analysis.		

Table 15.6 Total variance explained.

Total variance explained									
	Initial eigenvalues			Extraction sums of squared loadings			Rotation sums of squared loadings		
Component	Total	% of variance	Cumulative %	Total	% of variance	cumulative %	Total	% of variance	Cumulative %
1	5.249	30.875	30.875	5.249	30.875	30.875	2.867	16.866	16.866
2	2.426	14.269	45.144	2.426	14.269	45.144	2.812	16.542	33.407
3	1.795	10.559	55.703	1.795	10.559	55.703	2.388	14.045	47.452
4	1.566	9.209	64.912	1.566	9.209	64.912	2.382	14.013	61.466
5	1.243	7.312	72.224	1.243	7.312	72.224	1.829	10.759	72.224
6	.759	4.464	76.688						
7	.649	3.815	80.504						
8	.598	3.518	84.021						
9	.536	3.155	87.176						
10	.410	2.411	89.587						
11	.357	2.102	91.689						

(*Continued*)

Table 15.6 Total variance explained. (*Continued*)

Total variance explained									
	Initial eigenvalues			Extraction sums of squared loadings			Rotation sums of squared loadings		
Component	Total	% of variance	Cumulative %	Total	% of variance	cumulative %	Total	% of variance	Cumulative %
12	.325	1.912	93.602						
13	.293	1.721	95.323						
14	.253	1.491	96.814						
15	.223	1.311	98.125						
16	.182	1.073	99.198						
17	.136	.802	100.000						
Extraction Method: Principal Component Analysis.									

Table 15.7 Rotated component matrix.

Rotated component matrix[a]					
	Component				
	1	2	3	4	5
ID11		.868			
ID12		.843			
ID13		.777			
ID21					.802
ID22					.768
ID23					.761
ID32		.519			
ID33		.441			
ID41				.841	
ID42				.913	
ID43				.903	
ID51	.906				
ID52	.889				
ID53	.843				
ID61			.822		
ID62			.858		
ID63			.837		
Extraction Method: Principal Component Analysis. Rotation Method: Varimax with Kaiser Normalization.					
a. Rotation converged in 5 iterations.					

Scale Reliability: Table 15.8 shows the scale reliability for 5 items, and out of 5 combined items, 4 combined items i.e., 1, 2, 3, and 4 have Cronbach's α value above 0.70, and the remaining 1 combined item i.e., 5 has Cronbach's α value above 0.50 but less than 0.70. So, all the combined variables have been considered for the study as the scale is reliable enough [20, 21].

Table 15.8 Scale reliability.

Variables/ combined items	Anchor	Cronbach's α
1	3	0.913
2	5	0.816
3	3	0.876
4	3	0.865
5	3	0.663

15.4.1 Multiple Linear Regression

Data analysis and interpretation: Initially the impact of variables considered in the model 1, 2, 3, 4, and 5 have been analyzed by using multiple linear regression to test the hypotheses. Tables 15.9, 15.10, and 15.11 have shown the consolidated results.

Table 15.9 Model summary[f].

Model	R	R square	Adjusted R square	Std. error of the estimate
1	.752[a]	0.566	0.564	0.719
2	.597[b]	0.483	0.480	1.084
3	.751[c]	0.564	0.559	0.929
4	.614[d]	0.499	0.495	1.035
5	.484[e]	0.234	0.230	0.955
a. Predictors: (Constant), ID11, ID13, ID33				
b. Predictors: (Constant), ID21				
c. Predictors: (Constant), ID41, ID43, ID42				
d. Predictors: (Constant), ID52, ID51				
e. Predictors: (Constant), ID62, ID61, ID63				
f. Dependent Variable: D1				

Table 15.10 ANOVA[a].

Model	Sum of squares	df	Mean square	F	Sig.
1 Regression	350.339	3	116.78	226.088	.000b
Residual	268.592	520	0.517		
Total	618.931	523			
2 Regression	205.823	1	205.823	96.498	.000c
Residual	413.108	522	1.175		
Total	618.931	523			
3 Regression	438.521	3	249.63	126.929	.000d
Residual	180.41	520	0.864		
Total	618.931	523			
4 Regression	61.066	2	30.533	28.515	.000e
Residual	557.865	521	1.071		
Total	618.931	523			
5 Regression	145.035	3	48.345	53.048	.000f
Residual	473.896	520	0.911		
Total	618.931	523			
a. Predictors: (Constant), ID11, ID13, ID33					
b. Predictors: (Constant), ID21					
c. Predictors: (Constant), ID41, ID43, ID42					
d. Predictors: (Constant), ID52, ID51					
e. Predictors: (Constant), ID62, ID61, ID63					
f. Dependent Variable: D1					

Table 15.11 Coefficients[a].

Model		Unstandardized coefficients		Standardized coefficients		
		B	Std. error	Beta	t	Sig.
1	(Constant)	0.091	.144		0.636	.525
	ID11	.519	.039	.490	13.316	.000
	ID13	.317	.041	.300	7.674	.000
	ID33	0.081	34.000	0.078	2.354	.019
2	(Constant)	3.856	.162		23.819	.000
	ID21	-.101	.046	-.097	-2.227	.026
3	(Constant)	-.103	.210		-0.490	.625
	ID41	.764	.041	.657	18.604	.000
	ID43	0.260	.062	0.191	4.222	.000
	ID42	-.201	.062	-.152	-3.265	.001
4	(Constant)	2.738	.147		18.663	.000
	ID52	0.453	.072	0.48	6.261	.000
	ID51	-0.218	.073	-0.228	-2.972	.003
5	(Constant)	1.717	.162		10.602	.000
	ID62	.470	.067	.437	7.019	.000
	ID61	.243	.065	.212	3.717	.000
	ID63	-.173	.060	-.174	-2.903	.004
a. Dependent Variable: D1						

Model 1: Here hypotheses H01a, H01b, H01c, H03b, and H03c have been analyzed. Here trust level of middle-class depositors for banking institutions in India is D1 and restriction on funds withdrawal from a bank account is the main independent variable ID1 and irregularities observed in banking services is ID3 along with 5 overarching variables i.e., ID11, ID12, ID13, ID32, and ID33.

Model 1 (Table 15.9) represents 56.6 percent of the total variation of the dependent variable (D1).

Table 15.10 of ANOVA indicates the implication of model 1. Here significance value is less than 0.001.

Table 15.11 of coefficients revealed that variables ID11, ID13, and ID33 have significance values below 0.05. So, null hypotheses have been rejected i.e., H01a, H01c, and H03c, and alternate hypotheses have been accepted i.e., Ha1a, Ha1c, and Ha3c. Here variable ID12 and ID32 have significance values above 0.05, so accept the null hypothesis i.e., H01b and H03b.

The regression equation for model 1:

$$D1= 0.091+ 0.490*ID11 + 0.300*ID13 + 0.078*ID33 \quad (15.1)$$

Equation 15.1 reveals that one unit change in ID11 will impact of 0.490 unit change on the trust level of middle-class depositors for banking institutions in India, one unit change in ID13 will impact of 0.300 unit change on the trust level of middle-class depositors for banking institutions in India, one unit change in ID33 will impact of 0.078 unit change on the trust level of middle-class depositors for banking institutions in India.

It means that restriction on funds withdrawal from the bank account and irregularities observed in banking institutions have a significant impact on the trust level of middle-class depositors for banking institutions in India.

Model 2: Here hypotheses H02a, H02b, and H02c have been analyzed. Here trust level of middle-class depositors for banking institutions in India is D1 and the period of moratorium on banking services is the main independent variable ID2 along with 3 overarching variables i.e., ID21, ID22, and ID23.

Model 2 (Table 15.9) represents 48.3 percent of the total variation of the dependent variable (D1).

Table 15.10 of ANOVA indicates the implication of model 2. Here significance value is less than 0.001.

Table 15. 11 of coefficients revealed that variable ID21 has a significance value below 0.05. So, null hypotheses have been rejected i.e., H02a, and alternate hypotheses have been accepted i.e., Ha2a.

Here variable ID22 and ID23 have significance values above 0.05, so accept the null hypothesis i.e., H02b and H02c.

The regression equation for model 2:

$$D1= 3.856-0.097*ID21 \quad (15.2)$$

Equation 15.2 reveals that one unit change in ID21 will impact of 0.097 unit change on the trust level of middle-class depositors for banking institutions in India.

It means that period of moratorium on banking services has a minor impact on the trust level of middle-class depositors for banking institutions in India.

Model 3: Here hypotheses H04a, H04b, and H04c have been analyzed. Here trust level of middle-class depositors for banking institutions in India is D1 and failure of corporate governance in banking institutions is the main independent variable ID4 along with 3 overarching variables i.e., ID41, ID42, and ID43.

Model 3 (Table 15.9) represents 56.4 percent of the total variation of the dependent variable (D1).

Table 15.10 of ANOVA indicates the implication of model 3. Here significance value is less than 0.001.

Table 15.11 of coefficients revealed that variables ID41, ID42, and ID43 have significance values below 0.05. So, null hypotheses have been rejected i.e., H04a, H04b, and H04c, and alternate hypotheses have been accepted i.e., Ha4a, Ha4b, and Ha4c.

The regression equation for model 3:

$$D1 = -0.103 + 0.657 * ID41 + 0.191 * ID43 - 0.152 * ID42 \quad (15.3)$$

Equation 15.3 reveals that one unit change in ID41 will impact of 0.657 unit change on the trust level of middle-class depositors for banking institutions in India, one unit change in ID43 will impact of 0.191 unit change on the trust level of middle-class depositors for banking institutions in India, one unit change in ID42 will impact of 0.152 unit change on the trust level of middle-class depositors for banking institutions in India.

It means that the failure of corporate governance has a significant impact on the trust level of middle-class depositors for banking institutions in India.

Model 4: Here hypotheses H05a, H05b, and H05c have been analyzed. Here trust level of middle-class depositors for banking institutions in India is D1 and the role of bank staff for the a moratorium is the main independent variable ID5 along with 3 overarching variables i.e., ID51, ID52, and ID53.

Model 4 (Table 15.9) represents 49.9 percent of the total variation of the dependent variable (D1).

Table 15.10 of ANOVA indicates the implication of model 4. Here significance value is less than 0.001.

Table 15.11 of coefficients revealed that variables ID51 and ID52 have significance values below 0.05.

So, null hypotheses have been rejected i.e., H05a and H05b, and alternate hypotheses have been accepted i.e., Ha5a and Ha5b.

The regression equation for model 4:

$$D1= 2.738+ 0.480*ID52-0.228*ID51 \quad (15.4)$$

Equation 15.4 reveals that one unit change in ID52 will impact 0.480 unit change on the trust level of middle-class depositors for banking institutions in India and one unit change in ID51 will impact 0.228 unit change on the trust level of middle-class depositors for banking institutions in India.

It means that role of bank staff in the moratorium has a significant impact on the trust level of middle-class depositors for banking institutions in India.

Model 5: Here hypotheses H06a, H06b, and H06c have been analyzed. Here trust level of middle-class depositors for banking institutions in India is D1 and deterioration of the bank's image due to moratorium is the main independent variable ID6 along with 3 overarching variables i.e., ID61, ID62, and ID63.

Model 5 (Table 15.9) represents 23.4 percent of the total variation of the dependent variable (D1).

Table 15.10 of ANOVA indicates the implication of model 5. Here significance value is less than 0.001.

Table 15.11 of coefficients revealed that variables ID61, ID62, and ID63 have significance values below 0.05.

So, null hypotheses have been rejected i.e., H06a, H06b, and H06c and alternate hypotheses have been accepted i.e., Ha6a, Ha6b, and Ha6c.

The regression equation for model 5:

$$D1 = 1.717 + 0.437*ID62 + 0.212*ID61 - 0.174*ID63 \quad (15.5)$$

Equation 15.5 reveals that one unit change in ID62 will impact of 0.437 unit change on the trust level of middle-class depositors for banking institutions in India, one unit change in ID61 will impact of 0.212 unit change on the trust level of middle-class depositors for banking institutions in India and one unit change in ID63 will impact of 0.174 unit change on the trust level of middle-class depositors for banking institutions in India.

It means that the deterioration of the bank's image due to the moratorium has a significant impact on the trust level of middle-class depositors for banking institutions in India.

Excluded variables: Table 15.12 represents the information of excluded variables. ID12, ID32, ID22, ID23, and ID53 have been excluded based on their significance value as the significance value of all these variables is more than 0.05. So null hypotheses i.e., H01b, H03b, H02b, H02c, and H05c are accepted.

Table 15.12 Excluded variables[a].

Excluded variables[a]						
Model		**Beta In**	**t**	**Sig.**	**Partial correlation**	**Tolerance**
1	ID12	.067[b]	1.457	.146	.064	.392
	ID32	-.014[b]	-0.424	.672	-.019	.767
2	ID22	-.017[c]	-0.354	.724	-.015	.799
	ID23	-.009[c]	-0.185	.853	-.008	.823
3	ID53	0.053[d]	0.808	.419	.035	.395
a. Dependent Variable: D1						
b. Predictors: (Constant), ID11, ID13, ID33						
c. Predictors: (Constant), ID21						
d. Predictors: (Constant), ID52, ID51						

15.5 Conclusion

After an in-depth analysis of the collected primary data, the study concluded that the moratorium on banking services imposition by RBI has a highly significant negative impact on the trust level of middle-class depositors in India. Middle-class customers have limited sources of income and these customers deposit their hard-earned money in the bank for safety purposes and interest income. But restrictions imposed by RBI on funds withdrawal from their accounts demoralize the customers and these restrictions restrict the customers to avail banking facilities for a specific period. During the period of the moratorium, customers lose their trust level in banks. After the imposition of the moratorium, customers lose their trust in the bank's top management as well as the bank's staff as the moratorium was imposed due to the mismanagement of banking operations by the concerned staff members which hamper the image of the bank. Overall the study concluded that due to many prominent factors which have a significant impact on the trust level of middle-class depositors, customers lose their trust in banking institutions.

15.6 Recommendations

These are the recommendations proposed based on the study:

1. RBI, a regulatory body should be highly vigilant and monitor high-value transactions.
2. Top management of the bank should be more concerned about banking operations to minimize the effect of irregularities.
3. Bank staff should also be highly vigilant while assessing the creditworthiness of the customers to minimize the effect of non-performing assets and anti-money laundering activities.
4. Banks should identify the high-risk intensive customers on regular basis and monitor the transactions in their bank accounts.

15.7 Future Implications

The outcomes of this paper can be considered for further research in related studies:

1. This study can be significant for the study of banking irregularities.
2. This study can be significant for the study of the moratorium.
3. This study can be significant for the study of corporate governance failure in banks.
4. This study can be significant for the study of the deterioration of a bank's image.

References

1. Kumar, K.B., What is a Bank Moratorium, and when does it come into play?, 2020, Retrieved from https://www.thehindu.com/business/Economy/the-hindu-explains-what-is-a-bank-moratorium-and- when-does-it-come-into-play/article33151740.ece. (Accessed on 5th June 2021).
2. Basu, S., Why do banks fail? *Int. Rev. Appl. Econ.*, *17*, 3, 231–248, 2003.
3. Dayal, Y., Yes Bank Ltd. was placed under Moratorium, 2020, Retrieved from Moratorium on yes bank.PDF. (Accessed on 10th May 2021).
4. Sood, J., RBI Imposes Moratorium on Yes Bank: All You Need to know, 2020, Retrieved from https://www.outlookindia.com/website/story/business-news-rbi-places-moratorium-on-yes-bank-withdrawal-all-you-need-to-know/348340. (Accessed on 10th March 2021).
5. Mathew, G. and Verma, S., Moratorium on Lakshmi Vilas Bank: What does it mean for depositors, financial sector?, 2020, Retrieved from https://indianexpress.com/article/explained/lakshmi-vilas-what-a-failed-bank-means-7056518/. (Accessed on 26th March 2021).
6. Karthikeyan, S., RBI Extends Moratorium on PMC Bank Till December 22; Withdrawal Limit Capped At Rs. 1 Lakh, 2020, Retrieved from https://www.republicworld.com/business-news/india-business/rbi-extends-moratorium-on-pmc-bank-till-december-22-2020.html. (Accessed on 10th April 2021).
7. Sen, S., RBI extends restrictions on scam-hit PMC bank till March 31; receives four proposals for investment, 2020, Retrieved from https://www.dnaindia.com/business/news-rbi-extends-restrictions-on-scam-hit-pmc-bank-till-march-31-receives-four-proposals-for-investment-2862877. (Accessed on 10th February 2021).

8. Bansal, N., The impact of training programme of digital banking services to employees of unorganised sector and their acceptability in India. *Int. J. Electron. Cust. Relationsh. Manage.*, *12*, 3, 246–272, 2020.
9. Dayal, Y., Yes Bank Ltd. placed under moratorium, 2020, Retrieved from https://ypfsresourcelibrary.blob.core.windows.net/fcic/YPFS/PR2022OMD66B7AEEB3D849CEA7F5FF4EC757B41B.pdf. (Accessed on 10th March 2023).
10. Nair, V., Government Puts Yes Bank Under Moratorium, RBI Supersedes Board, Withdrawal Capped At Rs 50,000, 2020, Retrieved from https://www.bloombergquint.com/business/government-puts-yes-bank-under-moratorium-rbi-supersedes-board-withdrawals-capped-at-rs-50000. (Accessed on 9th March 2021).
11. Jagannath, J., *Lakshmi Vilas Bank brought under moratorium till 16 Dec; restricts withdrawals at ₹25,000*, 2020, Retrieved from https://www.livemint.com/companies/news/lvb-brought-under-moratorium-until-16-dec-withdrawal-capped-at-rs-25-000-per-borrower-11605619769547.html. (Accessed on 15th March 2021).
12. Nair, V., Lakshmi Vilas Bank Under RBI Moratorium, To be merged With DBS India, 2020, Retrieved from https://www.bloombergquint.com/business/rbi-places-lakshmi-vilas-bank-under-moratorium. (Accessed on 30th March 2021).
13. Bansal, N. and Pandey, K.N., Impact of password management strategies on the trust enhancement in the digital era. *Int. J. Bus. Perform. Manage.*, *24*, 3–4, 484–503, 2023.
14. Motiani, P., What Lakshmi Vilas Bank account customers should do post imposition of moratorium?, 2020, Retrieved from https://economictimes.indiatimes.com/wealth/save/what-lakshmi-vilas-bank-account-customers-should-do-post-imposition-of-moratorium/articleshow/79299602.cms?-from=mdr. (Accessed on 19th April 2021).
15. George, D. and Mallery, P., *SPSS for Windows Step by Step: A Simple Guide and Reference 17.0 Update*, 10th Edition, Pearson, Boston, 2010.
16. Malhotra, N., *Marketing Research – An Applied Orientation*, 5th ed., Pearson Education, New Delhi, 2008.
17. Hair, J.F., William, B.C., Barry, B.J., Anderson, R.E., Tatham, R.L., *Multivariate Data Analysis*, 6th ed., Pearson Education, New Delhi, 2009.
18. Churchill, G.A., Iacobucci, D., Israel, D., *Marketing research: A south Asian perspective*, Cengage Learning, New Delhi, 2010.
19. Nunnally, J., *Psychometric Methods*, McGraw-Hill, New York, NY, 1967.
20. Cavana, R.Y., Delahaye, B.L., Sekaran, U., *Applied business research: Qualitative and quantitative methods*, John Wiley & Sons, Australia, 2001.
21. George, D. and Mallery, P., *SPSS for Windows step by step: A simple guide and reference 11.0 update*, 4th ed., Allyn & Bacon, Boston, 2003.

16

Analyzing the Hindrances Associated with the Procurement of Used Products: A Circular Economy Perspective

M. Nishal[1], Sonu Rajak[1]* and K.E.K. Vimal[2]

[1]*Department of Mechanical Engineering, National Institute of Technology Patna, Patna, India*
[2]*Department of Production Engineering, National Institute of Technology Tiruchirappalli, Tiruchirappalli, India*

Abstract
The acquisition of used products has become an active search spearheaded by organizations that wish to reduce costs and be environment friendly. This, in a way, allows enterprises to achieve the twin objectives of increasing useful product lives and, as a result, decrease capital outlay, and at the same time, reduce the impacts on the environment. This approach as used here and that augments the tenets of a circular economy helps in reduction of waste and resource conservation. However, as with any concept, the purchase of used goods is not without its limitations, which hinder the proper implementation of the idea. This paper sheds light into the structural factors that include quality control concerns, legal factors, and practical challenges including compatibility issues and costs of inspections which are attached to buying used goods. Moreover, the contributed research analyses the risk arising from an unreliable supplier and the unavailability of essential paperwork. Mitigating these challenges is crucial for entities that are planning to purchase used goods. Thus, by defining and analyzing these particular obstacles it helps to develop plans to minimize possible threats and to maximize the value of gains provided by the phenomenon under consideration. This extensive review aims at unraveling the complex nature of such problems, as well as providing the best recommendations that can be applied to enhance the procurement of such items. With this reflection, we would like to make our part to the debate related to

**Corresponding author*: sonu.production@gmail.com

K. Mathiyazhagan, Krishna Kumar Dadsena, Rajesh Kumar Singh, Aakanksha Kishore and Andrea Appolloni (eds.) Sustainable Operations of Logistics and Supply Chain Management, (381–414) sustainable procurement in terms of a shift towards a circular economy. It seems that due to the mentioned challenges, the primary parameters that define pre-owned product procurement are orientation towards quality, reliability, and performance while maintaining sustainable goals and objectives at the same time, which should be addressed systematically.

***Keywords*:** Circular economy, sustainable supply chain, sustainable development goals, B2B purchase, used products

16.1 Introduction

The business to business (B2B) purchase of used goods has thus risen as the enticing model for enterprises that intend to reduce costs and embrace sustainability. Thus, when corporations prolong the existence of goods, they are able not only to significantly reduce the expenditures in the framework of capital but also to short-throw the impact on the environment. This approach inherently linked to the principles of the circular economy strengthens the principles of minimization of waste and conservation of resources. However, as it will exploit later on, this system of buying second-hand goods is not without difficulties that can hinder the successful undertaking of procurement. These have a vast array of concerns that include fear of the quality and reliability of the items being bought second hand to the challenges of legal and regulatory compliance [1]. Inconsistency and unpredictable state of used goods, possibility of meeting sellers with ill-intentions, and the issue of sufficiently inaccessible important documents and papers are some of the highest barriers that organizations face. Besides, there are challenges of operations for example compatibility check and other costs including inspection and certification of used products in the process of procurement. Understanding these issues is crucial therefore for priority associations planning to purchase secondhand goods. Understanding the sources and nature of this challenge is therefore helpful in the formulation of strategies that will lock the specific issues that cause it while at the same time also maximizing on the gains accrued from the practice. Thus, this extensive study attempts to shed light on the diverse ramifications of these problems to provide solutions for enhancing the efficacy and efficiency of the procurement of used items. This way, we seek to join the ongoing conversation in regards to sustainable procurement and circular economy shift.

The foremost barriers in B2B procurement of second-hand goods is the concern regarding the quality and reliability of these items. Organizations may perceive second-hand products as less reliable compared to new ones, leading to hesitance in making purchases. Organizations must navigate various regulations that govern the resale of used products, ensuring alignment with industry standards to avoid legal repercussions. This complexity can discourage businesses from engaging in second-hand procurement practices. The risk associated with encountering unethical sellers is a considerable concern for organizations in the B2B arena. The potential for fraud, misrepresentation of product conditions, or delivery of substandard goods emphasizes the need for thorough vetting of suppliers. Additional operational costs can be a significant barrier to adopting second-hand procurement processes. Expenses related to product inspections, certifications, and ensuring compatibility with existing operational setups can accumulate, counteracting the intended cost savings of purchasing second-hand goods. These costs may deter organizations from pursuing second-hand procurement options even when they align with sustainability goals.

16.2 Literature Review

Purchasing of used products has turned out to be a plausible way through which organizations can achieve cost savings and promote the preservation of the environment. However, it comes with a lot of difficulties that must be considered and properly planned for the practice to produce the desired results.

The first of these challenges is in establishing the means of evaluating the quality of the products. Contrary to products that are produced brand new, used products are likely to display different levels of usage, thus the need to develop strict assessment criteria that would enable an accurate assessment of their usage levels. It is mandatory to conduct thorough check on the received materials, test the equipment's performance, and conduct a detailed review diagnostic for any sign of failure in meeting the prescribed standards of quality and operational efficiency. Also, the credibility of the sellers in the used product market plays a significant role that should not be underrated [1]. Situations like these are where misrepresentation occurs, fraudulent practices take place, and there is no transparency at all and these situations will lead to worst procurement cycles where there is the possibility of experiencing big time losses and even operations may be coming to stand still. Therefore, prospective sellers should be properly vetted depending on their fitness to undertake the supply of the respective goods by considering vital aspects such as their reputation, performance standards, and other qualities that depict their credibility in business.

There is also the legal and regulatory compliance that is another major challenge that organizations must deal with whenever they are sourcing used products. Many fields experience strict rules and requirements concerning the safety of products and the environment as well as the performance standards. The applicability of these regulations to pre-owned items is of utmost significance as noncompliance has provided sanctions which lead to fines, legal risks, and eventual business shutdowns. Thus, the literature suggests proper evaluation of products and high concentration on compliance with rules and requirements for meeting the mentioned challenges. They do not only minimize risks but also benefit the enhancement of used product procurement programs. With market for buying and selling used item becoming even more global in the future, more researches need to be carried out and different set of norms needs to be worked out specifically for this practice. The cooperation of related manufacturers, suppliers, regulatory authorities, and universities can contribute to the development of overall principles, formalized certification procedures, and optimal practices adapted to the peculiarities of different industries.

By overcoming the difficulties connected with the definition of used product quality, the determination of the seller reliability and the fulfillment of legal requirements, organizations can optimize the usage of used product procurement [2]. This practice does not only provide a chance to save on the expenses but also meets the principles of sustainable development and circular economy grossing well on the efficiency of resources and impacts of the process on the environment. However, it is important to state here that like most business strategies, product procurement from used products have its own set of challenges [3]. The approach that is required for this practice entails a systematic approach that entails scrutiny, supplier assessment, and compliance with the law in order to avoid the pitfalls while reaping from it. The following section states the factors which need to be considered for procurement of used products for integrating the circular economy concept within a system.

16.3 Procurement Consideration of Used Products

Incorporating used goods into organizational operations presents several challenges that must be addressed. This research delves into the complexities of second-hand procurement, focusing primarily on product quality assessment. Unlike new items, used products often exhibit wear and tear, requiring rigorous physical inspections, performance tests, and documentation reviews to ensure quality. Additionally, vendor reliability is crucial, as

Figure 16.1 Factors to be considered for procurement.

deception and corruption can disrupt the procurement process. Legal and regulatory compliance further complicates matters, as pre-owned items must meet safety and environmental standards to avoid legal consequences [4].

To overcome these challenges, a robust strategy is needed—one that includes thorough product assessments, purchasing from credible suppliers, and strict adherence to regulations. While further research and industry-specific standards are essential, addressing these key issues can enable organizations to reap the benefits of second-hand procurement, such as cost savings and sustainability, while managing potential risks effectively [5]. The following Figure 16.1 shows the various factors involved in the procurement of the used products.

16.3.1 Quality and Reliability

1. Unknown Condition

Determining the actual status of products that have been sold and subsequently used is a difficult prospect indeed because such items come with a past that is often hidden and untraceable [6]. This lack of transparency of their prior usage and care means that their condition cannot be determined without an extensive check. For example, let there be a second-hand industrial machine, there could have been so many repairs, re-fixing of parts or alteration whose results do not show on the surface of the machine [7]. Such latent conditions may cause periodic failures or declining performance, and those will cost the acquiring organization a lot of money and system downtime.

Additionally, since there are no strict guidelines for the inspections and certification of used goods, the condition of the items is likely to remain ambiguous. What some reconditioned product buyers give or receive may depend on the kind of evaluation done by the provider and the strictness produced in reeling out findings on lifespan and reliability. To minimize such risks, management has to employ strict examination and testing protocols, which call for professional input as well as sophisticated tools to analyze the product's capabilities, tendency towards depreciation, and compatibility with other systems. Another option is to involve third-party independent experts or use the certification of operating companies, which can also speak about the condition of the product.

Lastly, an active and thorough identification process is vital to reduce the likelihood of several disastrous scenarios and to guarantee the successful incorporation of reconditioned items into diversified organizational processes.

2. Wear and Tear

Since the acquisition of pre-owned items is accompanied by the use of items, there is always some level of wear on the items, which may have an influence on the overall efficiency and utilization of the items. The level of this deterioration depends on a number of aspects such as age of the product, frequency of usage and sum of past maintenance. Damage is expected on the procured item, but severe loss can compromise the dependability and value for money of the operation. For instance, a used vehicle; while it actually means that the major parts and mechanisms of a car, including its engine and the transmission system, and braking system could be worn out and therefore prone to breakages or require more expenses on maintenance than others. Determining the further service life of these components is a difficult task that may sometimes need the help of professionals and/or specific instruments [8].

The identification of the precise rate of wear and tear is vital when purchasing secondhand commodities because it determines performance after purchase. Neglecting this aspect may result in the early failure of the products, frequent breakdowns, and additional operational costs that may eliminate any possible advantages of purchasing second-hand items. To avoid these problems, the strong inspection procedures should be used, including the application of the contemporary diagnostic equipping and the experience of the specific industry to determine the condition of the main components. Such measures as working with credible third-party inspectors or obtaining certifications based on specific requirements can add more credibility to the rest of the product's life and its performance capabilities [8].

3. Limited Warranty

New products and automobiles as they leave the manufacturing companies they are fitted with manufacturer warranties to protect them from being defective or dysfunctional. These warranties act as insurance of sorts, so that no matter what, there will be ways of dealing with what is wrong without having to spend more money of the buyer's. On the other hand pre-owned goods often do not include such extensive warranty guarantees or, conversely, the warranties may be restricted in some way Patel *et al.*, [9]. The lack of a sound warranty system that comes with the software actually shifts this risk to the purchasing organization in its entirety.

The problem with sales without warranty is that vendors/Manufacturers fully take the costs of repairs, replacements or any loss of business due to product failure. Such expenses can build up quickly, presenting a major fiscal danger, notably when obtaining large or essential commodities [10]. Lack of adequate financial safeguard in the matter discourages potential organizations and companies from bringing in second-hand products, because the costs of failure or even malfunction of a certain product could end up outweighing the monetary benefits to be derived from the acquisition of such a product. There is however a risk that some companies might opt for other strategies of risk management and include the following: Contracting for limited warranty after buying from providers who in turn sell them third party warranties [1]. It is also advisable to conduct adequate inspection and research on the used items in order to also foresee any looming problems and therefore apply adequate assessment on the purchase of used products.

16.3.2 Availability and Compatibility

1. Inconsistent Supply

Pre-owned commodities for some reason are characteristically unpredictable and are easily influenced by market forces, disposal patterns, and stock availability among sellers. Unlike products that are produced and manufactured and which can easily be ordered in large batches due to their new state, second hand items are scarce in the market and present a stiff challenge when it comes to their procurement. Such a supply chain can pose significant challenges as a firm tries to source a continuous flow of particular goods. Let me take you through an example of where a manufacturing enterprise is in the market to purchase second hand equipment that will intone their production processes. Uncertified steel may be produced in different procedures, and although it is possible to set standards for such a process, accurate models are rare, thus inhibiting such an endeavor and possibly creating operational inefficiencies, delays, and even redesigns and setbacks. This is because the purchasing of used goods is characterized by irregular market availability; therefore, the purchasing process highly depends on activity and contingency plans in case of potential interruption of supply chain [2]. This may make organizations have to seek for other sources of getting their products, keep several sources of vendors or possibly have a combination of both the new product sourcing the used product sourcing in order to be able to continue with their normal operation and actualization of production objectives.

2. Compatibility Issues

The need for ease of integration is noted as one of the most significant factors when integrating used items into existing frameworks or business models. The second-hand products that are obtained might have a core age that makes them incompatible with today's technologies, current industries' standards, or other attached components, which can act as barriers when integrating them [3].

This compatibility dilemma is especially challenging in industries where compatibility is a necessity than a preference such as in computer and technology systems, health care systems, and in manufacturing lines among others. Neglecting compatibility issues is a very serious mistake as it can result in decreased efficiency or effectiveness of the used products acquired hence affecting organizational operations. For instance, an organization that adopts the use of used computer hardware may find the equipment incompatible, with the old pieces of equipment not compatible with the latest versions of software or advanced connectivity standards. This may result in further investment into converters, enhancements, or transitional tools, which compromises efficiency of the buying initiative [8].

In the same way, compatibility issue might be a factor in the usage of pre-owned medical instruments because used instruments may not be compatible with the most modern diagnostic tool suites or electronic health record system. When such incompatibilities do arise, the usefulness and effectiveness of these devices can be rendered questionable, which can consequently have implications on the delivery of patients' care as well as their treatment. To avoid such compatibility risks, compatibility analysis and proper due diligent must be done, so that the acquired used products will be compatible with the existing systems and processes of the organization. It may require engaging with value chain players, best practice sharing or acquiring middle ware that create interfaces between systems. The failure to address compatibility issues will therefore negate all the advantages of used product procurement since the organization's operations, performance and even financial position can be worsened by the negative impacts [7].

16.3.3 Seller Reliability

1. Trustworthiness

Managing purchasing of used products entails great consideration of the credibility of centers for selling such products, and this field needs organization. In the case of new items that are directly from the production manufacturers or various authorized dealers, the second-hand products or used items may have a variable angle starting from full credibility to complete ethical practices to mere criminal traders. This unevenness, therefore, comes with a built-in risk that is confronted with literally shady folks who may or may not fake the state, the source, or the primacy of their merchandise [11]. This risk is worst in online selling platforms where the consumer who will never get to touch or feel the real product they are buying. Such kinds of deals are obscure and hence result to the relatively higher incidences of con artists, counterfeit products, and other forms of misleading advertisements; therefore, it is necessary to undertake thorough investigation in ascertaining the validity of the sellers.

Therefore, threats such as these mean that potential buyers should be very cautious and adhere to several precautionary measures. This may involve sometimes taking time and examining the reasons given by the sellers as to their legitimacy, ordering the sellers to provide feedback's from previous clients on the credibility of the suppliers, ordering the third party verification companies or partnering with business associations to ascertain the true status of the suppliers. Lack of compliance in this area may result in a huge amount of monitory loss, company operational nastiness, and legal ramifications that are always associated with the buying of substandard or misrepresented goods.

2. After-Sales Support

Due to the fact that second-hand or used products may be out from the factory for a while and bought second-hand, the availability and accessibility of after-sales services and technical support should form a significant and considerable part of the consumer evaluations and reflections. For unlike new product that has full support of the manufacturer in terms of technical help, parts back up and or maintenance schedules, used products do not have these benefits. Such scarcity of support resources can present problems in handling matters that may develop after the purchase is made. For example: if a firm purchasing old industrial equipment then, it can face some problems such as getting difficulties in finding necessary spare parts, or in getting necessary skilled technicians for repairing and maintaining those equipment's. Such challenges can result in long duration of operations shutdown, which in essence affects the organization's productivity and flow of work [12].

In addition, often it is lack of the definite support system which can turn the process of elucidation of various technical issues which may appear in course of product's life cycle in to a problematic one. Lack of sufficient expertise or instruments could be a challenge for many organizations who find it hard to tackle the above problems through their routine work and productivity. The above-mentioned risks can be managed by conducting a detailed assessment of the availability of support options when purchasing the used products and when planning for the products' use in critical applications or sectors whereby cost of downtime is high [13].

16.3.4 Evaluation and Verification

1. Inspection Costs

Evaluating the state of used or second-hand items is an aspect that has inherent difficulties. New products reputation is given at the point of entry, thus pointing to an important fact that used products need thorough examination in order to define their functional status. This evaluation process might be lengthy and could costs a lot of money if professional knowledge and/or equipment are necessary. For instance, it could be the assessment of used electronic equipment's. Sometimes, such an assessment may entail complex component and software testing and even highly stringent validation of the performance parameters. These detailed inspections usually require specific skills and may require additional professional or third-party companies to be involved, which increases the costs [9].

Furthermore, the types of these evaluations are usually more elaborate and exhaustive than simply comparing products and features and can greatly extend the procurement periods owing to the need for comprehensive review of the products. That is why this extended evaluation period can be quite problematic, as it may cause interference in the schedule of some projects and slow down the introduction of new systems or pieces of equipment. Hence, organizations need to consider the cost advantage of purchasing such products and the efforts and costs of conducting condition assessment to determine the viability of the decision to purchase such products. Achieving the right proportions crucial in conditions where risks are to be kept at an absolute minimum and added values obtained at their maximum possible levels, especially in such situations where the performance and reliability of products are of vital importance [10].

2. Lack of Documentation

The first known limitation of buying second-hand or used goods is that most of the paperwork may not be available most of the times. This enlists records of services rendered, instructions on the usage of the product, and certification documents which always accompany a brand new product. The absence of such records can significantly steer the efficiency of such a process, and it becomes rather challenging to provide solid evidence of the product's history, technical features, and conformity to the requirements of the existing standards [13].

From the example of buying a second-hand car, it will be possible to specify certain stages. When one lacks the records of the vehicle, he or she cannot be in a position to determine whether the vehicle has been maintained all through or has ever developed a problem that required serious repair during its operation. Such uncertainty may therefore be a risk since the problems may not be well documented or maintenance could be insufficient while the components could fail early or perform poorly. In the same way, lack of manuals or technical documents in the case of using complex machinery or equipment pose a high risk of inefficiency or inability to operate and maintain them in the best way possible. Lack of specific knowledge may cause confusion to the Operators on various aspects of operation, specific problem solving directives or suggested maintenance practices thus resulting in operation problems, safety hazards, or shortened equipment life.

Moreover, there is no guarantee of the product's genuine origin, which becomes a challenge in different industries due to high risks associated with the circulation of fakes or unauthorized modifications that can negatively impact safety, adherence to required standards, and protect ability of the copyrights and patents. In order to overcome these difficulties specific measures need to be taken: carrying out extensive researching, consulting with experts, or having high requirements to checks and verification's. They may also include resources for reverse engineering, documentation development or even a different procurement strategy to be on the safe side in case they need the help of the information for the acquired products.

16.3.5 Legal and Regulatory Issues

1. Compliance

Avoiding or dealing with the implementation of regulations is a crucial factor when purchasing used or labeled second-hand products. Since rules and regulations together with industry standards are not static but are normally revised and updated after some time older products may be found to be sub-standard. Purchasing non-compliant items also implies that organizations are at risk with legal consequences, penalties, or finances. For instance consider the case of environmental legal requirements regarding emissions in automobiles or some equipment. These standards may have been revised over time, to stricter models which means the older products may no longer meet those standards. Failing to meet the current standards of emissions may lead to legal consequences or limitation of the operation [14].

Another example can be seen in the regulation of safety for electrical equipment or the health care related instruments and devices for diagnosis and treatment. Since these industries involve operations that affect the society, regulatory authorities might come up with new standards or a new testing procedure that would improve safety. Thus, operating with second-hand equipment that does not fit safety requirements of the contemporary level may lead to dangerous consequences for the users and organizations, exposure to liability, or even disruptions. This difficulty is even more amplified especially where extensive documentation or even verification's from the manufacturer himself is inapplicable. This is because with minimal information on product specifications, production dates, or records of product alterations, the identification of an acquired item as one conforming to current standards is virtually becoming a herculean task.

To address these risks, organizations are obliged to undertake extensive due diligence measures; this can entail consulting the specialist, carrying out a detailed research, or turning to professionals who can perform testing and certification checks. Also, they may need to provide resources for changes in product designs or any little changes in products that do not meet these standards or as a way of achieving better and efficient compatibility with other manufactured items as a way of avoiding legal complications as well as operations.

2. Liability

Purchasing of reconditioned or used product has some risks associated with it and this is the fact that if the product fails or harms someone, who is to be held responsible? In contrast to new products, which are guaranteed by manufacturers, the purchaser of the used good is absolutely liable for any misuse, injury, or harm that may occur while operating the item or in the course of rendering the item's intended service. This liability exposure can be especially felt in industries or uses where product failure or premature failure would mean a disaster, for example, in medical, aviation, or construction. Suppose there is a healthcare facility that purchases a used medical device to use in diagnosing and or treating patients. In the case that this device would for some reason fail during a crucial procedure then the facility may be exposed to legal ramifications such as being sued by the affected patients, being investigated for non-compliance by the regulating bodies, or even sanctions for failing to meet set standards. While under a manufacturer warranty or having an influential support system, remedying the consequences is the healthcare provider's responsibility [15].

Likewise, in contexts of the specific economic sector of construction, the use of worn-out mechanical equipment or tools could also have severe consequences. If, for instance, a used piece of equipment were to break down while in use causing mishaps, loss of lives, or property damage, the construction firm could be legally be dragged to court for the outburst of consequences. This line liability exposure may also go beyond monetary implications and affect the company's reputation and regulatory fines. To avoid these risks, there is a need to have sound risk management factors when purchasing the used products especially when they will be used in critical applications. This may comprise of regular inspections, getting professional opinions, strict maintenance practices and having enough insurance. Further, it is important that the organizational trend of acquiring used items must be seen from the standpoint of probable outcomes of product failure and its implication to the company's economic gains.

16.3.6 Logistics and Transportation

1. Transportation and Acquisition Expenditure

Since the items that are bought or received may be second hand or used products, it is clear that they may entail higher handling costs than new products. Owing to wear and tear or their delicate nature, used products are likely to get even more damaged or become even more fragile during transportation; therefore, they will often need some special packaging or handling. This extra superintendence can lead to higher costs which may cancel out some of the expenses of procuring second-hand goods.

For instance, when moving a used item of industrial plant, machinery or equipment, custom build crates, padding, or temperature controlled transport may be needed to deliver that item in a satisfactory state. The added measures to handle these used products also increase its price and part of it must be included as part of the cost implication of buying the used product.

2. Limited Return Policies

The fact that buyers can purchase only second-hand products can be disadvantageous in a way that there are few return policies or even no return policies at all. New products on the other hand are launched with a well-defined return or exchange policy by the manufacturer or seller of the products but the used products are an exception in this case as they are likely to come with limited or none at all return possibilities. This in turn can raise risks for buyers as they end up using a substandard product that the seller cannot fix since it does not recognize the contract. Suppose there is an organization that buys second-hand furniture that is used in the office. Even if it is possible to determine the status and appropriateness of the items, it is possible to find out that the furniture does not fit in the planned location or the quality upon received is substandard. In case the seller has no return policy for used products, then the buyer is left with the challenge of looking for a way to solve this issue or owning the unsuitable products, meaning that he or she was just stuck with a premium price trying to avoid it in the first place.

Therefore, it is necessary for organizations to understand and research the restrictions of refunds or exchanges on the acquisition of used items before purchasing them. This approach actually helps in a more sober evaluation of the risks thus arriving at better cost/benefit ratios.

16.3.7 Perception and Acceptance

1. Stigma

Some industries or applications may have negative connotation, with reference to the use of refurbished or pre-owned item. This stigma can further have a negative prejudice on the procuring organization and its image in securing the customers or clients. Men could argue that the buying of used products portrays a lack of financial strength or a mere show of weakness, as well as the fact that a person is not serious when it comes to quality issues. For instance, a very luxurious hotel that intends to buy used furniture or accessories or even art pieces for interior decoration will be deemed to have made a wrong decision since most of its guests will not wish to associate with old or second-hand items due to the company's reputation of being very luxurious and classy; its guests are expected to get the best quality or new items only. Likewise, technology firm or an organization that uses old and used equipment would be considered behind in innovation, competition, and technology [16].

2. User Acceptance

Another key issue that may emerge in the management of used product acquisition is the resistance by the end-users or stakeholders. People may show resistance or delay in accepting the second-hand products because they may consider these products low-quality, unreliable, and may not function as new ones. Getting past these concerns and persuading consumers that the end product with be valuable and of good quality if often a major challenge for sites selling used products if they have had bad experiences with other preowned products. For example, in an office or working place environment, employees may not accept to work with used office equipment or furniture because often they experience more breakdowns, efficiency is low, or the organization seems to be reluctant to invest in equipment and furniture. Similarly, in the contexts of the healthcare delivery system, patients may raise concerns on issues that relate to health treatment and care that involves the re-use of the medical devices due to reasons of safety, effectiveness, and general quality of health care services.

Achieving broad acceptance in an established consumer base may entail the use of persuasive communication initiatives, the demonstration of the used product's reliability in use and performance, or the total eradicating of the few remaining barriers to its acceptance. Managers also have to be ready for these challenges and mitigate the risks and create a smooth process of adoption and transition to the use of remanufactured goods by the target consumers. The above various factors for procurement have been discussed and for these factors different mitigation strategies to be considered.

16.4 Mitigation Strategies

To address these hindrances, organizations can adopt several strategies to mitigate risks and enhance the benefits of procuring used products. Figure 16.2 indicates the various mitigation strategies which could be integrated with the system.

16.4.1 Thorough Inspection and Testing

The given products must not have flaws regarding their quality and functionality as for the case using pre-owned or second-hand items; inspection and testing are necessary. It is possible to dedicate resources to acquire diagnostic equipment and human capital to perform an analysis of companies for deal- making, detecting any flaw or deficiency that may exist before completing the business acquisition. For instance if a company is looking to purchase used industrial equipment for the purpose of its operations, it would be wise to make use of technical experts or people with related knowledge in the relevant industry; which have the capability to undergo a round check accompanied with operational testing, performance trial and a complete assessment of the specific components thus ensuring that the used equipment is in good working condition as and when purchase is made.

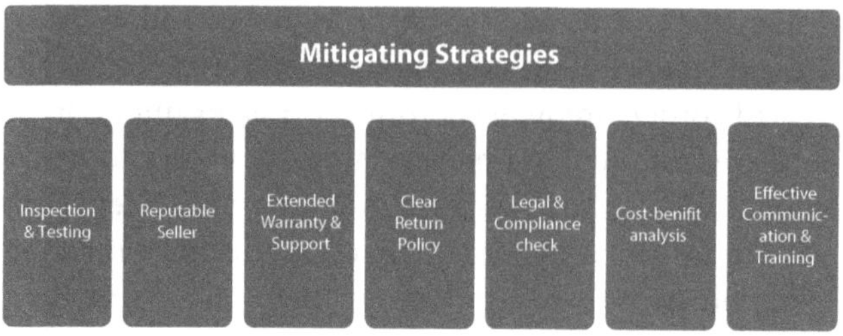

Figure 16.2 Mitigating strategies.

Thus, by inspecting and testing pre-owned products to a considerable extent, before purchasing them, organizations can reduce risks of failures or malfunctions during operation to the minimum. Thus, taking this action also minimizes the risks of time wastage or interruptions and maximizes the usefulness and durability of second-hand items; therefore, deriving better returns on investment. It is seen that, procurement of used products involves certain risks and undertaking a good inspection and test assurance program is one of the important risk management activities to be thought of and planned well while entering such deals where failure of the product may lead to major mishap [14]. The level of quality given and the guarantee of the state and performance of an item flagged give reassurance to the buyer and seller that the item will serve its purpose in terms of its performance characteristics.

16.4.2 Reputable Sellers

When buying pre-owned or second-hand goods, it is vital to establish association with a reliable and trustworthy seller. This requires a complete fact finding and reliability study of prospective sellers, preferably the one known for its consistent performance, transparency, and ethical dealings.

In this context, firms can concentrate their attempts on the used-product sources i.e. certified resellers, authorized dealers or well-reputed online marketplaces that provide guarantees, verification service/seller screening for its customers and in return demand strict conditions from sellers to join their platforms thereby making them accountable for the transaction and minimizing the risk of encountering a seller who may act dishonestly or irresponsibly. Moreover, working with the same trusted suppliers also helps to build confidence in the quality and legitimacy of the used items being purchased. After several positive experiences, and a track record of past successful deals, you know and trust these suppliers. You know how they work; you have a personal relationship; this helps to alleviate fears and navigate through the procurement process with minimal risk exposure.

In addition to this, the sellers who have created goodwill may also provide other benefits like warranties or after sale services or support. This will help you deal with the apprehensions regarding pre-owned goods to a great extent. If you make use of the knowledge and resources of reputable sellers, organizations will obtain improved and protected ways to purchase items.

In the quest for lowering costs and increasing the efficiency of operations, organizations must not compromise between value for money and the expectation of quality and reliability. Engaging credible vendors with good track records in dealing with pre-owned goods, and which practices ethical business, would go a long way towards ensuring a successful and risk-averse acquisition.

16.4.3 Extended Warranties and Support

Some of the risks that are related to the purchase of products, which are used or refurbished, can be avoided provided that the buyer selects a company that offers warranty and support services. These services are essentially associated with charges that have extra value added to them since they can act as an extra safety shield to the buyers and help them to avoid the financial repercussions in case of allergic reactions, product failures or other problems that might occur in future.

In a bid to choose the right vendors to deal with, organizations should consider those who offer warranty on the products they sell as used items. These warranties may help as a protective blanket since the steel mill will have to incur the costs of repair, replacement, and or rectification if and when a defect or malfunction occurs within the warranty period. This added protection can substantially reduce the costs that may be incurred when purchasing used goods since any problems will be the responsibility of the seller or manufacturer.

In addition, after-sales services such as support and technical help in the case of other products for sale can also be a deciding factor when dealing with a seller of second-hand products. It may be possible to intellectualize the fact that credible sellers can provide unique communication lines, help-desk or technical support or maintenance facilities that focus on the used items they are selling. Such a level of support can significantly improve the general dependability and productivity of the purchased commodities because any functional troubles and operational concerns can be solved with assistance from proficient personnel. For example, let us analyze a case of a company that is planning to purchase used IT equipment or some kinds of hardware. In this respect, cooperation with a seller offering a one-year guarantee and engaging in technical support services might be rather useful. If some problems related to hardware, or compatibility with other devices occur during warranty period, the company can address the seller for help, and within the shortest time possible, the problem is solved without affecting productivity.

Based on the theses that sellers with longer warranties and support services are preferred because they mitigate the risks implied by the purchasing of already used products, an organization can achieve the goal. Such an approach not only guarantees the financial shield but also safeguards the organization in ensuring that acquired products are service-worthy, effective and conformance with the organization's performance standards during its useful life.

16.4.4 Clear Return Policies

In other related products such as pre-owned or second-hand products that can be bought online or from physical stores, there is the need to set polices on return in a bid to avoid the probable risks and then to have an avenue to lay our complaints in case we are satisfied or the product does not conform to set standard. Return policies should be negotiated between the business's buyers and sellers and should cover issues like whether it is allowed; periods of time that can elapse before the sale can be returned, and charges if any for returning merchandise.

For instance, imagine an organization that is planning on the purchasing of second hand office furniture. In this regard, arriving at an agreement that permits the return of the products without penalties within a particular period – for example, 30 days – can prove to be useful if the items do not conform to the expected quality or cannot be incorporated appropriately into the workplaces. This clause gives the buyer the right to reverse any procurement errors or situations where the acquired goods are not appropriate for use; therefore, very few losses can be incurred [12].

Policies governing returns are in the interest of the buyer with an emphasis of guaranteeing a good experience in procurement. Thus, giving a guarantee that acquiring pre-owned product has little risks and making a sound decision when it comes to returns. This, in turn, helps to foster a less hostile and more constructive interaction between buyer and seller, since each is proceeding from the assumption that the contract has been carefully discussed and that it is both parties' mutual understanding of the terms and conditions of doing business together. Since individual sellers, industries and merchants have a different approach when it comes to return policies it becomes the buyer's responsibility to read and discuss the policies that would favor them including the acceptable risks. Thus, the possibility of an extension of the return window or better conditions for its implementation must be searched for in exceptional cases, and only when cooperating with reliable sellers or where the amount of a transaction is several tens or hundreds of thousands of dollars.

This paper contends that by focusing on the appropriate creation of the return policies, organizations are in a unique position to mitigate the vulnerability linked to the procurement of used items, all while enhancing the overall corporate honesty and credibility of the procurement networks.

16.4.5 Legal Compliance Checks

There is need to ensure that any used or second hand procurement meets all the legal requirements in compliance laws as this may reduce legal risks. It is the responsibility of the buyers to verify the compliance on matters related to the products to be purchased and this can be done by going through documents and certificates that bear compliance alongside regulations and guidelines that surround the usage of such products. Let us take a case of, a healthcare provider in need of purchasing used medical devices or equipment's. In this regard, it's sensible to verify whether the equipment that has been used and is being bought second-hand, meets the prevailing health and safety requirements of the country. This may require producing certification, approvals, or clearances from the appropriate governmental agencies, assurance that the equipment meets regulation set standards [11].

Lack of compliance to the law on purchasing second hand goods is dangerous since organizations can fall prey to legal repercussions severity including penalties, fines or other lawful consequences. Non-compliance in industries that require much regulation such as healthcare, aviation or construction industries will lead to drastic implications that include endangering patient lives, public health, or the construction project. With proper coverage of compliance checks and detailed documentation review, it is possible to reduce these risks and allow for the efficient implementation of the use of pre-owned products into organizations. Some of these steps could require using the service of regulatory consultants, reviewing standards and code of practices within the Industry or approaching the authorities to get familiar with the laws governing the Industry.

In addition, documentation that is kept consistently and accurately at every stage of the procurement cycle can help in case of an audit or litigation about the company's measure of compliance and diligence. Therefore, legal and regulatory requirements must be placed high on the agenda when sourcing used goods, because the implications of non-adherence could be dire. The issues indicated above mean that by taking the activity approach and carrying out the scrupulous check of the compliance with the requirements of the current legislation and the safety standards, the buyers will be able to include the used products to their operations without high legal risks and probable negative consequences for people.

16.4.6 Cost-Benefit Analysis

Before an organization is prepared to purchase used or second-hand goods, it should carry out a balanced score card to analyze not only the potential cost of the items being procured, but also the cost of having them, including the risks, costs and consequences of the organization's procurement choices. This evaluation should include such critical parameters as the probable expense of the inspection, repair/maintenance costs, the costs incurred in handling/transporting the equipment, and a probable influence on productivity.

For instance consider the case whereby a manufacturing firm planning to embark on the purchase of used machinery or equipment's for manufacturing line. Thus, in the given context, the cost-benefit approach would compare the aggregate of definite and estimated costs of acquiring the used assets together with the cost of sourcing the new, technologically advanced equipment all in consideration with the costs that may accrue from the downtime or productivity losses throughout its life cycle. By reigning in carefully the various distinguishable cost components above, the organization is helped to make its specific, sensible decision and at the same time bring about organizational improvement that balances its financial objectives, constraints, and needs. This analytical approach is helpful to make sure that the marginal cost of getting used products is not out compensated for by incidental costs or poor workflow. Moreover, cost-benefit analysis should not be limited and confined to mere monetary assessment and indicate some other effects, with possible influences on choosing the same including quality of the product, regulatory requirements, or the satisfaction of the customers. Mentioned above is an example of a manufacturing industry where product quality and uniformity play a critical role, and the risk of substandard performance attribute to the aging or worn out equipment may adversely affect the quality of the products, and hence the company's performance and thereby making more careful when opting for cost cutting in such expenses. That is why after performing a cost-benefit analysis; one is likely to come across vulnerable areas, which should be protected against unforeseen circumstances, and risk management strategies that should be taken in order to address unexpected problems.

These evaluation criteria enable decision makers to make a wise choice that ensures the acquisition of pre-owned goods addresses the organizational relevant strategies, needs, and financial objectives [12].

In conclusion, a comprehensive cost benefit analysis is the key decision-making aid with help of which, the intricacies of acquiring used products could be better defined and most of the possible cost advantages together with potential risks and impacts on business operations could be evaluated.

16.4.7 Effective Communication and Training

It is important to ensure the end-users and various stakeholders accept and enforce the usage of the pre-owned or second-hand procured products. It is up to the organizations to effectively convey to their employees and customers the relevance, dependability, and worth of such products; possible issues regarding these items are to be corrected by providing training and subsequent live demonstrations.

For instance, let us take a quagmire in which a firm has decided to incorporate used office equipment into operations. In this case, management can sensitize its employees through conducting training sessions on the analyses and findings of the research for them to accept the changes. While conducting these sessions, the organization can raise issues such as saved money, which is dependent on procurement of second hand equipment, and environmental impact of prolonging the usage of certain assets. Furthermore, the actual displays of operations of the used equipment where the functionality, performance, and reliability are of primary concern can help popularize, that which was once viewed unfavorably. Thus, live demonstrations of the equipment allow end-users to appreciate the practical benefits and potential of receiving pre-owned products. Besides, effective communication and training programs help to improve the level of user readiness and convert it into usage of reused goods within the organization. Addressing these potential concerns before they become defining factors can largely reduce the resistance and assure that the organizations' end-users have the essential knowledge and tools to get the best out of these assets.

Moreover, organization can also provide support through sustaining the communication channel after the development and implementation of the technology; it not only strengthens the user confidence but also allows the organizations to immediately respond to any issue that might emerge during the usage period.

In doing so, with openness in dialogue, modeling initiatives, and selective training approaches, organizations prepare the soil for better acceptance of pre-owned products in office environments. Such a strategic approach, proposed by the project, not only allows increasing operational efficiency and decreasing expenditures but also is aimed at improving ecological and social responsibility within the company.

16.4.8 Integrating Industry 4.0 Tools

AI tools play a pivotal role in enhancing the procurement of used products, especially in the context of integrating circular economy principles as shown in the Figure 16.3. By automating routine tasks, assessing quality, verifying suppliers, optimizing inventory management, and predicting market trends, AI facilitates a more efficient, sustainable, and strategic approach to second-hand procurement.

1. Automating Routine Tasks

AI can significantly streamline procurement processes by automating routine tasks such as order processing, invoice management, and purchase order generation. This automation reduces the administrative burden on procurement teams, allowing them to focus on strategic sourcing and decision-making rather than repetitive tasks. The efficiency gained through AI-driven automation supports a smoother procurement experience

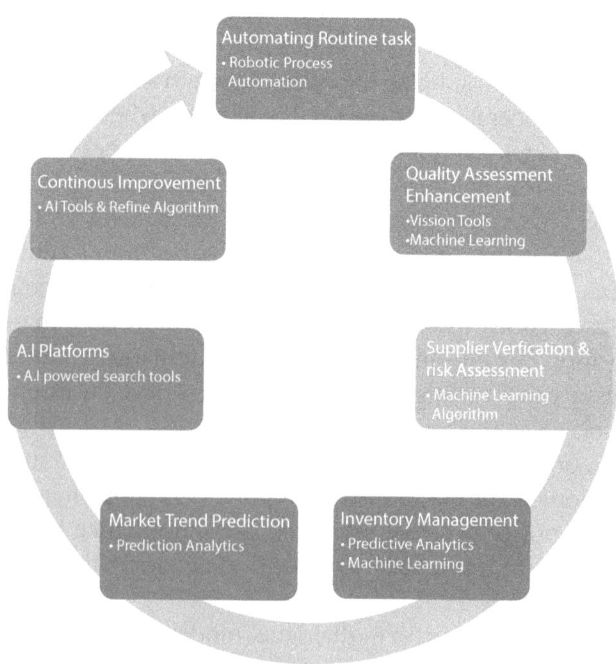

Figure 16.3 Phases to overcome the challenges in procurement of used products.

for used products. Robotic process automation tools such as UiPath or Automation Anywhere automate repetitive tasks like order processing, invoice management, and purchase order generation. These tools help eliminate manual errors and enhance efficiency, enabling procurement professionals to focus on more strategic activities.

2. Quality Assessment Enhancement
AI tools can enhance the quality assessment of used products by utilizing algorithms to detect contaminants, ensure accurate labeling, and perform early quality detection checks. This capability is essential in preventing issues related to quality and safety, particularly in food-related procurement. By improving the quality assurance process, AI fosters greater confidence in sourcing second-hand items, contributing to circular economy practices. Computer vision tools, integrated with machine learning algorithms, assist in assessing the quality of used products. For instance, tools like Inspectiv automate visual inspections and can detect defects or inconsistencies in products. This technology ensures that only quality items are procured and helps maintain standards within the circular economy.

3. Supplier Verification and Risk Assessment
AI is transforming supplier verification and risk assessment by analyzing supplier data from various sources, including financial metrics and compliance records. Machine learning algorithms can identify potential risks associated with suppliers, enhance supplier profiling, and ensure continuous monitoring of supplier performance. These measures safeguard organizations against fraudulent activities and ensure ethical sourcing, which is central to circular procurement. Tools like Sourcify leverage AI algorithms to analyze supplier data for risk assessment and verification. These solutions assess financial stability, compliance history, and operational performance, providing procurement teams with reliable insights to select trustworthy suppliers.

4. Inventory Management Optimization
AI tools optimize inventory management for used products by predicting demand, analyzing resource availability, and identifying recycling opportunities. Utilizing predictive analytics and machine learning, AI helps organizations maintain optimal inventory levels, reducing waste and ensuring that resources are effectively utilized. This optimization is particularly valuable in a circular economy, where resource recovery and reuse are prioritized. AI-powered platforms such as Netstock or Fishbowl

Inventory utilize predictive analytics and machine learning to optimize inventory levels. These systems analyze historical data and market trends to forecast demand, adjust reorder points, and prevent stockouts or overstock situations.

5. Market Trend Prediction
AI plays a crucial role in predicting market trends related to used products by employing predictive analytics models that analyze historical data. This insight enables procurement teams to make informed decisions, proactively identifying opportunities and understanding consumer behavior. By aligning procurement strategies with market trends, organizations can enhance their sourcing tactics for used goods, reinforcing their commitment to sustainable practices. Predictive analytics platforms like IBM Watson Analytics or Microsoft Azure Machine Learning utilize machine learning to evaluate market trends and forecast consumer behavior. These tools analyze various data points, including sales figures and social media sentiment, enabling businesses to make informed decisions about pricing and inventory.

6. Examples of AI Platforms
Several AI-driven platforms facilitate the buying and selling of second-hand goods, which support circular economy efforts. For instance, ThredUp employs AI-powered search tools to help customers find specific items based on descriptions or images, while platforms like Droom optimize the procurement process for used vehicles. These innovations demonstrate how AI can transform the landscape of second-hand procurement, making it more efficient and accessible.

7. Continuous Improvement and Adaptation
Implementing AI in the procurement of used goods within a circular economy requires continuous improvement and adaptation of technologies and practices. Organizations must regularly evaluate AI tools, refine algorithms, and update data to ensure they align with circular principles and enhance overall procurement efficiency.

In summary, integrating AI tools in the procurement of used products empowers organizations to embrace a circular economy by providing the means to automate processes, enhance quality, verify suppliers, optimize inventory, and predict market trends effectively. The potential to drive sustainable practices while achieving operational efficiencies positions AI as a critical enabler in the transition toward a circular economy. Also mapping the influence of this practice with the appropriate sustainable development goal will give much better view of the issue in hand.

16.5 Alignment Towards Sustainable Development Goals [10, 11]

The acquisition of such secondhand or used items for usage can be a noble one that is harmonious with and helps in the fulfillment of several of the Sustainable Development Goals or SDGs as they are commonly referred to by the UN. These global goals, which are centered on the idea of sustainable development and solving the world's problems, can in turn be helped by making careful purchases of used goods. In this section, the authors describe how procurement of fresh products can relate to particular goals of sustainable development.

16.5.1 SDG 12: Rooted in Sustainable Development Goal 12 that Speaks of a 'Responsible Consumption and Production'

Reduction of Waste:
Lifecycle Extension: Through buying and using second-hand or second products, organizations thereby support longer life cycle of products hence limiting production of new product and therefore reducing on production of waste. This practice effectively supports goal 12 of the sustainable development objectives, which require proper waste management, reduction, recycling, and reuse programs.
Resource Conservation: In essence, the consumption of used clothing reduces the demand of the materials and energy needed to produce new products. In this way, the purchase of used items enables organizations to stop using up scarce resources in extraction, processing, and production of associated consumables hence protecting the environment.

Promotion of Sustainable Practices
A circular economy model is therefore a shift from the more conventional linear economy often referred to as the 'take-make-dispose' model. In simple perspectives, the circular economy empowers the efficient usage and recycling of products, components, and materials to its optimum in its entire life cycle without creating much waste and without depleting resources.

The key aim of attaining the objectives of the circular economy heavily relies on the acquisition of used or second-hand goods. In essence, through acquiring and using goods that help in the elongation of their life span organizations are actively involved in the continuous circulation of resources. This practice not only decreases the call for new production but also assists in extending the application of parts and materials that otherwise would have gone through scrapping, hence decreasing the requirement for resource mining and processing. Also, the acquisition of used products contributes to sustainable procurement, which is in sync with the circular economy's main objectives. Through promotion of Product Recovery which involves reusing and adapting most of the products being used in the market, the impacts of resource extraction, manufacturing, and disposal processes are greatly reduced. It enhances the prudent management of the natural resources in the process halving the consumption of raw materials and reducing the amount of wastes and emissions produced.

In addition, the reuse activity leads to the creation of new economic models and services related to the renewal, restoration, rejuvenation of the object. These new IS not only open new economic niches and value streams but also grease the wheel of the Circularity Economy and promote the lengths of product lives and resource throughputs. Implementing the procurement of used products, organizations effectively participate in the circular economy transition that is pursued by society. Keeping with theories of circularity, this practice ensures that resources are used to the optimum level thus reducing wastage, recycling and redesigning the patterns of production and consumption.

16.5.2 SDG 13: Climate Action

Reduction in Greenhouse Gas Emissions

Consumers are encouraged to buy items directly and use second-hand products as a way of reducing the impact of production on nature. This is an area that is worsened by traditional manufacturing methods, which are most of the time characterized by high energy use that enhances bringing out of greenhouse gases. Managing directors and business owners can thus, use their organizations to down play on the demand of new products as well as deal with the issues of resource consuming manufacturing processes, by embracing the adoption of used products. This strategy of an organization also reduces the carbon emissions by playing its proactive role in the minimization of the carbon footprint of organizational operations. In this way, re-use of products also extends their useful life and thus the times between disposal and subsequent need for reproduction is reduced leading to more effectiveness in the decrease of emissions.

Energy Efficiency: The circulation of already used products together with their acquisition to be used reduce energy intensity needed in consumption of raw material to produce new products hence helping to ease climate change. Often, refurbishing or maintenance of used household items consumes significantly lower energy than the amount that is required to manufacture new items from scratch. This sharp decline in energy usage implies a lesser use of non-renewable resources such as fossil and in turn a reduction in negative greenhouse gases which are the main causes of global warming.

16.5.3 SDG 9: Industry, Innovation, and Infrastructure

Innovation in Product Lifecycle Management

The market for used goods creates the increase of innovative and environmentally friendly business strategies that focus on asset management across the product life cycle. Consumer goods are being offered as products-as-a-service, leasing product, or being offered by remanufacturing programs to potentially tap the values of end-of-use products. These fresh strategies ensure the efficient use of resources, reduction of wastes produced, and the enhancement of creative ways of designing products and methods of recovering them in the industrialization process. Besides, such models improve society's understanding of the concept of the circular economy and promote the change in the linear economy model to the circular one.

Infrastructure Efficiency: The incorporation of 'used' or 'second hand' products in business activities can greatly improve the functionality of infrastructure and output without standard calls for significant investments to buy new equipment. Buying second hand equipment, tools, machinery, or any other capital asset is a smarter move than having to pay for brand new items since it enables organizations to place their Cash flows better. It allows companies to align their infrastructure capacity with the requisite opportunities for enhancing productivity rates through the efficacy and versatility of refurbished goods without straining the company's capital resources through extensive purchasing of costly investment assets.

16.5.4 SDG 8: Decent Work and Economic Growth

Cost Savings and Economic Efficiency

The purchasing of second hand or used products creates the possibility of organizations to realize the goal of either cutting cost or using the saved cash in other better profitable ventures hence contributing to the growth of the economy. This practice is most useful to SMEs because most of them work under very tight budgets most of the time. Used products enable SMEs to acquire the equipment, machineries, or other assets needed for production at extremely cheap prices, comparatively cheaper to the new ones. The next benefit of cost leadership is that these cost reductions can be invested back into other segments of the business thus enabling growth, creativity, and diversification. As a result, effectiveness of used products' procurement contributes to SMEs success and overall business productivity and development.

The emerging demand of pre-owned, second/third hand products has pushed the refurbishment, repair and remanufacture markets. These sectors have the significant role in the prolongation of the further use of used products which are in circulation. With the rise of the demand for such services, there is creation of waged employment, which is able to fuel the economic developments and present decent employment chances. Technicians, engineers, and craft persons are required to determine value, working capacity, and general rehabilitation of used products to meet specified quality and performance characteristics. This economic structure not only but creates employment opportunities and the enhancement of skills and business-like portfolios that support people's livelihoods.

16.5.5 SDG 11: Sustainable Cities and Communities

Resource-Efficient Urban Development

Refurbishment of second-hand products to be used in the urban environments provides sustainable on the environmental impacts of the cities and communities. It also can contribute to the outcomes that make cities and towns more resource-efficient and effective, and generally, less vulnerable.

1. Consequently, one of the most effective solutions focused on sustainable urban development can be found in the implementation of second-hand goods consumption, which overcomes the linear model and implements the circular economy concept.
2. Through the process of elongation of the good's life cycle with a view of reusing and or re-applying it, this practice not only helps in conserving those few natural resources that are believed to be remain fixed but they also help in minimizing the problem of waste which is one of the many complications that arise thereof as a result of high population density in the urban cities.
3. The incorporation of second-hand products in people's way of life in cities contributes to changing the consumers' mentality to embrace sustainable resources, using strategies that embrace sustainable living principles.

4. In addition, the proliferation of second-hand product consumption leads to the emergence of new business solutions and services which actually contribute to forming new economic opportunities in rental, repair, and digital sectors, at the same time stimulating conscious consumption.
5. In the light of attempts to create communities that will be sustainable and clinically ready for the next stages of evolution whether in the next hundred years, this is a many-hued approach to dealing with the burden of consumption thus shaping a positive future for our cities.

Affordable Access to Goods

Thus, the upliftment of essential goods and services with cheaper used products can benefit the communities by making them more accessible to people with lower purchasing power and improve the standard of living of such segments.

1. Therefore, inclusive society is the extent to which there is equal provision of necessities for a human being regardless of his/her economic status. Low cost used products are a satisfactory solution, solving the problem of lack of demand for basic items for certain sections of the population.
2. The fact that there are cheap second-hand products enables the low-income earners to afford products they could not otherwise afford. These products range from home appliances and electronics for home, clothing for the body, books and other related products which provide the basic needs for people but are cheap due to people's limited income.
3. Furthermore, the flow of recycled products within the community is sustainable since it reduces the rate at which new items are manufactured and used consequently; the demand for the available natural resources is also reduced. This sustainable strategy not only has a positive effect on the environment but is also compliant with the principles of sustainable development focusing on the satisfaction of the present population's needs while maintaining the ability of the future generations to satisfy their needs.
4. Therefore, when communities ensure that they offer the market the required orders for cheaper used products, they are also supporting vulnerable people and giving them a purpose and hope in life. This can be done through carrying

out campaigns of creating outlets selling used clothes, opening up used car sale companies or simply using the internet through Facebook, and Twitter selling second-hand clothes at affordable prices.

5. However, the availability and accessibility of cheap second-hand goods can be considered as an effective and benefits the step towards creating a society free from significant social injustice for vulnerable and low-income population, and allows providing them with necessary means to lead a decent life and be included in community life.

16.5.6 SDG 17: Partnerships for the Goals

Collaboration and Partnerships

Building Collaborative Networks: Since the procurement of used products comprises of several individuals such as the manufacturers, refurbishes, suppliers, and the end buyers, it implies that their engagement is crucial. Thus, these collaborations complement informational exchange, foster the leadership standard implementation, and contribute to the shared advances towards sustainable development.

1. It is therefore important for manufacturers, refurbishes suppliers and buyers to build socially productive and efficient networks for the procurement of used goods. These are the stakeholders involved in the procurement process and they all work in a chain where they exhibit their special skills in the procurement process.
2. Manufacturers, especially the primary producers of products, are better placed to explain the design of products, the materials used and the processes used in the production of the products which are vital in the refurbishment and resale of products in retail markets. Refurbishes incorporate this into their practice to make sensible decisions in regards to the reconditioning process and quality.
3. Companies that buy used products are referred to as suppliers who facilitate the collection of used products from refurbishes and sale to consumers. Due to their experience and understanding of the market, they create the right

connections between the supply side and the demand side in various geographical areas or sectors.

4. Consumers across the spectrum of the population, from casual users to large-scale commercial companies, offer the demand for the market in used goods. The results also drive the consumer's preferences in the entire supply chain so that the stakeholders can learn and correct their mistakes in the future.
5. Due to the principles of openness, sharing, and practice, these collaborative networks can become a source of progress in the achievement of strategic goals of sustainable development, including the rational use of resources, the reduction of waste, and the implementation of circular economy models.

Global Trade of Used Products: Supporting international trade for reused products makes the countries to continue with their cooperation and come up with the best practices on trade.

1. Today, the practice of using products has no geographical barriers, and people from different countries come together to trade in the market thereby encouraging sustainable marketing on an international level.
2. Through international trade in used products, nations can optimize a set of similarities for favorable exchange ratio and maximum consumption and utilization of a consumption item globally.
3. This kind of global partnership fosters the exchange of information, ideas, technology, and the successful strategies in the management, distribution, or proper disposal of used products, thereby bringing positive improvements to sustainability.
4. Cross-border trade in second-hand goods is beneficial to emerging economies because it avails cheap consumer items and generates employment in re-sale and refurbishment industries.
5. Furthermore, the integration of the standards, the regulations, and the policies in the specific field of the cross-border trade which involves the used products can promote fairness, consumer protection, and environment conservation over the globe.

16.6 Conclusion

In conclusion, the procurement of used goods offers a strategic avenue for organizations to simultaneously reduce costs, enhance sustainability, and align with the principles of a circular economy. By extending the lifespan of products, companies can minimize their capital expenditures, reduce waste, and contribute to the conservation of valuable resources. This practice supports Sustainable Development Goals (SDGs), particularly responsible consumption and production, while fostering a more eco-conscious approach to industrial operations. However, despite these advantages, the procurement of used goods also comes with significant challenges that can hinder its successful implementation.

To fully realize the advantages of second-hand procurement, organizations must adopt a systematic and strategic approach. This includes integrating best practices such as conducting thorough product assessments, selecting reputable suppliers, ensuring legal compliance, and establishing clear return policies. Moreover, leveraging technological advancements, such as AI for quality assessments and market trend analysis, can further enhance the efficiency and reliability of second-hand procurement processes.

Despite these challenges, the potential benefits of second-hand procurement are significant. Organizations can achieve substantial cost savings, increase resource efficiency, and reduce their environmental impact. The extension of product life cycles through reuse and refurbishment supports a transition towards a more circular economy, where waste is minimized, and resource use is optimized. Additionally, procuring used goods can stimulate innovation in supply chain management, as companies develop new strategies for quality assurance, vendor management, and risk mitigation.

In summary, while the procurement of used goods presents various challenges, these can be effectively managed through a combination of rigorous quality control, strategic supplier relationships, and adherence to regulatory frameworks. By overcoming these obstacles, organizations not only benefit financially but also contribute to broader sustainability goals, helping to create a more resource-efficient and environmentally responsible economy. This practice embodies the core tenets of the circular economy, demonstrating that the reuse of products can be both a sustainable and economically viable strategy for modern businesses [11].

References

1. Chen, L. and Zhang, M., Technological Solutions for Evaluating Used Products. *J. Manuf. Technol. Manage.*, 29, 7, 1223–1240, 2018.
2. Foster, G., Circular economy strategies for adaptive reuse of cultural heritage buildings to reduce environmental impacts. *Resour. Conserv. Recycl.*, 152, 104507, 2020.
3. Fang, C., Liu, X., Pardalos, P.M., Pei, J., Optimization for a three-stage production system in the Internet of Things: procurement, production and product recovery, and acquisition. *Int. J. Adv. Manuf. Technol.*, 83, 689–710, 2018.
4. Green, P. and Wilson, R., Legal and Regulatory Challenges in Used Product Procurement. *J. Bus. Law*, 58, 2, 298–320, 2020.
5. Hart, A., Cost Savings through Procurement of Used Machinery and Equipment. *J. Ind. Econ.*, 45, 3, 231–250, 2018.
6. Johnson, A., Products Liability Reform: A Hazard to Consumers. *NCL Rev.*, *56*, 677, 1978.
7. Kim, S. and Choi, Y., Trust and Transparency in Online Marketplaces for Used Products. *Electron. Commer. Res. Appl.*, 36, 100894, 2019.
8. Miller, J. and Jones, L., Operational Risks in Used Product Procurement. *Oper. Manage. Rev.*, 52, 4, 402–419, 2017.
9. Patel, S. and Singh, R., Certification and Reputable Sellers in the Used Product Market. *Supply Chain Manage. Rev.*, 23, 4, 69–84, 2019.
10. Russell-Bennett, R., Rosenbaum, M.S., Fisk, R.P., Raciti, M.M., SDG editorial: improving life on planet earth–a call to action for service research to achieve the sustainable development goals (SDGs). *J. Serv. Mark.*, 38, 2, 145–52, 2024.
11. Sadic, S., Demir, E., Crispim, J., Towards a connected world: Collaborative networks as a tool to accomplish the SDGs. *J. Clean. Prod.*, 28, 142726, 2024.
12. Sasikumar, P. and Kannan, G., Issues in reverse supply chains, part I: end-of-life product recovery and inventory management–an overview. *Int. J. Sustain. Eng.*, 1, 3, 154–72, 2008.
13. Sivakumar, K., Mathivathanan, D., Nishal, M., Vimal, K.E., Subhaa, R., Pandian, R.S., Safar, L., Sopko, J., Krishnan, S., Gupta, S., Mathiyazhagan, K., Ensuring sustainability in industry 4.0: implementation framework, in: *Sustainable Manufacturing for Industry 4.0*, pp. 215–252, CRC Press, Boca Raton, 2020.
14. Smith, R. and Nguyen, T., Standardizing Evaluation Protocols for Used Products. *Int. J. Qual. Reliab. Manage.*, 35, 5, 789–805, 2018.
15. Wang, Y., Huscroft, J.R., Hazen, B.T., Zhang, M., Green information, green certification and consumer perceptions of remanufactured automobile parts. *Resour. Conserv. Recycl.*, *128*, 187–196, 2018.
16. Zhang, Y. and Li, X., Hidden Costs in Used Product Procurement: A Risk Analysis. *Bus. Strategy Environ.*, 29, 2, 130–143, 2020.

17

How does Personality Trait Affect Sustainable Logistics Management in the Banking Sector?

Navita Nathani[1*] **and Gaurav Soin**[2]

[1]*Amity Business School, Amity University, Gwalior, Madhya Pradesh, India*
[2]*Prestige Institute of Management and Research, Gwalior, Madhya Pradesh, India*

Abstract

The objective of this research is to investigate the impact of bank employees' personality traits on their sustainable logistic decisions. This study uses a survey method to assess the impact of personality traits on sustainable logistics management among banking employees in central India. A total of 200 valid responses were collected and structural equation modeling software Smart-PLS was applied to analyze the overall model while SPSS 17 was applied to check the effect of demographic factors. The empirical findings suggest that agreeableness, openness, extraversion positively and neuroticism negatively but affects significantly to sustainable logistic management decision while conscientiousness has no impact. The study further revealed that how bank employees' demographic factors like bank types, job levels, age and gender affects sustainable logistic decisions which disclosed interesting results that job levels and bank types do matters while age and gender do not. It offers a distinct viewpoint on sustainable logistics and the personal characteristics of bank employees contributing to the development of a more responsible and sustainable logistic ecosystem in banks. It also attracts future researchers to study the readiness of banks towards sustainable management practices.

Keywords: Big 5 personality traits, sustainable logistics management, bank employees, central India, demography, bank types, job levels

**Corresponding author*: drnavita810@gmail.com

K. Mathiyazhagan, Krishna Kumar Dadsena, Rajesh Kumar Singh, Aakanksha Kishore and Andrea Appolloni (eds.) Sustainable Operations of Logistics and Supply Chain Management, (415–436) © 2025 Scrivener Publishing LLC

17.1 Introduction

In the rapidly changing global economic environment, there's a growing recognition among banking institutions regarding the relevance of integrating sustainability principles into operations and support services. This understanding stems from the realization that financial success is deeply associated with environmental, social, and governance (ESG) factors, leading to a shift in how banks approach traditional logistics and investment methods [10]. Understanding the complexity of how personality characteristics affect the formation of banking policies and funding directions can turn into not only an academic endeavor, but also a rather substantial progress in terms of enhancing the further specific transformations of the overall financial system [8]. In today's financial environment, the incorporation of sustainability concepts is a critical factor for institutions seeking to align both their logistics and their financial strategies with ESG factors.

While exploring the wealth of knowledge available on sustainable financing and operation, what becomes conspicuous is that little is known about how every personality of a bank is involved in the provision of sustainable decisions at the employee level. The financial sector which is assumed to be diverse by nature found people with different personality traits concerning the attitudes, risk perception, and decisions for sustainable logistic initiatives and investments [6].

While a substantial body of literature examines the factors influencing sustainable investment and operational decisions, there remains a notable gap in understanding how individual personal characteristics impact the decisions made by bank employees in this area. As financial institutions increasingly emphasize integrating sustainability into their decision-making frameworks, it becomes essential to explore the nuanced ways in which employees' unique personality traits may shape their attitudes, perceptions, and behaviors regarding sustainable logistics management practices [16]. Despite the potential importance of personality traits in this context, a comprehensive study is necessary to address this knowledge gap and provide valuable insights for both academia and the banking sector.

The intention behind the study is to elaborate the study of personality traits that may affect the sustainable logistic decisions of the employees of banks. The research will examine important personality model, more specifically the five-factor model [15] that encompasses, openness, conscientiousness, extraversion, agreeableness, and neuroticism to reveal how these attributes influence awareness, preferences, and decisions in the banking industry.

17.1.1 Research Gap

As research on sustainable operations and logistics management continues to expand across various industries, a notable gap persists in exploring the banking sector. Though extensive research has been done to investigate the impact of the Big 5 inherent characteristics on financial decisions and investment behaviors, there is limited literature that measures these effects on sustainable logistics activities within banks. The banking sector presents distinctive challenges and opportunities that are not typically found in other industries, such as strict regulatory requirements, a strong emphasis on trust and reliability, and the vital role of sustainable logistics in ensuring an efficient banking system where personality traits plays a vital role in decision making. It also checks the readiness of bank employee towards sustainable logistics.

To bridge this gap, the paper seeks to explore the intricate relationship between the personality traits of banking employees and their contribution to sustainable logistics management, with a particular focus on below mentioned objectives.

17.1.2 Objectives

- To assess the impact of employee's big 5 inherent traits on sustainable logistic management of banks.
- To analyze the impact on sustainable logistic management across the demographic variables age, gender, job levels and type of banks.

17.2 Literature Review

17.2.1 Sustainable Logistics Management

The Big 5 inherent characteristics of banking employees are essential because banking operations such as sustainable logistics management largely rely on them. If the employees are capable of performing their duties they may align it with the Bank's goals of sustainable logistics management. But it's a pity that very limited research was conducted on the interaction between the Big 5 inherent characteristics and sustainable logistics decision-making within the banking sector. In the shifting terrain, the researcher's interest in logistics management is increasing day by day but from the findings of this literature, it becomes clear that logistics practices have to embrace environmentalism to foster such long-term sustainability and a dearth of research was found. One of the main topics is the application of green logistics strategies that include the selection of efficient transport routes, the usage of low-emission vehicles, and the implementation of energy-saving storage facilities in the banks [22]. Research has demonstrated that such practices are not only beneficial in minimizing carbon emissions, but also in saving costs, and enhancing organizational image [28]. The use of technology to support sustainable logistics cannot be overemphasized, as developments in information and communication technologies enhance live tracking, inventory control, and overall supply chain transparency [12]. Interorganizational relationships are also emphasized as a best practice because the resources are shared in implementing sustainability across the supply chain [5]. However, issues of high implementation costs, non-standardization, and resistance to change remain as influential considerations that require further research and policy interventions to popularize sustainable logistics best practices [3]. The literature states that the integrated solution incorporating technology, partnership, and policy measures is crucial to the effective application of sustainable logistics management in the banking sector.

17.2.2 Personality Traits

Sustainability in logistics operations within the banking sector is inherently tied to various personality attributes of bank employees. Personality encompasses the characteristics of an individual that lead to consistent patterns of emotional, cognitive, and behavioral responses. These patterns are closely linked to the personality traits of the individual, which are known to remain stable over time and are comparable across different contexts, particularly in research settings [4]. These five trait dimensions were initially introduced by D. W. Fiske in 1949, but were significantly expanded [21]. As a result, the FFM is considered the most widely utilized structural model in personality assessment and research.

Among all personality factors, these traits have a considerable impact on employees' attitudes, acceptance, and incorporation of sustainable practices when addressing sustainable logistics management in the banking sector. For example, employees with high conscientiousness can be more careful in their compliance with the sustainable logistics procedures and standards, while the openness to the experience may involve more creative solutions for sustainable logistics management [4]. They include extraversion and agreeableness which enable efficient people interactions, which are crucial when implementing sustainability programs involving representatives from different areas of the firm [6, 16]. On the other hand, high neuroticism may slow the rates of embracing sustainable practices because it induces stress and reduces the acceptance of change [21].

The relationship between these personality characteristics and sustainable logistics operations plays itself out given the role that such banks want to play in the enhancement of their ESG performance. Thus, with regard to account of personality theories, [15] identified that when training and sustainable initiatives are suitable matched with the unique personality profiles of bank's employees, sustainable practicing will be fostered effectively. The alignment likewise improves operating performance and strengthens the banking industry that would enable it to face and solve the problems of sustainability. Ref. [2] has identified 4 personality types, which indirectly relate to the level of sustainable social responsibility through bricolage: openness, conscientiousness, and agreeableness. Some of them proposed that these traits should be prioritized by enterprises when there is need to address issues to do with efficient utilization of resources and welfare of the stakeholders. SMEs that are family-owned should ensure that the resource tasks are allocated to those individuals who possess the personality traits that include openness, neuroticism, and conscientiousness because such individuals engage in bricolage.

17.2.3 Openness

Openness personality is associated with aspects like open-mindedness, imagination, and creativity. They continuously look for new idea, new aesthetics, and new anything [13]. This trait can prominently affect the actions within the banking sphere, especially in regard to sustainable logistics activities. This is particularly important since the openness element of the personality indicates receptiveness to fresh, sustainable ideas and practices among employees. This feature's effects are also present in the financial choices made for an enterprise. Ref. [20] also had similar experimentation with business school graduates and deduced that extroverts are therefore likely to trade more frequently and invest more in shares. This research pointed out that, interpersonal openness leads to the logistics decision-making to accept the idea of using heuristics such as the rule of thumb [24]. Some of the variables that they identified include; [23] observed that banking professionals with higher openness to experience perform better, in that, they are creative and more likely to make sustainable logistic decisions. They further argued that sustainable logistic practices mean embracing and implementing of change and that change is more preferred by extroverts. These aspects reveal that people belonging to this generation possess a creative mind and are more open to change, which will be crucial in coming up with and embracing sustainable logistics solutions. This understanding of the link between personality traits and the sustainability of operations can assist banks in improving their sustainability efforts, to optimally use the workers' strengths, which eventually improves efficiency and effectiveness when pursuing sustainable objectives [29].

17.2.4 Conscientiousness

The conscientious personality can be easily described with such characteristics as punctuality, persistence, goal orientation, reliability, and well organization, besides, people with such personality type hardly ever risks; though, major risks are supposed to be out of their sphere [20]. These traits are very useful in the context of banking sector logistics because they support the economy and reliability of sustainable operations. Self-directed employees are expected to follow the protocols in sustainability to the letter and would see to it that all the logistic processes are properly done systematically [29].

When it comes to financial decisions, conscientious individuals are personalities who should not be deceivable by other people or controlled by them as they make sound logistic decisions. According to [13], conscientious persons seem to be engaged in the decision-making process - which requires their time and effort, and cannot be regarded as sloppy or casual. This particular trait makes them more circumspect in their logistic decisions and wiser regarding sustainability [30]. Ref. [7] discovered that the anti-social personality had a positive correlation with logistics management behavior, a fact that shows that people with high conscientiousness are cautious and careful with their logistic activities. The study further continued that apparently conscientious subordinates are in a position to boost the efficacy of sustainable logistic implementation by their orderly and loyal nature. They are also supposed to play a leadership role in the aspect of sustainability where it is expected that operations of organizations will not only be effective but also sustainable in its usage of resources. Banks could build better training and development for the flow of serious and reliable sustainable practices through analyzing the integration of conscientiousness in sustainable logistics [17].

17.2.5 Extraversion

As stipulated by [21] and [18], extraverts are socially engaging, positive thinking, thrill pursuing, and comfortable in large groups. This personality trait must have a strong effect on patterns of logistic course of action typically for the banking industry. If a person is extraverted, his/her information processing is only the positive one, which affects the judgment of probabilities of success and provides overconfidence in logisticians' decisions [27].

In light of the above arguments, [20] proposed that extraverts are sociable and their risky disposition makes them participate in the management of the aspects of logistics more than intraverts. According to [7] show that personality trait such as extraversion has a positive relation to the ability of an individual in taking risks which are constructive in making of logistic decisions.

Ref. [4] examined the present study with the hypothesis that there is a connection between personality traits and logistics by analyzing the household's personality given that extraverted employees' optimism and sociability could be an asset. It may prompt them to support and engage in sustainability activities since they could be enthusiastic in promoting sustainable internal functions within the organization. Thus, their main weakness that has to be regulated in order to achieve the goals pertaining to sustainability is overconfidence and risk-taking. The usefulness of extraversion within sustainable logistics for the banking industry is again seen in the application of detailed guidelines to deal with both the benefits and drawbacks of extraverted employees in the specific context of a bank's operations. Furthermore, improving collaborative work as a result of the banking industry making it easier for their employees' energy to focus on sustainable objectives will increase the ability to implement sustainable logistics efficiently [9].

17.2.6 Agreeableness

Agreeableness is a personality attribute that defines social and interpersonal orientation, kindness, friendliness, generosity, and politeness [20]. Highly agreeable individuals are popular and prefer to defer to the authorities instead of deriving the logic themselves [6]. It brings about a positive perception of information as given by other people, especially as agreeable people usually do not go out of their way to look for trouble. Amiable staff share ideas and participate willingly in the implementations of sustainable development strategies in their organization. This personality domain entails aspects such as teamwork and cooperation, and can therefore enhance interdepartmental interaction, guarantee that sustainable logistics practices are adopted and implemented without compromise [21]. The positive aspects of the self can sometimes be problematic, especially when the person is reliant upon others' opinions, and avoids self-assessment. While employees who work well with others may embrace the strategies being put in place in sustainable management, other employees may require encouragement to exercise their independent decisions and even challenge the sustainability practices being used. Understanding this balance is therefore essential for the banks that wish to utilize the benefits of hostile employees while at the same time catering for their demerits. The impact of disagreeableness with sustainable logistics management can act as a guideline for banks to create effective training modules and develop an organizational culture that promotes collaborative problem-solving. Thus, by utilizing such opportunities, banks can improve their sustainability agendas and guarantee that their logistics processes are optimized for efficiency and environmental impact [18].

17.2.7 Neuroticism

This follows the effects that neuroticism which is a personality factor that comprises of traits such as emotional instability, anxiety, and mood swings has on sustainable logistics operations within the banking sector. High neurotics' failed to demonstrate significant strength in areas such as conceptual understanding, critical thinking, cognitive skills and analytical skills, and so feel fear and anxiety during risk taking [21, 32]. This fear and anxiety is likely to result in unfavorable logistic decisions thus its importance [11].

According to [25], neurotic people are inclined to make no sustainable logistic decisions. Following the work of [26], it is possible to find out negative link between neuroticism and risky behavior, which underlines the cautiousness of neurotic people in the context of sustainable logistic. Neurotic employees' reluctance and lack of willingness to take risks to limit their choices to low-risk options may cause them to act more carefully and avoidantly when implementing sustainability strategies. Although this precaution minimizes a hasty decision and assesses and implements best the sustainability initiatives, it could also lead to a delay on the implementation of more innovative and advantageous sustainability practices. Neuroticism to present sustainably on logistics operations allows the banking organization to build an approach to target neurotic workers including well-defined rules of working, low variability approaches, and stress-fighting tools. Therefore, catering for the particular needs of neurotic employees in the banking sector can ensure the availability of positive and efficient way of supporting sustainable logistics management [31].

H1: There is a positive correlation between Big 5 personality traits on Sustainable Logistic Decisions.
H2: There is a significant impact on sustainable logistic management across the demography (age, gender, and type of bank and job level).

17.3 Research Methodology

This study employs an exploratory approach using a survey research method to understand the inherent traits and sustainable logistics management among banking employees in the central region of India. The research focuses on banking staff from public, private, and cooperative banks across three levels-lower, middle, and higher within the four largest cities of Madhya Pradesh: Bhopal, Indore, Jabalpur, and Gwalior. Out of 279 respondents contacted through field investigators ensuring proportional representation from different types of banks and hierarchical levels, 200 banking professionals were selected using a stratified random sampling technique. Primary data was collected using a questionnaire on personality traits developed by [14] and the Sustainable Logistics Management survey by [1]. The questionnaires, based on a 5-point Likert scale, were administered both in hard copy and *via* Google Forms, depending on respondent preference. Secondary data was gathered from literature reviews and theoretical models. Data analysis involved reliability and validity testing, structural equation modeling and ANOVA.

17.4 Data Analysis

This study's hypothesis testing and data analysis were conducted using Partial Least Squares Structural Equation Modeling (PLS-SEM) with Smart-PLS ver3.0. The PLS-SEM analysis distinguishes between two types of correlations: outer model, which estimates convergent validity, discriminant validity, and reliability, and the inner model which also measures up the aforementioned elements according to [35].

17.4.1 Validity and Reliability of Results

The variable with reflective indicators is considered to have passed the test if both Cronbach's alpha and composite reliability are not less than 0.70 [33].

Table 17.1 Reliability metrics.

Latent variable constructs	Cronbach's alpha	Composite reliability (rho_a)	Composite reliability (rho_c)	Average variance extracted (AVE)
Agreeableness	0.799	0.811	0.908	0.832
Conscientiousness	0.810	0.811	0.887	0.724
Extraversion	0.814	0.818	0.890	0.729
Neuroticism	0.890	0.892	0.931	0.819
Openness	0.778	0.796	0.900	0.818
Sustainable Logistics Management	0.870	0.913	0.905	0.568

The reliability test results are displayed in Table 17.1; all the Cronbach alpha and reliability values are above 0.70 showing that all the study constructs are reliable. The underlying principle is that a construct measure (indicator) must have a high correlation. This is accomplished through convergent testing in Smart-PLS 3.0, as the value of all variables of the required construct exceeds a loading factor of 0.70 [33] as shown in Table 17.2.

Table 17.2 Factor loadings.

Latent variable constructs	Outer loadings
AG1 <- AG	0.898
AG2 <- AG	0.925
CO1 <- CO	0.843
CO2 <- CO	0.862
CO3 <- CO	0.849
EX1 <- EX	0.836
EX2 <- EX	0.842
EX3 <- EX	0.883
NU1 <- NU	0.899
NU2 <- NU	0.905
NU3 <- NU	0.912
OP1 <- OP	0.886
OP2 <- OP	0.922
SLM1 <- SLM	0.820
SLM2 <- SLM	0.817
SLM3 <- SLM	0.759
SLM4 <- SLM	0.875
SLM5 <- SLM	0.845
SLM6 <- SLM	0.882
SLM7 <- SLM	0.702
SLM8 <- SLM	0.802

17.4.2 Discriminant Validity

Discriminant validity primarily targets establishing the extent to which a set of variables diverge from each other in terms of different dimensions. [34] proposed that the value of cross-loading should be less than the square root of AVE for each factor. As shown in Table 17.3 and Table 17.4, the square root of AVE for the factors (in bold) is higher than the components' correlation. Consequently, the findings from this study support the preliminary conclusion derived from the preceding analysis that the instrument employed in this study passes both the convergent and discriminant validity tests.

17.4.3 Coefficients of Determination (R2) and Adjusted R2 (R2 adj.)

R-square is the measure that represents the degree of variations in an endogenous (dependent) variable explained by exogenous (independent) variables. It assists in measuring the adequacy of a selected model. The R-square value of 0.75 is considered a substantial (excellent) model, 0.50 as a moderate (medium) model, and 0.25 as a weak (poor) model. The adjusted R-square is applied to enhance the explained variance, which decreases the R-square value considering the addition of non-significant exogenous latent variables. As presented in Table 17.5, the model has a predictive accuracy (R^2 adjusted) value of 0.815 for sustainable logistics management [36].

Table 17.3 Discriminant validity.

	AG	CO	EX	NU	OP	SLM
Agreeableness	**0.912**					
Conscientiousness	0.725	**0.851**				
Extraversion	0.769	0.714	**0.854**			
Neuroticism	0.803	0.732	0.778	**0.905**		
Openness	0.572	0.708	0.654	0.582	**0.904**	
Sustainable Logistics Management	0.827	0.754	0.806	0.843	0.686	**0.754**

Table 17.4 Cross loadings.

	AG	CO	EX	NU	OP	SLM
AG1	**0.898**	0.674	0.662	0.663	0.526	0.696
AG2	**0.925**	0.651	0.736	0.795	0.519	0.606
CO1	0.588	**0.843**	0.613	0.624	0.739	0.673
CO2	0.626	**0.862**	0.620	0.636	0.539	*0.623
CO3	0.638	**0.849**	0.589	0.609	0.520	0.627
EX1	0.642	0.538	**0.836**	0.646	0.551	0.679
EX2	0.635	0.595	**0.842**	0.606	0.522	0.647
EX3	0.690	0.690	**0.883**	0.735	0.598	0.736
NU1	0.703	0.637	0.692	**0.899**	0.490	0.734
NU2	0.709	0.638	0.695	**0.905**	0.538	0.742
NU3	0.767	0.709	0.725	**0.912**	0.549	0.608
OP1	0.481	0.592	0.525	0.465	**0.886**	0.561
OP2	0.549	0.683	0.648	0.579	**0.922**	0.671
SLM1	0.740	0.647	0.696	0.771	0.597	**0.820**
SLM2	0.748	0.581	0.673	0.756	0.462	**0.817**
SLM3	0.575	0.597	0.574	0.614	0.576	**0.759**
SLM4	0.696	0.643	0.716	0.725	0.615	**0.875**
SLM5	0.719	0.646	0.628	0.695	0.471	**0.845**
SLM6	0.117	0.073	0.043	0.123	0.072	**0.882**
SLM7	0.514	0.543	0.586	0.510	0.596	**0.802**
SLM8	0.626	0.589	0.662	0.632	0.564	**0.802**

Table 17.5 Coefficients of determination.

	R-square	R-square adjusted
SLM	0.820	0.815

Figure 17.1 illustrates the Results of the PLS Structural Model, highlighting relationships between constructs, significance levels, and explained variance. Figure 17.2 presents the Structural Model of the Path Coefficient, emphasizing direct, indirect effects, and strength of associations among variables.

The results of hypotheses testing are listed in Table 17.6. Hypothesis 1 tests the impact of Agreeableness (AG) on Sustainable Logistics Management (SLM), T statistics of 3.527 and P value of 0.000 show the significant relationship between SLM and AG. Hypothesis 2 depicts the effect of Conscientiousness (CO) on SLM. The T value is 0.719 and P=0.472 shows no significant effect between the two variables. Hypothesis 3, which tests the impact of Extraversion (EX) on SLM is supported. There is a statistically significant relationship between the two variables at T=2.866 and p=0.004. Hypothesis 4 tests the relationship between Neuroticism (NU) and SLM. The p-value is 0.000, and the T statistic is 4.696, which shows a significant relationship between NU and SLM. Hypothesis 5 showcases the relationship between Openness (OP) and SLM. The T statistic is 3.322 and the P value is 0.001, which shows the substantial relationship.

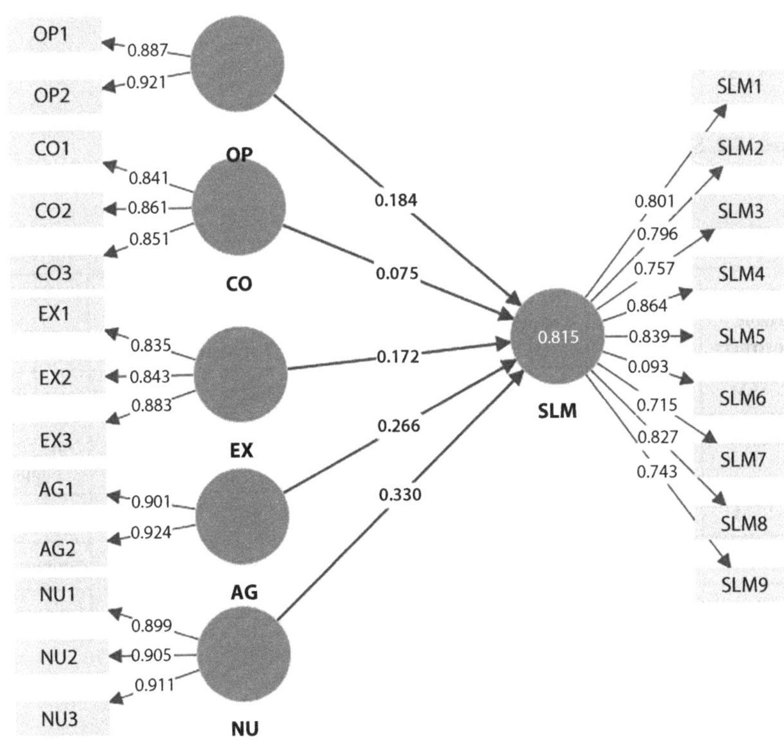

Figure 17.1 Results of the PLS structural model.

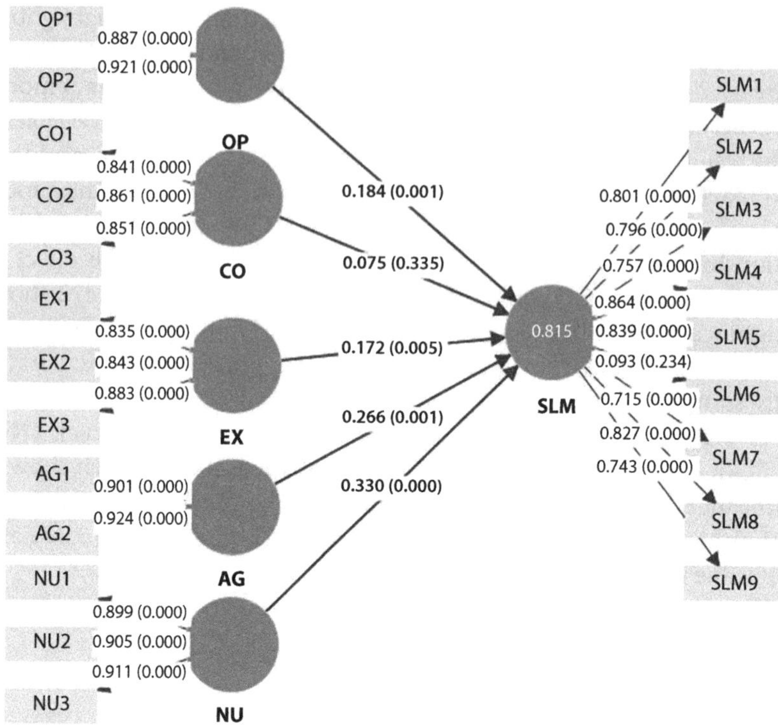

Figure 17.2 Structural model of the path coefficient.

Table 17.6 Results of hypothesis testing.

Latent variable constructs	Hypothesis	Original sample (O)	Sample mean (M)	Standard deviation (STDEV)	T statistics	P values	Decision
AG -> SLM	H1	0.282	0.279	0.080	3.527	0.000	Supported
CO -> SLM	H2	0.053	0.063	0.073	0.719	0.472	Not Supported
EX -> SLM	H3	0.170	0.164	0.059	2.866	0.004	Supported
NU -> SLM	H4	0.342	0.345	0.073	4.696	0.000	Supported
OP -> SLM	H5	0.178	0.174	0.053	3.322	0.001	Supported

The study's outcomes portray the considerable influence of inherent traits on sustainable logistics management within the banking industry, emphasizing the significance of employees' characteristics in shaping their sustainability approach. These results align with existing research on sustainable logistics management, which stresses the necessity of incorporating environmental considerations into logistics practices to achieve long-term sustainability [22, 28]. In particular, the implementation of green logistics strategies—such as optimizing transportation routes, curbing emissions, and utilizing energy-efficient warehousing—has been shown to diminish carbon footprints, yield cost savings, and bolster corporate reputation [28]. Moreover, the importance of technology and collaboration among supply chain partners has been recognized as essential in advancing sustainable logistics [5, 12].

In terms of personality traits, the results indicate that openness, extraversion, and neuroticism are statistically significant predictors of sustainable logistics management, while conscientiousness, although positive, is not statistically significant. Agreeableness, meanwhile, has a relatively strong impact compared to other traits. These findings are consistent with previous research on personality traits and decision-making. Individuals with high openness to experience are known for their creativity and willingness to adopt new ideas [13, 19], making them likely to innovate in sustainable logistics practices. Extraverted individuals, characterized by their sociability and optimism [18, 21], tend to engage more actively in logistic management and are more willing to take risks, which can be advantageous for sustainability initiatives [4, 7]. However, the results are contradictory, Conscientious individuals often fail to persevere when faced with difficult or unpleasant situations in the banks. Insufficient planning among banking professionals hinders effective sustainable logistic decisions. Due to the hostile environment in banks and the extensive workload banking professionals face, they lack time to make sustainable logistic decisions. These individuals often experience burnout, depletion of energy, and develop negative attitudes towards banking activities.

On the other hand, neuroticism negatively impacts sustainable logistics management, as neurotic individuals often experience fear and anxiety, hindering their decision-making abilities [21, 32]. This aligns with findings from [11, 25], who noted the cautious and risk-averse nature of neurotic individuals. Agreeableness, characterized by cooperation and helpfulness [20], facilitates better teamwork and communication, which are essential for implementing sustainability initiatives effectively [21]. However, the tendency to rely on others' judgments can present challenges in scenarios requiring critical evaluation [6].

The study's findings underscore the importance of understanding the interplay between personality traits and sustainable logistics operations. Banks aiming to enhance their ESG performance can benefit from aligning sustainability training and initiatives with the personality profiles of their employees, thereby fostering a supportive environment for sustainable practices [15]. By leveraging the strengths of employees' personality traits, banks can improve operational efficiency and contribute to a more robust and resilient financial ecosystem capable of addressing sustainability challenges. These insights are particularly valuable for designing targeted training programs, fostering a collaborative work culture, and developing strategies to support employees with varying personality traits towards sustainable logistics management [17, 31].

17.4.4 Demographic Factors and Sustainable Logistic Management

The results of the analysis revealed that demographic variables significantly affect the dependent variable, Sustainable Logistic Management (SLM) as shown in Table I (as shown in annexure). The overall model is significant, as indicated by the corrected model's F-value of 2.758 and a p-value of .000, suggesting that the predictors collectively explain a considerable portion of the variance in SLM ($R^2 = .386$, Adjusted $R^2 = .246$). Bank Type significantly affects SLM ($F = 3.476$, $p = .033$), implying that different types of banks and levels lead to different SLM outcomes. Gender and Level interaction is also significant ($F = 5.377$, $p = .005$), indicating that the relationship between gender and job level affects SLM. Age, Gender, Bank Type interaction ($F = 3.205$, $p = .043$) and Age, Gender, and Job Level interaction ($F = 3.173$, $p = .044$) are significant, suggesting that these factors influence SLM. Non-significant effects include the main effects of Age ($p = .913$), Gender ($p = .367$), as well as most of the interaction terms, implying that these factors do not individually influence SLM in this model.

These results are in concordance with previous research, which stipulates that the type of a bank, be it public, private, or cooperative highly determines the strategies for sustainability. Public banks tend to be keener in applying sustainable logistics since they are regulated stringently, while private banks may establish sustainable strategies to build a good image and to cut costs [28]. Since cooperative banks are primarily targeted to serve the needs of their members and society in general, sustainability is also considered as a part of CSR programs for cooperative banks. Further, the Gender and Job Level interaction ($F = 5.377$, $p = .005$) indicates that

SLM is affected by gender and position at the same time. This is supported by previous research concerning gender variations in sustainability leadership, where women in higher ranks are more likely to support the sustainability agenda [37]. The interactions of Age, Gender, and Bank Type ($F = 3.205$, $p = .043$) and Age, Gender, and Job Level ($F = 3.173$, $p = .044$) depict how the combined impact of these factors influence sustainable logistics decision-making, which are in parity with the findings [38] that that emphasizes the importance of considering demographic intersections when designing sustainability programs.

17.5 Implications

The implications of managing sustainable operations in the logistics of the banking sector, considering the relationship with banking employees' personality traits, are profound and multifaceted. Understanding how personality traits influence sustainable logistics decisions can lead to more effective and tailored strategies that align with employees' natural tendencies, thus enhancing operational efficiency and environmental responsibility. For instance, conscientious employees might excel in adhering to sustainable protocols, while those with high openness to experience could drive innovation in eco-friendly logistics solutions. This knowledge allows banks to design targeted training and development programs that leverage these traits, fostering a culture of sustainability within the organization. By aligning logistics management with employees' personality profiles, banks can improve job satisfaction and reduce resistance to change, further promoting a sustainable operational framework. Understanding and integrating personality traits into sustainability initiatives can thus create a more resilient, efficient, and responsible banking sector.

17.6 Limitations

The research may be constrained by the sample size and diversity, as a larger and more varied sample would yield more generalizable findings. The study is geographically limited to a specific region or set of banks, potentially overlooking the full spectrum of practices and personality influences found in different cultural or organizational contexts. The dynamic nature of sustainability practices and changing regulations also complicates the ability to draw long-term conclusions from the findings.

17.7 Conclusion

This study emphasizes the pivotal role of personality traits in shaping sustainable logistics management within the banking industry. By focusing on the Big 5 inherent characteristics, the in-depth analysis of the research provides valuable insights into how these characteristics influence employees' perspectives and behaviors toward sustainable practices. The findings indicate that openness, extraversion, and neuroticism are statistically significant determinants of sustainable logistics management, with agreeableness also having a comparatively strong effect. Although conscientiousness positively impacts sustainable logistics, it was not found to be statistically significant.

The study also reveals that age and bank type have a notable impact on sustainable logistics management, while gender and interactions do not. Grasping these dynamics is essential for banks aiming to enhance their environmental, social, and governance (ESG) performance. By aligning sustainability initiatives with the personality profiles of their employees, banks can cultivate a more supportive and effective environment for sustainable practices. This alignment can lead to improved operational efficiency, cost reductions, and a stronger corporate reputation, thereby contributing to the robust body of knowledge in establishing an environment-friendly financial ecosystem.

The study further highlights the importance of adopting a comprehensive approach to sustainable logistics management, integrating technological advancements, collaborative efforts, and strategic policy measures. Despite challenges such as high implementation costs and resistance to change, incorporating personality traits into sustainability strategies offers a promising pathway for banks to surmount these hurdles and achieve their long-term sustainability goals.

References

1. Ali, A.H., Gruchmann, T., Melkonyan, A., Assessing the impact of sustainable logistics service quality on relationship quality: Survey-based evidence in Egypt. *Clean. Logist. Supply Chain*, 4, 51–69, 2022, https://doi.org/10.1016/j.clscn.2022.100036.
2. Anwar, M. and Clauß, T., Personality traits and bricolage as drivers of sustainable social responsibility in family SMEs: A COVID-19 perspective. *Bus. Soc. Rev., 126*, 1, 37–68, 2021.

3. Björklund, M., Influence from the business environment on environmental purchasing — Drivers and hinders of purchasing green transportation services. *J. Purch. Supply Manage.*, 17, 1, 11–22, 2021.
4. Brown, S. and Taylor, K., Household finances and the Big 5 inherent characteristics. *J. Econ. Psychol.*, 45, 197–212, 2014.
5. Carter, C.R. and Rogers, D.S., A framework of sustainable supply chain management: Moving toward new theory. *Int. J. Phys. Distrib. Logist. Manage.*, 38, 5, 360–387, 2008.
6. Costa, P.T. and McCrae, R.R., The revised NEO personality inventory (NEOPI-R). *The SAGE Handbook of Personality Theory and Assessment: Personality Measurement and Testing*, vol. 2, pp. 179–198, doi:10.4135/9781849200479.n9
7. Durand, R.B., Newby, R., Peggs, L., Siekierka, M., Personality and risk: A study of financial decision-making. *J. Behav. Finance*, 9, 3, 152–158, 2008.
8. Eccles, R.G., Ioannou, I., Serafeim, G., The impact of corporate sustainability on organizational processes and performance. *Manage. Sci.*, 60, 11, 2835–2857, 2014.
9. Ferreira, S. and Schenk, S., Investigating short-term investment intentions through a sociological and behavioral lens. *J. Behav. Finance*, 22, 3, 193–210, 2021.
10. Friede, G., Busch, T., Bassen, A., ESG and financial performance: Aggregated evidence from more than 2000 empirical studies. *J. Sustain. Finance Invest.*, 5, 4, 210–233, 2015.
11. Gambetti, E. and Giusberti, F., The effect of anger and anxiety traits on investment decisions. *J. Econ. Psychol.*, 33, 6, 1059–1069, 2012.
12. Gunasekaran, A. and Ngai, E.W.T., Information systems in supply chain integration and management. *Eur. J. Oper. Res.*, 159, 2, 269–295, 2004.
13. Gunkel, M., Schlaegel, C., Taras, V., Cultural values, emotional intelligence, and conflict handling styles: A global study. *J. World Bus.*, 41, 2, 277–294, 2010.
14. Jiang, Z., Peng, C., Yan, H., Personality differences and investment decision-making. *J. Financ. Econ.*, working paper 31401, 2023, https://doi.org/10.3386/w31041.
15. John, O.P. and Srivastava, S., The Big Five trait taxonomy: History, measurement, and theoretical perspectives, in: *Handbook of personality: Theory and research*, vol. 2, Pervin, L.A. and John, O.P. (Eds.), pp. 102–138, 1999.
16. Judge, T.A. and Bono, J.E., Relationship of core self-evaluations traits—self-esteem, generalized self-efficacy, locus of control, and emotional stability—with job satisfaction and job performance: A meta-analysis. *J. Appl. Psychol.*, 86, 1, 80–92, 2001.
17. Lampropoulos, G., Anastasiadis, T., Siakas, K., Siakas, E., Personality traits and social media engagement: A review of the Five-Factor Model. *Pers. Social Psychol. Rev.*, 26, 1, 45–70, 2022.
18. Leary, Mark R., *Encyclopedia of Personality and Individual Differences*, 2589–2593, 2020, doi:10.1007/978-3-319-24612-3_2200.

19. Martins, N., Psychological and sociological theories of risk perception. *Disaster Prev. Manage.: Int. J.*, 11, 1, 43–48, 2002.
20. Mayfield, C., Perdue, G., Wooten, K., Investment management and personality type. *Financ. Serv. Rev.*, 17, 3, 219–236, 2008.
21. McCrae, R.R. and Costa, P.T., Openness to experience and ego level in Loevinger's sentence completion test: Dispositional contributions to developmental models of personality. *J. Pers. Soc. Psychol.*, 39, 6, 1179–1190, 1980, doi:10.1037/h0077727.
22. McKinnon, Browne, M., Piecyk, M., Whiteing, A., Green logistics – Improving the environmental sustainability of logistics. *Zeitschrift für Wirtschaftsgeographie*, 60, 1–2, 99–100, 2015, doi:10.1515/zfw-2016-0013.
23. Nandan, T. and Saurabh, K., Big five personality model: Comparative analysis in Indian context. *J. Manage. Dev.*, 35, 2, 227–240, 2016.
24. Nga, J.K.H. and Ken Yien, L., The influence of personality trait and demographics on financial decision making among Generation Y. *Young Consum.*, 14, 3, 230–243, 2013.
25. Niszczota, P., Determinants of the diversification of Polish investors' portfolios: The role of personality traits and demographic factors. *Econ. Res.-Ekon. Istraž.*, 27, 1, 752–771, 2014.
26. Pak, O. and Mahmood, M., Impact of personality on risk tolerance and investment decisions: A study on potential investors of Kazakhstan. *Int. J. Commer. Manage.*, 25, 4, 370–384, 2015.
27. Pan, C.H. and Statman, M., Investor personality in investor behaviour. *J. Invest. Consult.*, 14, 1, 48–56, 2013.
28. Rao, P. and Holt, D., Do green supply chains lead to competitiveness and economic performance? *Int. J. Oper. Prod. Manage.*, 25, 9, 898–916, 2005.
29. Rathi, K.N. and Geetha, D., The influence of intellectual capital on the financial performance of insurance companies listed on the Amman Securities Exchange. *J. Financ. Serv. Res.*, 49, 2, 275–298, 2023.
30. Sadi, R., Asl, H.G., Gholipour, A., Behavioral finance: The explanation of investors' personality and perceptual biases effects on financial decisions. *Int. J. Econ. Finance*, 3, 5, 234–241, 2011.
31. Wong, C.H., Chuah, C.Y., Kui, S.B., Soo, L.H., Ang, S.Z., The impact of personality traits on investment decisions of young potential investors. *J. Financ. Plann. Couns.*, 27, 2, 145–158, 2016.
32. Young, M.N., Peng, M.W., Ahlstrom, D., Bruton, G.D., Jiang, Y., Corporate governance in emerging economies: A review of the principal–principal perspective. *J. Manage. Stud.*, 45, 1, 196–220, 2023.
33. Hair, J., Ringle, C., Sarstedt, M., PLS-SEM: Indeed a Silver Bullet. *J. Mark. Theory Pract.*, 19, 139–151, 2011, https://doi.org/10.2753/MTP1069-6679190202.
34. Ab Hamid, M.R., Sami, W., Sidek, M.M., Discriminant Validity Assessment: Use of Fornell & Larcker Criterion versus HTMT Criterion. *J. Phys. Conf. Ser.*, 890, 162–163, 2017, https://doi.org/10.1088/1742-6596/890/1/012163.

35. Anderson, J. and Gerbing, D., Structural Equation Modeling in Practice: A Review and Recommended Two-Step Approach. *Psychol. Bull.*, 103, 411–423, 1988, http://dx.doi.org/10.1037/0033-2909.103.3.411.
36. Liao, J.G. and McGee, D., Adjusted Coefficients of Determination for Logistic Regression. *Am. Stat.*, 57, 3, 161–165, 2003, https://doi.org/10.1198/0003130031964.
37. Glass, C. and Cook, A., Do Women Leaders Promote Positive Change? Analyzing the Effect of Gender on Business Practices and Diversity Initiatives. *Hum. Resour. Manage.*, 57, 823–837, 2018, https://doi.org/10.1002/hrm.21838.
38. Nguyen, H.-L., *et al.*, Explorıng Vietnamese undergraduates perception of the social and emotional loneliness. *Int. J. Mech. Prod. Eng. Res. Dev.*, 10, 3, 9905–9912, 2020, https://doi.org/10.24247/ijmperdjun2020946.

Annexure

Table I Tests of between-subject effects.

Dependent variable: Sustainable logistics management					
Source	**Type III sum of squares**	**df**	**Mean square**	**F**	**Sig.**
Corrected Model	2631.431[a]	37	71.120	2.758	.000
Intercept	44030.630	1	44030.630	1707.394	.000
Age	13.572	3	4.524	.175	.913
Gender*	21.086	1	21.086	.818	.367
BankType	179.263	2	89.632	3.476	.033
Level	72.638	2	36.319	1.408	.048
Age * Gender	6.827	2	3.413	.132	.876
Age * BankType	36.454	3	12.151	.471	.703
Age * Level	13.392	2	6.696	.260	.772
Gender * BankType	91.655	2	45.827	1.777	.172
Gender * Level	277.347	2	138.673	5.377	.005
BankType * Level	187.815	4	46.954	1.821	.127
Age * Gender * BankType	165.284	2	82.642	3.205	.043
Age * Gender * Level	163.656	2	81.828	3.173	.044
Age * BankType * Level	248.388	4	62.097	2.408	.052
Gender * BankType * Level	172.942	4	43.236	1.677	.158
Age * Gender * BankType * Level	6.632	2	3.316	.129	.879
Error	4177.689	162	25.788		
Total	267740.000	200			
Corrected Total	6809.120	199			

a. R Squared = .386 (Adjusted R Squared = .246)

Index

Proof. To find $y*$ (optimal value), which maximizes $E\left[Z_1\left(y\right)\right]$, necessary condition is as follows:

i.e.
$$\frac{\partial E\left[Z_1\left(y\right)\right]}{\partial y}=0$$

$$y_1^* = \sqrt{\frac{E\left[G_3\right]}{E\left[G_2\right]}} \tag{11.26}$$

Hence, y_1^* is the optimal value.
Hence, Lemma 2 follows.

11.5 Numerical Analysis

A practical illustration is provided for industry professionals to improve their strategies for inventory management.

11.5.1 Example

$$f(d)=\begin{cases}25, 0\le x\le 0.04\\ 0, \text{otherwise}\end{cases} \tag{11.27}$$

$$f(\mathrm{q}_1)=\begin{cases}50, 0.01\le \mathrm{q}_1\le 0.03\\ 0, \text{otherwise}\end{cases} \tag{11.28}$$

$$f(\mathrm{q}_2)=\begin{cases}50, 0.2\le \mathrm{q}_2\le 0.7\\ 0, \text{otherwise}\end{cases} \tag{11.29}$$

$d = 0.1$, $i = \$\ 0.15$/unit, $q_1 = 0.02$, $q_2 = 0.02$, $C_a = \$\ 0.1$/unit, $C_r = \$\ 0.05$/unit,

Other parameters are same as that of Teng (2009) model:

$D = 3{,}600$ units/year, $c = \$\ 0.5$/unit, $K = \$12$/cycle, $p = \$1$/unit, $C_s = \$0.35$/unit, $h = \$0.2$/unit, $\alpha = 0.5$, $\lambda = 5{,}000$ units/year

The optimal order size $y^* = 580$ units/ cycle with corresponding $E^*\left[Z_1\left(y\right)\right] = \$440$ /year and $T^* = 52.02$ days respectively.

Index

Printed in the USA/Agawam, MA
September 16, 2026

910661.142